The Possibility of Norms

The Possibility of Norms

Social Practice Beyond Morals and Causes

CHRISTOPH MÖLLERS

OXFORD
UNIVERSITY PRESS

OXFORD
UNIVERSITY PRESS

Great Clarendon Street, Oxford, OX2 6DP,
United Kingdom

Oxford University Press is a department of the University of Oxford.
It furthers the University's objective of excellence in research, scholarship,
and education by publishing worldwide. Oxford is a registered trade mark of
Oxford University Press in the UK and in certain other countries

First published in Germany in 2015 with the title
Die Möglichkeit der Normen. Über eine Praxis jenseits von Moralität und Kausalität.

First Edition published in 2020

Impression: 1

Published in the United States of America by Oxford University Press
198 Madison Avenue, New York, NY 10016, United States of America

British Library Cataloguing in Publication Data
Data available

Library of Congress Control Number: 2019952620

ISBN 978–0–19–882739–9

Printed and bound by
CPI Group (UK) Ltd, Croydon, CR0 4YY

Word of Gratitude

This is an old project. Thank you to the Berlin Wissenschaftskolleg, especially its library services, for its generous support during my time as a fellow 2006/2007 and as a permanent fellow since 2012. Special thanks to my editor at Suhrkamp, Eva Gilmer, and to Eva Herzog and Ali Ighreiz for help with the English version, finally to Alex Holznienkemper for his translation.

Table of Contents

Introduction

On Norms—No More, No Less

> An instrument for possibility must be substantively more comprehensive and subtle than one for reality.
>
> Hans Blumenberg

> But then, were the world as it is supposed to be, the activity of willing would fall by the wayside. Thus the will in itself requires that its purpose also not to be realized.
>
> Georg Wilhelm Friedrich Hegel

> ... but never mind. Rules were made to be broken. Which meant, if that was a rule, that sometimes they should be observed.
>
> Edward St Aubyn

1. *What we Mean when we Talk about Norms*

We know so little about norms because we are so preoccupied trying to justify them. Our talk about norms is sustained by intuitions, both normative and other.[1] When we think of norms, we think of appropriate norms or of that which makes or could make them appropriate. It is difficult for us to separate our idea of what a norm is from our idea of what it should be. When we think of norms, we also think of something concrete which appears to us as exemplary for a norm. Talk of a "norm" is so opaque that we frequently resort to examples when we try to give an account of the concept. We take a written law, a behavioral rule, a religious command, a happy family, an unhappy family as an archetype for everything normative. But we avoid the concept of a norm or the normative as such since we can imagine too little under this concept.

[1] Concerning the history of this term, which is not of immediate interest here: Hasso Hofmann and Wolfgang H. Schrader, "Artikel Norm" in: Karlfried Gründer (ed.), *Historisches Wörterbuch der Philosophie*, vol. VI, Darmstadt 1984, pp. 906–20; H.E. Hasso Jaeger, "La norme d'après la doctrine des humanistes et des auteurs du droit naturel" in: Universidad de Navarra (ed.), *La Norma en el Derecho Canónico*, Pamplona 1979, pp. 291–346; Herbert Oppel, *Kanon: zur Bedeutungsgeschichte des Wortes und seiner lateinischen Entprechungen (Regula-Norma)*, Leipzig 1937; Leopoold Wenger, *Canon in den römischen Rechtsquellen und in den Papyri*, Vienna 1942, p. 70 ff.

The Possibility of Norms. Christoph Möllers, Published by Oxford University Press (2020) under licence; © this translation, Alex Holznienkemper; © the original German edition, Suhrkamp Verlag Berlin.
DOI: 10.1093/oso/9780198827399.001.0001

This impression is confirmed when we compare the ways in which we deal with norms and how we deal with statements.[2] Our idea of a statement is more certain, more formalized, and more comprehensive. It is primarily shaped by grammar. A statement is a sentence, consisting of a subject and predicate, potentially also in a combination between the two, a linking verb. Whoever has pondered language knows this form and can work with it. It is no coincidence that the propositional sentence remains the most fundamental unit of analysis in the philosophy of language. There is no corresponding form in the theory of the normative. Neither in the theory of the normative nor in our everyday lives is there a comparable unit of analysis as the statement in language. Any claims that commands, rules, judgments, or reasons for action might serve as the fundamental unit of the normative will most likely face resistance.

We recognize a similar discrepancy when it comes to the question of how a norm is justified or what makes it appropriate. A propositional sentence is "justified" if it is true. The truth criterion is contentious, of course. At times, it is even doubted whether the truth of a claim has any meaning for our language practice.[3] But despite particular contentions, the truth-theoretical debate about correspondence and coherence (concerning the condition that a statement must correspond to facts and/or cannot contradict other true statements in order to be true) accords stability to both the concept of truth and the form of statements.[4] This stability becomes tangible when it is compared with the situation of norms. The justification of norms knows no category that would correspond to a criterion of validity such as truth. Moral realism, the theory that understands moral correctness as factual truth, is one such model of ethics. Such a theory does not stack up to the truth concept of statements. Our ideas regarding the correctness of a norm are distinctly more heterogeneous than our ideas surrounding the truth of a statement.

Since we have the form of the statement, we can collectively evaluate statements from various contexts with certain methods, with the instruments of logic, language analysis, or grammar. We lack corresponding instruments for norms. We don't have a grammar for norms, at best we have a deontic logic, which is only of minimal meaning for most normative practices. Norms simply seem to be too diverse to be reduced to a manageable number of forms and criteria of correctness.

The reasons for this diversity are numerous. One might be that for us many norms appear less as facts than as artefacts, as products of social and cultural achievements that cannot be pinned down by true statements. Despite talk about the *fabrication of facts*, we take facts to be something that can be discovered or *found*. Whether norms can be found or must be made, however, is a highly

[2] This becomes apparent at the outset of modern philosophy of language, in which Frege doubts how imperatives are to be treated: Gottlob Frege, "Logik" in: Id., *Schriften zur Logik und Sprachphilosophie*, Gottfried Gabriel (ed.), Hamburg 1990, pp. 35–73, here p. 40.

[3] Doubtful: Nelson Goodman, *Weisen der Welterzeugung*, Frankfurt/M. 1990, pp. 31–4, 146–7.

[4] Wolfgang Künne, *Conceptions of Truth*, Oxford 2005, Chapters 3 and 7.

contentious question. A second reason for our problem might be that normative statements always receive a demanding doubling, as they draw on facts and simultaneously operate on a second, normative level. Put plainly: every "ought" sentence presupposes a reference to something that *is*, without being able to limit itself to that *is*.

In light of such complexity, it is in no way necessary to introduce a single notion of the "norm" for norms of such varied kinds as legal, religious, esthetic, political, and moral norms, or for social norms in a narrow sense such as the rules of etiquette. Nonetheless, we often do speak of "norms" and compare law, morality, religious commands and social conventions. I suspect that we often implicitly assume a shared concept of the normative. It is one of the goals of this book to make this assumption explicit.

The conceptual uncertainty in dealing with norms leads to its over-categorization. Due to the lack of determinable but open forms like that of the statement, as well as the lack of criteria like that of truth, attempts to grasp conceptually normative problems quickly become too narrow. Despite a large abundance of phenomena that we would intuitively characterize as normative in their own right, we resort to categories that exclude many of those phenomena. Theoretical reflection on norms centers on alternatives that are too exclusive for an appropriate description of social practice: are norms either set or found, are they reasonable or necessary, are they formalized or rather formless? Reflection on norms is hyper-categorical, or as a reaction to that, they are non-categorical. Over and against this, thinking about norms should take place in categories, but in ones that grant space to the phenomena.

1.1 Scope of the Topic

With this book, I am attempting to make a contribution to approaching this landscape of problems by elaborating a concept of the normative. That is, I aim to explicate what we mean when we speak of norms *as such*. Two limitations arise from this. For one, this book is only concerned with developing a concept of the normative, that is to crystallize that which makes a norm a norm. The book is not concerned with presenting a concept of the correctness of norms which could correspond to the truth criterion. Hopefully, if one can accomplish the former, it will become obvious why the latter is so difficult to accomplish. Secondly, I will restrict myself to shape a concept of *social* norms, that is of norms that have arisen out of a social context. That which is internal, which is so essential for the modern theory of moral action, shall remain on the margins—yet not completely outside, for the simple reason that a categorical distinction between inside and outside, between the internal and the social is not possible. My viewpoint on questions with which every practice of social norms sees itself confronted, however, is certainly to be compared and contrasted with philosophical theories of the morally appropriate.[5] What implication does it have for the value and accuracy of philosophical theories of morally right action that social norms need a location, a time, and a form of illustration, that one has to be able to perceive them? Along such a line of inquiry, moral norms will represent an important reference, though frequently only used as a contrast because—I would like to claim—social norms such as religious commandments, legal prescriptions, or rules of etiquette, operate quite differently from norms that are typically debated in practical philosophy. The commonalities of social norms are the object of this book.

These commonalities cannot consist in social norms somehow being justified—be it morally, be it by other means. Legal norms may well be unjust, political rules of the game undemocratic, religious precepts heretical or abstruse, and rules of etiquette impractical and antiquated. These kinds of deficits and this potential lack of a justification regardless of kind are—at the outset—not of interest here. That being said, the line of inquiry pursued does not need to prove itself as value free or non-normative. There may be good reasons to discuss the form of the normative itself in a justificatory or critical manner. On another level, one might explore whether certain reasons speak for or against the use of norms. One could ask whether it is "better" to raise children by means of prohibition and praise, or whether it is sensible to inhibit political processes by means of norms. This is where the normativity of the normative must justify itself. These questions will come up at the end of the book, but in order to understand what we mean when we speak of norms, we should avoid narrowing down the concept of a norm at the outset to correct or justified norms.

1.2 Thesis

Against this backdrop, it is necessary to develop a conceptual framework for (the analysis of) social norms that is sufficiently broad to accommodate diverse phenomena, while not becoming shapeless.[6] The assumption for which I will argue in the following is to understand norms as *positively marked possibilities*. Norms point toward a possible state of affairs or a possible event. To posit something impossible as the object of a norm is pointless. The positive marking of a *possibility* indicates that it should *be realized*. The supposition is that one can only speak of normativity where it is presumed that the world could be different than it currently is, and

[5] A reflection on the relationship between social-scientific and philosophical investigation of norms that has enjoyed far too limited attention can be found in Dorothy Emmet, *Rules, Roles, and Relations*, London 1966.

[6] On this—possible—virtue of the concept of norms also see Scott J. Shapiro, *Legality*, Cambridge, Mass. 2011, pp. 40–2; a unified concept of normativity is also advocated for by Christine M. Korsgaard, *The Sources of Normativity*, Cambridge 1996, p. 21.

where this presumption is marked as such. Normativity hinges on the possibility of a divergent *state of the world*, or a judgment of the world, the measure of which is not limited to the world as it is.

In his Letter to the Romans, Paul writes: "where there is no law there is no transgression."[7] The law fulfills the purpose of making the sinfulness of those recognizable who strive to follow it. The law is a negative foil for that which is meant by salvation through grace, and is thus part of the process of grace. Paul's declaration makes no substantive claims concerning what is to be done. At a different point, Paul advises the community of Corinth to distance themselves from others who don't share their faith,[8] or in a freer expression, not to associate themselves with the world. Both of these references—independent of any identification with Christianity—can give an initial impression of what this book is about. My interest in normativity does not concern the appropriate justification of certain actions or forms of life but rather the explication and reassurance of the distinction between that which is and a norm. Paul's remarks are of a systematic interest here as they do not stop at making commands but go on to introduce distinctions in virtue of which one can take a step back from the world while being within the world. Such means of self-distancing, I propose, make up the core of normative practices. The questions of concern in this book will be how exactly these means of distancing function, how norms are represented and realized, especially as they, at one and the same time, refer to an occurrence in the world while simultaneously distancing themselves from it. These questions are easily neglected if a theory of normativity too quickly turns its attention to the problem of justification.

This overall thrust of the argument, which itself will, for the moment, not be justified further, has numerous implications that also manifest themselves as pragmatic problems in our dealing with norms. Operating with possibilities is precarious as their ontological constitution is uncertain and their recognizability doubtful. For this reason, many problems in different normative practices converge on questions of a norm's representability, on the consequences of its written fixation, on the possibility to make recognizable the violation of a norm and its sanction, or on the role and importance of time.[9]

Articulating the normative in this way is an attempt at distancing myself from two dominant interpretations in the theory of norms; on the one hand, from a view that reduces norms to reasons, that is to entities that lack any spatial or temporal dimension, entities which at best manifest themselves secondarily or accidentally in the world, without this manifestation having any bearing on their actual nature

[7] Romans n 4, 15. The following stems freely from Rudolf Bultmann, *Theologie des Neuen Testaments*, Tübingen 1984, pp. 263–70, esp. pp. 266 ff.

[8] 2 Corinthians n 6, 17.

[9] The question of the recognizability of norms as norms is notoriously underestimated in its significance. The question is addressed in very fruitful reflections by Heinrich Popitz, *Soziale Normen*, Frankfurt/M. 2006, p. 69.

and character as reasons. On the other hand, I distance myself from a view that only seeks to describe norms by means of outcomes or effects. Against these two views, I understand norms as social practices in which a community distances itself from its own reality in order (not necessarily, but under certain circumstances) to change this reality, a project that, under yet further circumstances, sometimes succeeds. As a social form in its own right, so runs my central claim, norms can be reduced neither to moral reasons nor to causal effects.[10]

1.3 Expectations to be Disappointed by this Book

Theories of normativity often find themselves chasing after two phantoms. For one, they are searching for methods of an appropriate application of norms. In doing so, however, they operate in a space that is not particular to the realm of normativity. Due to their orientation toward practical realization, it may be especially urgent to establish appropriate standards for the application of norms. That is because under certain circumstances, we can better cope with the vagueness of a descriptive sentence than with a vague statute. Nonetheless, every attempt to find general rules for practices of proper application will prove to be futile. The fact that esthetic theory has made this realization far earlier and more thoroughly than legal and moral theory may be attributable to their differing levels of pragmatic urgency. And yet, acknowledging the futility of such general inquiry does not deny the possibility of arguments that speak for or against a certain type of application in a given context.

A second, structurally similar and similarly futile effort can be identified in seeking a practically manageable definition of the concept of a norm. Two things must be distinguished in this context. This book is concerned with answering the question of what we mean when we speak of norms, that is, what commonalities among legal, religious, esthetic, or other social practices we denote with the category of the normative. This, however, is something fundamentally different from an attempt to draw a clear line between normative and non-normative phenomena by means of theory in hopes of providing a manageable standard for normative practices.[11] The transition from a norm to a non-norm will prove itself to be rather murky. And the description of this transition will show itself to be a kind of description that will not provide any guidance in the practice of normativity. In this book, a game is described, not played.

[10] This concern is rarely found in the academic literature, for a recent exception see Geoffrey Brennan, Lina Eriksson, Robert E. Goodin, and Nicholas Southwood, *Explaining Norms*, Oxford 2013, pp. 15–19.

[11] To take but one seemingly unproblematic example: The assumption that a social rule might be established when it is recognized by a majority (Ursula Wolf, *Das Problem des moralischen Sollens*, Berlin 1984, pp. 16, 20) is much more presumptuous upon further consideration. Whence do we derive this rule of the majority? Are there no examples of effective social rules that are merely recognized by minorities? If there are, then the majority principle may still be useful for the question of legitimation, but not for the question of their existence.

1.4 Gains

So what is the point of developing at this level of abstraction a common conceptual framework for (the analysis of) social norms? On one level, such concept formation, if it proves to be plausible and coherent, can reframe many questions of norm theory in new ways and contribute to their solution. Are sanctions a prerequisite for the existence a norm? How might the "application" of a norm be reconstructed? What is the relationship between action-governing norms and so-called constitutive norms? How can we understand the distinction between "is" and "ought" in a way that is plausible for a social practice?

At a second level, the preconditions of an empirical investigation into the normative realm need to be explained. Here, we come up against a problem both practical and internal to the empirical-scientific inquiry of norms. While the empirical investigation of normative practices is a crucial object of study in the social sciences, it will become clear that it is often shaped by highly questionable theoretical assumptions deriving from practical philosophy which in turn affect the reliability of scientific findings. How exactly is it possible, as an adherent to a Humean or Kantian theory of normativity, empirically to investigate normative practices? A new definition of the normative may shed light on new parameters that are essential for the success or failure of describing normative practices.

This conceptual work also brings commonalities of norms into view which are significant for numerous paradigms in the humanities, social sciences, and cultural studies. The investigation by a common analytical framework of multifarious kinds of norms—political, esthetic, religious, and legal—might raise and harbor doubts with regard to strong models and claims of functional differentiation. That is because the attribution of norms to one of these (supposedly) functionally distinct systems is often uncertain or disputed. Human rights are an example of this, religiously inspired political programs another.[12]

Finally, common expectations vis-à-vis norms might be relativized in two important directions. On the one hand, norms are often expected to prove themselves by their outcomes. If they fail to yield an outcome, they count as mere fictions. But this misses the conceptual point. The practice of the normative persistently entails uncertain consequences due to its fixation on a possibility. Whoever wants reliably to bring about outcomes should try to set causes rather than norms. This might well be one of the main reasons why an instrumental conceptualization of norms explains very little. A norm might reveal a lot about who we are or strive to be; used as a means toward an end, though, it quickly reaches its limits. After all, the possibility of deviating from a norm is one of its most consequential practical characteristics. And yet, norms are expected to bring about tremendous achievements which quickly overburden them, for

[12] One might briefly ponder what counts as a "political" norm. Possibilities include norms that shape the political process yet are not legally inscribed, e.g. constitutional norms without juridical review, as well as political programs.

example "holding together" whole societies. A conceptually sharpened view will more precisely outline what norms can and cannot achieve in a given context.

1.5 Terminology

A word on the terminology already presupposed in this introduction. In the following, I will employ the terms norm and normativity—the property that makes a norm a norm—as overarching terms. Rules, commands and verdicts, judgments and valuations, State-sanctioned laws, moral imperatives and matters of taste are altogether norms. Evaluative and prescriptive acts alike fall into the realm of the normative.[13] Many divergent terminologies can be found in philosophy. There, the juxtaposition between moral norms that fulfil a universalization criterion and ethical values plays an important role.[14] That debate, however, is concerned with the appropriate kind of norm justification; it is hardly disputed that both norms on this understanding and values are normative. The concern here is exclusively with the commonalities that turn prescriptions and values into something normative.

In the following I will speak of "normative order" when I speak of a correlation between norms that can be traced back to common mechanisms. Normative orders consist in different kinds of norms, under certain circumstances even in norms that contradict one another. I understand social norms to be norms that come into existence in a social context, at a concrete time, and at a concrete place.[15] Social norms are taken as the overarching term for rules of etiquette, legal norms, as well as other socially relevant normative practices. Whether moral norms are social norms depends on whether they are conceived of dependently of social practices or not—a contentious question that cannot be answered here. It should be obvious, however, that there are many social norms that we do not need to follow for moral reasons.[16] Either way, moral norms conceived independently of existing social practices can develop social relevance and become social norms. It remains to be shown just how productive it is to subsume and investigate them under an overarching concept. The artificial term of normativity certainly has the advantage of not entailing too many connotations and prematurely narrowing the vantage point on these phenomena.

[13] Expressly, Herbert Schnädelbach, "Rationalität und Normativität" in: Id., *Zur Rehabilitierung des* animal rationale, Frankfurt/M. 1992, pp. 79–103, here pp. 88–93, referencing the description combining both in Paul W. Taylor, *Normative Discourse*, Englewood Cliffs 1961 (esp. pp. 279–82). Similarly, Georg Henrik von Wright, *Norm and Action*, New York 1963, pp. 1–16; in contrast, e.g. Wolf (n 11), *Problem*, p. 12.

[14] For example see Rahel Jaeggi, *Kritik von Lebensformen*, Berlin 2013, p. 36 ff. A concise historicization between antiquity and modernity in Korsgaard (n 6), *Sources of Normativity*, pp. 2–5.

[15] The distinction between social and moral norms is undertaken in very different ways (Wolf (n 11), *Problem*, pp. 8 ff.; Jaeggi (n 14), *Kritik*, p. 147, fn. 12). One could also conceive of moral norms as a subset of all social norms or distinguish social norms from moral ones, e.g. as Brennan et al. (n 10), *Explaining Norms*, Chapter 4. This results in religious norms—for instance and unlike the present approach—not being considered as social norms. See ibid., p. 76, fn. 49.

[16] Nicholas Southwood, "The Authority of Social Norms" in: Michael Brady (ed.), *New Waves in Metaethics*, London 2011, pp. 234–48, here p. 239.

I

PROBLEMS

1
Good Reasons?
Deficits of Philosophical Concepts of Normativity

> ... whether we can draw any distinction between the subjectively and objectively "good" does not enter into our determination of the sense of should-propositions.[1]

If categories from practical philosophy are of significance for understanding social norms and how these can be adequately described, then taking a look at the philosophical discourse will provide an entry point. Of course, speaking of practical philosophy as such is somewhat limiting in light of the sheer breadth of such discourse, even more so in that philosophical debates are contentious not only in their solutions but in the very definition of problems. Attempts to identify discursive commonalities in a critical manner quickly come across as futile or reductionist at the very least. Nonetheless, this will be attempted here, driven by the presumption that at least the identification of problems isn't too vague an enterprise in contemporary practical philosophy, and that it indeed plays a decisive role for a theory of the normative.

1. Norm Individualism: Norms as Reasons for Action

1.1 The Prominence of Reasons for Action

It is no coincidence that the question regarding why we *should* use reasons does not resonate strongly in philosophy. It would only lead to a meaningless doubling or to a regress while little could be drawn about reasons themselves. This is quite different for historians or sociologists.[2] Historians describe the evolution of social practices, and from such a perspective, the giving and taking of reasons is not self-evident. Admittedly, even in philosophy the term has only more recently gained prominence. Starting with the works of Stephen Toulmin,[3] the view of identifying

[1] Edmund Husserl, *Logische Untersuchungen*, Volume 1 (= *Gesammelte Schriften* 2), Hamburg 1975, p. 56 (transl. J. N. Findlay, New York 2001).
[2] Exemplarily, Charles Tilly, *Why?*, Princeton 2006.
[3] Stephen Toulmin, *An Examination of the Place of Reason in Ethics*, Cambridge 1950.

The Possibility of Norms. Christoph Möllers, Published by Oxford University Press (2020) under licence;
DOI: 10.1093/oso/9780198827399.001.0001

norms with reasons or reasons for actions has slowly established itself in meta-ethical discussions. On the side of theoretical philosophy, this idea merged with analytical theory of action rather well, but its effects were longer-lasting in practical philosophy. Currently, the philosophical debate about the essence of normativity is almost exclusively focused on the structure of reasons; it is concerned with how reasons for action are to be conceived, especially whether they must have an actual effect on an acting subject or not. Few ask for a more thorough justification of the concept itself, however.[4] Such dogmatization of reasons has become commonplace in Scanlon's claim that the concept of a reason is a *primitive*, most simplistically paraphrased by the axiom "counts towards."[5] At the very least, the characterization as primitive is dubious, as Scanlon himself has much more to say about the term than would be fitting for a *primitive*.[6] Most problematically though, this choice of term predetermines aspects of the constitution of the normative which, whether appropriate or not, are so significant that they would require an explicit justification. As opposed to other kinds of "carriers" or "forms" of normativity, such as law, rule, judgement, or, yet different, revelation, or beauty, the identification of norms with "reasons" for action, and the considerations following in this section are only concerned with such reasons, limits the concept of normativity in numerous ways from the outset.

The concept of a reason for action exclusively relates normativity to the justification of individual actions. Such a limitation is not semantically necessary. The word "reason" can be understood synonymously as "argument" and thus as a more general viewpoint not only referring to a single action. One could also read the above-cited passage from Scanlon this way. But if one examines the argumentation style, particularly the selection of examples in contemporary moral philosophical debate,[7] as well as the intellectual genealogy of the discussion arising from analytical theory of action, then it should be obvious that reasons for a single action of a person are implied when speaking of normativity in this context. Our parlance has established "Someone has good reasons for 'X'," and X denotes a concrete action.

Now one might be tempted to rebut this classification since there has been a long-lasting debate within practical philosophy concerning the distinction between values and norms. However, various deductive forms—rights, obligations,

[4] But also see Judith Jarvis Thomson, *Normativity*, Chicago 2008, pp. 158–60.

[5] Thomas Scanlon, *What We Owe to Each Other*, Cambridge, Mass. 1998, p. 17.

[6] Ibid., Part 1, Chapter 1.

[7] Exemplary for such commonalities beyond all other differences: Derek Parfit, *On What Matters*, Oxford 2011, Vol. 2, Part 6; Id., "Normativity" in: *Oxford Studies in Metaethics*, Vol. 1, Oxford 2006, pp. 325–80; Scanlon, *What We Owe*, pp. 17–77; Ralph Wedgewood, *The Nature of Normativity*, Oxford 2007, pp. 108–26; Jürgen Habermas, "Erläuterungen zur Diskursethik" in: Id., *Erläuterungen zur Diskursethik*, Frankfurt/M. 1991, pp. 119–226, here pp. 134–42; Rainer Forst, *Das Recht auf Rechtfertigung*, Frankfurt/M. 2007, pp. 23–53. Overview in R. Jay Wallace, *Normativity and the Will*, Oxford 2006, Ch. 1. Critically, Thomson, *Normativity*, pp. 158–60.

or ends—persistently point toward the figure of the reason for action.[8] Such is the case in Scanlon's theory which consistently takes reasons for action as implications of natural properties of objects and views values as a derived category that merges various bundles of reasons for action.[9] This is also the case for the value-focused approach of Joseph Raz. Here, too, all emanations of normativity are related back to actions.[10]

The parlance of good reasons also has a significant intuition in its favor; that is, the idea that a person acting, a person imbued with reason who makes a given decision, is to be taken as an elementary unit. Such a unit, in turn, serves as the departure point for both a theory of action analysis and for a synthesis toward establishing sweeping social-theoretical models. One could claim that within practical philosophy, action has assumed the role that the declarative sentence, the proposition, took on in analytic philosophy of language: that of the central explanatory category. To this, one would have to add the critical question of whether practical philosophy has similarly been able to supplement such a fixation on reasons for action with a practical perspective resembling pragmatics in the philosophy of language, which supplants the semantic focus on propositions. Such additions can be found in political philosophy but rather tend to compete with practical philosophy. In short, since the reference to reasons for action is so central for contemporary philosophy's understanding of normativity, what follows will be concerned with understanding which implications the identification of normativity with reasons for action can have, particularly how it limits the describability of/our ability to describe normative phenomena.

1.2 Self-Referentiality of the Debate

Let us begin with the dispute between two protagonists of the last few decades' meta-ethical discussion, Bernard Williams and Derek Parfit, concerning the understanding of moral reasons. The goal of looking at these two is not to take a stand and fine-tune the frequently reconstructed arguments about internalism and externalism,[11] cognitivism and non-cognitivism.[12] It is, rather, the commonalities linking these two approaches to the concept of the reason that are quite striking.

For Williams, it is inconceivable to think of a moral reason as something purely objective. An agent must make even the most practically plausible and factual

[8] Joseph Raz, "Right-Based Moralities" in: Jeremy Waldron (ed.), *Theories of Rights*, Oxford 1984, pp. 182–200' here pp. 183–6.

[9] Scanlon, *What We Owe*, pp. 78–107.

[10] Joseph Raz, "Agency, Reason, and the Good" in: Id., *Engaging Reason*, Oxford 1999, pp. 22–45, here pp. 24–8.

[11] Even if it is obvious that we are presuming that X is being conceived from the perspective of the subject, not of a community. Otherwise "inside" and "outside" could be inverted.

[12] See Wallace, *Normativity*, Ch. 5, for a reconstruction.

context his or her own in order for it to pass as a moral reason: the mere fact that my action brings about suffering for another person, in and of itself, is not a motivating reason to omit that action.[13]

Parfit, on the other hand, conceives a moral reason as a special form of an objective truth apt and rationally recognizable as fact. The fact that Paul, who is sitting in a burning hotel room, can only save his life by jumping from his window into a river, is such a reason.[14] The realization that Paul should jump out of the window is a true moral statement. Its truth is recognizable and does not depend on his inner sentiment.

Strikingly, the impression arises that the discussion is less concerned with the right understanding of normativity than with characteristics of the concept of a reason itself: in light of the claim of an objective reason for action, Williams asks why someone should take note of such a reason.[15] For him, a fact cannot be relevant for action without a further tie-in to one's own internal sensitivities. Thus, neither the fact nor the conviction of its correctness is sufficient for being a reason for action. What is indeed correct about this claim is that the German word "*Grund*" (even more so than the English "reason"), as well as connotated examples, persistently point toward a concrete action. On Williams' view, the person that is actually performing an action is neglected in place of the idea of an objective reason; there is no relevant role for the actor. The concept of the reason—just as it is used by Parfit in his examples—always refers to a specific subject and a concrete action. Other examples can scarcely be found in the meta-ethical discussion. Even in light of his own language usage and employment of examples, this brings Parfit's idea that normative reasons are always concerned with objective characteristics into question. The objective conceptualization of a reason for action only seems sensible in connection with a subject.

A similar tension in concept usage is apparent in Scanlon as well. Scanlon expressly differentiates between the reason as such, a "judgement-sensitive attitude," and an individuated reason for a certain person, a mere "biographical fact."[16] He views the latter as normatively secondary and not worthy of philosophical examination. This is irritating as he resorts to the idea of the reason as a category, one that is marked especially by its situatedness, that is, as a reason for action, only to immediately abstract from this situatedness.[17] The resulting concept of a reason without the actor's viewpoint is an odd composite. If the "idea of a cognition without a

[13] Bernard Williams, "Internal and External Reasons" in: Id., *Moral Luck*, Cambridge 1981, pp. 101–13, here pp. 106–13.

[14] Parfit, *On What Matters*, p. 283.

[15] See ibid., p. 417.

[16] Scanlon, *What We Owe*, pp. 18–20.

[17] The insight into the situatedness of reasons actually appears to be more established and important for sociology: C. Wright Mills, "Situated Actions and Vocabularies of Motives" in: *American Sociological Review* 5 (1940), pp. 904–13.

perspective is non-sensical in its own right,"[18] then doesn't the same go for the idea of a reason for action without a subject?

What is further striking is that when one finally moves on from discussing "reason" or "good reasons" in general and considers a concrete reason, this occurs in the form of conditionals. For example: "If X does not jump out of the hotel window into the river, then he will burn to death"[19] or "A will drown, if B does not toss a rope."[20] But conditionals are specified rules. In them, a result is tied to a certain condition. This is remarkable in so far as such parlance must immediately resort to a concept that is understood as derivative and secondary to the reason: that of the rule.

On the other hand, Parfit is able to point out that what Williams calls a reason can hardly be viewed as *normative* for the reason that Williams is ultimately invested in an actually realized tendency to carry out a specific action.[21] Williams not only reduces reasons for action to individual tendencies but even to tendencies that are realized in an action. Thus understood, reasons for action cannot become autonomous from motives. This may well be appropriate when reasons are understood as instruments for *explaining* human actions but one can only explain actions that are actually carried out. Such a limitation to the actual is too narrow for a normative structure. On such a reading, only that could become a normative reason which could also serve as a cause. Thus, the discussion substantially revolves around a normative and an explanatory conception of a reason without much being gained for the concept of the normative.

1.3 Action as the Foundation for Describing Social Phenomena

The problem lies in a methodical approach to questions of normativity which treats action as its fundamental unit only in order to use the idea of a reason, in turn, to develop a conception of normativity that scarcely considers the concrete circumstances of actions.[22]

This can be clearly seen in the treatment of rule conceptions.[23] Take a given rule R which states that one should utter a greeting upon encountering an acquaintance.

[18] Sebastian Rödl, *Selbstbezug und Normativität*, Paderborn 1998, p. 164.
[19] Parfit, *On What Matters*, p. 270.
[20] Thomson, *Normativity*, p. 256.
[21] Parfit, *On What Matters*, p. 287 f.
[22] In situationist theories one notes a desire to mediate between general normative requirements and particular contexts of action: Jonathan Dancy, *Ethics without Principles*, Oxford 2004, pp. 118–39.
[23] Exemplarily Marco Iorio, "Die Rollen von Regeln beim Handeln" in: *Zeitschrift für philosophische Forschung* 3 (2009), pp. 392–416; id., *Regel und Grund*, Berlin 2011, p. 181 ff. For a clear exposition of the problem: Edward McClennen, "Rationality" in: Alfred R. Mele and Piers Rawling (eds), *The Oxford Handbook of Rationality*, Oxford 2004, pp. 222–39, here p. 223 ff. Critically Frederick Schauer, *Playing by the Rules*, Oxford 2002, pp. 115–18, who rightly notes that a rule which dissolves in its situatedness can no longer be described as a rule.

With recourse to a plethora of mundane examples, it can be shown that each rule stands under the proviso of many concrete assumptions. People greet one another indoors but not if one is entering a play in progress, and not if one thinks the other is ashamed of the encounter. In light of these exceptions, the rule appears to falter. It is doubtful whether any concrete action can be explained or justified by the rule.[24] One might deduce from this that reasons for action represent a preferable (because more fundamental) category to rules in justifying and explaining actions.

Yet two issues arise on such a reading. For one, it is a circular argument. If one seeks to explain a concrete action, one will indeed have to resort to individualized constellations as the explanatory unit. But this, too, is subject to its context with existing rules. As we have learned from scientific theory, an event such as an experimental result is explained not merely by reference to a law of nature but by the combination of that law with a certain constellation or test arrangement.[25] From this, it does not follow, however, that natural laws are mere secondary categories of lesser explanatory power. The argument above draws a comparable conclusion concerning a rule, however. If an action can only be explained as a complex interplay of rules pertaining to a particular situation, then the conclusion that a certain rule only minimally determines the action (or doesn't at all)—as opposed to a reason being pivotal in determining the action—is faulty. It is as meaningless as saying that gravity is irrelevant, as it doesn't make any difference in the result of a certain experiment. Each concrete action is only imaginable in a highly specified situation in which many rules are applicable, and in which many other rules don't even count. Reasons for a concrete action might not necessarily coincide with this web of rules but might arise from the concrete circumstances for which no rule currently is available. But this does not make the presented argument any more convincing as it remains stuck in the circular claim that for a given path of action, only those rules that pertain to that situation are relevant, and that they condense to become reasons.

The second issue with this exclusive reference to action is related. With it, practical philosophy has neglected just how problematic it can be to define acts as actions at all without consideration of their social context.[26] While the theory of action since Wittgenstein has become sensitive to vagueness issues at the boundary between behavior and action,[27] this can hardly count as a serious consideration of social contexts. Even the identification of a spacio-temporally defined event as the action of a concrete person carries with it immense suppositions and is

[24] The attempt to differentiate reasons and rule categorically, so that rules cannot serve as reasons, can be found in Iorio, *Regel und Grund*, pp. 171–201.

[25] On the autonomy of the experminet, Ian Hacking, *Einführung in die Philosophie der Naturwissenschaften*, Leipzig 1996, pp. 250–77.

[26] A helpful reminder of Hegel on this can be found in Michael Quante, *Die Wirklichkeit des Geistes*, Berlin 2011, p. 204 f.

[27] Simply compare the influential examples in G.E.M. Anscombe, *Absicht*, Berlin 2010.

neither historically nor culturally invariant. In classifying an event as an action, I assert that the action was intended by a person and that he or she had influence on the action-event with his or her intention. The variously reflected details of the concept of intentionality are not of primary concern here, but rather that both presumptions—intention and influence—are established in many social practices by means of *rules* about ascription. Many social practices, easily recognizable in law or pedagogy, operate in an ad hoc-ascriptive manner.[28] This means that actions are the result of an ascriptive practice that seeks to differentiate between an action and an event in light of generalizable rules. Additionally, it means that criteria for action are developed on the basis of experiences, and that these criteria are to be corrected and adapted in light of practical outcomes. Such criteria do not merely arise out of a desire for consistency, even if that may be important for many practices, such as penal law. They also follow practical considerations such as responding to the question of how likely a certain limitation of bodily operability might cause a certain damage and how much such damage costs.

Actions result from social practices of ascription that process events which are understood to be actions, or not. Experiences in this practice of ascription lead to a continual adjustment of criteria for an action, such as the question of up to which concentration of alcohol in a person's blood intentional action can still be ascribed, or at which age childlike behavior should be viewed as an action potentially worthy of sanctioning.

What is decisive is that in addition to instrumentally rational considerations, we are faced with a *normative* dimension that is precisely not invested in the question of proper reasons for action. After all, the formation of ascription criteria always has to do with the idea of a community concerning behavior that *should* count as action. Aside from a situational assessment of consequences, practising ascription implies ideas of individual capacity. This concerns the expectations that can be imposed upon behavior to be understood as action, and it also reflects the flexibility a community has in shaping these expectations. What we come to classify as an action decisively hinges on who we want to be or who we believe we should be, such as a responsibly minded citizen or a loyal follower.

From this perspective, it is no longer necessary to treat reasons that drive or explain action as fundamental units of normativity, as the assumption of a present action already entails preconditions which must be understood as constituting action, not justifying action.

This goes against introducing a *methodical* individualism into practical philosophy, an individualism that on the quiet becomes a *normative* individualism in the context of *practical* philosophy. Many freedom-theoretical arguments point to normative individualism, but taking action as the theoretical basic unit does not

[28] Herbert L.A. Hart and Anthony Honoré, *Causation in Law*, Oxford 1959, pp. 58–78.

deliver this justification. Precisely for the description of normative practices that have an institutional framework, this model is hardly useful, as within it, normativity can only ever be thought inner subjective and situational.

Finally, the fixation of philosophical discourse on reasons for action is not inscribed into the nature of the discipline as it might be in sociology to only concern itself with phenomena between multiple people, or as in biology, which focuses on the living. If there indeed are such disciplinary orientations, and if they should particularly be found in philosophy, then the history of philosophical reflection on the normative itself shows that a fixation on reasons for action is not self-evident. One cannot find a division of labor that assigns a methodical action individualism to philosophy and a contrasting one to social sciences, for example. Philosophical investigations such as between values and norms, between *is* and *should*, and *doing* and *should*, between rules and reasons, between *rules of doing* and *rules of being*[29] show that even philosophical reconstructions of normativity neither need to restrict themselves to reasons for action nor to treat them as their basic unit. These differentiations provide conceptual offers which can easily be rejected by a fixation on the concept of the reason. Large segments of political theory would be cast out of the area of philosophy in that way. The theory of normative problems thus devolves into a practical philosophy straightjacketed as an analytical theory of action, without providing sufficient justification concerning the reasons and effects of this limitation. The fact that many social norms explicitly do not refer to actions but rather to group identities, to works, or to a belief system that might not even want to spell out proscriptions for actions, remains unappreciated.

2. *Norm Rationalism: Norms as Achievement of Reason*

2.1 Identification of Normativity and Rationality

In her exchange with Bernard Williams, Christine Korsgaard remarks: "It [internalism] does not require that rational considerations succeed in motivating us. All it requires is that rational considerations succeed in motivating us insofar as we are rational."[30] With this, Korsgaard offers a further characteristic of a normativity conception that is philosophically dominant, since reasons are frequently

[29] von Wright, *Norm and Action*, p. 14 (alluding to Nicolai Hartmann, *Ethik*, Berlin/Leipzig 1925, I/VI, Chs 18–19 and George Edward Moore, "The Nature of Moral Philosophy" in: Id., *Philosophical Studies*, London 1922, pp. 310–40, here p. 320 ff). See also the comment in Philippa Foot, *Natural Goodness*, Oxford 2001, p. 48, as well as the differentiation between norms of action and norms of objects in Herbert Schnädelbach, "Rationalität und Normativität" in: Id., *Zur Rehabilitierung des* animal rationale, Frankfurt M. 1992, pp. 79–103, here p. 84.

[30] Christine M. Korsgaard, "Skepticism about Practical Reason" in: *Journal of Philosophy* 83 (1986), pp. 5–25, here p. 15.

identified with rationality—of one or another kind—in philosophical discussion.[31] The realm of reasons is a realm of rational action. In the Anglo-Saxon discussion, the common linguistic core of individual *reasons* and *reason* writ large makes their identification particularly suggestive. Defining normativity in terms of reasons also suggests describing normativity as the result of a rational effort. Once more, a cursory glance at segments of contemporary philosophical discourse suffices as evidence. Certainly, this holds true for the tradition of political liberalism as well as for discourse ethics, in which the practice of politics turns into a particular form of pragmatically applied philosophy. This may also be the case, even if *ex negative*, for the post-structuralist critique of these traditions, which frequently conflates critique of rationality with critique of normativity. More pointedly, one could claim that postmodernity—with different premises—shares in the same fixation on reason that is exhibited by the philosophical traditions which it critiques, thereby being able to, in the end, dismiss every concept of normativity.[32]

Looking at the philosophical discussion from the outside, the identification of normativity with reason seems to also be a consequence of a certain limitation to which philosophy as a scientific discipline is subject, at least in its dominant traditions. That is because the philosophical treatment of social practices like art, law, or religion tends to describe these practices with recourse to categories of rationality. One could ask: how else should it describe them? As many other disciplines operate with categories of their own, so too is this imperative for philosophy. This does not imply accusing philosophy of a primitive rationalism. Of course, developed conceptions of rationality can be fine-tuned at will, and it is undeniable that the question of what is to qualify as rational is being disputed at a conceptually high level within philosophy. It also cannot be denied that a significant part of the Western philosophical tradition, all the way from the Greek Sophists to post-structuralism, has presented itself as a critique of rationality. Yet despite all the doubts as to whether this critique has reached the heart of academic philosophy, even this critique of rationality ties closely together rationality and normativity.

2.2 Quarrels between the Disciplines: Philosophy and the Others

If we thus, despite all care not to overgeneralize, continue to claim that contemporary practical philosophy identifies rationality with normativity, and if we further

[31] John Broome, "Is Rationality Normative? " in: *Disputatio* II/23 (2007), pp. 161–78 and Schnädelbach, "Rationalität und Normativität" p. 79 develop arguments for an indifferent relationship between normativity and rationality.

[32] An important exception can be found in parts of communitarian theory which, by means of highlighting the value of traditions or concrete political communities, has developed a theoretical offering in which rationality and normativity can be viewed separately from each other.

recognize in this an element of philosophy's disciplinary identity, then the question remains, what exactly is wrong about this close relationship (between reason and the normative)? After all, every discipline has its specific ways to approach problems and come to its conclusions. This would only be problematic if philosophy's world of categories, with its typical claim for universality, as applied to normative social practices, were only providing a distorted image of these practices. We will see that this is the case by taking a first look at domains of social norms, which are of concern in this book.

In political theory, the identification of legitimate politics with reasonable collective action has long been the subject of critique.[33] Practical philosophy's claim to assign appropriate institutions to self-determined political actors and to view these institutions' political rooms of maneuver that are undetermined by reason as something (purely) negative appears contentious. Can an open political process be reduced to the application of philosophical criteria of correctness? Crucial features of democratic orders, particularly the institutionalization of an opposition whose role it is to oppose, regardless of content, the opinion of the majority, cannot be reconciled with a conception of democracy that is fixated on good reasons alone.[34] Notably, Hannah Arendt urged to dismiss the disciplinary term "political philosophy" and to speak instead of political theory, so as to avoid reducing the question of good political ordering to simply applying a given pattern of philosophical rationality.[35] Arendt's conception of politics is not of immediate concern here. What is, however, is the observation that political theory deals with conceptions of normativity that seek to elude a philosophical claim to reasonableness and correctness. I will explicate this more concretely with the example of majority rule.

A second example can be found in the realm of art theory. Philosophical esthetics also enjoys a long tradition in which the *philosophical* reading of works of art is understood as a privileged access to truth.[36] Truth-esthetic theories measure the value of art in its ability to support a philosophical interpretation of the world. As such, it is not so much the art but the philosophy that brings about knowledge gains by means of art, and advancing that knowledge gain constitutes its decisive quality. In this case, too, other theoretical concepts can certainly be found, but the prevalence of truth-esthetic philosophical description of art is significant.[37] On such a reading, esthetic accomplishment, to employ a figure of normativity from

[33] Raymond Geuss, *Kritik der politischen Philosophie*, Hamburg 2011, pp. 56–81; Jörg Schaub, "Warum es einer von Idealtheorien unabhängigen Theorie politischer Legitimität bedarf" in: Anna Geis, et al. (eds), *Der Aufstieg der Legitimitätspolitik* (= Leviathan Special Volume, 2012), pp. 436–52.

[34] Isabelle Ley, *Opposition im Völkerrecht*, Heidelberg 2015, pp. 183–207.

[35] Clearly expressed in spoken word in Hannah Arendt, "Fernsehgespräch mit Günter Gaus" in: Id., *Ich will verstehen*, Munich 1996, pp. 44–70, here p. 44 ff.

[36] Lasting and convincing critique in Rüdiger Bubner, "Über einige Bedingungen gegenwärtiger Ästhetik" in: Id., *Ästhetische Erfahrung*, Frankfurt/M. 1989, pp. 7–51, here pp. 11–30. See also Martin Seel, *Ästhetik des Erscheinens*, Frankfurt/M. 2003, pp. 37–42.

[37] Overview in Reinold Schmücker, *Was ist Kunst?*, Munich 1998, pp. 27–46 and pp. 47–79.

the art realm, becomes a function of a philosophical pretense to rationality.[38] But one may certainly doubt "whether one adequately understands art if it is philosophically prejudged, and whether one better grasps philosophy if its borders to art are held open."[39]

A third example is offered by the realm of law. A long-standing philosophical tradition views law and its scientific description as a mere filler and placeholder for philosophically founded normative precepts. More specifically: legal theories that develop a conception of law distinct from morality push back the substantive claim of influence of practical philosophy; alternatively, morally minded conceptions of law ultimately identify law with a philosophical claim to rightness.[40] Mapping law onto a philosophical claim to rightness, too, is hardly necessary. It even seems to mark a point of modern legal orders to immunize themselves—by means of procedural rules and organizational structures—from all too fundamentally led philosophical lines of inquiry.

Among the debates analyzed here, the problem has most openly and lastingly been addressed in Christian theology, which knows a long tradition of rationality critique following Plato's *Eutyphron* which raised the issue of the relationship between divine will and reason.[41] That tradition can be found in late Scholasticism[42] or in the dialectical theology of the interwar period.[43] For theological reflection of a revelation-based religion, reduction to a model of rationality is a risky enterprise, no matter how demanding it were conceived.[44] This is particularly the case for the relationship of theology of revelation toward questions that concern practical philosophy. Christian theology cannot let itself be reduced to a universal ethics of reason without losing the distinguishing characteristics of its idea of God.[45] Thus, it not only enjoys a long-standing tradition of rationality critique, but more specifically of a critique of morality.[46]

[38] Or else, in a characteristic counter-movement, it is completely banned from the realm of the social: Christoph Menke, *Die Kraft der Kunst*, Berlin 2012, p. 14.

[39] Bubner, *Bedingungen gegenwärtiger Ästhetik*, p. 17 (Transl. AH).

[40] Particularly extensively, Ronald Dworkin, *Justice for Hedgehogs*, Cambridge, Mass. 2011, pp. 400–17.

[41] Plato, *Eutyphro*, 10a–11b.

[42] See briefly concerning Augustine and the outcomes, Kurt Flasch, *Das philosophische Denken im Mittelalter*, Leipzig 1988, pp. 39–43.

[43] For example, Karl Barth, *Die Theologie Schleiermachers*, Zürich 1978, pp. 429–31; see also, on Heidegger's view of the relationship between theology and philosophy, Ingold Dalferth, *Radikale Theologie*, Leipzig 2010, pp. 193–217. The philosopher schooled in aporias remains skeptical of this: Theodor W. Adorno, "Vernunft und Offenbarung" in: Id., *Gesammelte Schriften*, Vol. 10.2, Frankfurt/M. 1977, pp. 608–16, here pp. 611–16.

[44] A concise sketch of the relationship between philosophy of religion and revelation-based religion in Wolfhart Pannenberg, "Offenbarung als Kategorie philosophischer Theologie" in: Id., *Philosophie, Religion, Offenbarung*, Göttingen 1999, pp. 238–45. For a more recent discussion within Protestantism: Martin Laube and Georg Pfleiderer (eds), *Die Vernunft der Religion*, Loccum 2007.

[45] In an exemplary way, this revealed itself within Protestantism in the critique of Adolf von Harnack, *Das Wesen des Christentums*, Leipzig 1990.

[46] A current indication of the unease with a reduction of Christianity to moral commands can be found in Pope Francis, Apostolic Exhortation "Evangelii Gaudium", Rome, Vatican Press, 2013, p. 37 and fn. 48, referencing *Summa Theologiae* I-II, q. 107, a. 4.

2.3 Returning to Philosophy

On the flipside, the philosophical debate on the structure of normativity can also be understood as one concerned with an appropriate concept of practical rationality. It seeks to clarify whether obligations arise from subjectively fixed, instrumental contexts, or from objective claims of reason. The debate surrounding the structure of moral duties in philosophy strives to identify an appropriate model of rationality for actions. Yet the task at hand is not only to show that phenomena of normativity from realms such as politics, art, or law could be aligned with a conception of rationality. Rather, one would also have to name the price for such a reference to rationality in describing these practices.

Admittedly, Western philosophical tradition has chiefly been invested in objects that are not contingent.[47] By this token, however, the distinction between the description of an object with a claim to rationality and its categorization as rational ceases to be a matter of course. Philosophical models needn't deny contingency, but only rarely will they make the outcome of contingency an object of their investigation. The obviousness of this differentiation completely reaches its limits in the case of normative concepts. Here, the description of justification and the justification itself lose their differentiability. Other approaches come to mind, such as Nietzsche's thoughts on the genealogy of morals, as well as authors that extend from Nietzsche. But it appears that part of the consequences of such approaches is that they lead away from philosophy.[48] For at a certain point, historicizing philosophical truth claims or viewing them through the lens of sociology can no longer be accomplished by means of philosophy.

If these observations are indeed true, that is, if there is a philosophy-immanent access to the concept of normativity (or, expressed more cautiously, if there is an approach typical for philosophy) implicating the equation of normativity with some form of rationality, then is it not pointless to criticize such a tradition? Proponents of different disciplines are free to develop and apply their own conceptions (of normativity). Put differently: why should different disciplines not simply make different use of a concept, a use which accords to their particular interest, just as there is no problem in speaking of moral, esthetic, and legal norms that connotate different things and yet remain norms nonetheless? Why not simply keep things such that practical philosophy cares about the question of justifying practices and identifies it, by and large, with a notion of rationality, whereas sociology and jurisprudence respectively develop empirical and legal-dogmatic access to norms?

This would only be possible in so far as it wouldn't obfuscate a wider perspective on the concept of the normative. It would become problematic if empirically operating disciplines saw themselves confronted with a false alternative. If their

[47] Simply see Dieter Henrich, "Hegels Theorie über den Zufall" in: Id., *Hegel im Kontext*, Frankfurt/M. 1971, in more detail further along, pp. 163–5.

[48] See also Judith Butler's take in "Can the 'Other' of Philosophy Speak?" in: Id., *Undoing Gender*, New York 2004, pp. 232–51.

empirical access *either* led them to give up on the concept of normativity—for this would once more result in ceding the concept to a philosophical discourse oriented toward rationality—*or* if the treatment of an empirical access to norms were so noticeably influenced by philosophical conceptualization that the disciplinary division of labor became inoperable, as a philosophical understanding of the idea of normativity would guide which types of norms could be empirically grasped and which could not. Both alternatives, as we shall see, can be found in the empirical treatment of normativity. The influence of philosophical traditions that view normativity as a mark of rational achievement is so forceful that it would be negligent simply to ignore it in seeking out a conceptual framework for social norms. But maybe moral norms would be better understood as options within a rational blueprint for action, as opposed to being viewed as necessary results of rationality.[49]

3. *Norm Platonism: Norms in the "Realm of Reasons"*

3.1 Norms as Abstract Objects

Tied to identifying normativity and rationality is a claim about the ontology of the normative which states that norms are abstract objects[50] that have no spacio-temporal individuation of their own. Normativity can thus assume the form of an abstract duty, or of a practical consequence from a particular need, or of the content of a promise or a law. Common to all these emanations is that they, in contrast to social norms, do not have to realize themselves in events or objects. In the philosophical discussion of norms, this has found expression at least since von Wright's pioneering investigations of norm theory and the distinction between a norm and a linguistic formulation of a norm. The rule that obliges me to honor my wife must strictly be distinguished from the linguistic form in which it is expressed.[51] The linguistic form—the norm text—can have an abstract identity as a type, as a concept. And it can materialize in events such as a proclamation by a prophet, in objects such as the inscribing on a tablet, in a legal gazette, or a manners manual, which in turn can be multiplied and gain expression in a plenitude of objects. These copies, however, "are" not the norm, they are not even the norm text as such, but only copies of the norm text. These kinds of materializations of a norm—in the abstract form of a sentence or the realized form of writing upon a special sheet of paper—do not participate in the normativity of that which they materialize. At least, this is an

[49] As the case is made for by Gerald A. Cohen, "Reason, Humanity, and Moral Law" in: Christine Korsgaard, *The Sources of Normativity*, Cambridge 1996, pp. 167–88, here p. 181.

[50] On the concept up until this point Wolfgang Künne, *Abstrakte Gegenstände*, Frankfurt/M. 2007, p. 23.

[51] Georg Henrik von Wright, Norm and Action. A Logical Enquiry. Routledge & Kegan, London, 1977, p. 93 ff. Also Scott J. Shapiro, *Legality*, Cambridge, Mass. 2011, p. 103.

often unspoken assumption of philosophical norm theory. Normativity operates within the "realm of reasons." This realm is achieved and secluded through the distinction between norm and norm text or another norm symbol.

Wherein lies the problem with this assumption? Not in questioning the ontological status of abstract objects over and against an object and event materialism, that is, not in claiming that there is no concept of table, but only a spacio-temporally finite number of individual tables. I do not want to delve into this discussion but rather want to limit myself to the conjecture that the difficulties do not decrease when we do away with the assumption of abstract objects' existence.[52]

The distinction between a norm and its materialization becomes dubitable when it defines the space of the normative in such a way that the materialization devolves into a mere side effect, to a negligible epiphenomenon, when norms are described so that they are "actually" viewed as reasons that then become "embodied"[53] poorly rather than well in language and other objects. This view creates an ontological gradation in favor of a non-material norm conception, belonging to the realm of reasons, which stands in the way of grasping social norms.

The assumptions that the esthetic value of a painting lay in its embodying a thought,[54] or that a liturgy symbolize the rational content of a religious revelation, or that a political procedure serve the discovery of a moral truth, all have in common that a distinction is being made in them between an actual, rational and an unactual, material side to be located within time and space. I will try to show how unconvincing this is with recourse to three examples: the concept of procedure, the description of power, and the question of the social meaning of the giving and taking of reasons.

3.2 Generalization or Majority: On the Critique of Ideal Procedures

This critique can be nicely illustrated by the way in which philosophy tends to engage with the concept of procedure. Procedure as analyzed by philosophers is one which knows neither time nor place; it is an ideal procedure which operates like a thought experiment. For this reason, legal practices—comparable to literary works in their linguistic composition and their reliance on the extra-linguistic[55]—can

[52] Künne, *Abstrakte Gegenstände*, pp. 126–34.

[53] Jürgen Habermas, "Die Lebenswelt als Raum symbolisch verkörperter Gründe" in: Id., *Nachmetaphysisches Denken II*, Berlin 2012, pp. 54–76, here p. 58 ff.

[54] Surprisingly, one still encounters the accusation aimed at esthetic depictions that they are merely esthetic and neglect the actual moral problem of their object, see for example Martha C. Nussbaum, "Wie über Armut schreiben?" in: *Merkur* 766 (2013), pp. 250–7. On Katherine Boo, *Behind the Beautiful Forevers*, New York 2012. Here, however, we rather see a deflection of a threat to one's own kind of philosophy.

[55] On this, see further below pp. 149–56.

hardly be fully grasped without including the material conditions in which they operate; for example, when an original manuscript in the form of a legal gazette must be secured in order to guarantee the authority of a certain legal content. In a first step, such phenomena demonstrate that the inclusion of the material side is necessary for a sufficient description of the normative claim of art, politics, and law. For without question, there are no actual legal orders, artworks, political processes, or religious practices that function purely in the imaginary. But it is in the second step—and with it, we enter shakier foundations—no longer possible to separate this material side from its normative side. Therefore, the normativity of law is not a characteristic that can meaningfully be grasped without reference to the spacio-temporal side of procedures, to the possibility of applying force, and to law's written fixation. What makes law normative has to be conceived taking into account such features.

The difference between a philosophical conception of normativity building upon a standard of rationality and a social conception thereof can be illustrated by the discussion of procedural rules for political communities. Democratic constitutional States decide by majority rule in all kinds of institutional contexts among equals, among voters, parliamentarians, members of executive committees, and—frequently overlooked—among members of a panel of judges. From the frequent use of this decision-making rule, one can easily deduce an element of a concept of legitimation shared by these orders, one that supposes the interplay between the recognition of status equality and a decision rule that follows from such recognition. Such omnipresence of the majority rule in liberal democracies, however, stands in stark contrast to the critical or even dismissive treatment which it received within political philosophy, most prominently by Rawls.[56] For according to these accounts, decision by majority vote is "merely empirical,"[57] that is, it is limited to counting votes and processing existing preferences.

Majority rule operates as a genuine procedural rule, as a rule of an *actual*—not imagined—procedure, as it provides manageable criteria for action in a concrete, individualizable decision-making context. By that token it is distinct from generalizability rules in the vein of Habermas or from Rawlsian decision-making rules in the moment of conclusion of the original social contract, which also claim to be rules of procedure. Regardless of whether it is appropriate to dub the generalizability criterion a "rule of procedure" at all, the difference between it and the majority rule illustrates where the practical problem might lie: Not in the vacuity

[56] John Rawls, *A Theory of Justice*, Frankfurt/M. 1990, pp. 392–9. In Korsgaard, *Sources of Normativity*, pp. 34–7 one finds the differentiation between substantive and procedural moral realism. On my reading, the former also follows a model of ideal proceduralism.

[57] Here, I'm referring to a verbal comment by Jürgen Habermas. On the majority rule, see Jürgen Habermas, *Faktizität und Geltung. Beiträge zur Diskurstheorie des Rechts und des demokratischen Rechtsstaats*, Frankfurt/M. 1992, pp. 351–66. The degree to which this criticism also applies to Habermas depends on the difficult question of which systemic significance his social theoretical contributions hold for his democracy-theoretical reflections.

or formality of the criterion (much criticized following Hegel) but in the fact that it remains unclear how and why such a rule should ever be implemented in a concrete procedural context; that is, it remains questionable why all those affected by a given decision should have to apply the generalizability criterion if the same result could easily be brought about by a single philosopher properly applying the rule. Why do we even need a practice of political procedures if we have conclusive rationality tests for norms? In line with Kant, a generalizability theorist could point out that the rule itself commands as such. Such a reading would claim it as part of the generalizability rule's content that it be applied equally by all those affected, and that a philosopher king were thus excluded as a possibility.[58] So far, so good, but what happens when no consensus is achieved concerning the application of the generalizability rule—a consequence that is probable in light of the many uncertainties of its application?[59] Under the conditions of a democratic order, we are then thrust back upon a majority rule, and once again the above-raised and already negated question arises as to whether this circumstance might be viewed as the symptom of a deficient reality, or, to the contrary, whether the hierarchical priority of generalizability over majority rule falsely abstracts from the circumstances of political socialization. On this reading, prioritizing the rule of reason would be the result of a misplaced philosophical abstraction of the political process in complete disregard of (actual) political processes.[60] With the majority rule, however, we indeed stick to a specific form of approval control concretely delimited by local rules,[61] and in this way, Habermas' insistence on the rule's merely empirical character can be spun in a positive manner. Factual approval cannot be traced other than by means of a procedure that is spatially and temporally defined.

Against this, Rainer Forst has argued that the two conceptions of procedure do not exclude each other but instead could be carried out in tandem and

[58] This would seem to accord with the problematic reading of Kant by Ingeborg Maus, *Zur Aufklärung der Demokratietheorie*, Frankfurt/M. 1994. Critically on this, Wolfgang Kersting, *Kant über Recht*, Paderborn 2004, pp. 94–7.

[59] See the discussion in Dorothy Emmet, *Rules, Roles, and Relations*, London 1966, pp. 56–88.

[60] For me, the German Federal Constitutional Court plays a theoretically interesting (and problematic) game with the idea of proceduralism when it repeals decisions of legislators on the grounds of lacking procedural rationality which require that certain factual or normative aspects are included in the decision-making process. The appeal to the procedural nature suggests a reduced test limited to "formal" questions, thereby appearing to protect the legislator's freedom of decision while the court severely interferes with the latter. See Christoph Möllers, "Legalität, Legitimität und Legitimation des Bundesverfassungsgerichts" in: Matthias Jestaedt, Oliver Lepsius, Christoph Möllers, and Christoph Schönberger, *Das entgrenzte Gericht*, Berlin 2011, pp. 281–419, here pp. 395–9 (translation forthcoming).

[61] Unlike for any other philosophical work, this problem can be traced in the genesis of discourse theory through Habermas' work: what began as a theory of the normative preconditions for factual claims morphed into on concerning moral, political, and legal correctness. All four questions received, at their systematic core, the same answer, albeit with many important variations. See Christoph Möllers, "Demokratie und Recht" in: Hauke Brunkhorst, Regina Kreide, and Cristina Lafont (eds), *Habermas-Handbuch*, Stuttgart 2009, pp. 254–63, here pp. 257–60.

simultaneously.[62] The way I understand his point, the rule of actual procedure is to infuse actual decisions with legitimation yet also lead to a conclusive decision, whereas rules of ideal procedure—for example, testing whether the decisions made can be generalized—serve to develop criteria in order to critique the content of a given decision as well as in order to reach new decisions. What is certainly true on this account is that rules of actual procedure remain normatively empty in that they offer no objective indication whatsoever as to how things should be decided. A generalizability test along the lines of Kant could fulfill this task, but one also has to remark that this division of labor distinctly limits the potential contribution of philosophical criteria in two ways. For one, it shows that the above-mentioned (negative) philosophical evaluation of the majority rule misses its mark. This principle necessarily operates at a practical, social level so that it remains unclear how philosophical rules of ideal procedure could ever be used to serve as a critique of the rules of actual procedure in which these rules of ideal procedure can be actualized. This brings us to the second limitation. In one strong philosophical tradition, rules of actual procedure are viewed as deficient since they must account for the limited resources of time and rationality that are immanent to all things social. On the reading presented here, however, the opposite holds true. Criteria such as the categorical imperative or its heirs in contemporary discourse theory only gain social relevance in and through the practice of rules of actual procedure.

If both types of rules serve the end of justification, of legitimation, then their coexistence deserves further analysis. For what do the two, more specifically the majority rule and generalizability test, contribute to the justification of a decision? We can only reach an answer to this query if we first clarify what is meant by "justification." Such a clarification can only ever apply to one of the two procedures, not to both simultaneously, as both procedures can be imagined separately from each other and contradict each other in the end. In this case, a justification could be justified at one level and not the other. Now, it is hard to see how this persistent situation in practice could be solved at an institutional level for there is no spacio-temporal procedure in which one could approximate the ideal criterion of generalizability. For example, there is no empirically rigid insight according to which a group of people who sit in a circle and enjoy equal speaking rights for an unlimited period of time can more likely arrive at a generalizable decision in the end.

Of course, there is a tremendous difference between procedures in which participants have the opportunity to converse with one another, to inform themselves, and reflect before they take part in a majority decision, and those in which decisions are being made without such possibilities.[63] It is in this distinction that the

[62] Discussion at the Social-Scientific Class of the Berlin-Brandenburg Academy of the Sciences, 14 June 2013.

[63] There are very real instantiations of this difference, for example in the phenomenon of "(merely) electoral democracy" without open deliberation: Aurel Croissant and Wolfgang Merkel, "Formale und informale Institutionen in defekten Demokratien" in: *Politische Vierteljahresschrift* 41 (2000), pp. 3–30.

meaning of ideal criteria for political procedures finds its expression. For just as there can be no real procedures without criteria that are applied in them, so too no design of real procedures can fulfill its purpose without justifying reasons that speak for this procedure as opposed to a different decision procedure. Thus, underlying the majority rule there is a normative claim about the value and specific meaning of participants' equal status,[64] and also about the missing normative neutrality of the status quo that is to be changed by means of a decision.[65] A majority decision does not gain its legitimating content without such reasoning. But this does not affect the fundamental line that is drawn whenever an actual procedure is introduced. It also does not change the resulting limitation of the influence that the reasons for introducing certain procedures might have on the procedure itself. For it is precisely the limiting of the effectiveness of reasons that provides the essential justification for actual procedures. This ambivalence of actual procedures which, on the one hand, are to transport a legitimating content while, on the other hand, limit the influence of legitimating aspects on (the binding effect of) the decision is by no means an accident. Quite to the contrary: it is the practical purpose of any procedural solution. To discount this distinctive property of procedural solutions—without more specific consideration of concrete procedural makeups—as a mere loss through friction due to an imperfect reality would not amount to arguing for more justified decisions. Instead, it would amount to rejecting as a whole any decision-making and other modes of realizing normative demands. Herein lies the crux of any moral theory of procedure.

3.3 Power

Assumptions of practical philosophy have repercussions on the description of social norms. This is particularly the case when social norms are reduced to being reasons (for action). A look at Rainer Forst's theory of power will serve to substantiate this claim.[66] Forst takes power to be a phenomenon of "intelligible, spiritual" or "noumenal" nature, its "actual realm of existence is the realm of reasons," the sphere of justification. He who exerts power over someone controls that person's reasons for action. "Power rests on recognized, accepted justifications—some

[64] Wojciech Sadurski, *Equality and Legitimacy*, Oxford 2008, pp. 41–8.

[65] Cass R. Sunstein, *The Partial Constitution*, Cambridge, Mass. 1993, pp. 68–92.

[66] Rainer Forst, *Kritik der Rechtfertigungsverhältnisse*, Berlin 2011, pp. 21–4; in greater detail Id., "Noumenal Power", *Normative Orders Working Paper* 02/13, pp. 1–24, here p. 9. Is the "power" that will be of further concern here and in the following a normative phenomenon? Even if we cannot yet provide an answer at this point, due to the lack of our own concept of the normative, power certainly establishes the possibility of setting and enforcing norms. The debate surrounding the idea of power only addresses the question at hand and is not of further interest. For an overview, see Byung-Chul Han, *Was ist Macht?*, Stuttgart 2005.

good, some bad, some in between."[67] Only if someone has options for action can power be exerted over them. For that reason, violence and coercion need to be distinguished from power. The latter do not limit room for action but exclude it. If an agent follows an external command of power, then only because he or she recognizes that command as a reason for their action.

An immanent problem of this model seems to lie in that it identifies the concept of a reason, which concerns every possible action, with a mere motive, all the while clinging to the idea that reasons operate within the realm of justification—even if possibly failing at it.[68] As such, however, a motive lays no claim to justification. Can instruments of power such as temptation or the exploitation of hunger be taken to be justificatory offerings? This objection can also be applied to the theory of the subject and leads to the question of whether being a subject—beyond immediately operative coercion—merely consists in rationalizing justificatory options. Temptation, hunger, and mental pressure operate neither through immediate coercion nor justification. They are found within an intermediary realm that appears to be typical for many of our actions. For that reason, the model of the acting subject alleged here comes across as lacking in nuance.[69] According to this theoretical account, vastly different phenomena are being oriented toward a pre-existing stock of categories, imputed on the subject, and rationalized.[70] However, a notion of a reason for action that could simultaneously include the threat with a pistol, pain, an act of seduction, hunger, a proper argument, as well as a well-presented but false argument, offers no laudable descriptive value. It remains an empty *passe-partout* for the entirety of all actions—with a very broadly understood notion of action—whereas what is truly of interest among these phenomena is what distinguishes them from each other, and what is external to them. We are ultimately again confronted here with the problematic inference from a normative individualism to a methodical one. A theory that treats moral justification as the achievement of subjects in the tradition of Kant straightforwardly uses its categories in order to describe social

[67] Forst, "Noumenal Power", p. 13.

[68] Here we might make out a distinction from other theories of power that tie the idea to successful justification, not just with any claim to justification. See, for example, Hans-Peter Großhans, "Die Wahrheit wird euch frei machen. Zum Verhältnis von Religion, Wahrheit und Macht" in: *Zeitschrift für Theologie und Kirche* 104 (2007), pp. 336–56, here pp. 346–52. For this reason, the purported proximity between Forst and Spinoza, as seen in Martin Saar, *Die Immanenz der Macht*, Berlin 2013, p. 264 and fn. 53, appears dubitable. Forst's notion simply also includes irrational attempts at justification, in so far as they are used as reasons.

[69] In the paradoxical coexistence of coercion and action, Wittgenstein's remark: "If a rule does not coerce you, then you are not *following* a rule" (transl. AH) (*Bemerkungen über die Grundlagen der Mathematik*, Frankfurt/M. 2013, p. 413, italics in original) at least emphasizes the problem that cannot simply be solved in favor of one of the two alternatives.

[70] Christine Korsgaard's remark that "pain is the perception of a reason" points toward a similar strategy, see Korsgaard, *Sources of Normativity*, p. 149; contrast, however, with Ludwig Wittgenstein on perceiving pain, *Philosophische Untersuchungen*, Frankfurt/M. 2003, § 289 (p. 162).

practices and structures, but without explaining[71] how well these categories are suited to the task.[72]

The core of our problem, however, lies elsewhere. Forst conceptualizes power as a practice of justification. On his reading, power is based on factually accepted justifications. For him, power practices are like other social practices in that they are always normative because they are only possible by means of justification.[73] As such, however, the concept of justification loses its discriminatory content with respect to the practices to which it refers. In the end then, every action raises a normative claim. Only two descriptive levels remain then for analysis: the level of practice that is always already normative since it commands justification, and the level of moral justification or critique of said practice. What is missing, then, is a level of morally unjustified social norms that, under some circumstances, might not be adhered to but nonetheless remain relevant for social relations. It is precisely this level that will be of concern in what follows.

Let us assume, for example, that international law is recognized by all participants as the relevant normative order of international relations between States. At the same time, it appears questionable to all participants whether the existing international legal order can be fully justified morally. Furthermore, the practice of States not only frequently violates international legal norms. What is more, it often upholds certain norms vis-à-vis weaker States while not upholding them vis-à-vis stronger States, that is, only against Serbia and not against China, even though this is hardly reconcilable with the international legal axiom of the sovereign equality of all States. Forst would have to hold that this common practice in the international arena integrates the unequal distribution of power into its *justificatory* calculus. The practice accepts the unequal distribution as a reason for action, even if this reason remains legally and morally dubious, thus becoming normative on Forst's understanding. But this interpretation misses something. The practice of international relations indeed avoids the conflict with powerful States, as it is politically or economically risky. However, the distinction between such a practice of evasion and the level of norms of international law remains of immense import whenever actors in the international arena purport to act legally. The norms of international law can neither be reduced to a moral imperative, nor to the actual practice of States that at times violates them. The actual domain of

[71] The often-criticized dualism in Habermas' social theory, which integrates a sociological notion of systems, seems also indebted to the correct insight that the description of social practices cannot be simply achieved with the self-same conceptual instruments as the construction of a theory of justification.

[72] Concerning the ability of the concept to analyze structures, see Forst, "Noumenal Power", pp. 12–17. Presumably, such an analysis would have to reintroduce all of the differentiations that it had precisely excluded from its analysis by mean of its notion of reason.

[73] Ibid., p. 13.

social norms is found precisely in the area beyond moral justification and ad hoc justified practice. But this domain remains invisible if every practice is taken as normative.

Incorporating power into a theory of reasons and domesticating it for the purposes of philosophical discourse entails the price of significant losses in descriptive power. Every motive becomes a reason, every social practice becomes a normative project, and the rich world of power techniques is reduced to an ever-identical, rational internal matter. Social norms—practices of the counterfactual—vanish between facticity that is automatically interpreted as normative and its moral evaluation. In contrast, a substantive theory of power will also, if not primarily, have to engage with the external side of this phenomenon, for example with the fact that hunger has a physiological cause and that legal justifications generally are not the best justifications but are rather justifications under certain institutional circumstances. The problem of philosophical conceptualizing thus lies in the fact that it tends, in the name of coherence, radically to reduce given concepts referring to social practices—be it the concept of a norm, be it the concept of power—while at the same time refusing to give up the claim that the thus-reduced concept still provides a meaningful account of these practices.

3.4 Giving or Taking Reasons—on a Socially Relevant Distinction

A third example for the implications of philosophical conceptualizing is offered by Charles Tilly's observation that justificatory situations in social practice often result from situations of inequality.[74] On his reading, there is a profound practical difference between the giving and the taking of reasons, one that not only questions, but turns on its head the parlance of "giving and taking reasons," which at least in German has arisen following Brandom.[75]

The formula is brought into question in as far as it treats the giving and accepting of reasons as equal efforts. Doing so abstracts from a lot of what is socially meaningful in these procedures of justification—for example from the differences of a reason-giving political, legal, or religious institution on the one hand, and the addressee of these reasons on the other hand. One might object that behind the equal treatment of giving and taking reasons there are in turn concrete normative and cognitive reasons, namely the fundamental equality of all participants who, in

[74] Tilly, *Why?*, pp. 24–31.
[75] See Robert B. Brandom, *Making It Explicit. Reasoning, Representing, and Discursive Commitment*, Cambridge, Mass. 1994.

light of the objective worth or worthlessness of reasons, all owe reasons to one another. Even if one accepts this important point, it remains unclear why even political and legal institutions that rest on an egalitarian footing tend to organize duties of justification in a highly asymmetrical fashion. More specifically, in a democratic State, why are citizens not held to justify their voting behavior whereas courts must justify their verdicts? A substantive answer would have to combine an egalitarian theory with institutional considerations in such a way that neither side is prioritized as the "actually" normative one. Why?[76] Because a theory of normative social and political practices cannot relegate the characteristic features of the practical aspect to a subordinate role.[77]

The notion of giving and taking reasons should be turned on its head in so far as it suggests a symmetry which does not exist. The right to demand reasons is supposed to be matched by an obligation to give reasons. If one follows Tilly's analysis, then the possibility of giving reasons turns into a privileged status which is only accorded to actors of a certain social power and imbues upon them the power of definition over a socially unequal situation that is already in their favor. Seen in this light, the possibility of giving relevant reasons shows itself less as an obligation than a right, if not a privilege. One could see in talk of "giving and taking" of reasons a parlance which is not interested in such questions and is thus unworthy of such a critique. But my reading would differ: such parlance is applied to social practices, and yet it simultaneously abstracts from that which is socially relevant in these practices. It is not simply neutral but rather carries with it a notion of how social norms operate, a notion that is misleading.

In conclusion, the distinction between mutually independent moral and social concepts of normativity that do not conceptually interfere with each other becomes questionable in light of these examples. Forst's conceptualization of power has repercussions for the understanding of social practice, a practice that may also be empirically observed. The expression of "giving and taking" reasons, adopted from Brandom, implies an equality in the practice of justification which particularly ignores essential characteristics of this practice. The same goes for a notion of procedure based purely on reason that in fact ignores procedures. The descriptive claim of philosophical theories thus often reaches far into the empirical study of social practices, but suppresses practically relevant differences.

[76] Exemplary on the question of the obligation of justification in institutions, Christoph Möllers, *The Three Branches. A Comparative Model of Separation of Powers*, Oxford 2013, pp. 59–63.

[77] This, of course, is ultimately a Hegelian idea. When Hegel takes "law", and here we can take all normative practices as such, to mean "being of free will", as he does in the *Grundlinien der Philosophie des Rechts*, Frankfurt/M. 1986, § 29 (p. 80), then the meaning of being in this definition is not of secondary concern.

4. *Pan-Normativism: On the Normativity of Descriptive Propositions*

4.1 Normativity of Meaning?

The identification of normativity with rationality also raises the question of a delimitation of the normative and non-normative. This is even more the case as the category of the normative has migrated from practical into theoretical philosophy. Subjectivity,[78] intentionality,[79] and linguistic meaning[80] are taken to be normative phenomena.

In the following, I will limit myself to the case of meaning. If linguistic meaning can be explained by adherence to certain norms, then we must be dealing with something normative, such as if "yellow" were only *allowed* for the description of yellow objects. If, by making a given assertion, I decide not to assert a claim that goes against this linguistic norm, and if I, by describing a certain situation, take responsibility for it, then it would indeed seem appropriate to understand linguistic meanings in this way. But this reconstruction raises several questions.

For one, we should clarify whether the fact that the expression "yellow" only serves the description of yellow objects constitutes an obligation, or, more generally, what exactly does it mean to use an expression appropriately or to describe certain circumstances wrongly? Do criteria of linguistic correctness constitute a norm, or wouldn't more be needed for that? Am I *held to* express myself correctly? Of course, certain other obligations come to mind, such as a general moral obligation to truth. But this would be its own norm which would transcend the rules of linguistic meaning.

Another concern arises in the idea of linguistic *rules*. Nobody learns a language from a set of rules, and Willard Quine realized early on[81] that the search for linguistic rules quickly turns into the construction of ad hoc conventions that need to adapt to every practice; that is, they don't prescribe anything in the end but only reconstruct something.[82] Linguistic rules serve as instruments for describing language, not as normative rules. If at all, they resemble natural laws that are subject

[78] John McDowell, *Mind and World*, Cambridge, Mass. 1996; Rödl, *Selbstbezug und Normativität.*

[79] Differently, however, Brandom, *Making It Explicit*, p. 243.

[80] Representative for many, Brandom, ibid., pp. 18–30, developed from a different foundation, Allan Gibbard, *Meaning and Normativity*, Oxford 2012. Critically on that assumption, Kathrin Glüer, "Sense and Prescriptivity" in: *Acta Analytica* 14 (1999), pp. 111–28, here pp. 120–7; id., "Bedeutung zwischen Norm und Naturgesetz" in: *Deutsche Zeitschrift für Philosophie* 48 (2000), pp. 449–68, here pp. 454–62. In a practical context, Korsgaard, *Sources of Normativity*, pp. 132–40.

[81] W.V.O. Quine, "Truth by Convention" in: Id., *The Ways of Paradox*, 2nd edited volume. Cambridge, Mass. 1976, pp. 77–106, here pp. 88–97.

[82] A similar observation following Wittgenstein by Stanley Cavell, *The Claim of Reason*, New York 1979, p. 31: It is impossible for us to have assented to the conventions that shape our language beforehand. On the problem of the thereby implied norms, see below, pp.123–25.

to observable change. Some aspects, such as formations of poetic language, elude such rules.[83]

Donald Davidson added to this critique with the observation that for important speech practices there can be no rules, for example on the question of whether someone is lying.[84] My two-year old son might point to a green dot, yell "buue!" and laugh because he knows that the dot is not blue. Does this constitute a lie or a joke? Did he violate a norm, and if so, was it a *language norm*, or just a norm *within* language? After all, it is no coincidence that such norms are rarely spelled out explicitly in the philosophy of language, which presumes the normativity of language. Here we see a fundamental difference to the social practice of law. When describing the law, we are not constantly concerned with making presumably implicit norms explicit, since there already exist institutional mechanisms charged with that task. For this reason, language-theoretical claims about meaning and usage cannot simply be transferred into legal theory or into the theory of other social norms.[85] It thus remains questionable whether a model of normative regularity can be fruitfully applied to the practice of language. It is equally questionable whether we can sufficiently grasp practices of social norms such as (the rules of) etiquette or the law by employing language-theoretical models.

4.2 If Meaning is Normative, what then is not Normative?

Robert Brandom has developed an influential, pragmatic theoretical model of linguistic meaning which will bring us closer to some of the problems of an expanded usage of the concept of normativity. Brandom distinguishes three levels of normativity.[86] At the lowest level, a language community defines the appropriateness of a certain linguistic usage. The definition of these "norms," at a higher level, presumes that the members of this language community are treated as being empowered as well as bound by the language usage; that is, the model assumes that all members take a *normative attitude* toward the usage of language, according to which all language users must take responsibility for their language usage and may hold other users accountable for their language use. On a third level, the language community must develop its language usage in such a way that the mutual ascription of linguistic obligations and authorization functions properly.

[83] An admirably concise analysis of pragmatics of the notion of a rule can be found in Max Black, "The Analysis of Rules" in: Id., *Models and Metaphors*, Ithaca 1962, pp. 95–139, here pp. 120–3.

[84] Donald Davidson, "Kommunikation und Konvention" in: Ibid., *Wahrheit und Interpretation*, Frankfurt/M. 1999, pp. 372–83, here pp. 379–87.

[85] Scott Hershovitz, "Wittgenstein on Rules: The Phantom Menace" in: *Oxford Journal of Legal Studies* 22 (2002), pp. 619–40, here pp. 635–7.

[86] Summarily, Brandom, *Making It Explicit*, pp. 636–9.

It is only *within* such an elaborated model of a *normative* linguistic pragmatism that the distinction between normative and cognitive; that is, non-normative speech acts becomes neutralized. Brandom takes this distinction as analogous to the distinction between input and output, where a cognitive input refers to the realm of the descriptive, while output in the shape of actions refers to the realm of the normative in a narrower sense.[87] This differentiation is located within a factual social practice. Norms and non-norms participate in the world of facts.[88] For Brandom, norms are facts, but talking about facts unfolds and is made explicit in normative categories. Therefore, the cognitive side is more basic than the normative side,[89] for I can only strive for an action, something that aims to make true, on the basis of a cognitive achievement, a holding-to-be-true.[90]

The example of Brandom's model is of interest for a model that makes normativity an element of any meaning without wanting to sacrifice the differentiation between normative and non-normative propositions. If normativity and and the ability to be described can only be distinguished in the mentioned way, however, then it remains to be explained why normativity cannot simply lose itself in general social practice. Ultimately, Brandom provides a surprising answer to this question, with which he is clearly wrestling toward the end of his book:[91] the fixed point for normativity lies within facticity itself, more specifically, in the resistance of the objects to be described. It would lead to commonality of descriptions that makes sure that the normative claims to correctness of language practice weren't built on sand, that they didn't operate just self-referentially. According to Brandom it is only the shared perception of such objects that guarantees that it is sensible to make any claims to correctness. Claims to correctness, in turn, are then viewed as the foundation for all other forms of descriptive propositions and normative ones in a narrower sense.[92]

The answer is surprising because it implies that every form of normativity depends on the world being constituted in a certain way. Normativity is made contingent upon the factual beyond our command.[93] On top of that, normativity is a

[87] Ibid., p. 232 ff.
[88] Ibid., p. 625.
[89] Ibid., p. 232 ff.
[90] This seems to be a point in which Brandom digresses from the pragmatic theory tradition that is so important for him.
[91] Brandom, *Making it Explicit*, pp. 626, 633 ff., 648 ff.
[92] For a critique that begins from a different starting point but arrives at similar conclusions to what follows, see: Jasper Liptow, *Regel und Interpretation*, Weilerswist 2004, pp. 148–54. There, Liptow also mentions important doubts by Michael Esfeld concerning Brandom's model of supervenience, as it posits that normative dispositions are taken to supervene »correct« normative dispositions. (ibid., p. 154, fn. 57).
[93] Habermas quickly recognized that the crux of the scheme is in the truth-theoretical question and that this entails an »overly inclusive notion of normativity«: Jürgen Habermas, "Von Kant zu Hegel" in: Id., *Wahrheit und Rechtfertigung*, Frankfurt/M. 1999, pp. 138–85, here p. 148.

phenomenon to be developed out of things, so it is not a created or posited phenomenon. Its ultimate reason is found in the fact that the world is as it is.

Both assumptions follow from Brandom's pan-normativism. If one takes world description in its entirety to be a normative undertaking, then the delimitation of normativity becomes a problem almost impossible to solve, leading to theoretical conclusions that, despite departing from normative categories, end up in a factualization of the normative, even in theories from which one wouldn't expect such positions.[94] Segments of neo-Kantian philosophy seem to have failed in light of a similar dilemma. For these thinkers, the reference to normativity was an escape, all the while failing to reach a precise account of what they meant by this reference.[95]

For now, it thus appears more convincing not to treat every conceptual criterion as a normative criterion.[96] The assumption of a normative constitution of language, widely followed in analytical philosophy, attempts to get rid of the problem of normativity by generalizing the concept (of normativity). In doing so, the concept of normativity is mutilated according to the model of human language in order to be able to reconstruct language as something normative. All conceptual features and specifics of normativity are thereby blocked from sight by normativity's omnipresence.

5. *Norm Moralization: Moral Norms as a Model for Norm Theory?*

5.1 Morality as a Paradigm of Normativity

In our pondering of normativity, even in our practical dealing with norms, moral standards assume distinguished meaning. We know that there are many kinds of norms that do not make a moral claim or have a moral content, from table manners to traffic signs. In some cases, we might even expressly prefer them: "Manners before morals!" Oscar Wilde has Lady Windermere declare.[97] But upon closer inspection, even this quotation proves to be oriented toward morality. It expresses the idea that considerate behavior is morally more valuable than grandiose universal pretenses. Wilde's declaration is less of a critique of moral convictions per se than it is a critique of a false form of morality. As in other contexts, we discover a moral content here, lurking behind non-moral norms. If we almost necessarily

[94] Expressly different in Gibbard, *Meaning and Normativity*, p. 23, who sees no problem in understanding the distinction between norms and facts as a normative differentiation which prescribes what we are to do with them.

[95] Thus, the brilliant analysis of the theories by Rickert, Lask, and Windelband, with reference to current parallels with Brandom and others in Frederick C. Beiser, "Normativity in Neo-Kantianism: Its Rise and Fall" in: *International Journal of Philosophical Studies* 17 (2009), pp. 9–27.

[96] Formulated in this manner by Schnädelbach, "Rationalität und Normativität", p. 92.

[97] Oscar Wilde, *Lady Windermere's Fan*, Berlin 1947, p. 130 (4th act).

think of moral norms as paradigmatic for norms in general, then it is no surprise that the theory of the normative is primarily being shaped by practical philosophy, by the theory of morally appropriate action.

Other normative disciplines also orient themselves along moral models. An important line of debate in legal theory has long been treating the question of whether legal norms—possibly or necessarily—have a moral content, and if so, which one. Even proponents of a legal positivism that maintains a safe distance to morality rely on theories from practical philosophy in order to back up their claims, such as Hans Kelsen drawing on Immanuel Kant or Joseph Raz drawing on certain variations of value theory.[98] Legal theory's affinity to morality is all the more obvious in theories that ascribe an immanent moral content to the law, such as the models of Ronald Dworkin or Robert Alexy.[99] Moral norms also play an extraordinary role in the empirical social sciences. Talcott Parsons still assumed that the social distribution of moral orientations must be understood in order to be able to properly describe societies.[100] After all, the philosophical forefathers of the current meta-ethical discussion, David Hume and Immanuel Kant, remain significant in many paradigms of empirical social research, as we shall see in Chapter 2.

If we want to understand normativity as a social practice, as a form that must be divested among persons, then moral norms do not necessarily have to appear as a general model. One of the fundamental problems of the philosophical discussion of normativity, as we have seen, lies in how internal processes, chiefly the motivation for an action, can be brought into harmony with external processes, such as contexts that transport moral obligations. The debate about the constitution of moral reasons combines the question of the justification or moral obligation with the metaphysical question about the relationship between subject and world, and it thus imposes a burden upon itself that a theory of social normativity could not handle, even if it accepted that rationality plays an important role in this practice.

6. *Recognition and Acknowledgment of Moral Norms*

Recognizing a moral norm as a moral norm also means to *acknowledge* its binding effect in the context of practical philosophy. If I describe a norm as a moral norm,

[98] Joseph Raz, "Explaining Normativity: Reason and the Will" in: Id., *Engaging Reason*, Oxford 1999, pp. 90–117. The reference by H.L.A. Hart, one of the most important Anglo-Saxon legal positivists of the twentieth century, to *Ordinary Language Philosophy*, a piece of theoretical philosophy, represent an exception in its meta-ethical agnosticism. For a critique thereof: Sylvie Delacroix, "Meta-Ethical Agnosticism in Legal Theory: Mapping a Way Out" in: *Jurisprudence* 1 (2010), pp. 225–40. The question remains in how far such a legal theory is still a legal theory, and not a moral theory, especially in light of a legal practice that is promiscuous in terms of meta-ethics.

[99] Ronald Dworkin, *Law's Empire*, Cambridge, Mass. 1986; Robert Alexy, *Begriff und Geltung des Rechts*, Freiburg 2005.

[100] Talcott Parsons, "The Place of Ultimate Values in Sociological Theory" in: *International Journal of Ethics* 45 (1935), pp. 282–316.

at least in as far as I cannot delimit it from its specific context, then I must simultaneously accept that it binds me, otherwise something would be wrong with its description.[101] This explains why moral theories of normativity often describe and simultaneously justify their object in one step. I cannot both mark an action as morally necessary and simultaneously distance myself from it. Herein lies a further problem of moral philosophical models for a theory of social normativity, for such a theory has to be able to describe norms without having to justify them. This does not imply that they can be "value free" or normatively neutral. This is not the case, and the question of the normative claim of the theory of normativity to be developed here will continue to concern us. On the flipside, social norms also cannot be reduced to a proper theory of moral action. Against the claim made in philosophical discussion that a reason for an action must both explain and justify it,[102] it is necessary to distinguish between explanation and justification even when the two seem pragmatically inseparable. The goal of this book is to reach a *non-normative conception of normativity*, not one that simultaneously justifies a certain descriptive form of normativity as normatively appropriate.[103]

6.1 Socially Stabilizing and Destabilizing Potential of the Normative

It is an important tenet of many recent social theories that social practices or the existence of entire societies depends on the presence of moral bonds. Beyond a primitive moralism, Parsons formulated this claim early on.[104] In order to work, societies need a moral vanishing point. Parsons' contribution had a certain impetus, it served as a methodical critique of a utilitarian description of society. His objections to a purely instrumental conception of the social can be accepted without having to thereby deny that moral claims also have destructive effects on the operation of societies. That is, a social theory that accords a task to moral norms cannot restrict itself to seeing the functional side of morality while ignoring its dysfunctional side. Societies—this formulation will return at the end of the book—can be under-normativized or over-normativized. They can crumble under the weight of their own normative pretenses. This has certainly been recognized in sociology, as is evidenced by Max Weber's distinction between an ethics of moral conviction

[101] Unless I were able to limit its scope of validity, but then, too, I'm not saying that it doesn't count for me, but that it doesn't apply to my situation.

[102] Stefan Gosepath, "Praktische Rationalität. Eine Problemübersicht" in: Id. (ed.), *Motive, Zwecke, Gründe*, Frankfurt/M. 1999, pp. 7–53, here p. 10.

[103] Schnädelbach, "Rationalität und Normativität", p. 88 and p. 96, rightly emphasizes that this classically social-scientific concern is still not outdated, not even by the critique of the supposed value-neutrality of the sciences. It is rather dislocated as long as the description of phenomena is the goal.

[104] Parsons, "Place of Ultimate Values". Critically, but concurring in its basic approach, Hans Joas, *Die Entstehung der Werte*, Frankfurt/M. 1997, pp. 32–6.

and an ethics of responsibility[105] and—one-sided in the opposite direction—by Niklas Luhmann's reminder of the polemical character of morality.[106] To this insight, a philosophical discourse might respond with the distinction between real and false conceptualizations of morality and insist that moral pretenses that could bring a society to collapse are already false for that reason alone. But this differentiation is of little merit for a theory of normativity because it would extend the descriptive claim of a philosophical theory of the normative to unfathomable heights and it would suffer from a dramatic lack of differentiation. In fact, the insight of sociologists into the ambivalence of morality reaffirms the necessity of working on a non-normative conception of the normative which does not orient itself along moral normativity.[107]

[105] Max Weber, "Politik als Beruf" in: Id., Gesammelte politische Schriften, ed. by Johannes Winckelmann, Tübingen 1988, pp. 505–60, here pp. 551–9.
[106] Niklas Luhmann, *Paradigm Lost*, Frankfurt/M. 1990.
[107] Another sociological branching off could consist in looking for functional equivalents for morality and thereby turning the assumption on its head that there is something fundamental to morality: Niklas Luhmann, "Soziologie der Moral" in: Id./Stephan H. Pfürtner (eds), *Theorietechnik und Moral*, Frankfurt/M. 1987, pp. 8–116, here pp. 63–73.

2
Conceptual Baggage of Empirical Research

When philosophical theories of normativity miss the mark concerning the social practice of normativity, then they thereby miss a side of the normative that is empirically accessible and can be recognized and described in time and space. In order to substantiate this claim, four models will be examined more closely in the following chapter so as to explicate how they relate to the question of social norms' empirical recognizability.

1. After Kant: Rationalization of the Normative through Generalizability

1.1 Acting on Reason in International Relations

Kant and Hume are the most significant philosophical forebears of modern debates concerning the nature of normativity. At the same time, both their theoretical models exert great influence on the description of normative social practices. Kant's conception of moral normativity as acting *on* practical reason withdraws the normative from the sphere of empirical observability. As such, many of the following questions about practical philosophy concern Kantian theory—from the identification of the normative with the practically rational, to the fixation on reasons for action that can both explain and justify an action. Yet how can such a conception gain influence over the description of social norms?[1]

An important consequence of Kantian philosophy for any theory of social practice can be traced to the insight that the actions of persons and the operating of societies cannot be described by causal models alone but rather require a modeling which incorporates moral orientations, even if, strictly speaking, these preferences are empirically inaccessible. Thus, Kant had influence on the sociology of classical modernity, on Durkheim, Weber, and the early Parsons. Despite this influence, major lines of inquiry by these sociologists, such as Weber's concepts of rationality or Durkheim's concept of anomy, had to deviate from Kant's

[1] Kelsen, who views himself as Kantian, claims that it ultimately cannot in his engagement with the newly developing legal-sociological research field of Eugen Ehrlich (*Grundlegung der Soziologie des Rechts*, München 1913). According to Kelsen's rigid concept, one cannot empirically draw on law: Hans Kelsen, "Eine Grundlegung der Rechtssoziologie" in: *Archiv für Sozialwissenschaft und Sozialpolitik* 39 (1915), pp. 839–76, esp. pp. 845–56.

The Possibility of Norms. Christoph Möllers, Published by Oxford University Press (2020) under licence; © this translation, Alex Holznienkemper; © the original German edition, Suhrkamp Verlag Berlin.
DOI: 10.1093/oso/9780198827399.001.0001

ontology of the normative by distinguishing different observable forms of rationality without reducing these to their instrumental rationality. For Weber, who is very conscious of methodology, there is no problem in observing moral orientations of actors.[2] But his notion of value rationality, in contrast to Kant's notion of practical reason, has to manifest itself in causal connections in order to enable this.[3] We see something similar in the case of Durkheim, whose investigative unit of a *fait social* remarkably resembles the Kantian notion of law.[4] *Faits sociaux* are *general* formations that manifest themselves in the outside world and are implementable by *force*. It is precisely these three criteria that Kant uses to define his concept of *law*.[5] In contrast to his concept of morality, however, this denotes an empirically graspable phenomenon. Durkheim's designation of social facts, as well as the empirical research connected to it, thus also undergird an understanding of normativity that diverges from practical philosophy, even if it draws inspiration from Kant.[6]

1.2 An Empirical Research Agenda Drawing on Kant and Habermas

In more recent years we find newer approaches to empirical research of politics and law inspired by Habermas, which are closer to a Kantian modeling of the normative and thus closer to a connection between explanation and justification than classical sociology.[7] With his concept of communicative action, Habermas has developed a model of rationality that is aimed at communication. This model is supposed, on the one hand, to help justify the claims to validity raised by communicative actors, on the other, to be necessary in order to explain how social communication can take place at all.[8] According to Habermas, a reductionist approach that would limit itself to strategic, maximally instrumental action would neither

[2] Ultimately, what is being observed are degrees of freedom that are kept open by a naturalistic proceeding of causality. On this, see Dieter Henrich, *Die Einheit der Wissenschaftslehre Max Webers*, Tübingen 1952, pp. 48–53. Obviously, there were prompt objections to Weber, claiming that he must presume motivations which he could not observe. See Jürgen Kaube, *Max Weber*, Berlin 2014, pp. 298 ff., referring to Felix Rachfahl's critique of Weber's writing on capitalism.

[3] It remains tied up with a subject-philosophical concept in so far as the empirical description of norms aims to capture subjective ideas: Max Weber, "Der Sinn der 'Wertfreiheit' der soziologischen und ökonomischen Wissenschaften" in: Id., *Gesammelte Aufsätze zur Wissenschaftslehre*, Johannes Winckelmann (ed.), 1988, pp. 489–540, here p. 531.

[4] Émile Durkheim, *The Rules of Sociological Method*, New York 1982, pp. 58 f.

[5] Immanuel Kant, *Die Metaphysik der Sitten*, Frankfurt/M. 1977, pp. 336 ff. (§ B).

[6] On Durkheim's overcoming of Kantianism, see in brief: Hans Joas, *Die Kreativität des Handelns*, Frankfurt/M. 1992, pp. 80–9.

[7] On the Kantianism of his theory, see Jürgen Habermas, *Faktizität und Geltung. Beiträge zur Diskurstheorie des Rechts und des demokratischen Rechtsstaats*, Frankfurt/M. 1992, pp. 9, 45–52.

[8] Concerning the critique of the normative saturation of this notion of communication: Cristina Lafont, *The Linguistic Turn in Hermeneutic Philosophy*, Cambridge, Mass. 1999, pp. 188–225.

explain how communication ought to function nor even appropriately describe it. Even if the notion of understanding (*Verständigung*) opens up questions,[9] this assumption shall not be questioned here. Instrumental reason alone is neither sufficient for justification nor in explaining a plenitude of social norms.

The theory of international relations inspired by Habermas exemplifies the kinds of implication this has for an empirical approach to norms. Such theory positions itself between neo-realistic theoretical models for which States act as mere utility maximizers, and constructivist approaches in which international relations are explained with the help of institutions constituted by norms. With Habermas, generalizable moral convictions of participants are invoked with respect to both norms and institutions, factoring as powerfully explanatory units.[10] Now moral convictions that are brought up in communicatively oriented action are only discernible in a roundabout way. They manifest themselves with certain indicators and only appear in certain constellations. For this reason, their theoretical foundations shouldn't be examined in Habermas' theory of action, but rather in his theory of democracy.[11] They are not found in a pure form in international relations—nor are they found anywhere else.[12]

We see a differentiated attempt to empirically apply this model in Nicole Deitelhoff's work on the development of the International Criminal Court.[13] With this case, she demonstrates that the genesis of international cooperation cannot be explained simply by the idea that States pursue well-defined positions. Deitelhoff shows that in the negotiations about the foundational treaty, at least some State representatives exchanged generalizable arguments and changed their positions in doing so. The resulting international legal agreement is—at least partially—the result of rational discourse aimed at understanding.[14] While orientation toward understanding did not dominate this discourse, it did appear in discursive "islands of persuasion"[15] which were crucial for the continuation of negotiations. Of course, these kinds of "islands" are only possibly under certain institutional and life-world conditions, with the result that generalizable arguments only arise among experts that share similar life worlds; that is, the universalizable argument seems to be the function of a specialist context.[16]

[9] Strikingly similar: Robert B. Brandom, "Facts, Norms, and Normative Facts: A Reply to Habermas" in: *European Journal of Philosophy* 8 (2000), pp. 356–74; John Rawls, "Reply to Habermas" in: Id., *Political Liberalism*, New York 2005, pp. 372–434, here pp. 386–95.

[10] For an introduction on this discussion, see Thomas Risse, "Let's Argue!: Communicative Action in World Politics" in: *International Organization* 54 (2000), pp. 1–39.

[11] Nicole Deitelhoff, *Überzeugung in der Politik. Grundzüge einer Diskurstheorie internationalen Regierens*, Frankfurt/M. 2006, p. 282.

[12] Risse (n 10), "Let's Argue!", pp. 14–16, 18 ff.

[13] Deitelhoff (n 11), *Überzeugung*.

[14] Regarding the institutions thus arising: Deitelhoff (n 11), *Überzeugung*, pp. 255–69.

[15] Ibid., pp. 278 ff.

[16] Ibid., pp. 228–31, 273. There is a certain irony in this, as a universalizable morality proves to be only pragmatically possible in a highly specialized professional *ethics*.

A similar explanatory approach, traceable to Habermas, can be found in the literature on the highly contentious dominance of committees in the structure of the European Union, the so-called comitology. These committees are viewed as the epitome of non-transparent, bureaucratic power. For this case, too, a branch of empirical research has tried to provide evidence that representatives of European Member States not only represent nationally defined interests, but that they exchange reasons, argue under the obligation to justify, and change their positions.[17] The necessity to at least pretend to resort to generalizable arguments, such as the public interest or human rights, has the consequence that such declarations are taken at face value and the participants are tangled up in justification discourses that ultimately modify their positions.[18] This combination of generalizable semantics and alterable positions also fulfills the function of an indicator of communicative action in other models of deliberative democracy, and thereby the function as a criterion for the justification of decisions made and rules set in such procedures.

1.3 Why are these Investigations of Interest here, and Wherein Lies their Problem?

For starters, the question arises as to how the invisible moral motivation of Kant can be made visible by means of Habermasian theory. As we have seen, in the proceduralist rational model, this can principally only occur in two ways. On the one hand, through observation of a procedure that lives up to certain standards, one which gives all participants the same opportunity to articulate themselves and does not preclude any questions from the outset; on the other hand, by a comparison between the positions of participants *before* and *after* the procedure. Only if positions have changed can one verify the presumed conception of rationality as having been effective.

It is obvious that methodological problems arise, because it is not easy to determine the causal relationship between the procedure and the change in positions after the procedure. It can remain unclear to which degree position changes are of mere strategic origin and concessions were thus merely feigned, or whether they were prompted less by means of normative argumentation than by the sharing of cognitively relevant information in the procedure.[19] Were participants persuaded by arguments, or did they simply find out new information, or were concessions part of an instrumental calculation from the outset? Trying to integrate strategic

[17] Christian Joerges and Jürgen Neyer, "From Intergovernmental Bargaining to Deliberative Political Processes: The Constitutionalisation of Comitology" in: *European Law Journal* 3 (1997), pp. 273–99. A more recent overview in Thomas Risse and Mareike Kleine, "Deliberation in Negotiations" in: *Journal of European Public Policy* 17 (2010), pp. 708–26.

[18] Risse (n 10), "Let's Argue!" p. 32.

[19] The meaning of this point is quite established in this discussion, see ibid., p. 2.

action into such a framework brings about tremendous challenges, as the rationality content of various arguments must principally be able to be defined independently of participants' concrete convictions which are expressed in documentable expressions. The philosophical observer must know better than the discourse participant being observed, even though this "better," according to Habermas' theory, can only result from a procedure, a procedure which the observer cannot follow when conducting her empirical research. This is not an uncommon consequence of a rationality-focused explanatory concept of political processes, but certainly one that raises doubts concerning its empirical prerogative. Furthermore, the opposite deficit of the model reveals itself in constellations in which the examined procedure did not lead to position changes but under certain circumstances led to new reasons for a maintained conviction.

In addition to these methodological insecurities, it remains unclear what remains of such a demanding standard of rationality that needs to be so severely truncated in order to be of empirical use. While a central problem of explaining social norms via rational reasons consisted in its combination of explanations and justifications—or its merging with the difficult formulation of the forceless force of the better argument[20]—it is precisely this combination that leads to the main argument against any empirically usable conception of normativity that latches on to Habermas. In the present example, even if we assume that the negotiation process altered the positions of participating States—and our intuition would even hint at that, even if it is quite difficult to prove—then the question remains as to the precise justifying content of such an insight. One may well believe that an openly held discussion oriented toward understanding finds a justification in itself. But does the same hold for its results, more specifically, for the results of international negotiations? And can anything be said about these if one doesn't take a stand on the content of the arguments at stake? Is the International Criminal Court justified by the means through which it was negotiated? And how far-reaching is such a justification in light of certain practices of international criminal law? Is it only justified as an institution, but not in its concrete actions? Are comitology commissions justified because open discussion unfolds within them?[21] Was German reunification more justified at precisely that moment in which the Soviet Union gave up its resistance due to the United States pointing out the Germans' right to self-determination?[22] To make such claims, it is not enough to assume that recourse to

[20] Jürgen Habermas, "Wahrheitstheorien" in: Id., *Vorstudien und Ergänzungen zur Theorie des kommunikativen Handelns*, Frankfurt/M. 1984, pp. 127–83, here p. 161. On the same topic, also Jürgen Habermas, *Theorie des kommunikativen Handelns*, Frankfurt/M. 1982, vol. 1, pp. 47–50.

[21] Critically on this: Joseph H. H. Weiler, "Epilogue: 'Comitology' as Revolution: Infranationalism, Constitutionalism and Democracy" in: Christian Joerges and Ellen Vos (eds), *EU Committees*, Oxford 1999, pp. 339–50.

[22] This example is in Risse (n 10), "Let's Argue!" p. 27.

human rights and public interest entangles those people in arguments who themselves invoke these ideals. Even more so, one has to explain which legitimating content the invocation of such abstract entities has—a question that is highly contested in the context of human rights at an international level. Furthermore, one can imagine many results that could not be justified by such invocations, and we cannot know whether such invocations occurred subjectively with an intention of achieving an understanding. Thus, all we are left with is an assertion that certain invocations were made and had a certain effect. But the empirical search for communicative action in institutions is doubly limited. For one, as the evidence that a certain argument is supposedly oriented toward understanding can hardly be achieved. For another, because communicative action depends on factual conditions that aren't necessarily present in observed practices. This is not an argument against the normative claim of the theory. The theory of communicative action can even provide us with arguments when no-one is actually acting communicatively. But it runs against its own independent value for the *explanation* of a practice, a value that stretches beyond knowledge of the circumstances that enabled such action.

All being said, here we are neither concerned with a concrete international institution nor with an appropriate notion of its legitimation, but solely with the relationship between the observation and justification of norms. A discourse theory drawing on Kant combines models of explanation and justification in such a manner that appears to be empirically unreliable, as it assumes implications of certain observable practices that do not necessarily follow. If participants come out of a discussion with altered preferences, this only actually shows that these participants have malleable positions, and that these positions only changed *in the process of* the discussion, but even this is much less certain. This is not insignificant, especially in light of influential theories that claim that such positions are not malleable. Nonetheless, it remains unclear how more can be deduced from such observation than that which we have stated, especially how one can conclude that the resulting change in position of a participant indicates a higher normative value of the changed position, even more so if this higher value can only result from the procedure itself. This can also be shown in a countering thought example: Can a negotiation that falters despite its participants having changed their positions be similarly justified? And how do we assess procedures that began in a promising way, yet led to no result? On this theoretical model, the empirical analysis of micro-phenomena appears to be shaped by a normative macro-preference, such as one in favor of international collaboration, a preference that itself is not justified.

The methodological question thus remains unanswered as to how a concept of normativity that rests on good reasons can be made visible for empirical research. A model of normative justification is developed that is both too demanding and too modest: too demanding because we cannot be sure that democratic institutions themselves can live up to the high standard of communicative rationality demanded by it;[23] too modest because empirically, all that is required to fulfill this high standard is a discussion procedure open to its result. This is hardly sufficient for justifying a certain outcome, such as the precarious legitimacy of international criminal authority.[24] This simultaneous overbidding and underbidding of justification standards—this is the point—follows from a theoretical model that, on the one hand, spiritualizes normativity and detaches it from actually occurring elements of self-determination in practice, but on the other reacts to such spiritualization by treating relatively modest procedures as sufficient for justifying political institutions.

2. *After Hume: Preferences or the Empiricization of the Normative*

2.1 Preferences and their Effects

Another moral-philosophical model that was important for empirical research comes from David Hume and the utilitarian theories that ensued. These won't be spelled out in detail here; it will especially remain open in how far a theory of normativity ascribed to Hume does justice to his work as a whole.[25] For the theory lineage that remains tied to his name, normativity arises from subjective preferences that are connected to a conviction regarding certain factual contexts.[26] Our obligations arise out of that which we will or do not will, and from that which follows from such willing according to our conviction.[27] A norm gains its normativity by virtue of the fact that it has unpleasant consequences for me if I break it, or pleasant ones if I follow it. My needs reveal themselves in expressions and actions, and they explain these in turn. On a strong reading, these needs are neither accessible by justification nor alterable. They must be posited as a given and as unchangeable—an idea that became particularly powerful in neo-classical economics[28] and in the

[23] A standard traditionally employed in order to supposedly disappointedly turn away from parliamentarian politics: Carl Schmitt, *Die geistesgeschichtliche Lage des heutigen Parlamentarismus*, Berlin 1926, pp. 41–63.
[24] Christoph Möllers, *The Three Branches. A Comparative Model of Separation of Powers*, Oxford 2013, pp. 215–17.
[25] Specifically concerning the relationship between skepticism and instrumentalism in Hume: Elijah Millgram, "Was Hume a Humean?" in: *Hume Studies* XXI (1995), pp. 75–94.
[26] For a consistent current application: Peter Stemmer, *Normativität*, Berlin 2008, pp. 25–50; for critiques, see the contributions by Michael Esfeld, Thomas Schmidt, Marco Iorio, and Rainer Forst, including a reply, in: *Deutsche Zeitschrift für Philosophie* 58 (2010), pp. 145–69.
[27] A reconstruction of a purportedly Humean concept of normativity can be found by Michael Smith, "The Humean Theory of Motivation" in: *Mind* 96 (1987), pp. 36–61, here pp. 50–8.
[28] George J. Stigler/Gary S. Becker, "De gustibus non est disputandum" in: *American Economic Review* 67 (1977), pp. 76–90, who sought to prove that phenomena such as addiction, custom, advertising, and fashion are best described as stable preferences.

economic analysis of law.[29] Even if preferences prove themselves to be malleable, as is held more and more widely,[30] a change in preference does not follow as a result of rational insight.

The kinds of implications such assumptions have for the empirical treatment of norms can be shown with an example from the legal-realistic tradition in the United States, in which this theoretical approach still thrives.[31] If one identifies normativity with a constellation of individual preferences, then empirical legal research has to orient itself according to actors and their output, in the case of the legal systems, this primarily means along judges' decisions. It would thus be unrealistic to equate the normative side of law with written legal texts. The order of norms far more serves to predict future decisions. A quote from the church father of American legal realism that has already taken on proverbial status brought this insight into clear focus: "The prophecies of what the courts will do in fact, and nothing more pretentious, are what I mean by the law."[32] *The normativity of law reveals itself in the output of judges.* The decision of a judge is explained in light of her preference constellation, which does not necessarily have to be equated with the satisfaction of primary needs. The desire for recognition as a professional jurist by her colleagues can lead to the de facto convergence of individual needs and technical, professional interaction with the legal order. That is, the preference situation can coincide with a standard that is generally viewed as appropriate.[33] The use calculus is open to be fine-tuned at will which can then be empirically tested.[34]

But the description of a legal order within this framework remains defined by the systematic departure point of individual preferences. The norm is not a rule that leads to a certain decision-making practice, which can have relevance for the future, but at most a factor within an individual constellation of preferences that seeks to evade the professional criticism of colleagues in the case of law, or the derision of others in the case of manners. For the description of a normative order, this implies a different conception of rules. On such a model, a normative rule is also not an instruction but an *empirical hypothesis* by the aid of which future decisions can be predicted. It is thus indistinguishable from a descriptive rule or a law

[29] Already from a critical perspective, Hans Albert, *Marktsoziologie und Entscheidungslogik*, Tübingen 1998; Elizabeth Anderson, *Value in Ethics and Economics*, Cambridge, Mass. 1993, pp. 129–40; Thomas Nagel, *The Possibility of Altruism*, Princeton 1970, pp. 27–32.

[30] Christine Jolls, Cass Sunstein, and Richard Thaler, "A Behavioral Approach to Law and Economics" in: Cass Sunstein (ed.), *Behavioral Law and Economics*, Cambridge 2000, pp. 13–58, here pp. 14–21.

[31] Neil Duxbury, *Patterns of American Jurisprudence*, Oxford 1997, pp. 301–420.

[32] Oliver W. Holmes, "The Path of the Law" in: *Harvard Law Review* 10 (1897), pp. 457–78, here p. 460. A second canonical quote from the same context states: "We are under a Constitution, but the Constitution is what the judges say it is," Charles Evans Hughes, "Speech before the Elmira Chamber of Commerce, Elmira, New York (3 May 1907)" in: *Addresses and Papers of Charles Evans Hughes, Governor of New York, 1906–1908*, New York 1908, pp. 133–46, here p. 139.

[33] Thus runs the analysis by Richard A. Posner, *How Judges Think*, Cambridge, Mass. 2010, pp. 93–121.

[34] On this aspect of Mill's theory, see John Rawls, *Lectures on the History of Political Philosophy*, Cambridge, Mass. 2007, pp. 251–65.

of nature. The rule arises out of the coordination of preferences. The quality of the scientific description is determined by the quality of the prediction. In the case of jurisprudence, the achievement does not consist in conceptually systematizing a body of norms but in a maximally successful prediction of judicial behavior—an achievement which, in doubt, can obviously be taken over and methodically "naturalized"[35] by other disciplines of empirical social research.[36] The result is a base/superstructure approach in which the self-understanding of the participants remains insignificant, as might be the case for a judge who, as an applier of legal norms, sees herself as being bound by those norms.[37]

This kind of model offers a program capable of empirical research, which certainly remains contentious in its preconditions, but could potentially achieve greater descriptive success than approaches inspired by Habermas that empirically investigate norms. The measuring unit of a revealed preference is easier to wield than categories of communicative action and reasons. As a methodically consistent way to find out more about social practices such as the legal system, the Humean tradition deserves respect even if one remains critical of its preconditions.[38]

Yet this advantage has to do with the fact that a specific notion of normativity is lost in this model. The orientation along lines of actual preferences does not allow for the possibility of a divergence between normative pretense and practice. "Norms" are merely reconstructed after the fact from the expression of preferences. Because of its limitation to preferences, this model can only make norms visible from the perspective of factual norm *sanctions*. Norms become relevant for actions when they contain credible threats or incentives that act positively or negatively toward a given preference. On this model, the existence of norms manifests itself as a result of the reflex of individual, subjective preferences, the realization of which can be obstructed or supported by norms. A counterfactual understanding of norms is thereby excluded.

Before we will have thought about our own concept of the normative, this objection will remain of a preliminary nature. For now, it may well be an appropriate model for the description of norms' reality. But two objections can already be raised that bring into doubt such a reduction of norms to positive or negative motivating factors for individual behavior.

For one, there is the possibility of a change of preferences by means of norms. People come out of procedures with different preferences than the ones with which

[35] Brian Leiter, *Naturalizing Jurisprudence*, Oxford 2007, pp. 184–93, in line with Quine. Of course, the concept of naturalization is not so simple in Quine, on this see Sandra Laugier, *Why We Need Ordinary Language Philosophy*, Chicago 2013, pp. 6 ff., pp. 34–8.

[36] Regarding the considerable predictive quality of such models for decisions by the U.S. Supreme Court: Theodore W. Ruger, Paulin T. Kim, Andrew D. Martin, and Kevin M. Quinn, "The Supreme Court Forecasting Project: Legal and Political Science Approaches to Predicting Supreme Court Decisionmaking" in: *Columbia Law Review* 104 (2004), pp. 1150–210.

[37] Concerning rare empiricism: Peter Stegmaier, *Wissen, was Recht ist*, Wiesbaden 2008.

[38] Daniel A. Farber and Philip P. Frickey, *Law and Public Choice*, Chicago 1991.

they entered them. Such a change is more probable in some procedures than in others. It is more likely in the German Constitutional Court, which consults behind closed doors and in which preference alteration can be observed through consultation,[39] than in the US Supreme Court, in which by all accounts the positions of the justices rarely change in consultation and rulings can thus be better anticipated,[40] or in the Brazilian Constitutional Court system, in which judiciary bodies only consult publicly and in highly ritualized fashion.[41] Similar differences are likely in parliamentary systems.

A second obstacle that is difficult to integrate into the model is the self-description of people that have to deal with norms, with legal rules, with a guilty conscience, or with a critical argument. For them, even norms that run contrary to their needs can be of significance. This does not mean that a social theory must take any self-description at its word; after all, the situation might be marked by self-deception or rationalizations after the fact. But the danger of a theory of stable preference lies in its approaching preferences in a definitional way, thereby becoming irrefutable and ultimately unempirical. Preferences, then, are what individuals express because they express them. Even if many models do not run this risk, as they empirically test predictions, this objection applies to the basic model. The self-description of actors remains irrelevant in the name of an empirical model. In this way—and this is decisive—a divergence between norm and facticity that goes beyond an unsatisfied preference cannot be described. This would most likely prove itself to be too narrow of a conceptualization of a norm.

2.2 Conventions and Rules?

Theories that treat conventions as paradigmatic of the normative also see themselves as being in line with the Humean tradition. David Lewis defines conventions as regularity in a group's behavior in a given situation. A convention is found when all members of a group act regularly, when everyone expects that all the others do the same thing, and when everyone prefers to behave regularly, as long as others do it as well. All of this must furthermore serve to solve a coordination problem.[42]

39 Uwe Kranenpohl, *Hinter dem Schleier des Beratungsgeheimnisses. Der Willensbildungs- und Enscheidungsprozess des Bundesverfassungsgerichts*, Wiesbaden 2010, Part II.

40 See above, p. 39, fn. 36.

41 Virgílio Afonso da Silva, "Deciding without Deliberating" in: *International Journal of Constitutional Law* 11 (2013), pp. 557–84, here pp. 569–76.

42 David K. Lewis, *Conventions. A Philosophical Study*, Cambridge, Mass. 1969, p. 42. It is thus concerned with a problem that, due to the convergence of interests, is solved in favor of all participants if everyone employs a strategy attuned to each other. A handy depiction can be found in Nicholas Southwood and Lina Eriksson, "Norms and Conventions" in: *Philosophical Explorations* 14 (2001), pp. 195–217, here pp. 197 ff.

Are these kinds of conventions norms? Lewis recognizes that his definition itself contains no normative element, but he claims that it can be deduced from the definition.[43] For if a convention is established, I can expect that as good as all members of my group will follow it. In this case, I too want to do it, and will do it—and if as good as all others can count on my following the convention, then they too will want me to follow it, because that would solve the coordination problem. If all this is applicable, then there is reason to belief that it is in accord with both my preferences as well as those of the others that I follow the convention. For this reason, the convention is a norm.[44]

Even at first sight, it appears questionable whether one can detect many pure coordination problems in social practice.[45] This, at least, speaks against the explanatory value of an approach that strives to depict real preferences. And it remains unclear how the reference to no matter how highly qualified a majority[46] can uphold such a normative pretense, since strictly speaking, one single divergent preference would suffice to destroy the entire normative pretense. The preference holds only for the person who has it.[47] Beyond that, the normative pretense points to nothing more than the mechanisms which brought about the convention.[48] It thereby remains open why a coordination behavior that spontaneously unfolds should be taken to be normative.[49]

If the normativity of a rule arises out of my preferences, then the rule vanishes at the moment in which it no longer interacts with my preferences. Thus, for the robber who doesn't fear punishment for robbery, there is no prohibition of robbery.[50] If I change my preferences then I cannot remain tied to old

[43] Ibid., pp. 97 ff.

[44] It can certainly be doubted whether it is convincing to call someone rational who follows a rigid order of preferences, for this person can reasonably enter into obligations that contradict them: Amartya Sen, "Rational Fools. A Critique of the Behavioral Foundations of Economic Theory" in: *Philosophy & Public Affairs* 6 (1977), pp. 317–44, here pp. 326–33.

[45] It is not by coincidence that a jurist points this out: Gerald J. Postema, "Coordination and Conventions at the Foundations of Law" in: *Journal of Legal Studies* XI (1982), pp. 165–203), here p. 175. A different notion of convention is found in the French discussion: Luc Boltanksi/Laurent Thévenot, "Die Soziologie der kritischen Kompetenzen" in: Rainer Diaz-Bone (ed.), *Soziologie der Konventionen*, Frankfurt/M. 2011, pp. 43–68. Doubts concerning the coordinating function of norms also in Southwood/Eriksson (n 42), "Norms and Conventions" pp. 208–12.

[46] The question is whether "majority" is to be taken literally, or whether—at the price of circularity—it means "sufficiently many." It speaks against the first assumption that social processes shouldn't tip over precisely beyond a previously determinable portion of dissenters.

[47] On the problematic political possibilities that the individualistic departure point allows for individuals: Amartya Sen, "The Impossibility of a Paretian Liberal" in: *Journal of Political Economy* 78 (1970), pp. 152–7, here pp. 156 f. A concise overview of the economic debate around social norms in Peyton Young, "Social Norms" in: Steven Durlauf and Lawrence Blume (eds), *The New Palgrave Dictionary of Economics*, London 2008, pp. 647–51.

[48] Margaret Gilbert, *On Social Facts*, Princeton 1989, pp. 349–55.

[49] On this problem, see Russell Hardin, "The Emergence of Norms" in: *Ethics* 90 (1980), pp. 575–87, here pp. 579 ff.; this also counters an overly narrow modeling of the application field of norms in Edna Ullmann-Margalit, *The Emergence of Norms*, Oxford 1977.

[50] Explicitly, Stemmer (n 26), *Normativität*, pp. 177 ff. The critical example is found in Armin Engländer, "Norm und Sanktion - kritische Anmerkungen zum Sanktionsmodell der Norm" in: *Rechtswissenschaft* 4 (2013), pp. 193–207, here pp. 200 ff.

preferences. One finds many attempts to construct such mechanisms of self-binding in literature. They do not extend beyond the alternative between having to normativize the actual preference or being left without any model of normative commitment.[51] For the discussed solutions, it is characteristic that they end up filtering out certain preferences, so that ultimately, it is not empirical preferences that become relevant, but rather preferences that are normativized by the model.[52] The norm conception of the preference-oriented theory thereby dissolves.

2.3 "Is" and "Ought": Commonalities and Differences in Both Models

The traditions inspired by Kantian and Humean theories share two important commonalities which will be of further significance. For one, both postulate a categorical separation of "is" and "ought."[53] Both operate with—even if different—strategies of differentiation in order to distinguish the normative level from the descriptive. Both employ fundamentally different conceptions of the will as "bridging concepts";[54] one understood as an unjustifiable preference, one as the capacity for rationally generalizable decision-making.

This initial commonality provides an indication of demands for a reconceived notion of norms. Facts should not have direct access to norms, but simply shape them through controlled mediation. At the same time, norms should be defined in a way that is open to empirical evidence, that is such that they can be recognized in a methodically controlled manner—in the case of social norms in their realized form, not merely through subjective introspection.

A second commonality of these approaches is that they both locate norms in an acting subject, with the consequence that, strictly speaking, one cannot speak of independently existing norms but instead of individualized attitudes toward certain actions that create normativity. This is obvious in the Humean approach, as the concept of norm has vanished as part of subject-centered events here. The theory thus contains an empirically robust object, the normative character of which is

[51] A favorable overview of the Anglo-Saxon debate in Edward McClennen, "Rationality" in: Alfred R. Mele and Piers Rawling (eds), *The Oxford Handbook of Rationality*, Oxford 2004, pp. 222–39; see also the critique by Hubertus Buchstein, "Selbstbindung als verfassungstheoretische Figur" in: Jürgen Gebhard and Rainer Schmalz-Bruns (eds), *Demokratie, Verfassung und Nation*, Baden-Baden 1994, pp. 231–52, here pp. 246–52.

[52] Characteristically, Smith, "Humean Theory" p. 49, which understands the term *desire* in such a way that it also contains preferences that aren't actually perceived. This might well be an apt determination, but it throws a methodological shadow on the empirically solid pretense of the theory.

[53] However, convincing doubts whether this is true for Hume can be found in Alisdair MacIntyre, "Hume on 'Is' and 'Ought'" in: *The Philosophical Review* LXVIII (1959), pp. 451–68, here pp. 455–61.

[54] This term found in MacIntyre, ibid., p. 463.

uncertain, however. For Kantian theories, the opposite is the case. Here, the normative excess becomes more obvious, but it remains uncertain whether what distinguishes it can be empirically accessible.

3. *After Foucault: Power or the Absorption of the Normative*

3.1 Guizot's Concept of Power

François Guizot, critic of the Restoration and later the leading politician of the French bourgeois monarchy before 1848, stood before a theoretical dilemma in light of historical experience. The dramatic pretense of the great French Revolution, to restructure society completely from the outside according to a rational plan by means of politics, had failed. But he also found the restorative renunciation of any pretense to political change to be unacceptable. Society had to be changed, but the power that wanted to and should change it couldn't assume as diametrically opposed a stance toward society as the Jacobins had tried. That power first had to understand and intimately grasp what it sought to change. Here we quote Guizot at some length, so as to better reveal the proximity to current theorists:

> Governance is often subject to a curious mistake. It holds it to be sufficient to control its own power, its own life, not merely in distinction from, but independent of the powers in society on which it has an effect comparable to the peasant's plough on the soil that feeds him. What does a peasant need? Servants, horses, and ploughs. He has to move all of this on the ground, and the ground will submit to him. Governance takes itself to be under similar conditions. Ministers, prefects, tax collectors, soldiers, that is what it calls the means of governing; and it is surprised when it encounters obstacles and the people aren't capable of being owned like the own agents. I dare to say: This by no means denotes what I take the means of governance. If such were sufficient, what could governance possibly lament nowadays? It is plentifully supplied with such. Nonetheless, governance withers from weakness amidst its power, just as Midas does from hunger amidst his gold. This is because the true means of governance do not lie in governance's direct and visible means of action. They sit in the lap of society itself and cannot be separated from them.[55]

The young Guizot says it is a mistake to equate power with the external means of wielding power. Power could thus not simply affect society, which can only be

[55] François Guizot, *Des moyens de gouvernement et d'opposition dans l'état actuel de la France*, Paris 1821, pp. 128 ff (translation via German). Regarding its context, see Pierre Rosanvallon, *Le Moment Guizot*, Paris 1985, pp. 107–20.

governed from within, by political power understanding the laws that it controls. Power has to adjust to society in order to change it. It has to become internalized and absorbed by society.

This quotation is of interest for a number of reasons. It stems from a different constellation of problems than the models examined so far. Guizot is trying to draw a political lesson from historical experience. This lesson contains a theory of the normative, not in the sense of a justification of norms, but in the sense of how they operate. Norms only work if they adjust to the object that they are supposed to regulate. The key for functioning norms lies in the object to be regulated.

Guizot's theory, too, is a theory of the internalization of the normative. In order to work, norms have to become internalized. But this internalization does not occur in individual subjects but rather in society as a whole. Guizot thinks in historical patterns and he is far from the methodical individualism that connects Hume and Kant with the current debate on reasons. At the same time, it remains open on Guizot's account what becomes of the normative pretense that has to assimilate to its object. Guizot's time as French head of government is memorable not least of all for its horrendous corruption and politics' bowing to private industry. At least on the practical political level, the social internalization of the normative political pretense brought about the dissipation of the latter.[56]

3.2 Elias and Foucault

We also come across models of individualization or absorption of the normative without normative individualism in recent theories.[57] For Norbert Elias, the internalization of behavior rules creates the condition of possibility for renouncing violence in social interaction.[58] Aside from the concentration of violence in the decisive battle of feudal lords, out of which the modern State can originate, it is the invention of table manners and other internalized social rule codes that accounts for conflicts no longer being carried out in a violent way. The internalization of norms is neither morally valuable nor does it happen out of insight by the internalizing subject. It arises from a combination of deterrence and routine.[59] In this manner, social norms obtain effectiveness. They work because they have to be considered by agents before it can come to an externalized conflict. The similarity to the argument made by Guizot can hardly be overseen. It is only the norms that a society has

[56] François Furet, *La Révolution*, Paris 1988, vol. 2, pp. 180–6; Rosanvallon, *Le Moment Guizot*, pp. 305–32.

[57] A precise look at Durkheim would be important: Émile Durkheim, *Moral Education*, New York 1973, pp. 95–126.

[58] Norbert Elias, *Über den Prozeß der Zivilisation*, Frankfurt/M. 1976, vol. 1, pp. 65–109.

[59] Ibid., vol. 2, pp. 312–36.

internalized that can in turn affect said society. But does it make sense then to still talk of these as norms?

Michel Foucault's theory of governmentality also entails a similar conception.[60] While the centralization of violence and the internalization of rules are two sides of the same civilization process for Elias, the externally operating sovereign who sets rules and enforces them with physical might, for Foucault, is more of an unsuccessful development in the modern history of power. Power develops and refines itself through other strategies.[61] Furthermore, both theories (though Foucault more clearly) attempt to historicize the subjective side of power and thereby describe not only its subject-restricting, but also its subject-constituting effect.

In Foucault's work, we only find traces of a theory of the normative. In the third lecture on the theory of security, from 25 January 1978, he reflects on the pertinent notions. He does so in the context of the "dispositif" of discipline.[62]

> But I think it is necessary to show that the relationship of the law to the norm does in fact indicate that there is something that we could call a normativity intrinsic to any legal imperative, but this normativity intrinsic to the law, perhaps founding the law, cannot be confused with that we are trying to pinpoint here under the name of procedures, processes, and techniques of normalization. I would even say instead that, if it is true that the law refers to a norm, and that the role and function of the law therefore —the very operation of the law—is to codify a norm, to carry out a codification in relation to the norm, the problem that I am trying to mark out is how techniques of normalization develop from and below a system of law, in its margins and maybe even against it. [63]

And further along:

> In other words, it is not the normal and the abnormal that is fundamental and primary in disciplinary normalization, it is the norm. That is, there is an originally prescriptive character of the norm and the determination and the identification of the normal and the abnormal becomes possible in relation to this posited norm.[64]

[60] On parallels, see Claus Dahlmanns, *Die Geschichte des modernen Subjekts: Michel Foucault und Norbert Elias im Vergleich*, Münster 2008.

[61] Foucault is tremendously careful (if not vague) in articulating the relationship of the three apparatus of governmentality—the juridical, discipline, and security—both in terms of its systematicity and its sequencing. (Michel Foucault, *Security, Territory, Population. Lectures at the Collège de France, 1977–78*, Basingstoke 2009, pp. 5 f. and more frequently). Nonetheless, the judicial power comes across as external and weak in his model. His theoretical, not his political preference, for internalized techniques of power shines through.

[62] On Foucault's take on the dispositions, see the portrayal by Thomas Lemke, *A Critique of Political Reason: Foucault's Analysis of Modern Governmentality*, London 2019, pp. 64–85, 188–98.

[63] Ibid., p. 56.

[64] Ibid., p. 57.

The normativity of statutes manifests itself in that a law codifies a pre-existing norm, whereby the norm in this context denotes "an optimal model that is constructed in relation to a certain outcome." This imbues techniques such as analysis, classification, and control, which distinguish the dispositif of discipline, with a goal. It is only the norm that enables differentiation between normal and abnormal. Foucault describes such a process as a "normation," as opposed to a normalization. The "normation" is hardly distinguishable from a classical prescriptive rule.

For the dispositif of *security*, such terminology does not apply. Under the aegis of the security dispositif, categories such as case, risk, threat, or crisis create a statistical model of the most diverse normalities that are to be set in relation to each other.[65] First, these normalities arise, then a norm that stems from the interplay of normalities, as deemed appropriate. "The norm is an interplay of differential normalities." He calls this process a normalization "in the strict sense." He calls this process a normalization "in a narrower sense."[66] With recourse to the security dispositif, Foucault analyzes liberalism, which, as he maintains, takes laws to be "laws of reality,"[67] thereby not opposing reality through norms. Here we once again are reminded of Guizot. In the end, Foucault's concept of "normation" carries over a conventional concept of norm, though in contrast to the concept of normalization it cannot explain many phenomena of power, and is thus historically outdated by the latter.

A shared consequence of such highly complex conceptualizations[68] that permanently modify themselves according to historical material can be found in how they make the normative side of practice dissipate. In the process of "normation" and normalization, norms are *absorbed* in precisely these processes. This is the least case in juridical practices, which according to Foucault merely rest on "normation." But the juridical, which he largely, if also historically questionably, identifies with the sovereign power of absolutism,[69] assumes for Foucault the same role that the external "means of governing" take on for Guizot. Ultimately, neither of them get under society's skin.

[65] Ibid., p. 63.

[66] Ibid.

[67] Ibid., p. 48.

[68] One reads of Foucault's Darwinist nominalism in Phillip Sarasin, *Darwin und Foucault*, Frankfurt/M. 2009, p. 73.

[69] It would be worthy of its own study to show how Foucault identifies law with public law, that is the law posited and simultaneously made binding by a ruler (see Michel Foucault, *The Birth of Biopolitics. Lectures at the Collége de France, 1978–79*, Basingstoke 2008, pp. 1–27). Public law, however, represents a later exception in European legal history, whereas Foucault largely ignores civil law which operates more along the lines of his liberal paradigm of discipline. Approaches to such a critique found in Petra Gehring, "Epistemologie? Archäologie? Genealogie? Foucault und das Recht" in: *Internationale Zeitschrift für Philosophie* 1 (2000), pp. 18–33, here pp. 20–6. See also Lemke (n 62), *A Critique*, pp. 120 and fn. 72, as well as the reference to Alan Hunt and Gary Wickham, *Foucault and the Law*, London 1994, pp. 60 ff. For a historically convincing counter-history of European early modernity which can hardly acknowledge law posited by rulers before the nineteenth century: Thomas Simon, "Geltung" in: *Rechtsgeschichte* 7 (2005), pp. 100–37, here pp. 110–20.

But why does Foucault explicitly speak of the relevance of a norm in his analysis of "normation"? The present reconstruction should not distract us from the fact norms are nowhere mentioned explicitly in his work. It thereby follows that thoughts on normalization dominate his theory. But normalization, as a molding of subjects enabled by techniques of security, is a process in which that *toward which* one is to normalize can no longer be contrasted with that which is normalized. That which normalizes vanishes in normalization.

At this point, such a theory of the normative actually seems rather conventional, for the doubts about normativity's relevance for the social unites numerous otherwise different social theories from the second half of the nineteenth century. After all, the assumption that societies operate differently in reality than external normative forms would claim, is almost the common denominator of the critique of law and rules since Marx,[70] despite the differences among theories. It is also something of an unexpected commonality between Foucault and the tradition of subject-centered, practical philosophy, since the internalization of the normative remains the essential object of analysis for Foucault despite his interest in methods of governing.[71] Despite all the significance of his critique of an absolute and unhistorical understanding of subjectivity, the latter remains the decisive vanishing point of his project—even if only because subjects can be accorded a body. A theory of "subjectivity that is produced in order to be suppressed"[72] is also a theory of subjectivity. Both elements—the limitation to normativity's efficacy and the search for this efficacy within the subject or its constitutive practices—beg for more precise examination.

An initial problem is found in the fact that limiting one's focus on the efficacy of norms loses sight of the essential point of normative practices, namely that normative practices cannot be made dependent on whether they are effective or not.[73] Otherwise they dissipate behind that which occurs anyway, or like Guizot's politics, they become indistinguishable by their adaptation to the circumstances. In that case, one can simply forgo the notion of normativity, even if it is at the price of losing the ability to describe certain social practices. That wouldn't be a moral problem, but certainly a cognitive deficit of such a theory.

A further problem lies in the asymmetrical difference between the interior and exterior which Foucault shares with theories of moral interiority. Instead of allowing for a description of the operative interplay of external norms and subjective behavior that is open to the phenomena in question, such theories seem to entail

[70] Karl Marx, "Zur Kritik der Hegelschen Rechtsphilosophie" in: Karl Marx and Friedrich Engels, *Werke*, Vol. 1, Berlin 1981, pp. 201–336.

[71] Lemke (n 62), *A Critique*, pp. 109–18.

[72] Ibid., p. 116.

[73] Here, Martin Saar, "Genealogische Kritik" in: Rahel Jaeggi and Tilo Wesche (eds), *Was ist Kritik?*, Frankfurt/M. 2009, pp. 247–65, here pp. 261–5), recognizes the critical content in the affective mobilization of doubts, but this does not diminish the differentiation between both elements.

a fundamentalism of the interiorized which categorically classifies as secondary the achievements wrought by the formalization and materialization of norms. This is an unusual critique of Foucault which appears unfair insofar as he has inspired many unorthodox examinations of norms on which practical philosophy could not get a good grasp.[74] But particularly the later contributions by Foucault on the theory of governmentality remain remarkably theory-immanent, less proximate to practice than they claim to be. One finds little on the materiality of the normative in these works. At the same time, they reveal a stunning resemblance with some forms of moral philosophy. Describing power as a subject-constituting normalization, as Foucault does, and reducing power to reasons, as Forst demands, discloses considerable commonalities despite the differences in reasoning and cognitive interest.

One can also view these approaches as continuation of a previous line of theory about social relations which attempts to explain power primarily by a description of those who follow it.[75] In both cases, we are dealing with recognition theories, even if they distinguish themselves in their respective weak-factual (Foucault) and strong-normative (Forst) notions of recognition. As will be shown in Interlude I, this distinction is of little meaning for the description of social norms.

4. *Norms in the World: Moral Realism*

4.1 A Realistic Alternative?

Against these models, one could think of an alternative that could accommodate my critique; a conception that doesn't internalize normativity, but rather views it as a fact that does not fundamentally differ from other facts and thereby becomes empirically accessible. Why do we not treat normativity as one property among others?[76] Normative statements would thus be statements that have a truth value, that describe a certain property.[77] What speaks for this view is that it can do without any exceptional ontology of the normative, just as much as it can do without a theoretical construct of the will that separates the world of the normative from the world of the factual. Normative sentences need not thereby be extracted from the general model of statements that have a truth value. In their rationality, they are objective, and in their objectivity, they denote something that can be recognized

74 Exemplarily: Judith Butler, *Bodies that Matter*, New York 1993, pp. 32–6.

75 For example in Étienne de La Boétie, *De la servitude volontaire ou Le Contr'un*, Paris 1993.

76 Christoph Halbig concisely writes on this in: "Die Realität der Moral" in: *Information Philosophie* 36 (2008), pp. 17–29, and in more detail in: id., *Praktische Gründe und die Realität der Moral*, Frankfurt/M. 2007, pp. 236–76.

77 For an in-depth critique from the vantage point of an intention-oriented notion of normativity, see Ralph Wedgwood, *The Nature of Normativity*, Oxford 2007, pp. 58–79.

and observed in the world. Normative assertions also do not need to abstain from empirical, evidential experiences such as one's own or another's suffering, even if such experiences do not operate with the same reliability as other experiences. To be sure, we are not as strongly in agreement with each other on the question if a certain action is "cruel" as we are on the fact that a given leaf is "green." But it might well be negligible how much moral facts subjectively bear on us. This could be of as little importance as are all the other facts that do not reach us subjectively. Our blindness cannot alter the color of the leaf.

Such a model begins to lose plausibility when it is taken from the epistemological to the ontological level. If norms are facts then can it really be negligible for the existence of these facts whether they are acknowledged or not? More specifically, can we imagine the existence of moral norms without subjects being involved? A distinction at least seems appropriate, as there can be no norms for moral realism if there are not subjects toward whom the norms are oriented. Subjects are a precondition for the existence of norms. This doesn't hold true, however, for the truth claims of moral statements, which can also apply if they are not held to be true by anyone. According to moral realism, then, a distinction is to be made between objective properties that—like moral or esthetic qualities—apply to subjects and are not imaginable without them, and the objectivity of these subject-related properties. Practical properties of an object are distinguished from its theoretical properties by the fact that the former relate to actions. But that doesn't mean that both are not real. The fact that a prohibition of speculation on grain at a commodities future exchange will assure that less people go hungry even exists as normative when nobody recognizes it as such.

4.2 Social Norms Operate Differently

It is no coincidence that moral realism is a model of moral norms. Otherwise the theory would not be able to consistently treat norms as rational and as knowable *qua* rationality. I have already pointed out the deficits of norm rationalism.[78] For a theory of social norms, norms are not necessarily results of rational action. As such, however, there is no reliable form available that would allow us to recognize norms. It is thus of tremendous practical significance for any theory of social norms that we have no perceptive sense for norms, and that moral norms lack a robust phenomenal structure, as Halbig notes.[79] After all, it is for precisely this reason that we talk differently about norms than we do about facts.

Social norms at least partially appear to us as fabricated units. They are made, and even if something made can be treated as a fact, the possibility of access

[78] See above, pp. 10–14.
[79] Halbig, *Praktische Gründe*, p. 258–276.

through fabrication, as well as the corresponding possibility to remove norms from this world must have consequences for our dealing with them. Their factual being is more precarious, their existence if frequently contentious from the outset, not least of all because the insinuation of "making" norms entails numerous preconditions, as does the insinuation of "finding" norms.[80] For this reason, it would be rather impractical to treat norms as other facts. Of course, in the pragmatics of the normative, there are many examples of references to facts fulfilling a normative function. Such a deduction might be especially plausible for local norms, but certainly not for the moral norms for which moral realism was developed. For example: I account for the existence of a certain rule of social etiquette via reference to a practice or something that is taught in school—even when the rule appears absurd to me. I justify a legal norm via mere reference to a certain court verdict—regardless of whether I take it to be legally or morally appropriate. Such deductions, which make up a significant portion of normative justification practice, treat norms as facts. But they differ from the model of moral realism in two ways: first, they do not fulfill its demands for a moral justification. They remain limited to more or less local references. They are dogmas that operate below the level of philosophical standards of rationality. Secondly, such deductions generally operate by means of descriptive elements that explicitly mark norms as norms. What distinguishes them is that they make a normative pretense explicit—by formalizing, such as in law, or by certain communicative techniques, such as the rules of etiquette. The treatment of such norms as facts without a corresponding reference to their character as norms would remain unclear. For that reason, norms are *marked as norms* in social practice. As will be shown, this marking can take on the broadest array of forms. It does not need to correspond to a certain meta-ethical model. The practical necessity of such a marking makes any assimilation of our dealing with norms to our dealing with facts appear dubitable.

[80] On this, see the following "Interlude" pp. 61–64.

Interlude I: False Juxtapositions for the Description of Norms

In order to develop a notion of what marks a normative practice, in this interlude I will examine *pairs* of conceptual alternatives, alternatives between which many theories of normativity implicitly or explicitly take sides. I am not concerned with a critique of just one of the available alternatives but rather with a critique of the notion that norms could appropriately be described by reference to these alternatives or juxtapositions. That is because these alternative pairs—so I assume—are conceptually misleading in their exclusivity. Why such a cumbersome form of critique? Because in many theories of normativity one of these alternatives is presented as the exclusive explanatory option. Because the deficit of this approach doesn't simply lie in the quality of the explanatory option presented but is situated already in discussing questions of normativity within such a framework of alternatives. As distinctions, these alternatives have a limited descriptive capacity; as exclusive, counter-positional alternative pairs, they lead to lamentably narrow notions of social normativity.

1. Reason or Coercion?

In the alternative between reasonable norms and those backed by sanction or force, systematic questions once more come to the fore, questions we had examined under the keyword of norm rationalism and in the analysis of the Humean and Kantian paradigms. Concerning the question of where the normative is located, a traditional line of conflict runs along the distinction between norms as rational grounds or good reasons on the one hand, and norms as emanations of force or coercion on the other.

As an example, take the normative content of a court's verdict can be seen in its threatening, if necessary even forcible execution, or in its effect on the reputation of the person condemned; that is, in a coercive effect that corresponds with or runs counter to the addressee's preferences, as a positive or negative incentive. The normativity of the verdict consists in a psychological or physical effect which the person concerned cannot avoid. The identification of norm and coercion, which runs in the background, corresponds to the Humean paradigm. It can be linked to an instrumentalist understanding of rationality. An instrumental rationalist would not see anything irrational in such an understanding of norms as being reducible to forms of coercion. If one further assumes stable preferences of people, then they

The Possibility of Norms. Christoph Möllers, Published by Oxford University Press (2020) under licence; © this translation, Alex Holznienkemper; © the original German edition, Suhrkamp Verlag Berlin.
DOI: 10.1093/oso/9780198827399.001.0001

only become normatively approachable if there is a realistic threat of sanctions being tied to a given behavior. Such an interpretation of norms is widespread: in the economic analysis of law, in rational choice literature, as well as in the theory of effect esthetics, whose proponents, such as Edmund Burke, see the effect of a tragedy primarily in the degree to and quality in which it succeeds in replicating a terrible reality.[1]

The normativity of the verdict can, however, also be located in the reasonableness of the arguments which the court develops in its reasoning. By means of its reasoned character, the legal practice of judging reaches beyond itself and marks itself as a normative practice. This reading also has many versions in different realms of the normative: in the esthetics of reason, in deliberative democratic theory, or in those theories of law that take it to be an specific case or field of moral argument.

A vast amount of energy in the theoretical debate on normativity has been invested into the dispute about which side of this alternative one should take. But is it even plausible that making a choice is necessary?

Before getting to a critique of these alternative pairs, a few clarifications seem necessary. For one, the strong theoretical aspirations of both conceptions of normativity need to be highlighted. Neither is concerned with the mere—conceptually non-binding—observation that normative practices can contain elements of coercion with respect to rational reasoning, or that coercion and rationality are frequently linked to the normative practices of law, politics, or esthetics. Instead, both sides insist that the normative character of the practice as such is only *constituted* by the link to either reason or coercion. It is only the reasonable character or the coercive effect of a certain social practice that makes this practice a normative one. Each side of the alternative is treated as the necessary condition for something to be properly spoken of or treated as normative. For that reason, the models are mutually incompatible.

Considering the multitude of phenomena one would typically classify as normative, this irreconcilability is irritatingly exclusive. To take only one example: modern legal systems, in which reasoning both with an eye toward reasonableness as well as toward physical force are no strangers, are scrupulously concerned with *not* becoming too dependent on *either* element. The claim to validity of a legal system does not depend on whether its decisions and reasoning in a specific procedure can be—according to whatever standard—considered as reasonable. Obedience is expected even in the case of a wrongful conviction. Even a verdict that is mistaken according to the internal standards of the legal system which brought it about can have a binding effect, for example when an appeal is not filed in time. The 'coercion theorists' have made a lot of the circumstances that

[1] Edmund Burke, *A Philosophical Enquiry into the Origin of our Ideas of the Sublime and Beautiful*, Oxford 1999, pp. 43–5.

their theoretical forebear, Thomas Hobbes, observed so poignantly: authority, not truth, makes law.[2] But on the other hand, not only are all norms in a modern legal system not backed by coercion; what is more, legal systems do not even depend on their decisions to be viewed as binding. That is because they tend to avoid the physical execution of their decisions. This is less so in criminal law, where sanction and execution are tightly interwoven, but it does hold for most cases in which decisions by an administrative body or a civil court meet resistance.[3] The actual employment of force imposes too obvious limitations to the legal order. For that reason, systems viewed as well-functioning are held to make compromises, for example in the persecution of lesser crimes, or in the implementation of administrative sanctions.

Similar observations can be made about other kinds of norms. Rules of etiquette are neither respected purely out of a fear of sanctions, nor are they always rationally justified.[4] A different example, which may initially appear to be far-fetched, can be found in the process of esthetic canonization. This is the practice that seeks to define which works of art are to be viewed as worthy of engagement.[5] Is this practice driven by the coercive effect of a powerful object in the work of art in question, as is claimed by the esthetic picture theory?[6] Or is the process of canonization the result and expression of an objective standard of esthetic quality[7] that might be captured by a theory of esthetic reason?

Both alternatives underestimate the inner-esthetic mechanisms as well as the context. For example, let us examine the invention of the "trail" as a criminalistic vehicle by Arthur Conan Doyle, a narrative innovation that shaped the canon of crime stories for well over a century.[8] This esthetic norm cannot be reduced to either side of the alternative. It is so form-immanent that neither a rational content nor a specific effect can be attributed to it. The process of its canonization furthermore depends on external factors that also cannot be grasped through either side of the alternative—on distributive media like literary magazines, for example, on demand for these media, and on forms that enable us to compare and collect literary works without which no communicable canon could even come about.[9]

[2] Thomas Hobbes, *Leviathan*, Oxford 1998, p. 183.

[3] Ralf Poscher, "Verwaltungsakt und Verwaltungsrecht in der Vollstreckung", in: *Verwaltungs-Archiv* 89 (1998), pp. 111–36, here pp. 117 ff. See also, Niklas Luhman, *Macht*, Konstanz 2012, pp. 59 ff.

[4] See the reflections by Asfa-Wossen Asserate, *Manieren*, Frankfurt/M. 2003, pp. 17–32.

[5] Moshe Halbertal, *People of the Book*, Cambridge, Mass. 1997, p. 3, differentiates between normative, formative, and exemplary canons, with the third category located on a different level as the first two.

[6] Horst Bredekamp, *Theorie des Bildakts*, Berlin 2012, p. 51.

[7] Harold Bloom, *The Western Canon*, New York 1994, pp. 22–41; Gottfried Willems, *Der Weg ins Offene als Sackgasse*, Bonn 2000.

[8] This is a phenomenon explicitly identified as normative by the father of this thesis: Franco Moretti, "The Slaughterhouse of Literature", in: Id., *Distant Reading*, London 2013, pp. 63–90, here pp. 69–81.

[9] Fundamentals concerning the process of canonization can be found in Jan Assmann, *Das kulturelle Gedächtnis*, München 2013, p. 103–29. On the media conditions in the case of music: Martin Elste, "Neue Aspekte des Kanonischen im Jahrhundert des Lautsprechers", in: Klaus Pietschmann and Melanie Wald-Fuhrmann (eds), *Der Kanon der Musik*, München 2013, pp. 818–31.

Fundamentally, every form of esthetic canonization presumes a concept of the artwork in which its esthetic quality is to be manifested. This also runs counter to our discussed alternatives.[10] Ultimately, the emergence of a canon is a process that is difficult to correct. The situation in which a canon came to be is not repeatable; alternative works may get neglected even if they fulfill the criteria of other canonized works.[11]

Now, one can also read these two examples differently. One can understand the process of esthetic canonization as a social practice that has nothing to do with art-immanent criteria, that is as a practice that is not normative, thus being irrelevant for our considerations. One could also reject the normative claim of a legal order that produces wrongful convictions or of an order that cannot or does not try to enforce its decisions due to their lack of either one of these qualities—reasonableness or coercion.

With these kinds of strategy, certain elements are conceptually extracted from social practices which are then, in their isolation, taken as constituting the normative element as such. From the practice of legal decision-making is extracted either its justificatory elements capable of rationalization or its effects on the exertion of organized force. In the practice of esthetic canonization, those elements are isolated which, for whatever reason, are deemed as having been "rightfully" esthetically canonized. In doing so, these practices are manipulated in a way that has more to do with the descriptive theory than it does with the object they are supposed to describe. The different theories maintain their conceptual consistency at the price of an anemic view of practices, in which a practice—generally considered as normative—is typically only made possible because of a commingling of justifications and other effects. Put differently, it is precisely the focus on the complex interplay between the general duty to justify decisions and the threat of force, both typical for legal orders, that enables an appropriately substantive description of a legal system's operation; it is precisely the combination of a historically permanent esthetic judgment of a work of art, the possibility of its depiction in a collection, and the effects of the thus-collected works on readers and observers that explains the operation of an art-esthetic canon. If one opts for the excluding option, the theoretical preference for one of the alternative positions risks leading to a peculiar reductionism. Far from limiting oneself to a philosophical conceptualization, these models shape empirically minded research, which tends to make invisible underlying normative commitments or to affirm the observer's own theoretical preconditions.

This critique does not save us the conceptual work with regard to the normative. Indicating the hybridity of normative practices can only fulfill a negative task, but

[10] Fittingly, Rüdiger Bubner, "Über einige Bedingungen gegenwärtiger Ästhetik", in: Id., *Ästhetische Erfahrung*, Frankfurt/M. 1989, pp. 7–51, here pp. 32 ff.

[11] Franco Moretti, spoken statement.

cannot provide such a concept. What remains is that a rich account of social norms does not have to take sides between a reduction to either coercion or reason.

2. *Command or Recognition?*

In answering how norms arise, theories of normativity often oscillate between an ideal-type of recognition by a given community and that of a norm-setting commander. If we construct a norm purely as a recognition phenomenon, then it clearly dissolves in the practice of the factually recognizing community. The norm-setter and the addressee of a norm merge with each other, unless a conflict questions the recognition itself.

For this reason, theories of recognition resort to highly normative notions of recognition. In that case, one is not so much concerned with whether a norm is actually recognized but whether it "can" find recognition.[12] This "can" denotes a "should," a normative claim that provides an excessive rest, which points beyond a practice of norm recognition even when all participants are of one mind. The normative concept of recognition—a concept not of factual, but accomplished, well-reasoned, or otherwise justified recognition—lacks an empirical docking point. This systematic issue became apparent in the reading of Brandom who ultimately grounded his recognition theory in the factual commonality in the perception of objects. For a theory of normativity that seeks to understand social norms as intelligible practice, both variants of recognition offer an unwieldy criterion.

By the same token, the issue of a norm's intelligibility cannot be solved by pointing toward a positing source of authority; that is, by understanding normativity as a command technique. This strategy, for example, can be found in the legal theories of John Austin and Hans Kelsen.[13] These kinds of theory often find themselves compelled to stylize or formalize the figure of the norm-setter, for example by highlighting the procedures of a legal order or the customs of a political system. This is their only way to protect themselves against a peak behind the scenes of formalized norm creation revealing social practices of recognition after all. Let us assume that the most elementary form of any norm were the command: A commands B to carry out a certain action.[14] All the contexts of such commands—a personal relationship between the two, A's role as holding a public office with the

[12] Exemplarily, Immanuel Kant, *Grundlegung der Metaphysik der Sitten*, Frankfurt/M. 1977, p. 51 (BA 52); Jürgen Habermas, *Faktizität und Geltung. Beiträge zur Diskurstheorie des Rechts und des demokratischen Rechtsstaats*, Frankfurt/M. 1992, p. 47.

[13] John Austin, *The Province of Jurisprudence Determined*, London 1954, pp. 9–33 (Lecture I); Hans Kelsen, *Reine Rechtslehre* (1934), Tübingen 2008, pp. 68 ff. A convincing critique, to which the following owes great debt, can be found in H. L. A. Hart, *The Concept of Law*, Oxford xxx, pp. 50–78.

[14] Peter Stemmer, *Normativität*, Berlin 2008, pp. 155–98.

authority to issue orders, the favor that B owes to A from a previous transaction, etc.—that could explain why this command should establish a norm would inevitably result in integrating recognition elements into the description.

These challenges prompt us to keep an eye out for combination models. One example would be Max Weber's formula of the *likelihood of observance*, which constructs a relationship between command and recognition in order to gain an empirically compatible concept of normativity.[15] This is an appropriate path for empirical lines of inquiry, even if one can imagine cases for which it—like any method—will reach its limits. If no-one stops at a red traffic light, how can one respond to the question of whether a norm is still in place? On the one hand, the presence of a command—one that is generally recognized under most circumstances—can easily be determined in the case of a traffic light.[16] On the other hand, this command generally remains unobserved. There is a lack of adherence, but is there a likelihood that someone, at some point, will stop again? Do we need a "certain" likelihood to accept the traffic light as a norm again? How large would this likelihood have to be?[17] There is no general answer to this, but only different cognitive and normative expectations of that which can be demanded of a norm.

The description of norms presupposes their intelligibility. Without alleging a well-defined notion of the normative, one can assume that normative practices, in two types of situations, cannot or can hardly be intelligible. These situations each correspond to one of the ideals described above: for one, when the social practice fully lives up to the normative demands; for another, when these demands are completely neglected by and dissociated from the social practice. In both cases, an incongruence is missing, a demonstrable difference between the norm and the practice that either abides by or violates the norm. By contrast, a coexistence of instances of violation and adherence makes it easier to identify the existence of a norm.

The cognitive challenges that arise from both situations, however, are distinct. The case of complete observance could realize the ideal situation of a recognition theory, in which consensus concerning a pre-existing practice has been reached, even if it becomes difficult to recognize the normative element of the practice. Analyzing Brandom's engagement with the distinctiveness and identification of norms revealed that norms are more difficult to identify when a community simply controls them, can simply produce or change them. For if a social practice fully conforms to a norm, the suspicion promptly arises that this norm is actually not

[15] On the multifaceted nature of the notion of value and its use as an instrument for an empirical research program, see Max Weber, *Wirtschaft und Gesellschaft*, Tübingen 1972, pp. 12–19.

[16] For a norm, the existence of a practice conforming to the law is neither necessary nor sufficient: Geoffrey Brennan, Lina Eriksson, Robert E. Goodin, and Nicholas Southwood, *Explaining Norms*, Oxford 2013, p. 21.

[17] On the quantitative character of Weber's likelihood of observance and its ignorance by the interpretation of Weber, fittingly, Heinrich Popitz, *Soziale Normen*, Frankfurt/M. 2006, p. 227.

a norm after all but that one is faced with merely describing a regularity, or even a 'law of nature' bar any normative claim.

On the flipside, the case of complete violation of a norm raises the question of whether the presumed norm for this situation even exists.[18] If nobody were to stop at a red traffic light anymore, can I then assume the validity of the norm, even if the rules of the State would point toward its validity? In either case, it remains to be seen how a good cognitive criterion for normativity could be constructed.

Durkheim's speculation, that a society needs a certain measure of norm deviation, thus does not just provide a functional observation,[19] it also contains an insight into the conditions of any description of norms. These can only be intelligible (or at least are more easily intelligible) if they are neither perfectly adhered to nor violated in all cases. Since this raises the follow-up question, as we have seen, if and when the point has been reached at which we can speak of a normative practice, theories of command are better off as they can more easily immunize themselves against the multitude of social practices. They do so by pointing out an intelligible context of issuing commands. Recognition theories, on the other hand, have to quantify the Weberian "likelihood" of observance; that is, they have to explain how likely observance has to be in order to be able to properly speak of the existence of a norm.

3. *Autonomous or Effective? The Dilemma of Social Norms*

Whoever speaks of norms speaks of something that is distinct from facts, from something that claims a certain measure of autonomy from the latter without, however, completely falling outside the realm of the factual. For that reason, we should be able to draw a line between the two, or there should be some kind of transitory rule—itself, in turn, normative?—at our disposition. In philosophy, these kinds of rules are prominently labeled as the distinction between "Is" and "Ought,"[20] or as the prohibition of the naturalistic fallacy.[21]

The question of the relationship between the normative and the factual might be the central problem of any theoretical framework of the normative. Responding to it can also serve as an instrument for reconstructing the theoretical frontlines in a different way. After all, Humean and Kantian approaches share the assumption of a categorical distinction between norm and non-norm, albeit for entirely different

[18] The later Kelsen was riveted by the relationship between validity and effectiveness, leading to a relativization of his differentiations, which appears to narrow their merit. See Hans Kelsen, *Reine Rechtslehre*, Wien 1960, p. 10.

[19] Émile Durkheim, *The Rules of Sociological Method*, New York 1982, pp. 100 f.

[20] David Hume, *A Treatise of Human Nature*, Oxford 2011, Vol. 1, pp. 294 ff.

[21] George Edward Moore, *Principia Ethica*, Cambridge 1903, pp. 18–21.

reasons. Other theories of the normative, such as moral realism or Hegel's legal philosophy, take different routes.

With that, our question is only framed from one angle. Normative claims must not only reference the world, that is the facts, what is more they must also arise out of the world. Special ontologies of norms turn out to be quite dubitable efforts, at least as long as norms are supposed to have any factual relevance.

One central problem for juridical, theological, or esthetic models of normativity therefore consists in simultaneously distinguishing and connecting the normative and the factual, treating both autonomously and in relationship to each other. "My kingdom is not of this world"[22] remains contradictory, so long as the kingdom of God is also meant to be of practical import to this world. If it were taken literally, Christian teaching would be irrelevant to the world. Quite to the contrary, divine mercy even seems to positively demand divine intervention into the world. "It would be a merciless God, who would let injustice take its course."[23]

This relationship has implications for the intelligibility of norms—and here, we encounter yet another misleading alternative pair, in which norms are either immunized against the world, or reduced to their efficacy in the world. This pair, too, can be illustrated by cases of perfect norm compliance and cases in which norms are universally breached.

A first example: Article 67 of North Korea's constitution guarantees its citizens the freedom of expression. Is this really a norm, or is it a norm-fiction, a political ploy? Second example: a sign in the hallway of a post-war German university declares it forbidden to belt out Nazi songs. Let us assume that no-one has ever sung Nazi songs there. The sign was put up years after the founding of the university, but even without this sign, the practice would not have developed differently. Are we dealing with a norm in this case? Or is there merely a fixed behavioral pattern which was declared a norm after the fact?

On the one hand, we expect a certain independence of norms from their surrounding circumstances. Norms are to operate counterfactually, or better yet a-factually.[24] But can they, without losing their status as a norm, be a-factual to such a degree as the written guarantee of the freedom of expression in North Korea? On the other hand, norms are to bring about an effect, for without any observable effect, the existence of a norm becomes easily contestable. But also if a norm is reduced to its effects in the world, it vanishes; it dissolves in the practice which it set out to affect. A dilemma becomes apparent: the more successful a norm is by corresponding to the course of events, the less clear it becomes what *noticeably* distinguishes this norm from said course of events. "Everything that assimilates to

[22] John 18, 36.
[23] Eberhard Jüngel, *Das Evangelium von der Rechtfertigung des Gottlosen als Zentrum des christlichen Glaubens*, Tübingen 2011, p. 71. Of course, this claim also allows for the inverse argument.
[24] See the following below, pp. 75 ff.

something, in its assimilating, changes that to which it assimilates"[25] Theunissen observes in reference to Hegel's theory of the concept, calling this the "law of reversal of mimetic dependency relationships." It is precisely this that can be observed in the practice of the normative.

What will prove decisive for the unfolding of the argument is that this problem cannot be solved by an act of definition. The greater value one accords to autonomy from the world of facts in defining the normative, the more difficult it becomes to attribute certain effects to such a norm. And the more attention one pays to a norm's embeddedness in the world of facts in defining such a norm, the more difficult it becomes to identify its autonomy from the world.[26]

This uncertainty can manifest itself at different levels. The meaning of a given norm is often uncertain. What does it mean to love one's neighbor as oneself? Even before we reach this question, it is often unclear whether there exists a norm at all. Do we really have to wear a tuxedo to the party? What is more, it may also be unclear where exactly in a given practice a norm, whose existence is uncontended, can be located. Is a court verdict the application of a rule that is applied to a specific case, such that the normative character of the verdict arises out of the rule? Or does the act of the verdict itself constitute the rule?[27] For a theory of social norms, it is important to acknowledge at the outset such uncertainties that concern the existence, meaning, and location of a social norm. As will be shown, these uncertainties stem not least from the dilemma between autonomy and efficacy of the normative.

A model of the normative must tackle this dilemma but also accept the possibility of a norm's factual inefficacy. *One* specific effect—beyond a causal effect—is, however, entailed by all norms: they change the meaning of an action even if the action deviates from the norm. The action's relation to the norm imbues it with a further characteristic, that is, with the quality either to comply with or violate the norm. This additional characteristic, of course, assumes that a norm is actually in place. For the freedom of expression guaranteed in the North Korean constitution this is not the case. No-one seems to have conceptualized the constitutional guarantee as something that could have these or other kinds of consequences.

If one accepts that any model of the normative must maintain the tension between autonomy and efficacy, then this has implications for the development of the concept. For this tension can only arise if, as a consequence of its establishment,

[25] Michael Theunissen, "Begriff und Realität", in: Rolf-Peter Horstmann (ed.), *Seminar: Dialektik in der Philosophie Hegels*, Frankfurt/M. 1978, pp. 324–59, here p. 344. See also the observation of Robert Cover, "Foreword: Nomos and Narrative", in: *Harvard Law Review* 97 (1983), pp. 4–69, here p. 39.

[26] A similar observation, operating without the concept of normativity, is found in Christoph Menke's formulation that practical freedom gets tangled up in the paradox of skill and power. On this see *Die Kraft der Kunst*, Berlin 2013, pp. 151 ff.

[27] This is a highly contentious question, both in legal and in esthetic theory. On this, see Sabine Müller-Mall, *Performative Rechtserzeugung*, Weilerswist 2012, pp. 74–124. For a theory in which the notion of verdict seems functionally to replace the concept of the subject: Florian Klinger, *Urteilen*, Zürich 2011.

two possibilities exist for any norm: to be upheld or to be infringed. Here, we catch a glance of what will be systematically worked out in the following chapter. Without the *possibility of norm violation* there is no normativity. This thesis contradicts any conception of normativity which identifies it with coercion because coercion, even conceptually, knows no possibility of deviation. Herein lies the difference between "ought" and "must."[28]

4. *To Find or to Make?*

We already encountered the question of whether norms are found or made—at first sight, an odd alternative pair—while explicating moral realism. At least implicitly, this alternative is of immense import for all theories of normativity. Furthermore, in the last two centuries it has become the object of a fundamental reorientation.[29]

At first sight, there are different types of norms; those that *can* be made, and those that *need* to be found. An administrative decree controlling emission levels is a legal artefact produced in a given norm-setting procedure. This is not the case for universally valid moral norms such as the prohibition of harming others, or for rules of etiquette such as not eating with your hands, a rule rarely made explicit in Europe. Convincing examples can be identified both for the making of norms and for the discovery of norms.

At second glance, such descriptions appear incomplete. *Both* assumptions presuppose more, and when those presuppositions are spelled out, they become contestable. This begins with the fact that the reference point of the distinction is not obvious at all. In thinking of moral norms, the question of whether they're made or found concerns the problem of the proper norm justification. If there are universally valid norms then these are not made—unless they are made by God.[30] In thinking of social norms, things are quite a bit more complicated. We cannot simply say that they are made, and thus the product of a conscious positing. Many

[28] Seen this way, the replacement of "Should" with "Must," based on a Humean model, appears consistent, even if it remains inappropriately labeled under the headline of normativity, such as in Stemmer (n 14), *Normativität*, pp. 12 ff.

[29] The following contributions at least agree in rejecting and repealing this distinction as an alternative: Robert B. Brandom, *Reason in Philosophy*, Cambridge, Mass. 2009, p. 93; Michael Walzer, *Interpretation and Social Criticism*, Cambridge, Mass. 1993, pp. 3–32. For a critique of a cultural studies-driven constructivism in which everything is "made" see: Miguel Tamen, *The Matter of Facts*, Palo Alto 2001, pp. 13–28. We see a classical instance of American legal realism, in which it is claimed that law is made and not found, in Benjamin Cardozo, *The Nature of the Judicial Process*, New Haven 1929, p. 115. We find an attempt to pick up on this distinction without deciding it in Hilary Putnam, "Are Moral and Legal Values Made or Discovered?", in: *Legal Theory* 1 (1995), pp. 5–19, here pp. 8 ff. See also the analysis which ultimately opts for "making" (with differing terminology) in Max Black, "The Analysis of Rules", in: Id., *Models and Metaphors*, Ithaca 1962, pp. 95–139, here pp. 115–17.

[30] This is suggested for the sake of completion, whereby it can remain open whether it follows from the fact that a norm was made by God that it can only be found by all others, or whether it follows from the fact that it can only be found that it was made by God.

norms whose "made-ness" is empirically obvious rest on something that itself cannot be understood as the product of a conscious positing—such as when a law-maker penalizes the killing of a person. This is instead a process in which finding and making find each other. One can also think of liberalizing rules about family law, or the previously dominant, but slowly fading standards of artistic beauty.[31] In such cases of historic change, the making appears to trace or grasp something found. It is not only norms that change but also their formal reconstruction. What's more, the idea that norms are fabricated and thus to be described as artefacts[32] is relatively recent and has only gained prominence over the last 200 years. The emergence of both a subjective reception esthetics and an esthetics of genius, for which artistic rules are constituted by observers or artists, coincided with a corresponding development in the theory of law and politics. Paradigms of the seeking and finding of standards gave way to the paradigm of shaping and creating them. For a long time, standards were taken as given, be it in nature, be it in the text of a norm. Theories as diverse as Kant's Critique of Judgment or the legal realistic critique of a formalistic understanding of norms, however, propagated that acts of judgment *produce* the very standards which they claim to apply. They are performative. They make.

The backdrop of this theoretical evolution can be found in epistemological and ontological doubts about standards. Ontological doubts concern the instrumentalization of nature for moral, esthetic, or legal judgment.[33] Epistemological doubts concern the reliability of texts and other bearers of meaning for the content of a judgment. If the meaning of a text is contested, then one can hardly resort to the text itself to settle a dispute. The decision has to become productive and reach beyond the text.

However, if one traces the emergence of a concrete norm, then the claim that it is purely made will most likely face resistance as well. The claim here is that only those norms can indisputably be described as being made that originate in a highly formalized process—at least as long as one refrains from veering behind the façade of this process. The rule which prohibits Catholic priests from marrying can currently be found in *c.* 277 § 1 of the *Codex Iuris Canonici*. This is the result of a norm-setting process which came to its conclusion in 1983. However, claiming that this norm was made—as opposed to found—only makes sense as long as one focuses on the formal aspect alone. As soon as one looks behind the norm's coming to be, noticing that a similar norm is part of the *Codex* of 1917, as well as of medieval canon law since Pope Gregory VII, a new picture emerges. Gregory VII certainly

[31] Karl Rosenkranz, *Ästhetik des Häßlichen*, Leipzig 1990, pp. 11–16.

[32] Vividly, on the challenges of delimiting artefacts: Tim Ingold, "Materials against Materiality", in: *Archaeological Dialogues* 14 (2007), pp. 1–16, here p. 4.

[33] Christine M. Korsgaard, *The Sources of Normativity*, Cambridge 1996, p. 8.

did not view his Cluniac visions of church reform, of which celibacy was one aspect, as the product of a newly made doctrine, but rather as a return to a precondition of the priestly office, one that had been envisioned in the Gospels, but had since been forgotten.[34] To this day, the Catholic Church interprets this norm not as the product of medieval reform papacy but as a precept that is to be *found* as a recommendation of Jesus in the Gospels. Most Protestant theologians would most likely contend with this. It remains contested whether the norm is to be made or found, as its justification is contested.

Furthermore, it is not necessarily less demanding to claim that norms are made, if one thereby also has to claim that they arise out of nowhere. Theories of social constructivism[35] seem to underestimate[36] the fact that the ontological and epistemological difficulties which arise from the criticism directed at normative standards being treated as something *given* also concern the construction of standards understood as something having been *produced*. For it remains unclear as to where the standard that was produced originated. Did it arise out of nothing, or did its coming to be only consist in it previously existing, and then emerging in a changed context? Such a mere change of context would not be well described with notions such as making, producing, poesis.

Nevertheless, it is of little use to return to the paradigm of finding. "Making" and "finding" are images for the social updating of meaning, which partially renews itself, partially reproduces itself, but which also changes in its reproduction. Since both point toward each other, we cannot do without the distinction *as* distinction. We will thus take recourse to it, but employ it as a distinction, not as an alternative.

We thus have seen that social norms, too, are not always treated as if they were made, as if they had an identifiable author. Whether for good cause or not, they are often treated as objects to be discovered. Not every norm needs to have an *author*, but every norm commands *authority*. Further along, we will also see that the application of norms cannot do without its own *authorization*. Even a norm whose existence is uncontested and given has to be taken up and applied by someone. This usage has its own normative claim and import. But we will need to distinguish between authorship and authorization.

[34] See Matthew 19,12; 1 Corinthians 7, 32–34; and 1 Timothy 3, 2–5. Thus, Article 599 CIC explicitly points to the "evangelical council of chastity for priests." It remains doubtful that this justifies understanding celibacy as precondition of priestly consecration. Concisely on this, see Norbert Lüdecke, "Artikel 'Zölibat'", in: Hans Dieter Betz et al. (eds), *Religion in Geschichte und Gegenwart*, Tübingen 2005, Vol. 8, cols 1896'1898.

[35] Very helpful in clarifying these concepts, Ian Hacking, *The Social Construction of What?*, Cambridge, Mass. 1999, pp. 32 ff, among others, who highlights that the value of such theories depends on the degree to which processes and their scientific description can be taken to be contingent. "Constructed," in this benevolent sense, means "ontologically subjective," that is, dependent upon the presence of subjects (ibid., pp. 29–34). Of course, the concept of "construction" is actually more narrowly understood, as it implies intention.

[36] Explicitly, however: Tamen (n 29), *Matter*, pp. 16–19.

How we understand the authorization of a norm depends upon whether we take them to be made or found. Three variations are conceivable.[37] For one, we can do without institutionalizing the process of norm creation and derive the authority of a norm from its content. By virtue of its content, the norm becomes a norm, just like in the theory of moral realism. Some challenges remain: "But how can values that we *found* be distinguished from values that we *invented*?"[38] Secondly, we can derive the authority of a norm-setting institution from its distinct access to the justification of a norm, similar to how philosophers might claim distinct access to ethical reasoning. Here, the authorization to set norms arises out of a proven skilfulness in the finding of norms. Finally, we can bear in mind that ultimately someone must make a decision about a norm and that we therefore confer the task of positing a norm to a particular institution.

It follows that the decision between the making and the discovering (of norms) also has repercussions on an appropriate theory of the justification of norms. I can only treat norms as truth-apt if I take them to be discoverable contexts, thus principally corresponding to statements of fact. If I treat them as a product (of will), by contrast, this is not the case. The claim, however, is that our treatment of norms does not settle on one of the alternatives, as we cannot limit ourselves to a certain form of justification. On the contrary, we need room for various techniques, for moral arguments, practical routine, and strict formalization. We neither opt consistently for nor against a normative practice that treats norms as truth-apt. This is one of the most interesting circumstances regarding our social treatment of norms, which must necessarily be excluded from meta-ethical theories that aim at unambiguity.

5. *Form or Reality?*

The critique of formalism constitutes an important part of social-scientific and philosophical engagement with juridical, moral, religious, and esthetic norms since the nineteenth century, and it has experienced stimulus from such diverse theorists as Kierkegaard and Marx, and early empirical sociology.[39] In such critiques, norms were frequently viewed as so tightly wound up with their form, that the critique of the form was simultaneously a critique of the norm. Norms were

[37] Here, I follow the considerations of Jewish law by Moshe Halbertal (n 5), *People of the Book*, pp. 84 ff.

[38] Ingolf Dalferth, *Naturrecht in protestantischer Perspektive*, Baden-Baden 2008, p. 54.

[39] On the newer counter-critique empirically: Arthur L. Stinchcombe, *When Formality Works*, Chicago 2001; James G. March, Martin Schulz, and Xueguang Zhou, *The Dynamics of Rules*, Palo Alto 2000. See also Stanley Fish, "Das Recht möchte formal sein", in: Id., *Das Recht möchte formal sein*, Berlin 2011, pp. 112–70, here pp. 153–70.

stylized as illusory constructions that were to be scrutinized by means of an analysis of their political, economic, or moral foundations, or by reflecting on their own logic.

But what is meant by "form," and what part of it is to be dismissed? We can identify certain models as *formalistic* which only describe normative practices from an internal or immanent perspective. This perspective, in turn, abstracts from its own contextual conditions in order to distinguish itself from them. Furthermore, normative orders especially define themselves, that is what a norm is, where and how it can be found, or who is authorized to posit the norm. But the question of how clearly we can distinguish between a formal-immanent and a critical-external perspective is a question, the answer of which has much to do with the tension between world-distance and world-reference, which marks all normative practices.

The investigation into the alternative between finding and making norms has shown that the charge of being formalistic can be brought against *both* sides. The discovery of a prescribed norm has to take "the norm" itself out of its context and isolate it in a formalizing manner. That which is found remains independent of its discovery process. The presumption that a norm is made has to define a procedure for norm creation. As we have seen, a norm can only be understood as a product of such a procedure if the examination of context remains without consequence.

Thus, between form and formlessness, we also cannot posit an exclusive alternative. It would be particularly wrong to interpret the form in which a norm appears as a deficient mode of its reality. If norms refer to the a-factual, then the ontological status of norms is uncertain, and formalization techniques can counteract this uncertainty. If norms are to remain distinguishable, in order not to dissolve into social practice, then this demand can be met by formalization techniques. Then there is no point in interpreting form and norm in the metaphor of a "beneath" or "behind," that is as an un-actual emanation, an epiphenomenon of social practice.[40] On the other hand, recognizing the value of formalization does not mean following a formalistic conception of theory. Understanding norms as forms embedded in contexts can neither be done by reduction to their form nor by overcoming their form.

6. *Product of Continuity or of Rupture?*

Historically, many social norms develop by means of establishment and recognition of customs. Customs arise from repetition.[41] On such a view, the

[40] On such figures of thought: Hans Blumenberg, "Dies ist in Wirklichkeit nur jenes", in: Id., *Die Verfügbarkeit des Philosophen*, Frankfurt/M. 2005, pp. 37–48.
[41] See also Ludwig Wittgenstein, *Philosophische Untersuchungen*, Frankfurt/M. 2003, § 199 (p. 133).

factual repetition would mark a constitutive element of norms. On the other hand, the reference to repetition risks missing the normative element of a social practice, as the difference between a descriptive rule that describes a process and a normative rule that *pre*scribes the process gets lost from sight.[42] What happens once repetitions discontinue or are brought to an end by a deviating event? If our treatment of such a discontinuation operates differently in the case of a normative rule than in the case of a descriptive one, then the normativity of the rule cannot consist merely in repetition as such. Otherwise, the end of the repeating practice would not be able to question its normativity, and the repeating practice would be an example of the conceptual difficulties arising in cases of perfect norm adherence. Upon closer inspection, such a norm would prove not to be a norm, because it would be impossible to break it.

A weaker interpretation of the positive relationship between normativity and repetition could state that, on the one hand, the discontinuation of repetition cannot suspend the norm, but that on the other, the establishment of this norm would not be imaginable without the repetition of events. The repetition, however, would merely be an indicator of something that would need to otherwise reveal itself as normative. This interpretation only works for norms that concern more than a single event or an individual action, that is it would work for a rule, but not for a command, for a religious precept, but not for an esthetic judgment regarding a specific work of art. Additionally, we are faced with the problem of how to recognize instances of repetition,[43] as the notion of repetition implies the existence of at least two events and a given identifying concept in light and virtue of which both events are instances of "the same" and receive their meaning as its repetition. The identification of a repetition thus has to abstract from certain differences, especially from the timing of events that are to be repeated. Now, the identifying concept itself can hardly be of normative origin, otherwise the repetition would be constructed. But a norm, for which repetition is to function as an indicator, must be able to grasp repetition *as* repetition. That means that not only the deduction of a norm from a repetition is rich in preconditions, but that even the mere observation of the repetition is. And even if it succeeds, it certainly does not contradict the assumption of a one-time normative event. Here, too, it would be wrong to ascribe normativity to only one side of the alternative pair.

[42] On this distinction, Max Weber, "R. Stammlers 'Überwindung' der materialistischen Geschichtsauffassung", in: Id., *Gesammelte Aufsätze zur Wissenschaftslehre*, Johannes Winckelmann (ed.), Tübingen 1988, pp. 291–359, here p. 329; Iorio, *Regel und Grund*, pp. 14–18.

[43] From a norm-theoretical viewpoint: Heinrich Popitz (n 17), *Soziale Normen*, pp. 79 ff; illustrative on the problem of recognition within natural sciences: Michael Hampe, *Alfred North Whitehead*, München 1998, pp. 63–73.

7. General or Individualized?

To classify the command of an officer or a court ruling as a "norm" seems unusual. Are such singular events actually norms, or do they merely concern the application of norms?

Understanding norms either as general or as individualized presumes a notion of norm-appropriate specification, that is a proper number of people or contexts, or an appropriate time frame which the norm governs. Nothing indicates that the concept of a norm could supply such a specification.[44] Is a norm that governs 100 cases still a norm, and one that governs 2 no longer a norm? Or vice versa? There is no proper measure of specificity for norms. To counter this, one could claim that norms must be applicable in order to count as norms. From this would follow that, in order to count as norms, norms would need a scope or field of application, which would only be actualized in the moment of application. But once more, we must be cautious not to exclude certain phenomena from the notion of a norm because of otherwise unjustified intuitions. As long as we observe that a court ruling is used as a yardstick for other rulings, and that a biography serves as a model for other biographies, it is fruitless to choose between the alternative of specific or general norms. The contrary assumption is more convincing: normative orders have to be equipped with various degrees of specification. A legal order cannot merely consist of general laws, for instance. It is most obvious in the case of fashion. Following its rules demands both orienting oneself toward a general rule, as well as carving out one's own individuality.[45]

8. Norm Author—Norm Addressee—Norm Content?

The plurality of social norms excludes us from taking recourse to the passed-down alternative pairs when considering the development of the concept of a norm. Norms cannot be convincingly described by these pairs. Nonetheless, these alternatives play a large role in our conceptual thinking and in our imagination with regard to norms. Some of these alternative pairs are due to philosophical controversies about the nature of moral normativity. Others are grounded in our everyday intuitions about the coming to be and contours of norms.

One difficulty in dealing with these alternative pairs lies in the fact that they cannot be systematically ordered. Opting for one alternative can have reverberating effects on others, without these even standing in a strict relationship to each other. Of course, it is tempting to bundle these alternative pairs together into one single

[44] See also the reflections by Popitz (n 17), *Soziale Normen*, pp. 96–101.

[45] On this problem in fashion, see Elena Esposito, *Die Verbindlichkeit des Vorübergehenden: Paradoxien der Mode*, Frankfurt/M. 2004, pp. 79–84, 156 ff.

pair, such as the alternative between a voluntarist and rationalist theory of norms. Voluntarist norm theories take norms to be commands backed by sanctions; that is, they are viewed as cultural artefacts. Rationalist theories, on the other hand, view norms as the product of a rationality to be discovered and unfolded. However, even if one adopts one of these readings, other alternative pairs—grouping around repeatability, effectiveness, or formality of norms—will remain undetermined. For example, for both Hume and Kant, legal norms—not moral norms—are commands backed by coercion. Both theories share a strict distinction between "is" and "ought," that is an autonomy of the normative, but they operate with differing conceptions of effectiveness. Repeatability plays a role in the Humean theoretical tradition, a role in which repetition can stabilize expectations and define preferences. Not so for the Kantian tradition, in which each norm must pass the test of universalizability anew. The Kantian theory of command requires a certain kind of formalization because a universalizability criterion is essential for it, not for the Humean. All in all, the investigated alternative pairs are as suggestive as they are misleading. At least implicitly, though, they maintain a significant impact on norm theoretical discussion. They suggest certain characteristics of the normative.

Finally, these alternative pairs diminish the descriptive value of the distinction between norm author, norm addressee, and norm content. Being able to distinguish a norm based on its process of coming to be, its justification, and its application, proves to be a conceptually demanding task in light of the preceding discussion. Where exactly in a living room in which everyone is eating with fork and knife are the corresponding norms to be located? Where are they located in a court ruling, in which the judge applies to a particular case her understanding of the statute at issue in the name of the people? There is no obvious answer to these questions. The formalization of a legal order in the latter case may suggest a different understanding than the former. But even if such measures of formalization are of immense importance for normative orders, they do not succeed in completely dispelling in the latter case my doubts that originated in the former. Before examining such mechanisms of norm identification in Chapter 4, we must first develop our own concept of the normative.

II

CONCEPTS

3

The Possibility of Norms

A Conceptual Model

In this chapter, we will develop a two-part concept of norms. Norms consist of a possibility and a marking that affirms the realization of said possibility.

1. Introduction

1.1 Anscombe's Model

In her book, *Intention*, Elizabeth Anscombe develops a famous distinction.[1] A man walks into a store with a shopping list and is observed by a detective. She notes what the man is buying. A discrepancy between the purchases carried out by him and his list constitutes a mistake by the man. A discrepancy between the purchases and the report of the detective constitutes a mistake on her part. The man adjusts his behavior to the list, the detective adjusts her report to the behavior of the man. The man's list is normative. The report by the detective is descriptive.[2] What distinguishes them is their *direction of fit*.

This distinction, stemming from the theory of intentionality, as a rudimentary concept of normativity, is of pertinent interest for the question tackled here; both for what it captures and for that which it leaves out. The model offers an inclusive and wieldy notion of the normative. On my reading, this consists in the portrayal of a possibility that is to be achieved, in this case in the obtainment of the goods written on a list. It furthermore consists in an affirmative marking that strives for this possibility to be realized. Anscombe explicitly states that the object of the direction of fit is not limited to certain objects,[3] and that is does not have to refer to actions.[4] What is essential for the direction of fit is its orientation

[1] G. E. M. Anscombe, *Intention*, Cambridge, Mass 2000, pp. 56 f.

[2] The expression *direction of fit* is often accorded to the cited passage, but is not found there. Rather, it originally stems from J. L. Austin. The discussion surrounding this passage has centered on the question of distinguishability between *desire* and *belief*, and it hasn't so much been concerned with the meaning of the normative, or rather it has taken both terms to be normative: I. Lloyd Humberstone, "Direction of Fit" in: *Mind* 101 (1992), pp. 52–83; Nick Zangwill, "Direction of Fit and Normative Functionalism" in: *Philosophical Studies* 91 (1998), pp. 173–203, here pp. 195–7, here with the interpretation as a normative differentiation. A concise explication of Anscombe's argument context in Mark de Bretton Platts, *Ways of Meaning*, Cambridge, Mass. 1997, pp. 256 ff.

[3] Anscombe (n 1), *Intention*, pp. 69 f.

[4] Ibid., pp. 37 f.

DOI: 10.1093/oso/9780198827399.001.0001

toward the future.[5] A spatial or temporal distance between the intention and the intended is a crucial factor in every normative adjustment.[6] What the model leaves out, however, are reflections on the justification of the list with any kind of objective measure (are the items to be purchased healthy?), in any legitimizing way (who has the authority to send someone shopping?), or even its origin (was the man free to select these products, was the woman free to write them down?) and its meaning (can we speak of the list being "unambiguous," or is its content, just as its directive mode is, the—potentially faulty—result of an interpretation on the reader's part?). Anscombe expressly locates her model of practical reason outside of ethics.[7] It is also irrelevant whether the list was written by the man himself or by his wife, whether it constitutes his own intention or a command.[8]

This reductionism will prove itself useful for a theory of social norms. So as not to be misunderstood, all these questions have their own justification. They are relevant for the theory of norms, but not when we are concerned with developing the conceptual precondition of the concept of social normativity itself.

1.2 The Problem of a Norm's Recognizability

The question concerning the relation between empiricism and normativity presupposes a concept of normativity in which norms are recognizable in so far as they are divested into the social realm. In Part I we already marked this as a crucial feature distinguishing my theory from typical philosophical conceptions of normativity. Acts of justification and recognition do not need to take place *in foro interno* of a subject, but they can. However, they must be divested, that is they have to become part of some communication that takes place in time and space, in order to be recognizable by others. In being divested in this way, norms become part of social mechanisms that cannot be grasped with the categories of practical philosophy alone.

If a theory of morality accords a justificatory effect to a certain reason due to its content or form, then this argumentation may well apply. But from the view of a social practice model, there always remains a need for some degree of translation or representation. A moral-philosophical argument can be sound, even if it has not been articulated or thought of by anyone. For its practice, a norm can only be of meaning in so far as a place and time are available for its articulation. This shift in perspective does not result in a reduction of normativity to facticity. On the

[5] Ibid., pp. 42 f.
[6] Ibid., pp. 49 f.
[7] Ibid., pp. 48 f.
[8] Ibid., pp. 34 f.

contrary, it is imperative to grasp the curious circumstance that norms can claim their autonomy from this world *while being* part of it.

Models that describe norms with recourse to a scheme of norm setter and/or norm addressee and/or norm content proved to be too narrow in the analysis of false alternative pairs. For that reason, the following will develop a reduced concept of normativity, which consists in just two elements. Norms, so runs the claim, consist of the representation of a *possibility* and a positive evaluation of its realization, one that I will characterize as a *realizing marker*.

1.3 A Countercheck: Luhmann's Notion of Norms

For an initial explication, I will compare this approach with a well-known distinction as well as with an example. According to a formulation frequently invoked by Niklas Luhmann, *normative* expectations differ from cognitive ones in so far as the former, in contrast to the latter, are not adjusted when the expected event does not occur.[9] This brings back to mind Anscombe's notion of the *direction of fit*.

It becomes apparent, however, that the notion of expectation, if it is not further specified, points toward a *cognitive* capacity. An expectation consists in a prediction about a future development, the occurrence of which is not evaluated—in contrast to the clearly evaluative counter-notion of disappointment. According to Luhmann, norms establish the expectation that they be honored, which is why the role of norms lies in the stabilization of expectations.[10] In this way, Luhmann backhandedly deploys the concept of stabilization in a *twofold* manner. Norms are stable in relation to factual events, that is, they do not change when the expectations are not met, and norms stabilize these expectations.

Such a concept, however, proves itself to be both too close to descriptive categories and too demanding in terms of presuppositions,[11] because the positing of a norm does not necessarily have to be connected to an expectation of adherence to it. Norms can also serve as markings of practices that deviate from them, thus serving as "symbolic" positing of norms.[12] The pejorative aftertaste of this formulation should not distract from the idea that "symbolism" is not a deficient characteristic of the normative but rather at its core, namely its distinction from the factual. It is highly doubtful that anyone should believe that the norms "all state power derives from the people" or "you shall love your neighbor as yourself" will

[9] Niklas Luhmann, *Soziale Systeme*, Frankfurt/M. 1987, pp. 436–40; Id., *Das Recht der Gesellschaft*, Frankfurt/M. 1993, pp. 77–83.

[10] Ibid., pp. 124–64, especially in the context of law.

[11] Along the lines of Heinrich Popitz, *Soziale Normen*, Frankfurt/M. 2006, p. 81, we could also limit the discussion to "desiderative norms."

[12] Peter Noll, "Symbolische Gesetzgebung" in: *Zeitschrift für Schweizerisches Recht* 100 (1981), pp. 347–64.

never be broken again, just as it is irrelevant for their nature as norms. Rather, the affirmative marking of a future event needs to be distinguished from the expectation of the occurrence of said event. Some norms derive their pathos precisely from the difficulty of their realization, but this pathos is not necessary for marking it as a norm.

On the other hand, the idea of normative expectation is also too narrow, because it presumes that norms fundamentally aim at *stabilizing* expectations. This can be the case, but it does not have to be. One example of such stabilization of expectations can be found in State-sanctioned traffic rules, which traffic participants actually observe in the factual expectation that they will be followed by all others as well. This expectation, in turn, can become a norm—but this is a special case, it is not self-evident. With respect to the law, one should drive like someone who expects that all others follow the traffic rules.[13]

The achieved stabilization presumes that the norm, the norm's application, as well as an amendment of the norm are sufficiently distinguishable as it may—at best—be the case with regard to legal norms (and even there, such distinction is not always or typically manageable). The boundary between a changed norm and a changed practice of an unchanged norm is never obvious. As such, the stabilization remains elusive in many cases. For example, I might be surprised at what counts as "good manners" in a specific case. Norms take part in the general uncertainty of meanings; how could it be otherwise? But this has repercussions for their supposed stabilizing function.

Furthermore, normative orders can even work toward *destabilizing* expectations.[14] Some norms create procedures to simplify their own amendment. Other norms are supposed to enable certain social practices, even those that one is not even aware of; basic rights are an important example of this. Freedom of opinion and the guarantee of private property also protect actions that one could or did not imagine at the time of codifying such rights. Basic rights serve to simplify making society and the normative system itself more dynamic. Norms can function as expectation stabilizers, but they do not need to.

Finally, in the case of normative disappointment, the normative underpinning of existing expectations can also amplify the destabilizing effect of their disappointment. Imbuing an expectation with normativity can dramatize its disappointment so much that destabilization only follows from its normativity. Religious taboos are an example. The transgression gains its immensity not so much from the concrete expectation that it would be nearly impossible to break the rule. Anyone can tear down a veil or climb onto an altar. The consequences of a broken taboo are

[13] This is the so-called principle of trust: Peter Hentschel, Peter König, and Peter Dauer, *Straßenverkehrsrecht*, München 2013, § 1 Straßenverkehrsordnung, marginal nos 20–24.

[14] This should be viewed separately from the fact that norms can create conflicts, see Luhmann (n 9), *Recht der Gesellschaft*, p. 139.

dramatic because of the value accorded to the rule. This also cannot be grasped by the figure of expectation stabilization.

This critique of Luhmann's conceptualization should illustrate what we are concerned with in the following: confronting the work on the concept of the normative with a broad spectrum of phenomena, in order to develop a concept of the normative that neither moralizes normativity—as is the case with Luhmann—nor backhandedly factualizes it.

> But then one is never sure what is
> possible until it happens . . . [15]

2. *Element 1: Possibility*

2.1 Afacticity between Experience and Imagination

The first determining feature of a concept of normativity lies in its distinction from facticity. According to a widespread expression, norms are concerned with something *counter*factual. The prefix "counter," however, it too strong an expression if one does not want to imply that normativity and facticity stand in an antagonistic relationship. What runs counter to this idea is that we could hardly allow ourselves to imagine normativity in such a way that it would *displace* facticity. Norms may well be realized, but they do not thereby stand in for the facts in which they are realized. A norm that is adhered to does not lose its validity by virtue of its being followed. Normativity does not direct itself in opposition to the world as it is per se; rather, it opens up space both for deviations and correspondences. Facts can correspond to norms, without this resulting in the *existence* of both being brought into question, whereas the *evidence* of norms may very well be brought into doubt in that way. For these reasons, it is more fitting to speak of the *afacticity* of norms, in order to express the difference to (but not competition with) facts.

At an *ontological* level, we need not immediately be concerned that the juxtaposition of normativity and facticity belongs to the realm of facts. There is no immediate need for a particular ontology in order to speak of normativity and contrast it with facticity. On this view, the same holds for norms and for poetry: "The poetic world distinguishes itself from the empirical world, and nonetheless exists within it."[16] Beyond the question of how the two relate to each other, and whether inferences from "is" statements are permissible for "ought" statements, normativity is still part of the entirety of facts. It is a counter-world that is part of the world.

[15] Stanley Cavell, "Aesthetic Problems of Modern Philosophy" in: Id., *Must We Mean What We Say?*, Cambridge 2002, pp. 73–96, here p. 73.

[16] Heinz Schlaffer, *Poesie und Wissen*, ext. edition, Frankfurt/M. 2005, p. 147.

Practices as diverse as the use of the imperative, the justification of a moral obligation, or the investigation of a legal question do not require a separate ontology, even if they are subject to all the problems that are raised by an ontology of abstract objects and institutions.

2.2 Experience and Imagination

The designation of possibilities cannot get by without experience. Remembered experience is the most important substantive source of normativity. With the help of a memory concerning a past experience, we potentially have recourse to a condition of the world which deviates from the actual state of affairs. This in turn enables us to imagine conditions differently from their current state. However, the development of deviating strings of events is not limited to experience and memory of the past. With the help of our imagination, we are also able to develop world conditions with which we have had no experience.[17] Of course, our imagination also relies on experience. This is expressed nicely in Kant's characterization of imagination as "capacity to grasp an object even without the presence of the object."[18] Without experience, we cannot imagine anything. And yet our imagination is not bound to experience. We can also imagine conditions which we have never seen, even ones that we could never see, as they are not accessible to experience. Highlighting remembered and imagined conditions also leads to two kinds of normativity: normativity by tradition, and normativity by projection.

2.3 Philosophical Cross-Checks

If we take as our starting point for a model of normativity the determination of an afactual condition on the experience-rich basis of memory and imagination, then we seem to be ignoring a long discussion about the nature of normativity. We even seem to turn it on its head. One might even get the impression that the distinction between normativity and non-normativity is being dismissed by means of a definitional move, taking normativity as something that can be inductively deduced from concrete imagination. Across the various discussions concerning the nature of normativity, the starting point is certainly not to be found in the construction of afactual conditions on an empirical or imagined

[17] The distinction between memory and imagination is measured by the degree of its success: James O. Urmson, "Memory and Imagination" in: *Mind* 76 (1967), pp. 83–91, here p. 89.

[18] Immanuel Kant, *Anthropologie in pragmatischer Hinsicht*, Frankfurt/M. 1977, p. 466 (§ 25). For an explication of the imagination's decoupling from reason in the transition from the first to the third critique, see Petra Bahr, *Darstellung des Undarstellbaren*, Tübingen 2004, pp. 261–7.

basis. Normativity can arise from a desire, from good reasons, from established traditions, or from the capacity to examine an action maxim's universalizability and make it one's own. Common among all these is that they more clearly distinguish between normativity and facticity than the current model. This raises the question of whether the current reconstruction suffers from precisely the kind of pan-normativity from which we previously distanced ourselves, and whether it backhandedly argues for a softening of the distinction between the normative and non-normative.

To show that this is not the case, we will resort to an example of a moral concept that is generally not suspected of blurring the lines between normativity and descriptiveness, namely the Categorical Imperative. I presume that the Categorical Imperative is a procedure for deriving morally appropriate actions, not merely an argument for proving the possibility of moral action. Now one reading of the Categorical Imperative suggests reconstructing it as a purely rational inference: I cannot break a promise because I *cannot* imagine this action as generalizable without sacrificing the concept of the promise. I cannot lie because the maxim that brings me to lie must presume that others do not lie. On this reading, it remains unclear why I must want to uphold the institution of the promise or the disposition of truthfulness through my actions.[19] But the inference cannot do without an *idea* of the practical consequences of generalizing my maxim for action.[20] In applying the universalizing rule, one first imagines an action not yet carried out, then this imagined action is in turn imagined as a generalized action; that is, it is envisioned as though all acted in accord with this maxim. Finally, in a third imagination, the consequences of this universalization are examined with regards to their agreeability. On such a reading, the application of the Categorical Imperative requires experience and imagination. As Sebastian Rödl expresses it: "According to an idea that Kant inherited from Aristotle, a reasonable being does not merely act in accord with laws, but rather in accord with the imagination of laws."[21] For Rödl, this means that the normative merit of laws cannot be separated from the subjectivity to which they are addressed. What is crucial here is that even a conceptually formulated moral criterion, such as Kant's notion of the principle of generalizability, is contingent upon the capacity for imagination, that the business of forming maxims is essentially one of the imagination.

[19] But also compare, as an attempt to integrate these levels for the figure of the promise, Stephen Engstrom, *The Form of Practical Knowledge*, Cambridge, Mass. 2009, pp. 196–209.

[20] On the necessity of including empirical elements in this process, see Thomas W. Pogge, "The Categorical Imperative" in: Ottfried Höffe (ed.), *Grundlegung zur Metaphysik der Sitten*, Frankfurt/M. 1989, pp. 172–93, here pp. 190 ff.; on the precise analysis of the actual inference, Peter J. Steinberger, "The Standard View of The Categorical Imperative" in: *Kant-Studien* 90 (1999), pp. 91–9, here pp. 95–9. Regarding the question of whether the reference to "being able to think" or "being able to want" is appropriate: Dieter Birnbacher, *Analytische Einführung in die Ethik*, Berlin 2003, pp. 142–54.

[21] Sebasitan Rödl, *Selbstbewußtsein*, Berlin 2011, p. 156.

2.4 Norms as Concepts?

How do these reflections relate to the assumption that normativity is to be understood as something purely *conceptual*? The example of Kant's Categorical Imperative is as follows: however one understands the role of the imagination for its application, it ultimately becomes part of a conceptual generalization. Without a doubt, many normative practices, if not most of the ones which will be discussed in the following, must be understood as conceptual achievements. Law is the paradigmatic case of a discourse that explicates social norms in conceptualizing them. One could say that successful practice of law is the practice of successful engagement with legal concepts.[22]

Nonetheless, not all normative practices are conceptual achievements,[23] just as not all concepts are normative. If one were to take a social practice as a normative expression, a practice in which breaking with a convention in the realm of table manners (e.g. eating with cutlery) brings about curious looks, then that practice can also count as a *pre*-conceptual form of normativity. Of course, it depends on surrounding conditions. If a rule had been expressly stated, justified, and argued for, then an operation with concepts took place. If the behavior of the guest evoked displeasure, even though no other participants had conceived of the possibility of eating with their hands, then the experienced displeasure can provoke an explication and conceptualization of notions of proper behavior. In that case there would have been a pre-conceptual norm at play. By contrast, an explicit practice, such as rules imbued in a child, can fade into the background and in turn only reveal themselves by someone's deviant behavior and another person thereby being negatively touched. In that case, one would be dealing with a post-conceptual norm, with rules that can no longer simply be explicated in concepts.

I shall return to the relationship between norms and concepts. An initial impression is worth highlighting. If we accept that there are social practices which do not draw on conceptualization, so also this possibility should be accepted in the case of normative practices. The distinction between the conceptual and the non-conceptual then does not square or coincide with the distinction between the normative and other practices. Normative practices can be expressed in the form of concepts, but they do not have to be. Concepts might even represent an intermediate position in the genesis of social norms which arise pre-conceptually and are then made explicit, ultimately becoming implicit through being made routine, operating post-conceptually.

[22] Christoph Möllers and Hannah Birkenkötter, "Towards a New Conceptualism in Comparative Constitutional Law" in: *International Journal of Constitutional Law* 12 (2014), pp. 603–25.

[23] Examples for preconceptual action in Jocelyn Benoist, *Concepts*, Paris 2010, pp. 61–4; Hans Blumenberg, *Theorie der Unbegrifflichkeit*, Frankfurt/M. 2007, pp. 51–3 and more frequently.

In Kant's critique of teleological judgment, the rational achievement performed by dealing with concepts is defined as one of mediation between possibility and conceptuality.[24] In contrast to sense perceptions, concepts do not refer to the actual world but rather to a possible one; they aspire to the future. Applied to the theory of normativity, concepts explicate possibilities, and that means that with recourse to said possibility, they also explicate norms which reference possibilities. Pre-conceptual norms are thus imaginable, and it is also not difficult to find examples for pre- or non-conceptual normative practices. The explication of normative practices as norms, on the other hand, only works at the level of concepts.

What does that leave us with? Even a theory which values the distinction between "is" and "ought," between normativity and non-normativity, hinges on the representation of possibility, whether that be conceptual or non-conceptual. However, the starting point chosen here does not imply any rejection of the distinction. For the development of afactual conditions is a necessary, but not sufficient element of a concept of normativity. The question of distinguishability is therefore to be located elsewhere.

2.5 "Cognitive Norms"

Here we can provide an initial ordering of phenomena that stand on the boundary between the factual and the normative, phenomena that are reminiscent of norms without being norms.

Repetition and practice are examples of this. Custom and repetition often instil a presumed "normative force of the factual."[25] But the fact that certain procedures repeat themselves, in and of itself, cannot have any normative content; repetition can follow a descriptive rule, such as a law of nature. It is no longer thinkable to combine this reference to nature with anything normative, as laws of nature were often conceptualized as normative rules that had been posited by God.[26] Repetition's capacity for normativizing, on the one hand, is tied to how instances of repetition

[24] Immanuel Kant, *Kritik der Urteilskraft*, Frankfurt/M. 1977, pp. 353–8 (§ 76), relatedly Hegel's observation in his lectures on esthetics, cited in Jens Kulenkampff (ed.), *Materialien zu Kants Kritik der Urteilskraft*, Frankfurt/M. 1977, pp. 212–17, here p. 214; Howard Caygill, *The Art of Judgement*, London 1989, p. 216. See also Hans Blumenberg (n 23), *Theorie der Unbegrifflichkeit*, pp. 26 ff, 56 ff.

[25] The expression stems from Georg Jellinek, *Allgemeine Staatslehre*, Berlin 1914 (New edn, Kronberg 1976), pp. 337–60. The expression reflects a specific political sensitivity in the theory of the state in the German empire, which raises the question of legitimation yet has not theory of legitimation to offer up (Christoph Möllers, *Staat als Argument*, München 2011, pp. 15–17). Nonetheless, the expression extends beyond legitimation in its striking aphoristic quality.

[26] Michael Hampe, *Eine kurze Geschichte des Naturgesetzbegriffs*, Frankfurt/M. 2007, pp. 34–41; Andreas Hüttemann, "Regel und Naturgesetz" in: Marco Iorio and Rainer Reisenzein (eds), *Regel, Norm, Gesetz*, Frankfurt/M. 2010, pp. 83–94, here pp. 86–90. Loraine Daston and Michael Stolleis, "Nature, Law and Natural Law in Early Modern Europe" in: Ids., (eds), *Natural Law and Laws of Nature in Early Modern Europe*, London 2008, pp. 1–12.

show what deviation from the norm could consist in, namely in the ceasing of the repetition. On the other hand, every repetitive sequence of events contains a prognostic quality, that is it allows for concrete hypotheses about the process of the future. This too, as we shall see, is typical for norms.[27]

A second example, which stems from the legal sphere, is offered by *soft law*.[28] This is concerned with rules and definitions which formally do not belong to a legal order but are followed by actors who could also posit them as binding law. One of the frequently discussed phenomena in international law is that these kinds of "non-norms" display a high degree of adherence.[29] What this might tell us is that even the positing of such non-norms reveals a recognition of their content. In them, recipients are shown a certain content. The non-norms—in this, not dissimilar to a work of literature—offer a certain view of the world. And with this view, an agent who perceives his action options can cognitively narrow these options down from the outset, comparable to when someone marks out a path in some landscape, and without any obligation to follow this path, other pedestrians still orient themselves along it, "without *interpreting* this with every new step."[30] Administrative bodies, for example, are permanently confronted with having to prioritize problems and figuring out by which means to solve them. For them, such guidelines can supply an orientation that remains independent of the question of its formal binding effect. In this case, we can speak of "cognitive norms," of formally descriptive statements with a normative effect.

2.6 Does an "Ought" Presume Ability?

Not every presumably remembered or imagined process is suitable as a norm. Rather, further restrictions are necessary in order to develop a usable concept. A first such restriction might lie in the condition of *possibility* of an afactual process. Does normativity have to be limited to the possible? This is often assumed following a formulation by Kant,[31] which in turn has much deeper roots. Roman law already states: *impossibilium nulla obligatio*.[32]

[27] On repetition further below, pp. 169–71.

[28] The problem, which is not of immediate concern for us, concerns the fact that this expression both claims a form for itself (*Law*) and also denies said claim (*Soft*). See Jan Klabbers, "The Undesirability of Soft Law" in: *Nordic Journal of International Law* 67 (1998), pp. 381–91.

[29] Wherever they are not followed or heeded, this has less to do with normative contradictions and more with cognitive problems and missing resources: Abram Chayes and Antonia H. Chayes, *The New Sovereignty*, Cambridge, Mass. 1998, pp. 1–33.

[30] Ludwig Wittgenstein, *Bemerkungen über die Grundlagen der Mathematik*, Frankfurt/M. 2013, p. 414, italics in original.

[31] See the formulation in Immanuel Kant, *Kritik der reinen Vernunft*, Frankfurt/M. 1977, pp. 678 ff. (A 807, B 835).

[32] D 50, 17, 185 (Celsus), on this: Heinrich Honsell, *Römisches Recht*, Berlin 2005, p. 39, also Christian Wollschläger, *Die Entstehung der Unmöglichkeitslehre*, Köln 1970, pp. 186 ff. Doubts concerning the legal character in Martin J. Schermaier, *Impossibilium nulla obligatio*, unpublished manuscript 2006.

At first glance, it would seem nonsensical for a norm to refer to something impossible. Regardless of how we imagine normativity, whether as command, as self-obligation, as value, as norm sanctioned by force, as moral precept, as religious taboo, or as esthetic standard, it wouldn't fulfill its task if it aimed at something impossible. Thus, it is contradictory to penalize someone for the transgression of a norm that he or she was unable to obey. It appears just as nonsensical to formulate a political program that cannot be realized. In striving for what is possible, we might identify an important and defining commonality among various forms of normativity.[33]

Examining the possibility criterion, it initially depends on whether a normative precept is formulated with an eye toward action. A concrete action command that refers to something impossible appears pointless *prima facie*. But this is not due to the concept of normativity but rather to the concept of action. When we identify a given behavior as an *action*, we understand this as ascribing an *avertable* event to an acting subject. If the behavior ascribed as an action cannot be carried out then the ascription is rendered moot. For that reason, the impossibility rule in Roman law identified the limits of concrete contractual duties. A contract obliging me to fly off by aid of my own physical abilities without any means of propelling myself into the air does not have to be fulfilled. This has been the case until today in the majority of legal orders.

But as we have seen, not all norms refer to actions.[34] Norms can suggest judging a certain process in a certain way, without that judgment expressing itself as an action. Norms can serve as offers for identification. A religious symbol or a flag might not tell me anything about what to do, but only about who I am, in the sense of my belonging to a community that defines its identity by means of norms. But what to make of the limitation to the possible in such cases?

One form of the normative that expressly does not submit to the limitations of the possible is the political utopia.[35] There is nothing nonsensical about the paradoxical desire to imagine this world completely differently, that is to neither do without reference to current conditions nor to submit to them. The core of the utopian form consists in two elements, only one of which conforms to the demand of possibility. For one, a utopia could serve to motivate certain actions; utopias can provide exceeding reasons for action which do ultimately refer to possibilities. For

[33] Limiting normativity to the possible does not entail a questionable inference from "is" to "ought." For the descriptive statement that a state is possible does not imply that it is also normatively imperative, but only that it could be suitable as a normatively imperative state. A normative precept cannot be deduced from the assumption of possibility. See Georg Henrik von Wright, *Norm and Action*, New York 1963, pp. 92 ff.

[34] See also the relativization by Ralph Wedgwood, *The Nature of Normativity*, Oxford 2007, p. 91.

[35] See also the reflection from Rainer Forst, *Kritik der Rechtfertigungsverhältnisse*, Berlin 2011, pp. 220–2. For its comprehensive justification, Bloch employs an Aristotelian-inspired notion of possibility that is rich in presuppositions. See *Das Prinzip Hoffnung*, Frankfurt/M. 1985, Vol. I, pp. 258–88. For the following reference to Adorno: Theodor W. Adorno, *Negative Dialektik*, Frankfurt/M. 1975, p. 66.

another, though, utopias can open up a political imaginary space which does not want to be restricted to the facticity of our world. This second element certainly does not seem to demand a reduction of norms to the possible, and we will see that this also does not have to be the case in the first interpretation. When Adorno pits the possible and the utopian against each other in order to liberate the utopian from the restraints of reality, he tries to repress this correlation at the expense of a philosophically pointed concept of utopia, which only offers little political relevance, however.

Let us expand our speculation with a further example. The Christian command to love can be understood as a norm that has meaning for nearly every action. The late Augustine's theology of grace, however, casts divine grace as independent of individual actions.[36] On its reading, one cannot earn God's grace through actions.[37] It thereby loses any immediate relevance for action.[38] But does it thereby lose all normativity?[39]

These examples necessitate a narrower definition of the "possible" even when it is referring to actions. In this, the concern is less with rejecting the limitation to the possible for determining the concept of the norm, and rather with understanding which systematic relationship exists between normativity and the assumption of possibility.

2.7 Possible Worlds in Social Norms?

We have seen that, in referring to actions, it is reasonable to limit normativity to that which is possible. But what can we take "possible" to mean? Analytic philosophy speaks of the concept of the "possible world" as an entity oriented toward laws of nature. Possible worlds are worlds in which Al Gore would have won the American presidency in 1998, but not worlds in which there is no gravity. It is on this basis that the concept of possible worlds gains its value for logical enquiry.

[36] Kurt Flasch, *Logik des Schreckens*, Mainz 1995, p. 63–83. Udo Schnelle speaks of the insight of Paul that justice is not a "concept of action, but one of being" in: Id., "Die theologische und literarische Formulierung des Urchristentums" in: Friedrich-Wilhelm Graf and Klaus Wiegandt (eds), *Die Anfänge des Christentums*, Frankfurt/M. 2009, pp. 168–200, here pp. 184 f.

[37] See also Eberhard Jüngel, *Das Evangelium von der Rechtfertigung des Gottlosen als Zentrum des christlichen Glaubens*, Tübingen 2011, pp. 152–69.

[38] Of course, in his sociology of religion, Max Weber tries to show that one can reintroduce this. This sociology is primarily a theory of modern rationality: Peter Ghosh, *Max Weber and* The Protestant Ethic: *Twin Histories*, Oxford 2014, pp. 102–28.

[39] Traces of Augustinian theology lead from the existentialist theology of grace of the 1920s to Rawls' posthumously published early theological work *A Brief Inquiry into the Meaning of Sin and Faith: With "On My Religion"* (Cambridge, Mass. 2010), and from there to his main work *A Theory of Justice* (Cambridge, Mass. 1999), in which "merit" only figures as a practical motivation but plays no normative role.

For a theory of social practices of normativity, this concept is dissatisfying, however. This is because the delimitation between possible and impossible worlds doesn't usually manifest itself as clearly in the context of social relations as is supposed in the theory of possible worlds.[40]

Furthermore, a concept of the possible which takes its cue from laws of nature has the remarkable consequence that the question of whether an event or object is *possible* is to be answered with the same means as the question of whether an event or object is *real*.[41] The concept of possible worlds approximates the cognitive means of the real and the possible by means of causal laws. It is not concerned with the concept of possibility, but rather with the variability or variations of realities.[42] In order to enable logical operations, the possible has to be treated as the real. Barbara Vetter rightly observes: "The so-called possible worlds of modal logic are a useful device to produce a formal model, but they are neither worlds, nor do they have any more intimate connection to possibility than they do to any of the other phenomena that they can be used to model: knowledge, obligation, vagueness and a wide variety of others."[43]

This approach seems obvious for the purposes of logic, which does not need to concern itself with questions of empirical uncertainty. But it is fruitless to employ this reduction of the possible in contexts in which the question of what is possible or not cannot be straightforwardly answered. This is the case with social normativity because in these contexts the notion of possibility primarily serves a temporal task, namely to keep open alternative *future* developments, or to insinuate that such developments had been open to alternatives, even if these were not realized.

2.8 Reversal: An "Ought" Determines Ability

The ambiguity of the possible applies to action commands as well as other normative contexts. For actions, however, this consideration plays a special role, as we are

[40] Hampe (n 26), *Geschichte des Naturbegriffs*, pp. 131–4; on the intrinsic normativity of the current debates in the natural sciences, Dominique Pestre, *À Contre-Sciences*, Paris 2013, pp. 101 ff.

[41] Thus, for Nicolai Hartmann, reality and necessity ultimately merged into one due to the principle of sufficient reason. See *Möglichkeit und Wirklichkeit*, Berlin 1938, pp. 24–27.

[42] Exemplarily: Precisely the determination that all modal statements are existence quantifications about possible worlds fails to provide us with a concept of possibility. We are rather concerned with expressing modal categories, such as "possible" and "necessary," in a quantifying-logical way as non-modal statements. The philosophical debate between modal realists who even accord possible worlds a status as actual (David Lewis, "Possible Worlds" in: Michael J. Loux (ed.), *The Possible and the Actual*, Ithaca 1979, pp. 182–9), and other theorists who deny this, despite all differences regarding questions about the ontology of the possible, share that their respective categorization of something as "possible" implies the relation to a defined, natural-scientific criterion. This is also noted in the logically formalizing analytical philosophy, see the ensuing quote from Barbara Vetter below. For an overview of the state of this debate, Charles S. Chihara, *The Worlds of Possibility*, Oxford 1998, Chapters 1–4.

[43] Barbara Vetter, *Potentiality and Possibility*, Manuscript, Oxford 2010, pp. 166–7.

already casting a possibility judgment when we attribute an action to a person.[44] It must have also been possible for that person to *not* perform the task at hand in order for that action to qualify as such. In responding to the challenging question of whether acting differently was possible, however, we do not apply laws of nature but rather experiential knowledge from which we derive measures for what we deem to be possible. Laws of nature—for the time being—are not available for questions of intentionality and attribution.

But we don't merely operate with experiential knowledge when we ascertain a possibility measure. For we frequently also pose the question of how a person *should* have acted, or what we could have expected of a "*reasonable* person" or an "*honorable* merchant." Furthermore, we take the broader context into consideration. Was the agent prepared, well-slept, and sober?

For this reason, a community can withhold sanctions if it is confronted with the situation in which a behavioral standard that its members have established can hardly be observed by anyone. The measure of responsibility we accord to a person thus does not merely arise from the experiences we have made but also from the normative conceptions we envision. Maybe we do not *want* to live in a community in which people are addicted. So we outlaw addictive substances, even though some or many cannot abide by this prohibition. The standard of prohibiting drugs is factually not enforceable. It is upheld, because the community does not want to be one in which drugs are allowed. The functionality of this law is dubitable. In many cases, communities will tend to adapt the rule. But what is decisive is that the norm transports an *assumption of possibility*. The norm does not ignore possibility but rather stipulates it. In most cases, many people will live by the rule, but not all. With this, no general statement concerning the possibility or impossibility of living up to the norm is indicated. This is standard case for a normativization. If everyone were to follow the rule, it would be redundant.

So, on the one hand, an "ought" presumes ability, since we do not postulate obligations that cannot principally be upheld. On the other hand, ability also presumes elements of "ought," as the concrete delineations of individual capacities for action and of the capacity of a society to shape itself are not simply descriptively ascertained, but normatively posited.[45] For the assessment of moral and

[44] See, for example, Ernst Tugendhat, *Selbstbewußtsein und Selbstbestimmung*, Frankfurt/M. 1997, pp. 348 ff. However, this interpretation is far from uncontested, see its critique Michael Pauen and Gerhard Roth, *Freiheit, Schuld und Verantwortung*, Frankfurt/M. 2008, pp. 48–52. Different conceptions of causality lie behind these differences, especially regarding the degree to which causal statements themselves presume counterfactual statements. Comprehensively on this, and ultimately skeptical in it analysis: Michael S. Moore, *Causation and Responsibility*, Oxford 2009, pp. 391–425. For our purposes here, suffice it to note that causalities could not be represented without counterfactual statements, even if they could be established without them.

[45] Behind this, we might detect a practical take on an Aristotelianizing ideal of practice against a weak will, dictating behavioral standards that can to be learned and trained. (John McDowell, "Virtue and Reason" in: Id., *Mind, Value, and Reality*, Cambridge, Mass. 2001, pp. 50–73; see also Myles Burneat, "Aristotle about Learning to be Good" in: Amélie Rorty [Ed.], *Essays on Aristotle's Ethics*, Berkeley 1982, pp. 69–92, here pp. 82–8.

legal misbehavior, answering the question of what is subjectively possible is also a consequence of such normative expectations.[46] The fact that these in turn can be corrected based on empiricism—for example, if it turns out that no-one is able to live up to them, or if more could be demanded from everyone—only confirms the truth of this very claim.

Social possibility statements remain uncertain. They call for a construction of counterfactual courses of events. Possibility statements are neither provable nor capable of empirical confirmation or refutation. For this reason, the relationship between the normative and the possible is more complicated than is expressed in the assessment of ability being presumed in every "ought." On the other hand, this assessment remains crucial for understanding what we are dealing with when positing and operating with social norms. Only in the realm of possibilities is it sensible to make use of normative figures.

2.9 Epistemic Possibility

With resort to a proposal by Ian Hacking, we can distinguish between two kinds of possibility.[47] M1 has the form: it is possible that p M2 has the form: it is possible for A to X. Hacking paraphrases M1 with the word "probable," so that p is possible if we can say of p that p does not stand in contradiction to our current state of knowledge. Philosophical discussion, rich in forms of possibilities, is concerned with *epistemic* possibility.[48] We speak of this because the assessing of possibility depends on our state of knowledge. Hacking identifies M2 as permissibility. It is possible for A to arrest me, or it is possible for B to rise socially.

According to Hacking, there are essential differences between these two forms of possibility. Since the first form of possibility refers to an epistemically unclarified object, ontological uncertainties arise, though they do not stem from the notion of possibility, but from the reference to an uncertain object. We are not faced with such an uncertain object in the second form. Here, the possibility refers to something that is not epistemically uncertain, even if it contingently happened to arise in the actual and social world.

How do the two forms of possibility stand in relation to the difference between norm and non-norm? Hacking's differentiation can help in clarifying the complex

46 Similarly in end result in Michael Kühler, "Sollen impliziert Können—begrifflich?" in: Martina Fürst et al. (eds), *Analysen, Argumente, Ansätze,* Frankfurt/M. 2008, pp. 363–70, here pp. 368–70.

47 Ian Hacking, "All Kinds of Possibility" in: *The Philosophical Review* 84 (1975), pp. 321–37, here pp. 322 ff.

48 See also the definition in Ian Hacking, "Possibility" in: *The Philosophical Review* 76 (1967), pp. 143–68, here p. 149. A condition is possible if it is unknown that it does not exist, and when no practical investigation could prove that it does not exist. Critically regarding the question of which difference exists between it and logical possibility: Paul Teller, "Epistemic Possibility" in: *Philosophia* 2 (1972), pp. 303–20.

relation discovered between "ought" and ability. The claim that "ought" presumes ability only draws on the first possibility form, M1. As stated: it is pointless to obligate someone to something that is impossible.

At the same time, and in addition to Hacking, norms serve as a form that practically deals with this epistemic uncertainty. Since we do not know where exactly the realm of the possible ends, but we cannot sustain a practice in the context of such indecisiveness, we use norms which posit the possible and impossible. The possibility thus posited represents M2 then. Here, the permissibility of a certain condition is stipulated and receives an evaluative marking. Of course, the two provisions can diverge. It can especially be the case that newly gained knowledge can prove a possibility of the second kind impossible in the sense of the first kind. "He could not have appropriately reacted to the collision." In this case, there is indeed reason for adjusting the measure of possibility, as it would otherwise not refer to a possibility. As such, the following relationship emerges between the two kinds of possibility. M2 presumes M1. But since the determination of M1 is uncertain, as we do not know M1 in detail, we take recourse to M2 in order to deal with this uncertainty, thereby delimiting M1 more precisely in pragmatic terms.

Both possibilities—this is a second addendum to Hacking—can thus also be alternatively qualified with reference to a given *normative order.* M1 functions as a *norm-external* possibility which norms themselves cannot factually limit or expand.[49] M2, on the other hand, functions as a *norm-internal* possibility, because the question of what is *permissibly* possible itself can be determined by a normative order. As a legal order, this makes it possible for a judge to determine a legal consequence, or as a social order, it enables a host to change the seating order.

Do epistemic possibilities entail particular ontological problems? Let us consider an example from Nelson Goodman, and first examine a circumstance which we do not know. We are waiting on a train. The train could be delayed. We describe it as possible that it is delayed because we do not know whether it is. Let us take a second case, in which we know what the situation is, but we make counterfactual speculations. The train has arrived on time, but because of a different event—there was severe weather—we claim that it also could have arrived late.[50] For Goodman, both statements are part of an actual world. They both describe the characteristic of a train which under certain circumstances *could have been* delayed.[51] How do we know this? The answer is that from experience we have with trains and severe weather. For Goodman, such knowledge does not exhibit fundamentally different

[49] Here we are also confronted with a science-theoretical problem, namely the question of whether, pragmatically speaking, we can really determine rules with which we in turn determine M1 and can call "natural laws" without normativity. That is, can we do so without normative rules concerning the transmission of knowledge. Doubting this, Dewey saw natural laws as practical instructions for appropriate arranging of experimental set-up, see Hampe (n 26), *Geschichte des Naturgesetzbegriffs*, pp. 142–50.

[50] Nelson Goodman, *Fact, Fiction and Forecast*, Cambridge, Mass. 1983, pp. 49 ff.

[51] Ibid., pp. 49–58.

characteristics than those at play in the description of facts. This is surprising, for after all, the statement that the train could be late appears to us to be easier to ascertain and to be relied on than the—necessarily counterfactual and unverifiable—statement that it could have arrived late. In light of Hacking's conceptualization, both these statements express epistemic possibilities. They do not run counter to our momentary state of knowledge, which is different from the statement that, in order to make up for a delay, the train could have gone airborne. There is not much more to be said in that regard. For both Hacking and Goodman, highlighting possibility does not entail any further epistemic problems. Of concern is how we deal with uncertainty.

The practical meaning of such possibilities reveals itself in Goodman's suggestion that our communication is rarely just concerned with the truth of a statement.[52] We often shorten our statements or leave them vague because it is practical or because we have no other option. We primarily have to be understandable, relatable, or pointed, but not necessarily truthful. These doubts about the relevance of truth undermine us in two ways. For one, they illustrate that the abandonment of facticity represents a normality even outside of the realm of normative practices. For another, they confirm the suspicion that possibility and reality in normative statements can be more complexly interwoven than is expressed in the passed-down statement that every "ought" presumes ability.

As previously indicated, one implication of such a conception of possibility lies in its exclusion of ontological problems deriving from the semantics of possibility. For doubts about a conception of possibility often arise as doubts about its ontology, as they are expressed in Quine's famous question: "How many possible men are standing in the door?"[53] With Hacking and Goodman, we can place this question outside of the realm of modality. It arises from the *uncertainty* that marked the first notion of possibility. We can only respond to the question of how many possible men are standing in the door on the basis of what we otherwise know. All men that stand in the door had this possibility; whether we also accord such possibility to others depends on the further circumstances.[54]

But what is the reference point of the possibility that is the object of normativity? We've seen this much: a limitation of norms to mark only possible actions is too simple. Norms can strive for characterizations and conditions that cannot be reduced to actions, and they can also prescribe the condition of possibility of actions.[55] Can objects also be the matter of a norm? And if so, what about possible objects? Of course, it is easy to imagine a norm that demands the production of a certain object. What thus becomes apparent is that the reference point of a norm

[52] Nelson Goodman, *Ways of Worldmaking*, Cambridge, Mass., pp. 120–9.

[53] W. V. O. Quine, "On What There Is" in: Id., *From a Logical Point of View*, New York 1963, pp. 1–20, here p. 3.

[54] Hacking (n 47), "All Kinds" p. 327; Id., "Possibility" pp. 164 f.

[55] See above, pp. 7–10.

can be determined differently without there being a conceptually necessary preference for one reconstruction over another. A norm can refer to an action or to the end result of an action. There are practical reasons for formulating a norm one way or another. It could be, for instance, more expedient to orient a command toward a certain action, because we are interested in prompting an attempt, even if it is uncertain whether it will lead to the desired result.

A theory of normativity thus requires an epistemic conception of possibility. Epistemic possibilities result from uncertainties that can also be dealt with normatively. For as long as a society is unaware of what is possible, it can only define a normatively preferred possibility from its existing ones. It is not only possible that these possibilities might not be realized but also that they might prove themselves impossible after the fact. So this conception of possibility defines possibility as a presumption of possibility that can also be quite contentious. Not every presumption of possibility is plausible, not every possibility presumption that realizes itself in hindsight encounters broader recognition.

2.10 Excursus on the Historicization of the Possible

The epistemic conception of possibility allows for a historicizing perspective.[56] For Reinhart Kosseleck, the idea of the future as a realm of action possibilities is the product of a turning point that we observe after 1750 in Europe.[57] According to this reading, it is only at this point that the concept of possibility gains an emphatic meaning for individual freedom to act and political formation. What does this mean for our concept of the normative? On the one hand, the historicizability of the normative is an essential element in the current approach. If we treat normativity as social practice then historical change plays an important role for it. On the other hand, our notion of normativity does not hinge on Kosseleck's classification of epochs. Even though it appears conceivable that societies can also do without normative practices, our conception of the normative may well encompass larger epochs than does the notion of future as a realm of possibility. While the reference to the future will yet prove to be important for our notion of normativity, in light of the abundance of premodern and antique normative practices, it would appear odd to synchronize it with the epochal turning point of Kosseleck's 'Saddle Period'.

Nonetheless, this turning point could have impacted at least Europe and North America regarding their conceptions of normativity. Summed up in one

[56] See also Hans Blumenberg, "Wirklichkeitsbegriff und Möglichkeit des Romans" in: Id., *Ästhetische und metaphorologische Schriften*, Frankfurt/M. 2001, pp. 47–73, here pp. 49–54, 61 ff. A historicization of the normative could be tied into this.

[57] Reinhart Kosseleck, "›Neuzeit‹: Zur Semantik moderner Bewegungsbegriffe" in: Id., *Vergangene Zukunft*, Frankfurt/M. 1979, pp. 300–48, here pp. 321–39.

phrase: norms change from being an instrument for the restitution of a lost or corrupted state of affairs to being instruments of creative change.[58] We could speak of the dissolution of a mimetic understanding of norms, which saw the task of norms as one of imitation and amplification of a naturally given state of the world, although both always seem possible;[59] that the mirror image should resemble nature, and that nature should resemble the mirror image.[60] One important example is the shifting understanding of a constitution, from a blanket term describing the condition of political institutions to a document that enables political change. We only begin to find such a politically understood conception of a constitution at the end of the eighteenth century.[61] We will see that such a conception carries a higher normative claim than its predecessor as it more clearly distances itself from a mere description of a state of things. The notion of a constitution also hints at the systematic context of Kosseleck's periodization. For an understanding of the future as an open realm of possibilities systematically presumes a theory of freedom to act and political subjectivity as it develops during the seventeenth and eighteenth centuries. For many modern theories of normativity, such a concept of subjectivity is a necessary precondition for any form of normativity, but not for our current theory.[62] Both the existence of normative practices which make do without an emphatic notion of subjectivity and the missing normative impetus of the notion articulated here rule out such a limitation.

2.11 Reality, Transgression, and Contingency

Since the real is possible, norms can also refer to that which is real. It is the case that norms refer to the real when they are observed. The affirmation of an existing condition or an established practice is a common application of norms. Such an affirmation can become socially relevant in two ways. For one, by giving the affirmed condition a new meaning through the norm. It conforms with the norm, is made explicit by the norm, and is explicitly affirmed.

A second result of the affirmation is that the normativization of the actual condition also contains the statement that this condition can *possibly*, but does *not*

[58] Vividly regarding the conception of law: Diethelm Klippel, "Die Philosophie der Gesetzgebung" in: Barbara Dölemeyer and Diethelm Klippel (eds), *Gesetz und Gesetzgebung im Europa der frühen Neuzeit*, Berlin 1998, pp. 225–47, here pp. 234, 243 ff.

[59] In "Local Knowledge: Fact and Law in Comparative Perspective" (in: Id., *Local Knowledge*, New York 2000, pp. 167--234, here p. 211), Clifford Geertz describes a notion of norms as "silent perfection of the community consensus."

[60] Franco Moretti, *Signs Taken for Wonders*, London 1988, pp. 66 ff.

[61] Ulrich K. Preuß, "Der Begriff der Verfassung und ihre Beziehung zur Politik" in: Id. (ed.), *Zum Begriff der Verfassung*, Frankfurt/M. 1994, pp. 7–33, here pp. 15–18. The question of whether this is tied to the turn to expressivism is an apparent one (see Charles Taylor, *Sources of the Self*, Cambridge, Mass. 1988, Chapter 21).

[62] See below, pp.228–34.

necessarily exist. By being part of a norm program, an actual condition receives a norm-specific interpretation. While it is real, it is not necessary. The normativization of a condition thus underscores two aspects: the contingency of the condition it addresses and the alternative possibility of a divergent path. Neither implication should be underestimated in their significance. The norm robs its object of its necessity, and it highlights its own vulnerability. This is particularly the case with prohibitions which draw their content from the deviant behavior that defines them. It also applies to other norms which contain an idea of what it could mean to transgress them. The *possibility of their transgression* is an important, implicit or explicit, content of any normativization. In other words, norms create a *doubling of courses of events.* They indicate their respective other possibility. If they are transgressed, they indicate the possibility of adherence; if they are adhered to, they hint at the possibility of transgression.

This thought process provokes a search for counterexamples: is a normativization of necessary states of affairs thereby excluded? Does normativity ultimately only refer to contingent phenomena that are neither impossible nor necessary?[63] States of affairs to which norms refer are possible. At the same time, it appears obvious that they cannot be necessary. If they were necessary, their realization would be inevitable. Admittedly, one can also assume an affirmative or critical stance toward an inevitable development. But even this attitude is only imaginable in light of at least imagined alternatives. What are critique and affirmation to mean if I cannot imagine alternative developments or if a deviant development could only be deviant from a necessity? Of course, we can take things as they come, without reflecting on it. But a normative access has to generate alternatives, even if these are factually excluded.

This also applies to historical philosophical schemes with a normative claim. The philosophy of history commonly has to argue on two temporal levels. In the long term, nothing escapes the historically necessary course of events. Historical-philosophical outlines draw considerably on the future. This makes them vulnerable but immunizes them against events proximate to the present which don't fit into their scheme. They thus never claim to be able to integrate everything into said scheme. Rather, they consistently leave room for inner contingency, that which Hegel calls "colorful bark" in the preface to his legal philosophy.[64] Necessary developments become noticeable temporally only in the distant future and determine their content only in long and broad lines. Concrete, individual events in the past, present, and near future, however, often deviate from the broad lines in

[63] Rüdiger Bubner, "Die aristotelische Lehre vom Zufall" in: Gerhard v. Graevenitz and Odo Marquard (eds), *Kontingenz. Poetik und Hermeneutik XVII*, München 1998, pp. 3–21, here pp. 5–8.

[64] Georg Wilhelm Friedrich Hegel, *Grundlinien der Philosophie des Rechts*, Frankfurt/M. 1986, Preface (p. 25).

which necessary developments proceed. The normative aspiration of a historical-philosophical scheme then only lies in the assessment of its remaining contingencies. Deviations of the determined course of the world can be reinterpreted as wriggle room within an incompletely determining plan, for example if "providence" has room for a hero.[65]

And what do we ultimately make of fortuitous events? If we define coincidence as the colliding of uncoordinated paths of action, as in the Aristotelian notion of *tyché*, then such fortuitous events can be related back to and evaluated in light of the purposes of the respective actions.[66] Hegel's theory of absolute coincidence differs. According to Dieter Henrichs,[67] it constitutes a quietist ethics that demands to accept developments as they occur, and to make neither the fruitless attempt to intervene nor to improperly attributing them to oneself. The norms of such an ethics, however, do not refer to random events but to one's own capacity to act, and to its limitations. In both cases, the random event is not itself object of a normative disposition.

3. *Element 2: Realization Marker*

3.1 Possibility as Necessary, but not Sufficient Determining Characteristic

Every norm denotes a possibility, but not every possibility denotes a norm. The reference to possibility is a necessary but not a sufficient condition for the presence of a norm. The concept of a norm requires a further qualification. One can call it a marker, distinguishing between a normatively charged possibility and a mere possibility. What is the content of such a marker? The marker must positively affirm the *realization* of the possibility,[68] for what distinguishes a pure possibility from a norm is the assessment of its realization. I refer to this second element as the *realization marker*.

It is not obvious how the two elements of the norm concept relate to each other. On the one hand, a norm can only refer to that which is possible, otherwise the concept would lose its meaning. On the other hand, it is uncertain what we can presume to be possible, and one way of dealing with this uncertainty is to stipulate

[65] See the structurally similar observation that even the moral authority of "nature" can only figure where natural laws allow for leeway, in Lorraine Daston and Fernando Vidal, "Doing What Comes Naturally" in: Id. (ed.), *The Moral Authority of Nature*, Chicago 2003, pp. 1–20, here p. 6 ff

[66] Aristotle, *Physics*, 196b10–197a37; Wilhelm Windelband, *Die Lehren vom Zufall*, Berlin 1870, pp. 68–78.

[67] Dieter Henrichs, "Hegels Theorie über den Zufall" in: Id., *Hegel im Kontext*, Frankfurt/M. 1971, pp. 157–86, here p. 180.

[68] The conflation of realization claim and effectiveness has brought much confusion into the legal theoretical debate. Only the former belongs in the realm of the normative.

the possibility normatively. The realization marker can affirm a possibility, in some circumstances it is only thereby marked as a possibility.

So we need a marker of possibility in order to mark it as normative. A central topic of meta-ethics is the composition and necessity of the marker.[69] Various elements figure as marker, even if not under this term: an individual need, the generalizability of an action maxim or objective characteristics of an action which may or may not be recognizable. Beyond the realm of practical philosophy, however, we see very different forms of markings: the inclusion in an official public bulletin, the addendum that a certain demand is actually a "command," a facial expression, or the inclusion of an object in a museum.

For now, it can remain open which form of marker is appropriate at which point. What is crucial is the commonality of the various figures, which consists in the demand that the thus marked possible condition be realized. That is, that the possible state of affairs become an actual one, that possibility and reality merge with each other, or stay merged. On this reading, the interest in the possible becomes illuminated from a different angle. We denote those practices as normative with which we express the affirmation of a realization, a *favorable attitude with respect to the realization of a possible state of affairs.*[70]

Now the distinction between possibility and marking is an analytical one, serving to determine normativity. We cannot objectify it. The marking is not an arrow that has to be fastened to a possibility so that it becomes a norm. The array of social norms allows for a diversity of possibilities to illustrate a norm in our present understanding. Nonetheless, we have seen that the recognizability of a norm *as a norm* is crucial for social practice. As a necessary conceptual element, the marking can thus become a marking in a very literal sense: as a deictic instrument that pragmatically illustrates that a norm is present.

For certain normative practices, the necessity of a realizing marker appears obvious, for others less so. It is obvious for commands, as they consist in a defined action and realizing marker for which the declaration "This is a command!" provides the grammatical form or military custom. The same can be said about an open and egalitarian deliberative decision, for example a lawmaking body, regardless of whether it contains a command or not. For in this case, too, a certain content is being given a certain form that marks its content as normative.

[69] Timothy Schroeder, "Donald Davidson's Theory of Mind is Non-Normative" in: *Philosopher's Imprint* 3/1 (2003), pp. 1–14, here p. 3 ff, makes a similar distinction and discusses the marker as a "force-maker" that is determined differently in various meta-ethical models.

[70] For this expression, Donald Davidson, "Actions, Reasons, and Causes" in: Id., *Essays on Actions and Events*, Oxford 2001, pp. 12–19, here pp. 12 f.; for a further meaning in comparison with "desire," see Michael Smith, "The Humean Theory of Motivation" in *Mind* 96 (1987), pp. 36–61, here p. 55.

3.2 Ascription of Identity as a Norm?

Certain social practices could cause trouble for our model because the conception of normativity does not accord to them. What about ascribing an identity? Can we take a national flag to be a norm? Toward which possibility does it point, and with which marking? Let us assume that we are in agreement that this flag is to express the political identity of a State. Is this content normative? Or does it merely refer to historical facts? Is it concerned with the realization of a condition? Is this the case only for certain flags, like the Catalonian flag which appears to demand independence from Spain? Does it not apply to others, for example the German flag after reunification? We need to distinguish different kinds of questions. For starters, the affirmation of a possible condition does not preclude the affirmation of the *status quo*.[71] It, too, is possible after all, and it can be *strengthened* by a norm. Realization then means the containing of an existing condition. This meaning is normative as it is not indifferent to the question of whether a given political identity successfully maintains itself. It expresses something that is distinct from the statements of a statistical yearbook of the same State, which is also a form of grasping one's identity. In a yearbook, not even the murder rate entails an evaluative stance. It is irrelevant whether a flag entails an action reference or not. A flag can be taken as a demand for certain actions, but it is just as possible to read it as mere affirmation of a community's identity.

3.3 Affirmation as Elementary Evaluation

But what is meant by "affirmation"? Which requirements does a realizing marker have to fulfill? In ethics[72] and in the doctrine of criminal law,[73] debate surrounds the distinction between merely foreseeing a future wrong from actually wanting said wrong. Connected to this is the question of whether and when someone has the obligation to intervene in a foreseeable string of events. What begs explanation, in other words, is what is to be demanded of an affirmation, and what can figure as its medium.[74]

We understand an affirmation to be the positive marking of one possible state of affairs. This presumes more than the expectation that it occurs because this latter

[71] Here we find a fundamental difference with theories that operate with the difference between "desire" and "belief" and presume that they exclude each other. See, e.g. Smith, "Humean Theory" pp. 55 ff.

[72] Critically on the moral relevance of the decision for State action, David Enoch, "Intending, Foreseeing, and the State" in: *Legal Theory* 13 (2007), pp. 69–99.

[73] Kristian Kühl, *Strafrecht. Allgemeiner Teil*, München 2012, pp. 93–120.

[74] See also the distinction between normatively free-standing and normatively embedded commands, in Jürgen Habermas, "Versprachlichung des Sakralen" in: Id., *Nachmetaphysisches Denken II*, Berlin 2012, pp. 7–18, here p. 13 fn. 10; regarding "weak normativity" of language, see "Die Lebenswelt als Raum symbolisch verkörperter Gründe," in: *Nachmetaphysisches Denken II*, pp. 54–76, here p. 66.

attitude does not operate with alternative developments, but remains focused on the single path of future events. We recognize a marking in its advocating for an expectation under the condition of assuming a possibly different development.

But if an expectation is insufficient for constituting a norm, what about an intention? I have the intention to do something. Does this intention sustain a marking that is sufficient for our ends?[75] One could argue as follows: only if I can assume responsibility for my actions can I develop intentions. I have to take responsibility for them, thus they turn out to be normative. But this argument falls short. In the end, it leads to similar objections as the claim that concepts are normative. It is not obvious why more than that should be brought into connection with the falling short of an intention. Not realizing an intention can have consequences which in turn, and for different reasons, could be normatively preferable—even for the acting agent. In an intention, one can see a form of articulating a possibility. In that sense, intentions can indeed figure as elements of a norm, but they are not sufficient to constitute a norm. This becomes more apparent when compared with a wish.[76] With a wish, we have an additional element to the articulation of a possibility,[77] namely the positive disposition which we also bring into connection with the term "affirmation." The wish connects a state of things with a realizing marker.

How coherent is this demarcation? Can I intend to do something even though I do not want to? We can find examples. I am intent on going to hold my lecture, even though I feel no desire to. Why do I go to the lecture? Maybe out of a duty of obligation, or out of fear of sanctions by the executive committee, or because the students would otherwise not pass their exams? Do such motives create a norm?

My intention of going to lecture does not constitute a norm, in so far as I describe it as mere intention. I will go even though I do not want to. This is a description. The factors that compel me to go could serve as realizing markers if they provided an evaluation. But this qualification does not just arise from my intention. These elementary evaluations would also stand even if I weren't to follow them. But isn't there such an evaluation behind any intention? By doing something, I express a preference that could suffice to count as an affirmation. And on the flipside, if I stay in bed, do I not thereby affirm that possibility? Are we thus concerned with an intention, or with something normative after all?

No, for it remains unclear why everything that I intend to do is affirmed by my doing it. I can do something that I think is wrong, I can also do something that I do

[75] To answer this question, we can initially gloss over the fact that an intention is always expressed only within a practice that makes it meaningful in the first place. A corresponding critique of the normativity of intentions, such as Robert B. Brandom (*Making It Explicit. Reasoning, Representing, and Discursive Commitment*, Cambridge, Mass. 1994, pp. 253 ff.), thus misses the question.

[76] On the problem of the temporality of wishes in an action theory, however, see Rödl, *Selbstbewusstsein*, pp. 43–54.

[77] On the flipside, the wish that strives for something decidedly impossible cannot count as a norm.

not care about. These kinds of phenomena confront practical philosophy with the problem of weakness of will. It arises when an agent takes a certain decision despite the fact that she or he—after a complete investigation of all circumstances—came to the conclusion that a different decision would actually be better.[78] If reasons only counted as reasons when they actually bring about an action, there could be no such thing as weakness of will; but under such conditions, would they still be reasons in a normative sense? However, if reasons had no bearing on my action at all, the reason loses its connection to the actions actually carried out.

This doesn't change the fact that I can make a decision yet hold it to be wrong. Internally, for me, this might be irrational. I might not understand myself.[79] But this crux only arises for a philosophical theory of action that views rationality as the best element for describing subjectivity. It can also happen that irrationality is perceived internally, but that this perception cannot be transmitted externally. Maybe weakness of my will may ultimately even lead me to a decision that is evaluated more favorably by a community. For a theory of normativity, for which the possibility of transgression is central, weakness of the will thus doesn't necessarily have to pose a problem. Under certain circumstances, it might actually prove to be part of a solution. The phenomenon of weakness of my will could help me gain an awareness of my own irrationality, instead of rationalizing all my actions ex post.[80] The fact that there are intentions for action from whose rationality I suffer speaks in disfavor of viewing intentions as such as normative.

3.4 Markings without Subjects?

One further constriction of the concept of the realizing marker should be avoided. In light of the discussion concerning wish and intention, one could gain the impression that the affirmation, which is the requirement of a norm, is necessarily ascribed to a specific subject who either posits or acknowledges the norm in question. But we have also seen that the limitation of normative practices either to a command or a recognition model falls short. The more challenging question concerns whether we have to ascribe the realizing marker to the attitude of a subject at all. This will most likely not correspond to the basic intuition to be developed here. According to that intuition, social practices are not only to be understood as functions of the condition of individual subjects, and normativity is not to be taken—in a Kantian way—as a function of subjectivity.

[78] Donald Davidson, "How Is Weakness of the Will Possible?" in: Id. (n 70), *Essays on Actions and Events*, pp. 25–43, here pp. 34–43.

[79] Ibid., pp. 41 ff.

[80] On both phenomena, see the observations by Alison MacIntyre, "What is Wrong with Weakness of the Will?" in: *Journal of Philosophy* 103 (2006), pp. 284–311, here pp. 292–302.

But this makes the concept of the realizing marker seem all the more odd. Is it a voluntarist figure that has lost its subject? After all, I cannot imagine an affirmation, a favorable attitude without someone holding such an attitude. It is possible, however, to express a favorable attitude that does not draw on an act of will. For example, we could claim that a certain sexual practice were "unnatural" and thereby express that and why its realization should be opposed. One can similarly argue with recourse to traditions and customs and operate with markings that are not accorded to any subjects.

Two levels need to be distinguished, and at the same time their repercussions on each other should be kept in mind. At the first level, we are addressing how norms or normative reasons can be derived. It is a philosophical dispute with consequences for political theory which either accepts reasons, values, preferences, or traditions as normatively relevant. At the second level, the normativity of these benchmarks is not simply socially evident.[81] No-one can count on the mere indication of one of the mentioned categories being sufficient for general agreement on the presence of a norm. For this reason, the second level needs a marking in order to distinguish a normative impetus.

But maybe this last statement is only true in certain historical situations in which the question of a norm's genesis is contested? After all, we could imagine a small, cohesive community in which the mere statement "God wants it" contains a normative content. In this case, the descriptive sentence extends beyond mere description. Analytically, it is true that a possible condition ("it") is enhanced by a marker ("God wants"). In this community, one can simply deploy God's will as a marker that grounds normativity. Trivially, this does not free one from the necessity of actually doing so. The reference to God contains a norm, but this reference itself has to be communicated in order to count as a norm in this community. In a different community, the question of grounding normativity could be so contentious that, in addition to a norm formulation, one would have to explicitly add that said norm is a norm. But this addendum does not necessarily have to be understood voluntarily. How it is understood depends on the normative circumstances in which one communicates. Claiming that a practice is "unnatural" may provoke the follow-up question of what is meant by nature, because after all, other things are quite unnatural, for example the command of loving one's neighbor which is unknown to nature. The answer might be "unnatural" means that one shouldn't carry out this practice. The necessity of an articulated realizing marker thus ultimately also applies to compact, normatively homogenous communities.

[81] Insightful concerning the notion of evidence in another context: Wolfgang Künne, *Abstrakte Gegenstände, Semantik und Ontologie*, 2nd edn, Frankfurt/M 2007, pp. 205–13.

3.5 Norms as Affirmed Possibility: Too Broad or too Narrow?

Before analyzing further implications of this concept of norms, it might be prudent to take a step back and examine its plausibility. Is the concept developed here too narrow or too broad?

It would be analytically too narrow if we could imagine neglecting one of its preconditions without entailing consequences. If we sidestep the element of possibility, the concept collapses. It would not be clear what the realizing marker was referring to. If we sidestep the marker, we are left with mere possibility. This also does not suffice for the demands of a useful concept of normativity.

What might we gain from applying the model to various phenomena? Let us take the example of concepts. Concepts are not norms. The wrong use of a concept does not indicate anything other than the wrong use of a concept. Possibilities of future usage are anticipated in concepts themselves, they process what is possible beforehand[82] but provide no indication of an alternative for their own usage. Nothing is to be realized in the concepts themselves. There are also no general obligations to use concepts correctly.[83] The case of concepts is of particular interest as concepts might be the only categories that are widely taken to be something normative but do not fall under the notion of norms developed here. This also suggests that the notion of norms developed here may rather tend to be too broad than too narrow.

So is the definition too broad? It would be analytically too broad if we were missing a qualifying attribute for its sufficient determination. That attribute could not sneak in a substantive criterion that would narrow down the group of social norms to those which contain a justification in the matter, be it political, moral, legal, or esthetic in nature. This would miss the point of the current enquiry which is seeks to develop a non-evaluative conception of social norms.

A narrowing down of the concept might be gained, however, by distinguishing between a *norm* and a *normative pretense*. With different semantics but regarding the same issue, one could also distinguish between norms with or without validity, and norms with or without binding character, only according normativity to the latter. But this would entail a conceptual doubling that fulfilled no function. What would a norm without normativity be? These kinds of formulations probably do not aim for a characteristic but instead for a procedure. Put differently, wouldn't it be more helpful to distinguish between successful and failed attempts at establishing a norm?

[82] Jocelyn Benoist, *Concepts*, Paris 2010, pp. 182 ff, and above p. 136, the reference to Kant. See also Blumenberg (n 23), *Theorie der Unbegrifflichkeit*, p. 26. See also the comments in Wittgenstein, *Philosophische Untersuchungen*, § 195 (p. 131), and in John McDowell, "Wittgenstein on Following a Rule" in: Ibid., *Mind, Value, and Reality*, pp. 221–62, here p. 233.

[83] See above, pp. 25–28.

In order to respond to that, it might once more be helpful to examine the example of wishes. An expressed wish, one carried into a social reality, fulfills our requirements for a norm. A wish defines a state of affairs and furnishes it with a realizing marker. But why should the wish contain a normative content? Whom can it hold to obligations? Wishes can remain without any social relevance as long as they are not uttered by anyone. But it is obvious that the expression "I sure could go for a coffee," uttered under my breath and overheard by my neighbor who is so kind to promptly bring me a coffee, can be taken to be a social practice in which an initially merely imagined state of affairs is being realized subsequently.

Nonetheless, the normative effect of the wish remains open. Was there an obligation for my neighbor to bring me a coffee? Hardly. It might be that he got the coffee for his own amusement; it might also be that he felt obliged by a sense of neighborly love. But in either case, the normative import of my utterance cannot be derived from the wish itself.[84]

However, the existence of a norm cannot depend on whether a sense of obligation existed on the part of the addressee, or whether there was some other normative attitude.[85] What if the addressee herself could not provide any information about her motives in following the wish, for example simply acting "spontaneously, just like that" or for a plethora of motives, one of which was empathy for the thirsty co-pilot? The search for an objective moral or social obligation, too, cannot serve as precondition for the presence of a norm. These two aspects are neither insignificant for adequately describing the situation, nor are they trivial. Nevertheless—and this is important for my line of argument—a concept of social norms would become unfit for the purposes pursued here if tied to them, because the concept seeks to also capture norms that are neither justified in some way nor factually accepted.

But can the concept of a social norm really make do without a criterion of factual establishment? Let us test this assumption with a theory that solves the problem differently. H. L. A. Hart develops this kind of criterion for a social norm.[86] According to his view, there is a need for an "internal aspect" of a rule reference, meaning that at least part of the addressees of a norm, specifically official representatives of the order from which the norm derives, have also to recognize this norm as a generally obligatory part of said order.[87] Certainly, addressees of a norm often follow it without referencing it, that is, without explicitly obeying it; others employ the

[84] One could also ask whether wishes and moral feeling don't so much bring about moral rules as they are brought about by those rules. Thus the assumption by Friedrich Nietzsche, "*Morgenröthe*" in: Id., *Sämtliche Werke: Kritische Studienausgabe*, Giorgio Colli and Mazzino Montinari (ed.), München 1999, Vol. 3, pp. 43 ff, 45 ff (Nos 34, 35, and 38)

[85] This is the crux of social concepts of norms that make norms dependent on their own adherence. See for example the determination by Cristina Bicchieri, *The Grammar of Society*, Cambridge 2005, pp. 11–14, and the convincing critique in Geoffrey Brennan, Lena Eriksson, Robert E. Goodin, and Nicholas Southwood, *Explaining Norms*, Oxford 2013, pp. 21–8.

[86] Not only for a legal norm: H. L. A. Hart, *The Concept of Law*, New York 2012, pp. 82–91.

[87] Ibid., pp. 88 f.

norm strategically, they treat it without developing any kind of relationship to the question of its general validity. Nonetheless, according to Hart, every social order of norms requires a qualified minority of officially authorized actors that explicitly accept a rule as binding. This necessitates an attitude that becomes apparent to the outside which recognizes the order as valid.

This success criterion for social norms sounds plausible but has its weaknesses. For one, the strong formalization, which Hart's model presumes for establishing norms, clearly oriented toward cases of law, is of little use here. For in many social orders of norms, there will be no official representative, quite in contrast to a formalized legal order. Who would be the "official" that recognizes and represents table manners and thereby makes clear that this or that norm is actually in force?[88] It is certainly not the person who accords polite silence to every norm transgression by his or her rude guest. Such enforcing roles often do not exist in normative contexts. They thus also cannot serve as a criterion for the existence of a social norm.

The decisive weakness of a factual success criterion, however, lies in the fact that it makes the concept of a norm dependent on the adherence to it. As with other attempts to place the concept of a norm under certain conditions of success, Hart's criterion distracts from the perspective in which a deviation from a norm needs to be just as possible as its adherence.[89] If norms are marked possibilities, and if they are distinguished by the fact that their existence does not hinge on their being adhered to, then this kind of success criterion ends up hollow.

A conceptual strategy that makes the presence of a norm depend on its practical establishment starts at the wrong end. It seems more suitable to begin with a less demanding concept of norm in order to see whether a norm, regardless of how primitive it may be, can be established, or whether it dissolves again in social communication. For even a fleeting norm is momentarily a norm. It existed even if it couldn't establish itself. The flipside of such a broad conception of norms, of course, is that it also entails practices that are socially completely meaningless, for example a person desiring a certain state of affairs that is expressed but to which no-one paid any attention. In the end, the criterion of social relevance does not help to elucidate the concept of norms as such; after all, many solidly established norms are irrelevant—codified laws that no-one observes, commands that don't concern anyone. We can describe the missing social meaning of these practices without denying their normative character.

The distinction between a norm and a normative pretense thus collapses into itself. The assumption that only a norm could be transgressed, and not a normative pretense, or rather the assumption that a norm would first have to be established before it could be disobeyed, remains unnecessary. The establishment of a norm is

[88] The lack of such a figure is also noted by Asfa-Wossen Asserate, *Manieren*, Frankfurt/M. 2003, pp. 19 ff.

[89] Although he is aware of this aspect: Hart (n 86), The *Concept of Law*, p. 94.

always dependent on mechanisms of expression and stabilization, but such establishment has to be distinguished from its characterization as a norm. From an outside perspective, the continued validity of any norm proves to be precarious and in need of permanent institutional efforts at actualization. The presence of a norm, its observance, and its keeping-in-existence need to be distinguished from each other.

3.6 Repetition and Custom

Above, I have tried to show why repetitions as such cannot bring about norms. Can this be further substantiated in light of the conceptualization developed here? Norm transgressions can repeat themselves, and they repeat themselves without the norm being affected. But the fact of repetition grounds the impression that further repetitions of the process might be possible. If a process repeats itself and follows a certain pattern that we can call "regular," then we can describe it with such rules and allege a certain persistence that could speak for classifying it as a norm. Both elements of the norm concept are indicated by repetition. The repetition points toward repeat*ability* and thus indicates a resilience of the repeated event, that is its support by factual circumstances which could be an indicator of a realizing marker.[90]

Something similar goes for custom. A glance at legal theory of customary law is helpful in illuminating the connection. In certain areas of law—in European private law of the nineteenth century and in international law to this day—customary law plays a vital role and is the object of significant theoretical disputes.[91] It is undisputed that mere custom cannot create law—just as the serial killer does not create a rule allowing to kill—but the customary act must be accompanied by the consciousness of acting in accordance with the law (*opinio iuris*).[92] This requirement fulfills the role of the realizing marker.

Repetitions and customs can thus point toward an underlying normative practice without acting as a normative practice itself. While repetitions per se cannot bring about norms, norms can account for events establishing themselves as repetitions, in cases where this might not be self-evident.[93] The definition of sins, of

[90] An ethics that operates in such a manner can be found in Nietzsche ("*Morgenröthe*" pp. 21–52). For a brilliant analysis in a surprising location: Eckart Goebel, *Jenseits des Unbehagens. "Sublimierung" von Goethe bis Lacan*, Bielefeld 2009, pp. 109–21.

[91] These, however, chiefly concern the legal normative value of scientific description of the phenomenon: Kenichi Moriya, "Zum römischen Gewohnheitsrecht bei Georg Friedrich Puchta" in: *Zeitschrift der Savigny-Stiftung für Rechtsgeschichte Romanistische Abteilung* 128 (2011), pp. 298–338, here pp. 315 ff.

[92] Concisely, Klaus F. Röhl and Hans Christian Röhl, *Allgemeine Rechtslehre*, Köln 2008, pp. 554–7.

[93] "If from one day to the next someone promises: 'Tomorrow I will give up smoking,' does he say the same thing every day, or every day something different?" Wittgenstein, *Remarks on the Foundation of Mathematics*, Cambridge, Mass. 1989, p. 276.

criminal offenses, or of manners enables precisely this: norms create categories that become preconditions for the recognizability of repetitions.

3.7 Ambiguity of the Norm Concept

Phenomena like customs show that the distinction between normative and non-normative practices is difficult because many practices find themselves at the threshold between outright affirmation and mere observation or neutral expectation. This problem cannot not be solved conceptually without losing sight of precisely these interesting borderline cases, that also provide a field for social experimentation and maneuvering. The continuous transition from perception via approval to affirmation is typical for normative practices. The ambiguity of concepts like "recognition" (between perception and endorsement) and "intention" (between observation of one's own horizon of action and its normative strengthening) is practically inevitable. It frequently corresponds with the fluid transition from non-normative to normative practices.[94]

4. *Sanctions*

4.1 Norms without Sanctions

We take norms to be the affirmation of the realization of a possibility. For Humeans, sanctions serve to set positive or negative incentives for subjective motivation, without which there can be no normativity. For Kantians, sanctions have no morally constitutive function, whereas they are part of the enforceability of legal norms.[95] For the concept of norm developed here, however, sanctions do not constitute a necessary element.

Every norm, by virtue of its normativity, contains a "sanction" in a weak sense, because every deviation of reality from the precepts of a norm enables that series of events to be described with an eye toward the broken norm. The series of events can be taken as a deviation and gains a different meaning than it would without the norm. The same goes for a series of events that is in accord with the norm. Regardless of whether an agent consciously follows the norm or the series of events happened to unfold as it did, the unfolding of events can be compared with the

[94] Niklas Luhmann, *Soziale Systeme. Grundriß einer allgemeinen Theorie,* Frankfurt/M. 1984, pp. 437 ff.

[95] For a critique along Kantian lines with a broadly defined notion of sanctions, see Gottfried Seebaß, "Die sanktionistische Theorie des Sollens" in: Id., *Handlung und Freiheit,* Tübingen 2006, pp. 81–110, here pp. 93–106; Armin Engländer, "Norm und Sanktion—kritische Anmerkungen zum Sanktionsmodell der Norm" in: *Rechtswissenschaft* 4 (2013), pp. 193–207, here pp. 198–205.

norm. Whether this consequence of normativizing, of providing a measure, as such deserves the term "sanction" or not is a terminological question. Our observation certainly makes it clear that norms always have consequences that should neither be conflated with causal effects nor with explicit notices of sanctions, but rather lie in the evaluation of alternative series of events which each norm contains. *In the broadest sense*, no norm can be imagined without such a sanction. Thus, we cannot define a norm by means of sanctions in a narrow sense, because these can only be perceived if they are already referring to a norm.[96]

4.2 Sanctions in a Narrower Sense

This brings us to the central function of sanctions *in a narrower sense*, that is, of consequences expressly connected to the transgression of a norm. They underline the meaning and relevance of a norm by reacting to its transgression. Under conditions of uncertainty in terms of the reach of norms, we have to think of sanctions primarily as reminding posts. Normative orders establish institutions that keep a community informed about their norm content, by, for example, establishing professional norm watchdogs such as guardians of public morals or public prosecutors. Sanctions and their application serve as points of reference for this public visualization and realization of a community's norms and thus play a prominent role in normative practices. The sanctioning responding to a norm transgression highlights both said transgression and the existence of the norm. Sanctions are special forms of the application and updating of norms. More precisely, a sanction cannot (directly) serve to implement the norm, as it only kicks in after the transgression. Primarily, it should remind the community of the existence and value of the norm. It plays an assuring and expressive role.

We can imagine many intermediate steps between sanctions in a broader and narrower sense. It cannot be ruled out that a community is implicitly more or less in agreement that a norm was broken without wanting to react to it. It can also occur that they realize that a transgression occurred only after a long delay. Sanctions in a narrower sense can be understood to be a conscious reaction to a norm transgression, with this reaction either being expressly stipulated by the normative order, or at least made because of and with reference to the transgression having occurred. Even a lynching could be a sanction in this sense if it draws on a past norm transgression. Sanctions can already be included in the formulation of a norm, as in the case of a written legal order or in the sentence: "If you don't go to bed, there will be no Christmas presents tomorrow." Explicit sanctions can take the shape of measures internal to the normative order in question, or as consequences external to it.

[96] A different view can be found in Popitz (n 11), *Soziale Normen*, pp. 69–73.

In many cases, a formalized order will refer back to itself, with the sanction merely consisting in determining that a violation of the order has occurred. One thing or another is "contrary to the norm"—but this only really formalizes the norm violation. The threat of a punishment, however, places the consequence of a norm transgression in the realm of the factual, in which children go to bed and adults go to prison, but it remains open whether the threat of such sanctions makes adherence to these norms more likely.

The reason that sanctions in a narrower sense do not constitute a necessary precondition of a norm is not only because we can also imagine sanction-less norms. Rather, the curious dialectics of expressly envisioned sanctions lies in their hope of supplying a certain reassurance of norm adherence yet also bringing about new uncertainties. In every normative practice that extends beyond the mere self-reference "... is forbidden," the step from the breaking of a norm to the sanction against that transgression entails many preconditions. If I demonstrably stop greeting my neighbor because he let the air out of my tires, but he is unaware that I know, the connection between norm transgression and sanction remains concealed to him. The sanction is my own decision and does not arise from the common norm of not letting the air out of others' tires. With their high degree of formalization, laws suggest an intimate connection between norm violation and sanction, but this is not self-evident. On the contrary: even in highly formalized orders of norms this connection is frequently mediated, both in normative and cognitive respects: both in terms of the justification of the sanction and the recognizability of the interplay between norm transgression and sanctioning.

4.3 Adequate Sanctions?

Hegel clearly recognized this problem in his philosophy of law. In his theory of punishment, he highlights the distinction between the punishment itself, as a reaction to the violation of law as law, and the development of the appropriate penalty.[97] Only the former is worthy of philosophical reflection.[98] But can these two aspects really be so neatly separated from each other? Can we say anything meaningful about a specific norm if we remain silent about its sanction? Every sanction requires justification. A missing justification of a sanction would not only be insufficient for the norm violator but also for the one affected by the violation. It becomes clear why this is the case if we take a sanction as a medium for emphasizing the validity of the violated norm.[99] The sanction shouldn't merely

[97] Hegel (n 67), *Grundlinien*, § 99 (p. 188).
[98] Ibid., §101 (p. 193).
[99] Günter Jakobs, *Norm, Person, Gesellschaft*, Berlin 1997, pp. 98–102.

be marked by a formal relationship to the transgressed norm, brought about by procedural rules, but by a substantive relationship to it. Otherwise, any arbitrary reaction could count as a sanction. Establishing such substantive relationships is only easy at first sight, however. One example: a guest is misbehaving at a dinner. An appropriate sanction might be to prevent a repetition of this norm violation. The man is not invited in the future. To avoid the recurrence of a norm transgression might seem as an obvious reaction. But upon closer inspection, there is no conceptual link to the norm transgression itself but merely to the possibility of its repetition. As a penalty, it would be missing its point if a penalty is to affect a given action. Otherwise, one could also penalize people who have done nothing, but threaten to do something—and one couldn't penalize people from whom one would not anticipate a repeated action. Generally speaking, a person who kills her husband out of jealousy will generally only do so once. The culprit is penalized, even if one can exclude the possibility of a repeated offense.

So how then do we arrive at a reasonably adequate sanction? It could be appropriate to employ a sanction to recover the original condition before the norm was violated. But strictly speaking, such a recovery is impossible, and many examples, be it the effort involved in a court case, or the emotional burden it can cost to obtain an apology from someone for breaking a politeness rule, all serve to illustrate that the impossibility of undoing something that's already happened embodies one of the central problems for implementing sanctions. At the end of the day, the jug remains broken.[100] For this reason, money is necessary as an abstract substitute in order to unite the content of the norm violation with the content of the sanction, and it is simultaneously clear that this medium cannot always convincingly provide such a service.

The greatest substantive proximity of a sanction to a norm transgression is provided by the retaliation by means of the same act. Yet beyond all moral objections, the deficiency of such sanctions is actually grounded in what is intended as its justification, namely its *similarity*.[101] Why would one want to multiply an evil? A dilemma arises. Systematically, we expect an appropriate sanction to both establish an objectively plausible connection between the content of a norm and its sanction and to maintain a distance to the norm violation, that is not to repeat it in the disguise of a sanction. In this dilemma, we once more encounter the problem of world reference and distance to the world, which is part and parcel of every normative practice.

[100] Heinrich von Kleist, "Der zerbrochene Krug" Scene 12, l. 1970 ff., in: Id., *Sämtliche Werke und Briefe*, Vol. 1, Peter Staengle and Roland Reuß (eds), München 1993, p. 244.
[101] Hegel (n 67), *Grundlinien*, §101 (pp. 192–4).

4.4 Cognitive Uncertainties

On the one hand, the sanction serves as a reminder of the existing norm, it makes clear that the norm is still relevant; in certain cases, it should even help implement the norm, if possible to approach a condition that is in accordance with the norm. This explains why an instrumental understanding of norms, which views them as means toward an end, values the establishment of sanctions so highly. An element of the norm materializes in the sanction.[102]

On the other hand, precisely this web of realization is difficult to establish. Aside from the open question of how a sanction can be appropriately substantiated, there are *cognitive* problems. As long as a norm does not operate like an electric fence, but rather has to refer back to possibilities, the ascription of a sanction to a norm transgression is complex. It requires separate decisions. In the world of norms, we frequently ask ourselves why someone acts one way or another, and we are unsure whether we have become addressees of a norm. In many cases, a norm also leaves it open whether or how it is sanctioned.

Once an ascription has been made, once we can rely on a certain event being understood as a sanction of a norm violation, it remains unclear whether that sanction will serve to stabilize the norm. The sanction itself can change our view of the norm in many different ways. It might be the case that the content of the norm no longer seems plausible to us in light of its sanction. Such irritations are no rarity in the history of criminal law. Here, a given punishment frequently reminds us that the sanctioned norm is inappropriate or old-fashioned. By attaching a certain consequence to a norm violation, I sometimes create a need to adjust and change the norm's meaning. Thus, the assumption that sanctions are always means for stabilizing norms is not tenable.

4.5 The Example of Laughing

Laughing is a consequence of the disappointment of an expectation, sometimes of a normative expectation. Some laughter is in response to a norm transgression and operates as a sanction. It is rather common that actions are avoided out of fear of exposing oneself to ridicule. This kind of laughter, however, follows other mechanisms than the more *schadenfreude*-driven laughter about slipping on a banana peel. The fearful anticipation of a group's impending laughter hints at the presence of a norm. An intuition about when a group will laugh about certain behavior may

[102] A norm understanding fixated on sanctions leads to the alleged paradox that norms are particularly needed yet difficult to establish where people are not willing to concern themselves with the collective well-being. Summary and critique thereof: Geoffrey Brennan and Philip Pettit, *The Economy of Esteem*, Oxford 2005, pp. 270–9.

be a helpful instrument for recognizing the presence of said norm. In other words, the flipside of this is that it is hardly promising to ask a person, who for specific reasons fears the laughter of a group and acts accordingly, to outline a rulebook that outlines when such laughter will occur. The fear of others' laughter is often the fear of a sanction for the transgression of a rule that one doesn't know well. Does this stand in contradiction to the minimal meaning that we accorded to sanctions in our conception of norms, or does the sanction prove itself to be constitutive of the norm after all?

Once again, it is worth turning the perspective on its head. Laughter was the reaction to a norm violation, where the question of what precisely the norm consisted in, that is for what precise reason people laughed, is often unclear. This is not to be confused with the assumption that the sanction itself constitutes the norm. We can imagine a norm violation that would have led to laughter at every other family gathering but not at this current one, as it is for a funeral. In this case the norm violation has merely yielded silence, but has led to no obvious reaction, except that all participants had made a successful effort to ignore it such that we cannot be dealing with a sanction even though the norm violation was generally perceived to be dramatic. By now we should no longer be surprised by the fact that sometimes even the gravity of a norm transgression itself can be the very reason why no sanction will follow. After all, it has already become clear that there is no self-evident relationship between a norm and the sanctioning of its violation. The violation of a highly valued norm is so difficult to sanction precisely because the sanction either trivializes the violation or the norm violation calls for a sanction that would draw the integrity of the sanctioning authority itself into question. For this reason, we often feel more secure when punishing a burglary or common murder, as opposed to the violation of human dignity by acts of torture, which afflicts more than mere physical injury.[103]

Sanctions cannot be described by means of the distinctions between theory and practice, norm and reality, or *Norm in Action* and *Norm in the Books*.[104] Sanctions neither make norms effective nor does the norm become real in them. It is no new insight that there is no linear relation between the following of a rule and its sanction, that sanctions do not necessarily make norms more effective. Nonetheless, this insight does accommodate with our notion of norms as possibilities and the corresponding emphasis on the reminding and expressive function of sanctions. If sanctions, more precisely: the threat of sanctions prevent norm violations, this would speak in favor of a causal model of the normative. While it would be absurd to deny that the threat of sanctions can have consequences, the empirical idea, in terms of kinds and locations of norms, comes across as so incohesive that no

[103] Christoph Möllers, "The Triple Dilemma of Human Dignity: A Case Study" in: C. McCrudden (ed.), *Understanding Human Dignity*, Oxford 2014, pp. 173–87, here pp. 182–4.

[104] Roscoe Pound, "Law in Books and Law in Action" in: *American Law Review* 44 (1910), pp. 12–36.

general conclusions can be drawn.[105] Any identification of sanctions with the "reality" of the normative is also conceptually mistaken. The assumption that only effectively sanctioned norms are real obfuscates the fact that sanctions only operate as part of an existing norm. Even norms that are only secretly sanctioned or whose violation is only occasionally prosecuted are still real. In any case, norms make the possibility of their violation explicit in their sanction.

5. *Normative Order, Norm, and Norm Application*

5.1 "Norms" in a Normative Order

Not all norms are part of a normative order, and it is to be counted among the deficits of many theories of normativity to underestimate this circumstance. A norm can be established without additional norms necessarily being connected to it. Norms can prove themselves to be fleeting entities. This is not trivial, as we have to redefine the preconditions for norms differently—more modestly—for an individual norm than for the preconditions of a normative order developing, if the latter can be defined at all.[106] Some types of norms rely on normative orders. This is the case for legal norms, for example, but this is because of the concept of law, not because of the concept of a norm. Norms can merge into orders and orders can also be used to create norms that form part of these orders. There is no priority between these two. In the following, we will consider the relationship between an established normative order, a norm, and its application. I will address the question of when and how a normative order becomes established later.

The previous chapter discussed "normative phenomena," "normative practices," and "norms," without having clarified their relationship to a normative order. It is a difficult task to locate exactly where a "norm" is between its normative order and its application. Let us imagine an order of norms, the norm, and its application as dots on a continuum that is arranged according to the reach of the normed object. The reach denotes the temporal, personal, and subject-matter dimension to which the norm refers. It can span from universal to punctual-local. When the one flows into the other would be a matter of custom. At any rate, the middle would contain a unity that contains more than a specific situation but less than the totality of the order, that is a form that we would label with the term "rule" (to be understood not necessarily in a normative sense).

[105] For example, see Wesley Skogan, "Crime and Criminals" in: Peter Cane and Herbert Kritzer (eds), *The Oxford Handbook of Empirical Legal Research*, Oxford 2012, pp. 37–63, here pp. 43–7. Up until now, the deterring effect of the death penalty remains empirically uncertain. On this, see the meta-study by Gebhard Kirchgässner, "Econometric Estimates of Deterrence of the Death Penalty: Facts or Ideology?" in *Kyklos* 64 (2011), pp. 448–78.

[106] On this, see below, pp. 240–47.

The example of law can help to illustrate how to deal with such distinctions, as legal orders are marked by a high degree of formalization and depend on the highest possible degree of clarity in their differentiations. But even in legal orders, the difficulties—familiar from other social normative orders—in identifying and ascertaining the existence of a norm do arise. Using a concept common in German law, one can grasp a norm by way of a "norm sentence " (*Rechtssatz*) and take this to be the connection of a defined state of affairs with a given legal consequence.[107] This is simply a different terminology for a conditional in which the antecedent defines a set of conditions and the conclusion defines the consequences that the legal order envisions when these conditions are met.[108] When two convergent declarations of will have been issued, a contract exists. If someone intentionally kills another person, then one legal consequence consists in us defining this act as "homicide," and another—the sanction—in this action being subject to a punishment. At first sight, it seems obvious to read such a written down rule as the formalization of a *norm*. Upon closer inspection, however, follow-up questions arise. For one, definitions of conditions and consequences scatter themselves across various parts of a legal text. Most of the sentences that we read in legal codes formulate incomplete conditionals. Norm sentences like the ones just mentioned are reconstructions and aren't to be found in most legal texts. In the first example, the conditions of issuing an effective declaration of will are defined in another part of the German civil code. In the second example, questions arise as to where the norm with the wording "Whoever kills another person . . ." begins and where it ends. That is because the antecedens ("intentionally killing another person") contains many other norms within itself, such as a legal conception of action, of intentionality, and of causation, which determine when we are dealing with an intentional killing, when there is merely negligence, and especially when there is no action, but mere accident, an unintended event. The same goes for the end of the sentence: "is punished." Who punishes when? The legal consequence presumes a whole complex of other norms that organize the criminal justice system and define procedural rules for court proceedings. It would be conceivable, though rather impractical, to incorporate all these rules into the norm sentence regulating manslaughter, in order to complete it thus.[109]

Even in such a highly formalized system such as codified legal orders, the distinction of one individual norm from another is a practical question of presentability, and not a problem that can be solved according to the internal logic of the norm system. For formalized legal norms, a holistic perspective is imperative,

[107] For an exemplary analysis, see Jochen Bung, *Subsumtion und Interpretation*, Baden-Baden 2004, pp. 31–5.

[108] On the conditional form of rules: Frederik Schauer, *Playing by the Rules*, Oxford 2002, pp. 23 ff.

[109] Why this doesn't necessarily mean denying their character as rules which apply to more than one case is shown by Richard Holton, "Modelling Legal Rules" in: Andrei Marmor and Scott Soames (eds), *Philosophical Foundations of Language in the Law*, Oxford 2011, pp. 165–83.

in which the knowledge of one norm is impossible without the knowledge of all other ones. If this is the case for a codified legal system then it is the same for non-codified legal orders and other social orders. The delimiting of one norm from another can occasionally be achieved more or less convincingly, but it always follows from the practical criteria of presentability. The distinction between norms and the normative order is thus not fully articulated, and at the same time, in most cases practically unproblematic. Norms are elements of normative orders, normative orders consist in norms. The concept of a norm serves as an analytical unit in making the order more manageable.

5.2 Norm—Norm Application—Norm Actualization

The distinction between a norm and its application is more troublesome. Let us recall: at first sight, the application of a norm can be nothing but a concrete formulation of the norm itself, which stands in relation to the norm as the norm does to its order of norms. But with the help of an example, let us look more closely in order to clarify the concepts. Let us say that our norm were a rule inscribed on a sign, which stated that one must not smoke in this location: "Smoking Prohibited!"

If we assume that no-one is actually smoking at said location, the question arises: is the norm actually being followed by smokers or simply ignored by non-smokers? Only in the former case does it seem to make sense to speak of the norm being applied. In the latter case, the agreement between norm and practice could just be mere coincidence. Under application, then, we understand *a reference to a norm with a normative pretense*. Such a determination is weak because it makes no guidelines of whether the reference is appropriate or not. The question of the proper meaning of the norm is left aside. At the same time, we can imagine different options for dealing with a norm, which could come in question as candidates for application. Someone lights a cigarette and the grounds-keeper points toward the sign; an anthropologist walks by and takes note that a prohibition is in place.

These variations encourage a further distinction. Norms can be actualized both normatively and non-normatively. The mere indication of a norm's presence, we shall call this its *visualization* or *actualization* in the following, is non-normative. In this sense, we could point out a prohibiting sign as a description of the norm, as a reminder of its existence, though without taking a stance toward it. The visualization of such fleeting entities as norms, as we have seen, is important for practice, even if it only occurs with a descriptive intention, and it can even occur with a descriptive intention when the person indicating it endorses it. After visiting a foreign country, I can recognize and acknowledge its social norms by highlighting them. Doing so can contain a normative element, such as the desire to introduce similar rules at home. But simply highlighting these rules does not constitute an application of the norms in question. Rather, I would like to understand the *application* of a norm as a normative practice in its own right. The application of a norm itself is normative. As remains to be shown, it creates a further norm. The *enforcement* of a norm, however, does not entail a normative pretense. This is irritating, but results from the modal characteristic of the normative. After all, enforcement knows no more *possibility* of deviation. Whatever the means by which enforcement proceeds, it ultimately consists in a causal chain of events that only allows for one effect.

The application of a norm contains two elements that can neither be reduced to each other nor played out against each other. The application cannot create something completely new, as is claimed in varieties of performance theory. The application of the norm *also* draws its normativity from the norm to which it refers. Yet on the flipside, the normative content of the application cannot dissolve in the norm that it references, as is claimed in the classic notion of rules.[110] The application cannot necessarily be derived from the norm. It is neither pure "finding" within the norm nor pure "creating" of a new norm.[111] In applying a norm, a new normative content also arises.[112]

So how exactly does a new normative content arise from the application of a norm? Couldn't we simply say that a sign which prohibits smoking has answered all questions, and that pointing out the sign adds nothing to this? But undeniably, such a sign also highlights other norms, such as the ones that authorize the person who hung up the sign. Within the order, there could be reasons why this sign does not address a certain person in a certain situation, for example the one authorized to hang it up and who thus might be authorized to ignore it. Now if a person applies the rule, by telling another person with a claim to authority that the norm on the sign prohibits smoking, then the question regarding the meaning of the norm *for this situation* is thereby answered. This does not mean that this answer is appropriate according to the internal logic of the order of norms. What is decisive is that something changes in the normative order because of the application of the command inscribed on the sign, that is with its own normative, situational reference.[113] A new—in this case, more concrete—norm arises, which adds to the set of norms in the order. The act of application excludes the possibility that the norm was understood differently, or that no-one was willing to recall it for the specific situation.

In a narrow sense, the expression "norm application" is not quite correct. In the case we just described, we are faced with norm creation on the basis of previously

110 This is an essential component of what Brandom criticizes as "regulism" in *Making It Explicit* (n 75), pp. 18 ff.

111 On the application of legal norms in light of Perice's concept of abduction, see Joachim Lege, *Pragmatismus und Jurisprudenz*, Tübingen 1999, pp. 445–84.

112 It is no coincidence that these kinds of questions became infectious around 1900: in the theory of legal decision-making, as well as in the theory of theatrical performance, and in both cases they are expressed as a crisis of work or rule formalism. See Erika Fischer-Lichte, *Ästhetik des Performativen*, Frankfurt/M. 2004, pp. 42–57; on law, see Cornelia Vismann, *Medien der Rechtsprechung*, Frankfurt/M. 2011, pp. 19–71.

113 Charles Taylor, "To Follow a Rule" in: Id., *Philosophical Arguments*, Cambridge, Mass. 1995, pp. 165–80, here p. 178.

existing norms.[114] And the opposite holds true as well: in most cases, norm creation is actually a norm application, for we almost always refer to other norms when we create a norm. Norm creation *ex nihilo* is impossible.[115] Intuitively, we distinguish between creation and application in terms of the temporal sequencing (first creation, then application) and by specification (application as the specific form) which, at least in our example, reaches a personal, temporal, and spatial point: *you* may not smoke *here now*. However, we will also immediately see that application needn't mean specification. The docking of one norm onto another can specify it and make it more concrete, but it can also abstract and generalize it.

5.3 No Application without Authorization

A further differentiation arises from our example. Not only does the application of one norm create a new norm that simultaneously references a preceding one; the application itself also makes a claim for its own authority. No order of norms assumes that the existence of a norm as a matter of course also implies the universal authorization to apply it. Let us assume that it were factually uncontested that smoking harms other people, even if they enter a room later and the smoke is simply lingering in the air. Let us further assume, as was the case in the natural law tradition, that there were an objectively justifiable norm that prohibited everyone from harming each other.[116] So let us say that the prohibition of harming others required no authorization because it was simply "right." The application of this general norm by means of a sign, and the application of the sign by referencing the norm would both participate in the truth of the norm and be justified by it. But even in this eccentric example of a presumably obvious and objective norm, the question remains open as to who is authorized to apply it and for what reasons. Just as we accord no-one the moral right to instruct everyone else at all times on moral obligations, so we would presumably struggle to draw from the correctness of the two norms—the prohibition on harming others and the prohibition to smoke—the idea that everyone has the right to put up respective signs everywhere. Such doubts may arise from the suspicion that every application could also affect the rights of others. All the more, the application on other, less obvious cases requires

[114] This argument generalizes a thought from Kelsen's legal theory. The application of a law by administration or courts brings about new, in most cases more concrete norms. See Hans Kelsen, *Reine Rechtslehre* (1934), Tübingen 2010, pp. 84–99.

[115] One could view this differently in terms of a purely voluntaristic norm creation. But even in such cases, the reference to other norms, as opposed to merely stating "because we like it this way," is inevitable. On the end of this kind of justification in French absolutism: Simone Goyard-Fabre, "La rationalisation de la loi en France au XVIII siècle" in: Barbara Dölemeyer and Diethelm Klippel (eds), *Gesetz und Gesetzgebung im Europa der frühen Neuzeit*, Berlin 1998, pp. 55–70.

[116] "Neminem ladere," see e.g. Samuel Pufendorf, *Über die Pflicht des Menschen und des Bürgers nach dem Gesetz der Natur*, Frankfurt/M. 1994, pp. 72–7.

an authorization that doesn't stem just from the applied norm itself. The applying reference always needs its own authorization. If, upon my first visit to some friends, I immediately call for adherence to certain manners, I am lacking in authorization even if the rule itself is viewed as appropriate by all involved. The norm invoked by me is justified, but it is not due to me to invoke it.

These considerations complete the view of norm application. Every act of norm application creates new normative material with reference to pre-existing material, such that in light of the applied norm, both a constitutive excess and a constitutive lack arise from this application. The excess consists in the new normative content, the lack from the necessity of a continuing authorization that doesn't merely arise from the applied norm. The excess of normativity entails the lack of authorization.

5.4 Abstraction and Analogy

If the application can be taken to be a productive referral to a norm with a normative intent, then we have a conceptual framework that is broad enough to allow for other forms of application than concretization. That is, a form of application becomes conceivable that proceeds by way of *abstraction* from a specific norm to be then applied to a different situation. In the philosophical tradition, we often encounter the term analogy in this context, which is traditionally viewed with suspicion.[117] This suspicion stems from the fact that the analogy needs an intermediary step, which concretization does not require. The norm refers to constellation A and is to be applied to constellation B. This requires a justification. The analogy between the two constellations has to be specifically justified. For the application to constellation B, it needs to be clarified why two different cases should be treated equally with regards to the norm. This could unduly expand the field of application of the norm. If a sign tells me that I shouldn't smoke here, what about when someone explains to me that this also implies unhealthy drinking and takes the glass right out of my hand?

But this example is misleading. Before I explicate this, it should be mentioned that the application of a norm by way of abstraction is by no means unusual. This is not only illustrated by new legal doctrine being developed by means of court rulings, it is also apparent in that norms are often established in their breaking or, in other words, in experiences of injustice. Just as I can understand my request for a person to take their feet off the table as a norm that can also be applied to other people in the room, so a court ruling or an "exemplary" punishment in

[117] On the question of the compatibility with logical standards: Karen Gloy, "Versuch einer Logik des Analogiedenkens" in: Id. and Manuel Bachmann (eds), *Das Analogiedenken. Vorstöße in ein neues Gebiet der Rationalitätstheorie*, Freiburg/München 2000, pp. 298–323, here pp. 315–23. On the theological history of this figure: Wolfhart Pannenberg, *Analogie und Offenbarung*, Göttingen 2007.

an authoritarian system can serve as precedent for other cases. The same can be observed in other normative forms, such as role models or fables. In all of them, what is exemplary serves as a normative guideline which is applied by way of abstraction, not in a concretizing manner.[118]

But can concretization and abstraction thus simply be equated with each other? Intuitively, the rule emblazoned on the sign—not to smoke in this space—could be applied to all people at any given moment. The plea not to drink here, by contrast, is not as obviously derivable from the same sign. One might think that concretization operates fundamentally differently, as a rule already exists for the process, whereas a rule first has to be created in the case of an application by way of abstraction. But the capacity that is necessary for concretizing a norm does not operate like a logical conclusion. The fact that we are so assured of the sign's meaning is the result of our experience with similar signs and the observation of other people's reaction to them. The command to do or refrain from doing something at times is taken as an expression of a more general rule, sometimes even of a more narrowly defined norm. In its biblical version, "Thou shalt not kill"[119] was expressed in general, but did not mean to exclude killing in the case of self-defense or the killing of a soldier in times of war. In other cases, we take rules to be directed toward abstracting applications from the outset. This is the case with legends about saints, which cannot be read other than individual stories that have a normative appeal to those listening. It is also the case for the way in which the expert discourse on fundamental rights reads constitutional law, namely that "free speech" also protects the written word, as the freedom of press does for digital media, and freedom of opinion does for at least some factual claims.[120] Lawyers wouldn't even classify such approaches to fundamental rights as reasoning by way of analogy. The concretization creates a new norm, and the analogy continues to refer to a norm that is being applied. The difference between an immediate, even better concretizing, and an analogous application presupposes a clarification of the norm's meaning. From the perspective of those preoccupied with its

[118] Role models are an important example of pre- or non-conceptual norms. They are reconstructions of an individual life deemed worth emulating which cannot be boiled down to a concept, but rather derive their normative claim from the individuality of its object. Even though role models are normative in that they aim to orient toward a life plan to be realized in the future, it is also the case that a role model cannot be achieved and that its distinctness cannot be touched by its emulation. "I have set you an example that you should do as I have done for you" (John 13, 15). This sentence indeed demands to view Jesus as a role model; it precisely does not demand to become Jesus. Role models pose similar application problems to those that embrace them as do concepts that find expression in the question of how a role model would act in a specific situation. Ian Kershaw, *Hitler 1889–1936*, Stuttgart 1998, pp. 665–7, employs the phrase commonly used in national socialism, to "work toward the *Führer*." With this formulation, the system in place was able to operate without concrete command and radicalize and make its domination dynamic. More generally regarding the more conceptually minded function of role models in anticipating the future, see Thomas Macho, *Vorbilder*, München 2011, pp. 19–38.

[119] Deuteronomy 5, 17.

[120] For an overview, see Norman Dorsen, Michel Rosenfeld, András Sajó, and Susanne Baer, *Comparative Constitutionalism*, St. Paul 2010, pp. 847–97.

application, however, this meaning still waits to be established in the first place. We are thus dealing with an external differentiation, both sides of which share the reference to a norm.

5.5 Judgment and Imagination: A Detour Via Kant

Following Kant, the application of a norm can be considered an exercise of judgment. For Kant, of course, all claims are judgments, that is those in the realm of perception as well as those in the realm of practical and theoretical reason. Kant refers to the capacity for appropriate application as power of judgment.[121]

Two Kantian ideas help to approach the challenge of applying norms. First, rules do not themselves regulate their appropriate application.[122] The application does not operate like a logical conclusion, it cannot be rationally stabilized, but is rather a matter of experience and observation of one's own exemplary decision-making custom.[123] Precisely because Kant has a stable notion of a rule, one uncontested by any skepticism regarding the determinacy of meaning, the realization that the process of application itself cannot be regulated is important.[124] Experience stemming from experience, however, is of dubious epistemic value as it is unreliable. It is a practically necessary evil of our practice of judgment.[125]

Secondly, Kant's differentiation between determining and reflecting judgment shows a remarkable congruence to that which I call application by way of abstraction or concretization. While the determining judgment enables the application of a general rule to a particular case, judgment by means of reflective judgment brings about its own foundation in the first place,[126] which, however, doesn't operate at a conceptual level. Rather, the esthetic judgment is formed by the free interplay of

[121] Explained for a normative context in great detail by Wolfgang Wieland, "Kants Rechtsphilosophie der Urteilskraft" in: *Zeitschrift für philosophische Forschung* 52 (1998), pp. 1–22, here pp. 5–10. For Wieland, the problems inherent to reflective judgment prove to also be relevant for the judicial application of rules.

[122] Compare also with Aristotle, *Nicomachean Ethics*, 1141b15–36. In this context, Charles Taylor speaks of a "phronetic gap": "To Follow a Rule" (n 113) p. 177.

[123] Kant (n 31), *Kritik der reinen Vernunft*, pp. 184 ff. (A 133 ff., B 172 ff.)

[124] It anticipates much of the discussion following Wittgenstein, on this see David Bell, "The Art of Judgment" in: *Mind* 96 (1987), pp. 221–44.

[125] Jocelyn Benoist, "Appliquer ses concepts" in: Jean-Marie Vaysse (ed.), *Kant*, Paris 2008, pp. 91–127, here pp. 97 ff., 124; see also Manfred Frank, *Einführung in die frühromantische Ästhetik*, Frankfurt/M. 1989, pp. 88 ff. Training with the help of examples is also mentioned by Wittgenstein (n 30), *Bemerkungen über die Grundlagen der Mathematik*, p. 418.

[126] Immanuel Kant (n 24), pp. 87 ff. (A XXIV ff., B XXVI ff.). For reasons of the work's genealogy, the relationship between the two forms of judgment is also not clear. Does the *Critique of Judgement* also investigate judgments which are significant for *The Critique of Pure Reason*, namely judgments of reason, or does it limit itself to judgments of the esthetic and teleological judgment, that is artistic and natural phenomena? On this discussion, see Jens Kulenkampff, "Metaphysik und Ästhetik: Kant zum Beispiel" in: Andrea Kern and Ruth Sonderegger (eds), *Falsche Gegensätze. Zeitgenössische Positionen zur philosophischen Ästhetik*, Frankfurt/M. 2002, pp. 49–80, here pp. 54–9.

reason and imagination in light of a sensory-perceptible phenomenon. The judgment of taste does not constitute a new concept.[127]

According to Kant, both for determining and reflective judgment, *imagination* plays a crucial role. In order to make the determination whether an object in the realm of my perception falls under a certain concept, one has to make a *comparison* between this object and other objects[128] that could fall under this category or concept. It is only such comparative labor with imagined objects that allows me to come to a result in the question of application, which—in the form of a judgment—then enables a decision about the applicability of a given concept.[129] This central role for imagination and comparison supports the idea that abstracting and concretizing norm applications are fundamentally equivalent. The supposed additional achievement required for an analogizing or abstracting application of a norm—as opposed to a "mere" concretization—proves itself to be the normal case, necessary for both kinds of application. This is because the comparative imagination that allows us to put a specific norm in a context outside of its specification is no different from a comparative imagination that brings a specified norm into yet more specific circumstances. On this view, there is no categorical difference between an "immediately" concretizing and an analogous application. Norm and norm application are merely sequentially distinct, the application refers to the norm regardless of whether the norm to which it refers is broader or narrower in scope than the application that follows it.

Thus, I cannot simply deduce from the norm whether a given context is suitable for an analogous application. If the norm itself cannot define the conditions of its application, then this suggestion would refer back to the problem.[130] In order to justify the applicability of a norm to another case, I have to imagine[131] its application, and I have to compare it with other applications that are already practice or that might only have been envisioned in light of this case, in order to identify arguments for or against this instance of application.[132] The application either works constructively and concretizing, or exemplarily and abstracting.[133] There is no epistemic hierarchy between the two forms.

[127] Kant (n 24), *Kritik der Urteilskraft*, pp. 142 ff. (A 17 ff., B 17 ff.)

[128] On the underappreciated meaning of comparison: Beatrice Longuenesse, *Kant and the Capacity to Judge*, Princeton 1998, pp. 111–30.

[129] Bell (n 124), "Art of Judgment" pp. 228–30; Benoist (n 23), "Concepts" pp. 108–24.

[130] Gerald Postema, "A Similibus ad Similia: Analogical Thinking in Law" in: Douglas E. Edlin (ed.), *Common Law Theory*, Cambridge 2007, pp. 102–33, here pp. 113–16; Frances M. Kamm, "Theory and Analogy in Law" in: *Arizona State Law Journal* 29 (1997), pp. 405–25, here pp. 413–18; Cass Sunstein, *Legal Reasoning and Political Conflict*, Oxford 1996, pp. 62–91.

[131] Again, Bell (n 124), "Art of Judgment" pp. 228–30.

[132] On the meaning for the normative practice of law, see Wieland (n 121), "Kants Rechtsphilosophie der Urteilskraft" pp. 7–10. The scheme of subsumption, widespread among jurists, downplays the problem because for it, the comparative-imaginative work of application remains unseen.

[133] Benoist (n 23), *Concepts*, pp. 80–2.

Two further reasons speak in favor of the equal footing of concretizing and analogous arguments in the realm of the normative. First, a child's acquisition of concepts seems to operate by way of analogy, that is by a comparative treatment of objects,[134] though this doesn't only concern normative concepts. The more specific reason consists in a typical situation of social normativity, namely the obligation to apply a norm without any explicit norm being available. We are often called to apply a norm without having one at hand. Someone is obliged to make a normative decision. But his or her authorization hinges on their recourse to an existing norm. Since they cannot do so, they must argue by way of analogy. Law has been aware of this constellation ever since introducing the prohibition of the denial of justice around 1800. Courts have to reach decisions on the legal questions before them, even if there are no explicit rules applicable.[135] But this situation is also commonplace in other social practices in which the normative expectation insists on acts of judgment that cannot draw on any relevant norm. The paradigmatic case for the beginning of any normative practice—instances of disappointment—is an example for this as well. The one who is disappointed first has to conceptualize and articulate which expectation has been disappointed, and this conceptualization will go beyond the concrete experience of disappointment.

5.6 Distinct Practices—Explication—Formalization

At a conceptual level, we are missing the point in positing a priority of the regular over the exemplary, a priority of the concretizing over the abstracting, or a priority of subsumption over analogy. *Practically* speaking, however, such hierarchies between different methods of application can indeed be established. A normative order can enact a rule that stipulates that a norm may only be deduced from another norm, if this norm aims to regulate more than one case. The attempt to establish a hierarchy between abstracting and concretizing applications may have political or institutional reasons on its side. In this sense, some institutions are more capable of concretizing contexts, others are better at laying out fundamental principles by way of abstraction.[136] Theories concerning when this is the case are at the center of the political-legal distinction between legislative and judicial procedures[137] and strive

[134] Susan Carey, *The Origin of Concepts*, Oxford 2009, Chapter 2; Douglas Hofstadter and Emmanuel Sander, *Die Analogie*, Stuttgart 2014, Chapter 4.

[135] On the meaning of this order: Ekkehard Schumann, "Das Rechtsverweigerungsverbot" in: *Zeitschrift für Zivilprozeß* 81 (1968), pp. 79–102. The idea that compulsory legal decision-making could make repercussions for legal argumentation less clear was expressed by John L. Austin, "A Plea for Excuses" in: Ibid., *Philosophical Papers*, Oxford 1979, pp. 175–204, here pp. 188 ff.

[136] For an institutional theory of this distinction, see Neil K. Komesar, *Imperfect Alternatives*, Chicago 1994, pp. 53–152.

[137] Christoph Möllers, *The Three Branches. A Comparative Model of Separation of Powers*, Oxford 2013, pp. 80–101.

to rationalize when it is appropriate to establish general rules and when it is not. In many legal orders, we find a prohibition against reasoning by way of analogy in criminal law, allowing courts to render criminal sentences only under the condition that they are based on general, previously specified and written parliamentary laws to be applied in a concretizing manner.

These kinds of formalizing techniques can shape the standards of appropriate application in manifold ways. Some normative orders present themselves in the shape of general rules, whereas others are made up of cases, anecdotes, or even unsolved disputes. The means of portrayal in turn affect the way in which the process and task of application is understood. For it is norms of varying generality that are offered up for application. But the fundamental problem remains: even the prohibition of reasoning by way of analogy cannot clearly delineate its own limits.

5.7 Form of Application and Entanglement of Norms and Facts

We understand the application of a norm to mean that this norm is invoked in a situation. In this context, "invoke" merely denotes the circumstance that, in the act of application, we make reference to the norm. Invoking a given norm can be more or less convincing, but this broad notion of application should not be taken to imply a strong skepticism regarding the determinacy of meaning. But it certainly clarifies that the norm cannot force its own application, and that the application is an act itself. Temporally, the application comes after the norm. It contains its own normative pretense, it is a norm in itself, just as the applied norm which it invokes derives from yet another norm.

An important problem concerning the application of norms lies in identifying the situation for which an application is suitable. Is this situation simply a purely factual condition? In practically applying norms, we often distinguish between factual and normative questions, yet this differentiation is notoriously contentious. This poses a problem for all normative orders; in legal systems it is made explicit, and the differentiability of normative and factual questions is presumed, for example when an appellate court is only allowed to review legal questions, but not the particular circumstances of the case.[138]

What exactly is the problem here? For one, the things to which we refer as facts or circumstances are heavily affected by their normative context, even simply by virtue of them being expressed in a normatively shaped language. What is more, in formalized orders, "facts" are shaped by a procedure, that is because they need to be presented to a certain institution in a defined form.[139] These then are not

[138] Kim Lane Scheppele, "Facing Facts in Legal Interpretation" in: *Representations* 30 (1990), pp. 42–77, here pp. 43 ff.

[139] Niklas Luhmann, *Legitimation durch Verfahren*, Frankfurt/M. 1983, pp. 17–26.

brute *facts as such*, for which an application is suitable, but only facts that become relevant for the norm by virtue of the norm. This is the one side of things. On the flipside, the referral to a norm, which then shapes the selection of facts, already hinges on a previous appreciation of the circumstances. I do not simply resort to some norm and some procedure, only to thereby find criteria for the selection of factual circumstances, to which I then once more apply the norm. This would be circular.[140]

The problem takes care of itself as soon as we recognize that the norm and 'its' circumstances initially arise together, such as in a painful disappointment or a concrete wish. They can only be analytically disentangled to a certain degree, which usually occurs when the norm is made explicit. Then I begin to justify a claim, and only in this justification do I distinguish between the temporal and spatial circumstances in which the norm is invoked and the norm itself, or I charge a formalization process with the task of justification, a process which claims to be able to clearly distinguish between normative and factual questions, and which frequently is indeed successful at making this distinction plausible, such as when a concrete event or an object to which the norm refers is identified and isolated by the process.

These kinds of analyses can operate at two levels. At an initial level, a norm can employ normative and non-normative concepts. A rule that prohibits walking into a mosque with shoes and a rule that prohibits "bad" behavior employ different kinds of concepts. Whether we succeed at analyzing the concept of bad behavior with regards to normative and descriptive elements is secondary.[141] For most norms, in either case, both normative and non-normative concepts are simultaneously at play. A second level concerns the relationship between these concepts and the facts to which the norm is supposed to refer. It is not so much of interest whether the concept is normative. Both kinds of concepts can be applied. We ask ourselves whether a concrete object is an "animal" in terms of the law, or whether a certain behavior at a funeral is "worthy" of such an occasion.[142] Questions of proper understanding arise at both levels. The interwovenness of facts and norms is at play both in the use of normative and non-normative concepts in the norm, and in the act of connecting a norm to a given situation.

The normative and factual sides cannot be completely disentangled. One reason for this is that we simply do not command a vocabulary that is both sufficiently

[140] A vivid description of this can be found in Sabine Müller-Mall, "Fall und Urteil" in: Thomas Hilgers et al. (eds), *Konturen des Kunstwerks*, München 2013, pp. 249–62; see also the distinction between "*enthalten*" (containing) and "*bestimmt sein*" (being determined) in Friedrich Carl von Savigny, *Vorlesungen über die juristische Methodologie*, Frankfurt/M. 2004, p. 108.

[141] On the limits of such analyses, see below pp.127–30.

[142] This sheds light on what McDowell identifies as a distinction between interpretation and understanding in Wittgenstein, and what is discussed as the distinction between subsumption and interpretation in legal discussions of methodology: McDowell (n 82), "Wittgenstein" pp. 238–43; Bung, *Subsumtion und Interpretation*, pp. 37–41.

nuanced and neutral. Even the concept of normativity developed here cannot and is not intended to meet this demand. Nevertheless, practically speaking, we cannot neglect the distinction between these two as long as we want to describe normative practices as specific practices that are distinct from others. We also cannot completely analyze away the entanglement since we will never be able to keep the norm free of the demands of application, which are always empirically contaminated from the outset. That is because factual elements are part of every norm's origin—as the application of other norms—and they stay with them in every instance in which reference to a norm is made with a normative pretense. I can only speak of a pure norm if I am treating it as a fact, that is as removed from all normative context. If I want to apply the norm, realize it, then I confront it with and connect it with facts.

5.8 Applying Subject?

One could interpret an instance of applying the breaks when a traffic light turns red as a reflex, as a mere causal effect. Does this contradict the concept of a norm developed here, which also includes the possibility of refusing, of transgressing the norm? In line with Kant, Hannah Ginsborg has described abiding with norms with the concept of *primitive normativity*. According to her, we can speak of an instance of norm application when the action in question is accompanied by a moment of subjective acquiescence, by an inner affirmation,[143] expressing a normative attitude toward one's own actions.

For the present conception of social norms, this hypothesis is both too demanding and too modest. It is too demanding in that nothing precludes us from viewing even the "blind," reflexive stopping at a traffic light as a variant of norm application. There can be many practical reasons for some drivers to consciously, in Ginsborg's sense even normatively stop at the red light while others do not. This does not affect the categorization of such behavior as the application of a social norm as long as it remains possible that some drivers will run the red light. If the hypothesis demands that *every* addressee assumes a normative disposition, then it is too strong for a concept of social norms. It is also of little use to divide up the practice at a red traffic light into individual events and to only—post hoc—assume a norm whenever the respective driver has indeed consciously stopped. In this interpretation, the thesis is too modest, as it subjectivizes the establishment of a norm, that is, it demands no more than an individual disposition. This in turn, by itself, is unsatisfying as a model of social norms and would

[143] Hannah Ginsborg, "Primitive Normativity and Scepticism About Rules" in: *The Journal of Philosophy* 108 (2011), pp. 227–54, here pp. 233–8.

lose sight of questions concerning the depiction, tradition, implementation and upholding of norms.

5.9 Wittgenstein and the Rule: A Productive Debate?

Only now, quite a long way into this book—and only quite selectively—do I get around to what is arguably the most important philosophical debate concerning the figure of norm application, namely Wittgenstein's discussion of rule following, from his *Philosophical Investigations*, and the debate attaching to it.[144] This is certainly no coincidence, yet it is in need of justification.

To begin with, after what has been said it appears inappropriate to use as a starting point for an investigation into the problem of norm application the notion of the rule because this would conceal that in normative orders both punctual and general norms coincide with each other. The rule is neither the natural point of departure for a normative order nor is it static. The rule knows no immanent limits. Both can be understood as lessons from Wittgenstein's analysis which we have already incorporated here.

Furthermore, it is disconcerting for a theory of social norms to see how philosophical disputes tend to equate very different kinds of rules. Namely, the *Philosophical Investigations* are concerned both with mathematical rules and natural language, two practices that operate very differently.[145] Interestingly, both have precisely this in common, that they do not represent normative orders. We discussed the case of language earlier. The same holds for mathematical practices, such as addition, which Wittgenstein treats in his *Philosophical Investigations*, because we know successful mathematical practices that are entirely deterministic, that is, non-normative. The social practice that we have put in place through the invention and programming of computers is drastically different from the practice of social norms.[146] We might be unsure of whether we have correctly applied the addition rule, but we certainly do not treat our engagement with the addition rule as our own decision. We also do not require an authorization to apply it, since we take the addition rule to be a description, not an evaluation. The addition rule is more like a natural law than a social norm. If norms were to operate as calculations, they would no longer be norms but would be social algorithms that had nothing to do with how we handle norms in court cases or in our everyday lives.[147] It might seem

144 Precisely, Wittgenstein, *Philosophische Untersuchungen*, § 201 (pp. 133 ff.)

145 We find a rare critique of Wittgenstein's selection of examples, especially of strings of explicit rules that even for normative practices are quite untypical, in Andreas Kemmerling, "Regel und Geltung im Lichte der Analyse Wittgensteins" in: *Rechtstheorie* 6 (1975), pp. 104–31, here pp. 127–9.

146 On the problem of application to reflexive practices, again see Scott Hershovitz, "Wittgenstein on Rules" in: *Oxford Journal of Legal Studies* 22 (2002), pp. 619–40.

147 John Mc Dowell also wants to integrate mathematical phenomena into his general theory (see "Non-Cognitivism and Rule-Following" in: Ibid., *Mind, Value, and Rationality*, pp. 198–218, here

fitting to equate the two forms from the perspective of the philosophy of language, but all relevant social characteristics are thus lost.

Kripke's skeptical reading of Wittgenstein claims that we cannot know whether a rule was followed. The core of his argument asserts that we can only justify the aspiration inherent to norms, which points toward a determination of future results, after the fact. This ties his argument into Hume's critique of the inductivity of natural laws.[148] However, Kripke also emphasizes the practical operation of norms in a social context. While we wouldn't be able to know whether we follow a norm, in the context of a norm-applying community, we could orient ourselves toward the others.[149]

If we compare this observation with that of an eminent opponent in the debate, it becomes yet more clear why this debate has little to bring to our investigation. John McDowell doubts the preconditions of Kripke's skepticism.[150] According to McDowell, we understand a rule if we know what it means for someone to adhere to it, albeit without us thereby being able to predict how they would behave.[151] We can learn such knowledge. But Kripke is concerned with making possible correct predictions.

Both authors ultimately arrive at ideas about determination of meaning to be a specific achievement of social communities. For Kripke, meaning arises from factual consensus, for McDowell via learning processes that extend beyond mere agreement. But neither help us any further: neither can we take social norms to be an exercise at conditioning that reliably commits us on certain meanings because, we have seen, the sanction mechanisms that alone would allow for such conditioning are steeped with way too many practical uncertainties. Nor can social norms be understood as the product of a learning community of sensible and autonomous persons. In a theory of social norms, a space has to remain for dissent within an interpreting community[152] as well as for a practice in which consensus reaches its objective limits.[153] To engage with uncertain meanings, which also express the uncertainty with regard to the question of what seems possible for a community, is a fundamental function of social norms. Uncertainty, which is constitutive of the epistemic notion of possibility, is central to every normative practice. Whether we can know what a norm prescribes is irrelevant, as long as we can deal with such uncertainty.

p. 208). If we could treat social norms like we do mathematical laws, however, we would have to find different terms for social norms or we could do without them.

[148] Saul Kripke, *Wittgenstein über Regeln und Privatsprache*, Frankfurt/M. 1987, pp. 83–9.
[149] Ibid., pp. 113–43.
[150] McDowell (n 82), "Wittgenstein" pp. 221–62, here pp. 226–32.
[151] Ibid., p. 251 with reference to Wittgenstein (n 30), *Bemerkungen über die Grundlagen der Mathematik*, pp. 316–18.
[152] In Kripke, however, the community comes across as very compact: Kripke (n 148), *Wittgenstein*, pp. 118 ff.
[153] This is the all decisive point for McDowell (n 82), "Wittgenstein" pp. 249–57.

5.10 Application and Boundaries

Maybe even more so than for descriptive concepts, for normative concepts we expect to allow the drawing of boundaries, that is to exclude certain consequences. Why should we make use of norms, one might ask, that do not define any boundaries? In terms of a theory of meaning, however, the same holds true for normative concepts as for others. This does not mean that norms have no boundaries, but it means that these boundaries can only arise from the application itself, and that boundaries cannot be spelled out for every imaginable scenario. Boundaries only result from application, and this application cannot be justified ad infinitum. Rather, the application puts an end to the justification.[154] We never define the boundaries of a term merely by making reference to its immanent meaning.[155] There is always the possibility of a usage which is not determined in its specific context. Concepts, on Friedrich Waismann's reading, are "porous,"[156] that is, they can always be confronted with contexts for which their purview is not determined.[157] The norm cannot be applied to everything, but it nonetheless does not contain a defined boundary within itself either.

Since the identification of a norm points toward an entire order of norms, it can be ruled out from the outset that the meaning of a norm ever remains unchanged and stable over time, whether because it is applied and as such is set within a new frame of reference, or whether other parts of the order of norms are applied and thereby create a different context for the norm, or whether just the non-normative context changes. An immutable norm is impossible. It is no coincidence that the search for norms that have been valid at all times has yielded no success.[158]

Orders of norms can be structured to contain their own amendability within certain boundaries, with the help of techniques that maintain a close connection between the norm and its linguistic formulation by making their binding effect conditional on their written fixation, or by targeted socialization, the conditioning of future norm appliers, by sanctions or other mechanisms that back up the norm.[159] These kinds of techniques have an effect on the development of the order, but they do not affect the mutability of the order in principle. We should think of normative orders as fields of references, which convey to that to which they refer, the norm, through that which is making reference, the instance of norm

[154] This is what Wittgenstein seems to mean, see *Philosophische Untersuchungen*, § 217 (p. 139 ff); see also id., *Über Gewißheit*, Frankfurt/M. 2012, § 204 (p. 59).

[155] Benoist (n 23), *Concepts*, pp. 152–6.

[156] Friedrich Waismann, "Verifiability" in: Antony Flew (ed.), *Logic and Language*, London 1951, pp. 117–44, here pp. 118–24. In the original, the concept is in German. This concept has little to do with a problematic reading by H. L. A. Hart in his distinction between core and vestibule of a concept.

[157] For such an interpretation of Wittgenstein: James Conant, "Wittgenstein on Meaning and Use" in: *Philosophical Investigations* 21 (1998), pp. 222–50, here pp. 239–44.

[158] See Popitz (n 11), *Soziale Normen*, p. 62.

[159] Wittgenstein (n 154), *Über Gewißheit*, § 349 (p. 91).

application, a new actuality and relevance, by this both perpetuating and changing the norm.

5.11 Implicit Norms: Negation and the Coming to be of Norms

Some norms seem to be coming into being only in the moment of their application. An experience of injustice defines a moral standard, an esthetic or legal judgment develops a standard in the course of their production. Even more pronouncedly, many experiences of norms begin with their breach. It is only the act of transgression that brings about a constellation that allows for a norm to be identified. Georges Canguilhem puts it more radically: "In anthropological experience a norm cannot be original. Rule begins to be rule only in making rules and this function of correction arises from infraction itself."[160] But how can something be broken that, according to Canguilhem, only came to be by virtue of its transgression? The obvious answer is that the norm had already been in place but it was only perceived after its transgression that it had *implicitly* been in place. But implicit norms appear random as constructions ex post. They only appear at the moment in which they were disregarded.[161] For a theory that holds the recognizability of norms to be an important feature, this is unsatisfying.

If implicit norms can only be recognized in their breaking then they arise because an unexpected event explicates an expectation that otherwise would not have been made explicit.[162] The thus appearing norm then shows itself to be the positively marked continuation of a course of events that has been expected, which expectation, however, has been disappointed. It begins as a highly specified entity. It may take the shape of an expectation that a sentence end with a certain word, of an experience of disappointment which brings about an awareness of a certain wish, or of the observation of an outrageous atrocity that triggers the semantics of human rights. With regards to the arising of implicit norms, we thus have to distinguish two phases: the *discovery* of a norm through the event of unexpected disturbance,[163] and the *abstraction* by which the concrete experience of transgression

[160] Georges Canguilhem, *The Normal and the Pathological*, New York 1991, p. 241; On the differences between the dissertation and his epilogue inserted later, see Guillaume Le Blanc, *Canguilhem et les Normes*, Paris 1998, pp. 78–89.

[161] A stricter, yet practically less problematic notion of implicit rules views these as unuttered logical consequences of explicit rules: Max Black, "The Analysis of Rules" in: Id., *Models and Metaphors*, Ithaca 1962, pp. 95–139, here pp. 124 ff. (Rules taken there as a synonym for norms).

[162] Michael Tomasello (*Origins of Human Communication*, Cambridge, Mass. 2008, pp. 212 ff.) defines norms as mutual expectations including pressure to conform. The latter, in light of the reasons developed above between pp. 171–9, seems too demanding, even if norms practically arose in such a manner.

[163] Thus, implicit norms can only be discovered, not created, as any creation would require their explication before the disturbance.

is expanded to other cases that have become more easily imaginable after and by means of said disappointment. Even the disturbing event can become an object of dispute, in the course of which the supposedly disturbing character of the incident can be rejected by the community, or remain contested, or prompt the community formally to acknowledge the disturbed norm, thereby moving from the process of finding a norm to one of positing it.[164]

Now the question arises as to how this process is distinct from one that unfolds in light of purely cognitive expectations, why we should take implicit "norms" to be norms at all. If the assumption of a norm simply required a certain expectation along with its disappointment, then the difference between a norm and an expectation would be irrelevant. Not every surprise points toward the existence of a norm. One feature might lie in the subjective reaction. If the disappointed expectation causes an emotional reaction, such as outrage, this might indicate a normative, not a cognitive expectation. In many moral value theories, such a viewpoint sustains the thesis that, in reality, all norms can be traced back to values and the affects attached to them. There would thus at least be a genealogical priority of values over other types of norms.[165] But this criterion is not very helpful, not only because of the difficult classification of emotional states; it probably also does not always yield correct results. If a scientist conducting an experiment arrives at insights which undermine his hypothesis and thus frustrate entire years of his work, this might well affect his emotional state far more forcefully than a severe instance of someone's human rights being violated in a far-off country of which he hears on the news. But the first emotional state does not refer to a normative expectation because that would have to presume—from the outset—two developments as equally possible in practice. The indication of disappointment alone is thus neither a sufficient nor a necessary condition for the unfolding of a norm. At most it is an explanation for the success in establishing certain norms. The classification of something as normative, however, must be measured by the criteria which we developed earlier on. A course of events that diverges from the expected course of events cannot denote any normative content if this course of events proceeded with necessity. We know that in scientific experiments, a different course of events is impossible if conditions stay the same.[166] In the mindset of a scientist, the fact that the experiment runs in a certain way excludes the possibility of a different course of events.[167] This then shows that the expectation in question is not of a normative nature.

[164] Highlighted by Hauke Brunkhorst.

[165] Exemplarily, Hans Joas, *Die Sakralität der Person. Eine neue Genealogie der Menschenrechte*, Berlin 2011, pp. 253–60; see also the observation by Christine M. Korsgaard, *The Sources of Normativity*, Cambridge, 1996, p. 4, that values represent an attractive form of normativity, whereas obligations represent a repelling form.

[166] The sociology of knowledge, of course, has its empirically grounded doubts which go back to the lacking reproducibility of many famous experiments. (Pestre (n 40), *À Contre-Science*, pp. 19–42). It remains to be seen whether this indicates a return to a normative notion of natural law.

[167] This would be qualified for experiments concerned with probabilities.

Now let us assume that a given behavior of some person meets with disfavor of other people in a community without this disfavor ever being made explicit. Are we then dealing with a normative practice? Yes, if this disfavor points toward an alternate course of events, which would have avoided said disfavor. Let us now assume that we are sitting at a dinner table. One of the people present is speaking quite loudly, something that is a new experience for the others, which immediately prompts widespread rejection. Since the situation has previously never been seen, reflected, and assessed, there is no explicit social norm for its assessment.[168] What exactly am I saying about this situation when I take it to be an instance of a constellation that creates a norm? Three readings appear conceivable, as follows.

We either could link our rejection to normative preferences that had previously been in place.[169] If this were not so it would already be unclear, in which way I can treat the reaction to be referring to the transgression. Or, secondly, we take the situation to create a new norm that must refer to future situations, not to the incident which prompted me to stipulate it.[170] The third possibility would see an implicit norm at play that had existed in hiding and then only became visible in its transgression. The problem with this third assumption is that it would contribute nothing to the description of the situation, because it remains unclear what the difference would consist in between the situation being described as one in which a norm referring back to the past situation only arises in the moment of its breach, and a situation in which the event is described without any recourse to a social norm. To speak of an implicit norm then gives the impression that one could speak of a sanction without being able to identify what said sanction is referring to. If I have no means of identifying a norm other than a reaction to it, then I shouldn't classify the event as a "reaction."

Speaking of implicit norms is thus pointless as norms only arise on the basis of an experience which combines a negative evaluation with a generalization pointing *toward the future*. What we can take from these considerations is how essential the *negation* of reality, how essential *disappointment* is for the coming to be of norms. Norms do not have to negate reality, they can also affirm it. But in practical terms, the development of a norm cannot be imagined without experiences of disappointment and their negation. "In the act of *negation, reality's decision regarding the consciousness of possibility* is taken note and made aware."[171] The same doesn't hold

[168] If one looks more closely, one will realize that the norm in question was the object of people's own bringing up as children, and that the example probably doesn't operate in the same way in all European countries, not to speak of other continents. This goes to show that the breaking of social rules which don't follow an explicitly normative course in which a norm arises *ex ante* might not be as easy to identify as the observation from Canguilhem mentioned earlier in the section presumes.

[169] Max Black ("Analysis of Rules" p. 130) rightly highlights that it would hardly be possible to recognize implicit rules without having explicit ones in front of oneself, which can then be compared with candidates for an implicit rule—"rules" here are taken to be synonymous with norms.

[170] On the problem of retroactive norms, see below, pp. 192–93.

[171] Blumenberg (n 23), *Theorie der Unbegrifflichkeit*, p. 76 (highlighted in original, translation by AH).

for a positive surprise, as the own normative demands and reality coincide in it, even if unexpectedly so. The possibility of denying reality thus marks the departing point of every normative practice. Affirmation as a normative form always builds on negation. The recognition that something has been realized is only conceivable under the condition of its possible negation, that is, on condition of its not being realized. Affirmation is reflection upon a negation having been omitted, not vice versa. The base operation of the normative is negative. It rejects the world in its current state.[172] Without this operation, norms are inconceivable.

6. *Norms and Facts*

6.1 Dichotomy or Distinction?

At two points along the way we have encountered reasons to doubt that the normative and factual sides of a practice can be clearly distinguished from one another: at the fluid transitions from perception, intention, and affirmation in determining a realizing marker, and also in the dense entanglement of norms and facts in the process of applying norms. Some doubts seem granted concerning the question if norms and facts can be categorically distinguished, but this does not necessarily lead to our giving up on this distinction; without the distinction, there could be no meaningful critique of the dichotomy.[173] But we would like to know more precisely what exactly is being distinguished when we observe the entanglement of norms and facts in social practice.

We hear the following argument from neopragmatic philosophy: if we could neatly distinguish norms and facts, then norms would no longer participate in the rationality standards which we accept for the establishment of facts.[174] That is because, according to this model, a norm would then consist of a truth-apt factual statement and an evaluation that could not be rationalized.[175] As such, the practice of the normative would become idiosyncratic in a way that we cannot observe in practice. The objection is indeed significant but does it not look eerily similar to our two-part notion of a norm consisting of a possibility and a marking?

This is not the case, for precisely two reasons, each of which concerns one of the features of our notion of a norm. For one, the affirmation—the realizing marker—does not practically need rationalization but it is open toward it. The model developed here does not preclude norms from being convincingly argued for or justified,

[172] Hauke Brunkhorst, "Touching the Void—Kritische Theorie als logischer Negativismus" Paper 2013, pp. 22–5.

[173] Hilary Putnam, *The Collapse of the Fact/Value Dichotomy and Other Essays*, Cambridge, Mass. 2002, pp. 9 ff.

[174] McDowell, "Non-Cognitivism and Rule-Following" pp. 207 ff., 212 ff.

[175] Ibid., pp. 200 ff.

but rather simply maintains that this is not always expected of social norms, that it does not always occur, and that it would not always be useful. And even if the justification of norms reveals commonalities with the justification of statements of fact, it does not follow that a science akin to physics could be developed out of normative arguments.[176]

The second reason is that the affirmation of a norm does precisely not refer to a fact but rather to a possibility. We are thus not assuming a positivism of facts here, but instead are mindful of the many uncertainties surrounding "facts," and of norms being an important form of dealing with this uncertainty.

Even if norms and facts are entangled with each other, it does not follow that arguments within this context would not have to abide by certain rules and cannot fail.[177] Even if one has good reasons for doubting the strict Is/Ought distinction, drawing an "ought" from an "is" always requires a justification. The following is concerned with a critique of arguments that, from the insight into the entanglement of the factual and the normative, seek to extract more normativity than is possible and appropriate.

6.2 Hybrid Concepts

Hilary Putnam speaks of a "collapse of the fact/value dichotomy."[178] But what is meant by "collapse," and what is meant by "dichotomy"? For one, Putnam has to resort to the *distinction* of facts and values in order even to be able to describe its collapse. What is more, terms in which normative and descriptive elements converge, may well—and at times usefully—be analyzed with an eye toward these two aspects. We now want to do this with two examples. Putnam's example is the term "cruel," which both describes and evaluates a certain behavior.[179] Leaving ontological problems aside,[180] there is nothing stopping us from analyzing this term. We call someone cruel who gains pleasure from the suffering of others.[181] Strictly speaking, no necessary evaluative element is contained in the concept of "cruelty" itself.[182] A sadistic person might well employ it with honest recognition as a

[176] Hilary Putnam, *Reason, Truth, and History*, Cambridge, Mass. 1981, pp. 145 f.

[177] Alisdair MacIntyre, "Hume on 'Is' and 'Ought'" in: *The Philosophical Review*, LXVIII (1959), pp. 451–68, here p. 463.

[178] Putnam (n 173), *Collapse of the Fact/Value Dichotomy*, pp. 28–45; see also the formulation in Putnam, "Are Moral and Legal Values Made or Discovered?" in: *Legal Theory* 1 (1995), pp. 5–19, here p. 12.

[179] Putnam (n 173), *Collapse of the Fact/Value Dichotomy*, pp. 34–45.

[180] One can certainly agree with Putnam that it does not speak against a term that it appears ontologically unthinkable, see Id., p. 39, referring to Mackie's critique of such awkward grands (John L. Mackie, *Ethics: Inventing Right and Wrong*, London 1977, pp. 38–42).

[181] This is only a more recent meaning among many others: *Deutsches Wörterbuch von Jacob und Wilhelm Grimm*, Leipzig 1958, Vol. 4, Sec. I, Part 5, Cols. 2200.

[182] The term could even live up to content-neutral standards for norms, at least according to Allan Gibbard, *Wise Choices, Apt Feelings*, Oxford 1992, pp. 196 ff.

positive description of another sadist. But the term is easy to analyze on both readings. It describes a certain disposition, and on Putnam's reading it also marks said disposition as negative. Even if we could identify many terms with more complex relationships between their description and evaluation,[183] this would not prove the impossibility of analyzing them with the help of other concepts.

One might object that the word "cruel" is only properly understood by those who feel the moral and emotional distance that accompanies it. The proper usage of such hybrid or "thick" concepts,[184] so runs the theory, presumes a participatory perspective, that is, membership in a community in which it is employed.[185] This argument is well placed as a defensive strategy against highly formalized arguments for ideas of universal norms and values, because it carries the proper insight that there is no Archimedean point from which one could disassemble all hybrid concepts into normative and factual components. However, there is also no Archimedean point from which we could determine whether or to which degree we belong to a certain community. The presumed community in the argument seems to be rather unrealistically homogenous and to deny the normality of contradictory practices. I can understand a purely descriptive use of "cruel" by a sadist without having to incorporate this usage myself. He and I could belong to the same community, even if we are divided on elementary moral evaluations. We also do not know the degree to which the knowledge that we need in order to analyze a concept has to rely on normative versus factual reality, the distinction of which is still permitted. It thus holds that the possibility of failure in analyzing concepts provides no argument against attempting such analysis.

A completely different example of hybridity is provided to us by the magisterium of Catholic ecclesiology. On its own reading, the Church is both "community of faith, hope and love" *and* "visible structure."[186] It is only the one side—the "community"—that can seamlessly refer to God and be understood normatively. The other—the "structure"—acts under the conditions of the sinful world to which it belongs and remains reliant on the fact of a partially morally degraded church. In the same spot, it states that the church is a "complex reality that grows together out of human and divine elements."[187] From the outset, this formulation of conciliar

[183] The term "progress" would be a better candidate for illustrating Putnam's argument.

[184] The English term is "thick concepts" (Note by translator: Möllers' use of the German term *dicht* also denotes "dense" in English), compare with the distinction by Bernard Williams, *Ethics and the Limits of Philosophy*, London 2011, pp. 143–5; Putnam (n 173), *Fact/Value Dichotomy*, pp. 34–43.

[185] We find this argument in McDowell (n 174), "Non-Cognitivism" p. 210 ff, and in Korsgaard (n 165), *Sources of Normativity*, pp. 71–4.

[186] *Lumen Gentium Dogmatische Konstitution über die Kirche*" in: Karl Rahner and Herbert Vorgrimler (eds), *Kleines Konzilskompendium*, Freiburg 2008, pp. 123–200, here pp. 130–2, esp. p. 130. On the twofold nature of the Church, see concisely two representatives of the magisterium: Gerhard Ludwig Müller, *Katholische Dogmatik*, Freiburg 2010 (Special edn), p. 577; Walter Kasper, *Katholische Kirche*, Freiburg 2011, pp. 74–6.

[187] *Lumen Gentium* (n 186), ibid. (Translation by AH).

dogma is oriented toward suspending this distinction in such a manner that it doesn't completely eviscerate in light of this suspension. Catholic theology can neither allow itself to justify everything that happens in the Church as divinely sanctioned, nor can it sacrifice a normative notion of Church that extends beyond the Church's empirical self-portrayal. Neither, finally, can it do without the divine and secular sides of the church. This solution does greater justice to the fact/value problem than does Putnam's "collapse." The synthesis provided in the last citation underscores that the church, which a Catholic Christian encounters, can be described by means of a distinction, but not in terms of separation. Both elements of the notion of church are even less capable of being isolated from each other than in the previous example, and nonetheless it is the distinction of the two elements which enables a sufficiently rich description in the first place. Of course, many questions remain, as they always do in the case of a reform discussion: which parts of the church can be accorded to which aspect, and for which reasons? Not least, the distinction also allows us to address the unattainable character of its normative pretense.

This can be further illustrated by an example. If the Church consists of a spiritual and a secular side, and if the spiritual side also carries the normative burden, then this could have consequences for the organization of the Church. For the spiritual side of the Church can only be understood as a unit. Does this not suggest that the Church should be constructed as a unit and be centrally organized? This line of argument continues to be fiercely debated within the curia.[188] This is of interest for our own considerations as the content of double conceptuality entails normative consequences for the Church's actual organization, if it is assumed that the unitary notion of the Church indeed necessitates to be realized in a unitary organization.[189] Without stepping into these discussions too deeply, we can say that they unfold along three lines of inquiry as follows. Does the universal church have precedence over local churches? How does the socially operating, empirically visible Church relate to the normative-spiritual one? What implication does a response to the first two questions have for the concrete organization of the Church among pope, curia, dioceses, and local churches? Here, the descriptive and normative indeed are entwined, as it cannot

[188] Compare, on the one hand, Walter Kasper, "Zur Theologie und Praxis des bischöflichen Amtes" in: Werner Schreer and Georg Steins (eds), *Auf neue Art Kirche sein*, München 1999, pp. 32–48, here pp. 41–4; on the other hand Joseph Ratzinger, "Die große Gottesidee ›Kirche‹ ist keine ideologische Schwärmerei" in: *Frankfurter Allgemeine Zeitung*, 12 December 2000, p. 46. Summarily: Kilian McDowell, "The Ratzinger/Kasper Debate: The Universal Church and Local Churches" in: *Theological Studies* 63 (2002), pp. 227–50. What appears to serve as inspiration for both sides is the critique of national conferences of bishops in: Henri de Lubac, *Quellen kirchlicher Einheit*, Einsiedeln 1974, pp. 81–90.

[189] This does not mean that there cannot be other arguments for or against a centralized church organization, such as in Matthew 16, 18 ff. Here, we are concerned with the argumentation that begins with hybrid concepts.

be excluded that certain spiritual contents can only be expressed by means of a certain practice. This is particularly the case with the treatment of sacraments, as the Eucharist is exclusively celebrated in particular local parishes, never by the Church as a whole.[190] While people agree that the normative and empirical sides are to be distinguished from each other, it remains disputed both whether something follows for its spiritual notion as a result of the historical practice of the church, and whether something specific follows from the spiritual notion for the constitution of the Church. It is obvious that the spiritual Church is realized in the social organization of the Catholic Church,[191] but it remains unclear when and how.

Concerning social practice, both examples give rise to the question of how to recognize the normative marking. In the first example, it remains implicit; it has to be analyzed out of the term "cruel." In the second case, it is made explicit by the reference to God, however its scope is disputed. This becomes concrete in the ceaselessly debated question which institutions are necessary from a theological standpoint, and which aren't. In the permanent negotiation of this question, a marking—to be imputed to God—is made explicit.

What can we draw from this analysis? Hybrid concepts do not have to constitute a naturalistic fallacy.[192] On the contrary, they can make the intertwined relationship between facts and norms explicit and nurture them for further discursive engagement. For this, of course, it is necessary to maintain the assumption of a border between facts and norms, even if the question of its precise location cannot be satisfyingly clarified. Hybrid concepts that evade all analysis, even analysis that only claims a preliminary and tentative character, by contrast, can no longer be recognized as normative. They even go on actively to conceal the source of their normative pretense. No-one seems to be responsible for their authorization. As we will see at the end of this book, this proves in turn to be a normative problem in its own right. At this point, it at least reduces their utility for helpful analysis.

Do concepts that combine the descriptive and normative with each other in a certain way provide a more precise description of social norms since social practice itself does not neatly distinguish the two elements? Indeed, many social theories hold that any fruitful empirical study of normative practices would have to call the distinction into question. They insist that theories which heavily emphasize the distinction between facts and norms by doing so lose sight of reality. We will now turn to such theories.

[190] Critically, concerning this aspect: de Lubac (n 188), *Quellen kirchlicher Einheit*, pp. 50–4.

[191] Compare once more the formulations in *Lumen Gentium* (n 186), pp. 130–2.

[192] On this, Birnbacher (n 20), *Analytische Einführung in die Ethik*, pp. 363–9.

6.3 Normativity of Historical Progression: Rational Reconstruction I

An initial example is provided by the notion of "normative reconstruction," as exemplified by the social-philosophical considerations of Axel Honneth,[193] whose line of inquiry into the operating conditions of social norms comes very close to our own. Honneth investigates the reality of social norms, and the procedure of normative reconstruction is aimed at identifying those routines and institutions that are indispensable for the reproduction of a social practice.[194] Normative reconstruction thus denotes a process of thought that wants to grant its due to the world as it is, and thus seeks to unearth traces of normativity purely from within the existing world, in clear contrast to deontic theories, which seek to develop normative criteria on a blue print, detached from the world. Programmatically, Honneth maintains: "One of the greatest limitations, under which political philosophy currently suffers, is the detachment from social analysis, and thus the fixation on purely normative principles."[195]

The process of normative reconstruction traces historical developments in which a norm factually materialized. It establishes a history in which, in the process of its realization, the normativity of the norm is established. Consequently, Honneth's central notion of social freedom can only be justified, if incompletely, as one of realized freedom. If a social institution is "indispensable for the reproduction of a social practice," then according to Honneth, it is thereby marked as normative. Social, actually experienced freedom is thus to be understood as a precondition for other forms of freedom. We can make practical use of these freedoms only if we are brought up in relations of social freedom.[196]

But the normative reconstruction provides no criterion for which aspects of a historical process can be taken to be normatively successful and which cannot. For Honneth, historical facts serve as evidence for such success or failure. What seems to ultimately serve as the criterion is the "social" itself, in which freedom is realized, and in which it, as the substratum of realized normativity, cannot err. In this way, Honneth looks back on the beginnings of National Socialism and remarks

[193] On the origin of this figure and its justification, Daniel Gaus, "Rationale Rekonstruktion als Methode politischer Theorie zwischen Gesellschaftskritik und empirischer Politikwissenschaft" in: *Politische Vierteljahresschrift* 54 (2013), pp. 231–55. But of course, norms can also be reconstructed by other methods and according to divergent models of rationality: Geoffrey Brennan, Lina Eriksson, Robert E. Goodin, and Nicholas Southwood, *Explaining Norms*, Oxford 2013, Chapter 6, not without skepticism regarding their explanatory value.

[194] Axel Honneth, *Das Recht der Freiheit. Grundriß einer demokratischen Sittlichkeit*, Berlin 2011, pp. 23, 106.

[195] Ibid., p. 14.

[196] Even if Honneth's claim should hold, that is that negative freedom and the institutions which realize it depend on social freedom, then the normative value of freedom would not be able to be reconstructed with its help alone. It would remain presumed. This is no trivial point, particularly concerning how freedom normatively relates to equality. Concisely on this: Ibid., p. 35, fn. 1.

that after 1933 "the democratic majority was at once drawn into the horrors of the Second World War ignited by Germany."[197] Here, it is not so much the kind of explanation of National Socialism that is of interest, but rather the place of the normative in the historical assessment. Social freedom could not be realized in the "seizure of power," this would seem obvious. But how does this line up with the claim that freedom only justifies itself in its social realization, while this realization requires social acceptance? This only works if we hold that there was no normatively relevant social acceptance of the Nazi seizure of power. But this responds to the empirically open question of factual acquiescence to the system with a normative presumption. This is a conclusion from a "should" to an "is," a reversed naturalistic fallacy. An argument that first draws on reality then immunizes itself against it. On such an account, the shift to National Socialism could not have been a voluntary act of majorities; otherwise, social freedom would have been expressed in it. With this reversal of the explanatory direction, how I recognize social freedom in historical reality becomes questionable. Normativity is not explained, but rather the explanation is normativized. The theory has to select events from a historical development according to normative criteria, which themselves, according to the theory, should only arise out of the historical development itself.

6.4 Normativity of Generic Terms

This conception of the normative further becomes doubtful when taking a not necessarily historicizing view on social institutions, such as the market or family.[198] We can either view these institutions as specific realizations of traditions and recognition structures which themselves are normatively marked. In this case, they contain no immanent normative value. Or we refer to such institutions by a notion that is both descriptive and positively evaluative. The concept "family" then identifies family with successful family, whereas an unsuccessful family would not fall under the concept of family.[199] Aside from the open question of why generic concepts such as family or market should at all be normatively charged in the first place, this strategy gives rise to various problems.

For one, though the semantic ambiguity that arises from a conception, in which a bad family is not considered a family, or a bad State is not considered a State, may be systematically trivial, these ambiguities, however, are quite difficult to navigate in practice. North Korea is a State, and it is even useful to describe it as a State, in order to compare it with other States. It is precisely this comparability, which is

[197] Ibid., p. 598. For an attempt to resist a structurally overcharged explanation of Hitler's power grasp: Hans Boldt, "Januar 1933" in: *Der Staat*, 50 (2011), pp. 608–20.
[198] Honneth (n 194), *Recht der Freiheit*, pp. 277–316.
[199] Rahel Jaeggi, *Kritik von Lebensformen*, Berlin 2013, pp. 182–99.

fundamental to every substantive description of examples of a genre, that is made more difficult by a normativization of a generic concept. For a theory that values giving an account rich in reality, this poses a problem.[200]

If, however, one assumes that even bad States are still States, then the question arises as to how these can be recognized as States. The historical development of a successful exemplar of this genre should help us give an answer. The unity of the concept is derived from a "history of deformation,"[201] in the process of which this institution could not uphold its original normative pretenses. Despite the fact that the normative and descriptive are suddenly differentiated in this process, it is remarkable that this strategy only allows for histories of decline. A bad State could be described as the continuation of a good one, but describing a good one as a continuation of a bad one seems utterly impossible. For conceptual reasons then, German history would have to narrow its scope to the time between 1919 and 1945. Here, too, the normativization of the concept shapes its descriptive power.

If normativity did indeed presuppose social success, then the failure of immanently positive institutions could only be explained by external factors.[202] How would such an institution fail on its own if its positive character was precisely constituted and defined by its own durability and capacity to reproduce itself? If a family fails, it was not a successful example of a family, but if it wasn't a successful example, was it even, according to above's reasoning, a family? And if there are no obvious historical examples of a successful institutional practice, how can I even include this institution in my catalog of institutions of social freedom?[203] The market would be an example of this. The normative charging of social institutions carries with itself a conceptual logic, which has devastating implications for every social-scientific empiricism. For the desire to conclude—as a matter of conceptual truth—that a certain kind of institution can only fail due to external reasons excludes from the outset every empirical rebuttal. And it remains unclear how the institution is to be isolated from its environment, such that this thesis could ever be positively proven.

Let us compare this with Michael Thompson's considerations on the construction of generic concepts in biology. Is an assessment normative which classifies a three-legged animal to the category "horse" and simultaneously notes that the missing of a leg does not represent and constitute the category? If an existence appropriate to the species in question is part of what defines the concept of a horse, including the possibility of galloping on a pasture, in which a three-legged horse is lacking, then the answer would have to be affirmative. The classification as "horse"

[200] Correspondingly, Jaeggi's formulations come across as indecisive in light of this challenge, ibid., p. 183.

[201] Ibid., pp. 190 ff.

[202] Here, norms also always seem to be implicitly confounded with the sanctions of norms, which highlight the social consequences of breaking a norm.

[203] Honneth (n 194), *Recht der Freiheit*, III.2.

is the classification as belonging to "well developed horse." A horse *should* have four legs. A giraffe *should* have a long neck.[204]

Taking a generic concept as normative certainly does not allow us, as Thompson rightly remarks, to extract more out of it than what is meant by our practice of species determination.[205] Horses have four legs. This horse does not have four legs. The attempt to normativize this observation provides no further substance to the concept "horse." Thus it stands that two questions need to be distinguished: the difficult question, which interests Thompson, concerning the definition of certain kinds of generic concepts that are appropriate to the phenomena they classify and the question of the concept's normativity. Responding to the first question, which isn't of primary importance for our purposes, it may be necessary to define categories that include a temporal element, for example categories that incorporate a typical course of life of the exemplars in question. The second question we should negate along with Thompson. Even if the concept of family itself would yield criteria for a good family, the criteria for belonging to the category "family" would be different from those for its evaluation, because even if one wanted to believe in the immanent normativity of this generic concept, it would remain unclear whether it actually brings about blended normative-descriptive propositions. The observation that this is a bad family can simply be divided into the two statements: "This group of persons belongs to the category of family" and "This group is a failed example of the category family."[206]

The figure of normativity being inherent in a concept thus is faced with great difficulties, unless one honestly admits its inherent normative pretense, thus limiting oneself to a purely functional understanding, but even this quickly reaches certain limits. Of course one could claim that a car with an operable engine is "better" than one with a broken engine,[207] in so far as the car of concern serves the purpose of transportation, as opposed to standing around in a museum for its beauty. But this conclusion doesn't follow from the concept "car." It is the functional perspective that alone carries the normative claim. If someone talks of a "good" contract killer, everyone would probably still understand what is meant by this. But for ambivalent practices, for plastic surgeons or lawyers in authoritative systems, this becomes unclear and similar ambiguities would probably appear within social institutions such as families or political communities. If we observe that in the twentieth century the genre 'family history' for large parts coincides with the genre 'mafia movie', then this can be taken as a strong hint that there is little to gain from the immanent

[204] Jaeggi, (n 199), *Kritik von Lebensformen*, p. 171.

[205] Michael Thompson, *Life and Action. Elementary Structures of Practice and Practical Thought*, Cambridge, Mass. 2008, pp. 73 f.

[206] This is precisely what also happens in formulations that claim that norms become effective in life forms, in which a normative content is isolated after all, see Jaeggi, (n 199), *Kritik von Lebensformen*, p. 151.

[207] We see an analysis of these kinds of arguments, which distinguishes between predicative and attributive usage, in Judith Jarvis Thomson, *Normativity*, Chicago 2008, pp. 19–33.

normativity of the concept of family, particularly because these movies tend to take the family structures quite seriously. The normative quality of a family cannot in any helpful way be determined by recourse to the concept of 'family' as a genre.

6.5 Naturally Good?

We may maintain that a horse with three legs, or a giraffe with a short neck is incomplete. But what do we think of a person with only one leg? Hopefully it is indisputable that we would categorize this being as a human being, even if for some even this doesn't seem to be self-evident. It certainly is not self-evident if the functional aspect of the category human is normatively charged. Then the untypical and the impractical become normatively significant. To this, one might respond that the danger of an implicit functional or moral devaluation of a one-legged person has nothing to do with the normativization of the concept, for a purely descriptive notion of human being would ultimately operate even more fatally. In that case, a person with one leg would not be an incomplete human, but no human at all. But this objection rests on a fallacy, since it at the same time presupposes and disputes the classification as human.

It would be more consistent to limit the concept of human being to denote the belonging to a certain genre, that is, to treat the concept as a generic term. Then we would simply have to affirm the question of whether a one-legged person falls under the concept or not. A normative reading, by contrast, would claim to say something about the thriving as a human in addition to its belonging to the generic category. This would open up space to employ a range of meanings in between—a field of unsuccessful forms, some of which might include dying young, or missing a leg.[208] Such a normative reading thus tends to invite misuse, reducing the descriptive and delineative value of the concept and obscuring the reason for the normative pretense invoked by it.

If the normativity of human existence consists in its serving no end, then we could deduce from the concept of human that classification under the concept should not be made to depend on any condition of thriving.[209] It is not about whether humans have any value but rather whether the categorical concept "human being" contains this value or whether we have to add something else to the categorization: freedom, reason, creation.[210] With Thompson, it remains that

[208] Exemplarily, see the formulation in Sebastian Rödl, "Norm und Natur" in: *Deutsche Zeitschrift für Philosophie* 51 (2003), pp. 99–114, here p. 114: "If a life movement thus terminates, the subject of this movement misses its nature. It deviates from itself."

[209] Immanuel Kant, *Grundlegung zur Metaphysik der Sitten*, Frankfurt/M. 1977, p. 61 (BA 66 ff.).

[210] For a critique of Korsgard's reading of Kant, see the remark by Gerald A. Cohen, "Reason, Humanity, and the Moral Law" in: Korsgard (n 165), *Sources of Normativity*, pp. 167–88, here pp. 172–4. Cohen claims that the Kantian theory overshoots the essence of human nature.

the normative content which we derive from the categorical concept is simply that which we previously have imputed into it.[211]

A strong intuition urges us to view physical health as a normatively positive and primordial phenomenon. This is highly contentious, of course. From an analysis of medical theoretical history, Georges Canguilhem, for one, develops the claim that there can be no genuinely physical definition of health. Health cannot be reduced to blood levels or other measurable parameters. While the medical field of the nineteenth and early twentieth century was able to establish statistical norm values for certain bodily functions, it was, according to him, never able to remint these insights into a normative understanding of healthy and ill. Canguilhem lists two reasons for this. For one, different normality parameters depend on each other; it is frequently impossible to assess them in isolation, but only in the context of other measurement values. Secondly, the measurement values are tied in with the respective life situations of those whose values were measured, including their age and other factors. Finally, according to Canguilhem, being able to adjust to changing circumstances is part of what makes a healthy life: "Health is a margin of tolerance for the inconstancies of the environment."[212] Ultimately, health can only be determined by reference to the realm of action and the needs for adjustment of an individual person.[213]

The value of these considerations reveals itself in its confrontation with Philippa Foot's theory, which stems from the Aristotelian tradition and locates a certain normative content in the natural predispositions of human beings.[214] Her notion of a "natural goodness" is not meant biologically, and thus does not stand in direct confrontation to Canguilhem's critique of a physical conception of health.[215] However, it traces the notion of goodness back to characteristics of categories from which normative principles can be deduced.[216] Regarding such characteristics of human beings, Foot names human diligence and persistence in the context of finding food and practices such as love and friendship.[217] For her, the

[211] Foot, *Natural Goodness, Natural Goodness*, Oxford 2001, pp. 133 ff., and Rödl (n 208), "Norm und Natur" p. 108, quote Thompson in support of their view, but see above pp. 133 ff. and fn. 205.

[212] Canguilhem, *The Normal and the Pathological*, New York 1991, p. 197 transl. of *Le normal et le pathologique*, p. 130: "La santé, c'est une marge de tolerance des infidelités du milieu."

[213] On newer medical-theoretical discussions, see Thomas Schramme (ed.), *Krankheitstheorien*, Berlin 2011. The compiled contributions (especially from Schramme, Boorse, and Hucklenbroich) tend to bring together biological, individual, and social criteria, under certain circumstances species-specifically, in order to forge the concept of sickness

[214] Philippa Foot (n 211), pp. 38–51.

[215] Michael Hagner, "Georges Canguilhem und das Problem der Medizin" in: Georges Canguilhem, *Schriften zur Medizin*, Zürich 2013, pp. 115–43, here, pp. 132 ff., shows that this is not to be conflated with a critique of modern conventional medicine.

[216] The same goes for a modernized Catholic teaching of natural law, one which has detached from naturalisms and conceives of nature as "realization of nature": Franz-Josef Bormann, "'Natur' als Prinzip ethischer Orientierung?" in: Christoph Böttigheimer et al. (eds), *Sein und Sollen des Menschen*, Münster 2009, pp. 335–56, here p. 353.

[217] Foot (n 211), *Natural Goodness*, p. 44.

rhetorical question arises: "Why then should there be surprise at the suggestion that the status of certain dispositions as virtues should be determined by quite general facts about human beings?"[218] That is, if human beings generally have the tendency to foster friendships, then the justification of human virtues cannot unfold without the inclusion of such characteristics.

Two reactions to Foot's rhetorical question come to mind. The first is that referring to "general facts" obfuscates the problem because are we really dealing with "facts"? For one, this is doubtful concerning the terms "friendship" and "love," as they are not purely descriptive, and it is also not clear in which way they would unfold normatively. Some people might kill out of love, others might lead a virtuous life without love or friendship. The conclusion from the fact of love to the virtuousness of the one loving does not seem necessary.

Secondly, one must pay attention to the *recognizability* of such facts for a theory of social norms. Are we still in the realm of the good when dealing with the friendship between Berlusconi and Putin, or with the love between Bonnie and Clyde? Or do we have to upgrade the theory ad hoc?[219] From the standpoint of the theory, was it even "real" friendship or love? It is not by chance that a formulation by Honneth provokes a similar objection: "Members of a society are treated all the more equally, more confidently, and more comfortably, the more they are tied into the public will formation, the further along the realization of social freedom in personal relationships and economic interactions has progressed."[220] Here, a pre-stabilized harmony is presumed between the personal and the social, the contradictions[221] of which are a standard topic of social sciences and the bourgeois novel.[222] Or are different normative criteria simply being multiplied by their reciprocity, such that, in doubt, they can be relativized if reality no longer follows the model? Whenever things get concrete, the concept of immanent normativity develops a striking sleekness.

One final objection: if we interpret Canguilhem's claim about health in light of Foot's theory, then we would have a notion of health that could be individualized and contextualized, but wouldn't be able to substantially draw

[218] Ibid., p. 45.

[219] This could be shown with Foot's analysis of Nietzsche's treatment of immorality: Foot, ibid., pp. 103–15.

[220] Honneth (n 194), *Recht der Freiheit*, p. 618, similarly pp. 614 ff.

[221] The conflict between institutional roles and the necessary voluntarism of their perception is lucidly described in Michael O. Hardimon, "Role Obligations" in: *The Journal of Philosophy* 91 (1994), pp. 333–63, here p. 343.

[222] Simply see Eva Illouz, *Der Konsum der Romantik*, Frankfurt/M. 2007. Her investigation can be read as a diagnosis of the "social and cultural costs of marketing romantic love," as Axel Honneth does in the preface to this book, ibid., pp. 7–21, here p. 18. But Illouz' study supports neither the assumption that there is a solution to the problem which leaves both sides of the equation unchanged, nor does she justify such a pessimistic reading. Illouz soberly dismisses her proclaimed cultural pessimism in ibid., pp. 318–25. Also see, exemplarily, the analysis of Henrik Ibsen's dramas by Franco Moretti, *Der Bourgeois. Eine Schlüsselfigur der Moderne*, Berlin 2014, pp. 242–67.

on an individual patient's needs without neglecting the need to draw normative criteria from the objective characteristics of the genre. By contrast, Canguilhem's understanding of the medical differentiation between ill and healthy points toward a social realm of possibility tailored to individuals. For him, there simply are no "quite general facts about human beings" that could sufficiently determine a concept that has an affinity toward naturalizing theories, such as health.

For my analysis, this contradiction is significant as it documents the uncertainties of a notion of nature which, even in such an open and reflected formulation such as Foot's, comes up against empirical resistance.[223] Physical nature and self-determination collide in the concept of health. The advantage of Canguilhem's theory lies in the convincing power of his scientific-historical findings being greater than that of the philosophical argument. For him, the argument against a biological notions of health comes about by taking biology—viewed as a purely quantitative and measurable understanding of health—seriously, only to then show that it cannot be maintained, even by those who believe in it. Of immediate concern for us is the distinction between norms and non-norms, the way in which it is constructed, and its effects on the practice of normativity. Our example demonstrates that the individual needs of a patient have higher practical relevance and salience than the supposedly general categorical characteristics of human beings.

No cultural practice has as strong and suggestive an effect on our normative intuitions as does medicine with its distinction between health and illness.[224] It seems impossible to imagine Doctor Rieux, who in Camus' *The Plague* battles the epidemic, thus impersonating the resistance to the German occupation, as a lawyer. It is just as difficult to imagine replacing the medical metaphoric usage in conceiving the good life with a legal one without losing a certain effect, given the latter to be seen as a somewhat grey and morally ambivalent field. However, such metaphoric usage says more about the theory than about the reality of a professional practice which, from cosmetic surgery to the decision about life-extending measures, has more and more problems to solve for which neither obvious moral standards nor recourse to nature are available.

The irony arising from this is worth mentioning. In the name of theories that claim the distinction of norms and facts to be blind to reality, categories of the normative develop, which can no longer capture the normative complexity encountered by factual developments.

[223] Dieter Birnbacher, *Natürlichkeit*, Berlin 2006, pp. 42–56.
[224] This doesn't only imply a metaphorical usage: Susan Sontag, *Illness as Metaphor*, New York 1978.

6.6 Constitutive Norms

Constitutive norms are norms that constitute an object by, for example, defining which actions count as the conclusion of a contract or as a decision. John Rawls employed an analogous category in order to free utilitarian theories from their fixation on actions.[225] According to him, the utility of an action cannot simply result from its consequences, but sometimes only arises due to an institutional framework that extends beyond the individual action. This insight fits with our critique of the misplaced fixation on action which many theories of norms exhibit. John Austin and John Searle, who introduced the term "constitutive norm" to the discourse, are interested in the category for different reasons. They are concerned with the reality-grounding effect of language, that is, that speech acts do not simply refer to something but actually intervene in developments.[226] According to them, a constitutive norm creates a new part of social reality.

Now the question arises as to which normative content constitutive "norms" have, that is whether they are more than a means to more accurately describe social facts. One could claim that the concept "marriage" constitutes an institution and thereby creates a norm. Would we say the same of a norm for screws that determines that only a screw of a certain length and width can be meant by DIN ISO 8676? If yes, then all categorical determinations would be normative. But why *should* a screw accord with this norm? Who would be bound to shape it thus? These kinds of questions are the object of more subtle theoretical debates which seek to establish the normative content of constitutive norms.[227] Now we can imagine that a standard attaches itself to certain duties of action. Whoever uses screws in a building, those who did not accord with a recognized standard can be held liable even though the standard itself is not recognized as a legal rule.[228] But this does not change the fact that the standard, the constitutive "norm" itself, is not a norm, and that the liability norm does not turn into a norm by virtue of referring to the standard.

These problems dissolve when we accept that norms do not have to refer to actions. Then constitutive norms prove to be norms that both define and affirm a condition or an object, that is as concepts with a realizing marker, which express that which ought to be, or in Max Scheler's formulation, a "*Seinsollendes*,"

[225] See John Rawls, "Two Concepts of Rules" in: *The Philosophical Review* 64 (1955), pp. 3–32, here pp. 5–12, who differentiates between practice and an action in this practice.

[226] John R. Searle, *The Construction of Social Reality*, New York 1995, pp. 43–51; John L. Austin, *How to do Things with Words*, Oxford 1975, pp. 53–66.

[227] Thoroughly, Garson Reuter, "Konstitutive Regeln—normative oder nicht? Ein Blick auf ihre Rolle in Praktiken" in: *Normative Orders Working Paper* (03/11), esp. pp. 14–21. Reuter limits himself from the outset to actions when he looks for normative consequences. He can only observe side effects of such rules. We find a clear analysis of the possible action elements in constitutive rules (with other terminology) in Marco Iorio, *Regel und Grund*, Berlin 2011, pp. 106–9.

[228] On these questions, Harm Schepel, *The Constitution of Private Governance*, Oxford 2005, pp. 339–401.

the being of an ought.[229] The difference between a merely descriptive standard, which determines how a certain type of screw is constituted, and a constitutional norm defining marriage as the "permanent union of two persons," consists in the fact that the standard limits itself to determining the object, whereas the determination of marriage in a constitution not only defines this institution, but also affirms it. The order is not indifferent toward marriage but it is toward the screw, even if it applies the screw norm as a vehicle for other norms, such as in tort law.

Thus it would be misguided to deny wholesale any normative status to constitutive norms. It would also be wrong to view them as a weakened form of the normative. The harmless example of an industrial standard, or the widespread reference made in the literature to rules of games, should not make us overlook that constitutive norms are "constitutive," that is they can affect the inclusion or exclusion of actions and people. An example by Navid Kermani shows this.[230] The religious precept not to drink alcohol can be understood either as a command for action or as a constitutive norm. In the latter reading, if I were to drink in spite of the norm, I would no longer be a norm-violating member of the religious community, but rather no longer its member at all. The transgression removes me from the community. The proper understanding of the precept thus depends on the sanction attached to its violation. If this is not explicitly regulated, then this forces us to clarify the status of the norm. In so far as they define communities normatively, constitutive rules can determine membership of these communities and thereby seem more drastic than norms regulating action. The normativity of the constitutive rule arises out of the regulatory context to which the identity refers, this context therefore affirming the object and identity constituted by the rule. It is this difference—between a screw and a religious community—that grounds the different possibilities to normatively charge constitutive rules.

Ultimately, the concept of an action itself can be the object of a constitutive norm, thus constituting an entity or possibility that, at least in liberal orders, is positively affirmed. It is better to act, that is to make use of one's freedom, than to merely drift along. The epitome of a constitutive norm, then, is the Hegelian "Be a person,"[231] a norm that does not demand an action, but rather the condition of possibility for action, the actor.[232]

[229] Max Scheler, *Der Formalismus in der Ethik und die materiale Wertethik*, Halle 1921, pp. 208 ff.

[230] Navid Kermani, *Wer ist Wir?*, München 2010, pp. 17 ff.

[231] Hegel (n 67), *Grundlinien*, § 36.

[232] On the constitution of physical and non-physical actors through norms, Miguel Tamen, *Friends of Interpretable Objects*, Cambridge, Mass. 2001, pp. 97, 105–16; Kelsen (n 114), *Reine Rechtslehre*, pp. 63–71.

6.7 Explanation and Justification: Rational Reconstruction II

Jürgen Habermas provides a different kind of "rational reconstruction," which seeks to bring together explanation and justification.[233] On his reading, the rational reconstruction captures an empirical social practice of justification and makes explicit which normative assumptions the participants in this practice must presume in order for this practice to be meaningful in light of its own premises. This kind of reconstruction is supposed to contribute to explaining and justifying said practice. In this way, both the figure of communicative action[234] and the democratic State under the rule of law[235] can be reconstructed in a kind of rational "simulation."[236] This process intends to point toward a way out of the dilemma of modern normative social theories in which all justification discourse either is dissolved into facts by empirically proceeding social-scientific Enlightenment, or remains in a social vacuum of idealized presuppositions.[237] Compared to Honneth's understanding of reconstruction, which directly refers to functional conditions, this process is less susceptible to a practice's factual conditions for success. If a world worth living in succumbs to systemic imperatives, this does not so much speak against the standards of this world, its failure does not discredit it normatively. In this way, not only is the normative standard liberated, but the curious repercussions to supposed empiricism are avoided, which were at play in Honneth. Habermas' notion certainly corresponds more with a viewpoint on normativity which is oriented toward the possible.

But even on this kind of reading, the rational reconstruction closely ties together the *explanans* and the *explanandum* on the one hand and the *justificans* and the *justificandum* on the other, because the process of rational reconstruction purports to operate *empirically* when observing the self-understanding of participants in communicative action and the democratic State under the rule of law. These self-descriptions, however, themselves are normative. And the standards according to which the reconstruction orients itself follow the criterion of communicative rationality, ultimately the same standard that is being reconstructed in the first place.[238] The concern is not so much the concrete, actual self-understanding

[233] On this, Markus Patberg, "Suprastaatliche Verfassungspolitik und die Methode der rationalen Rekonstruktion" in: *Der Staat* 53 (2014), pp. 401–24; Gaus (n 193), "Rationale Rekonstruktion."

[234] Jürgen Habermas, *Theorie des kommunikativen Handelns*, Frankfurt/M. 1981.

[235] Jürgen Habermas, *Faktizität und Geltung. Beiträge zur Diskurstheorie des Rechts und des demokratischen Rechtsstaats*, Frankfurt/M. 1992.

[236] This expression employed by Patberg (n 233), "Suprastaatliche Verfassungspolitik" p. 417.

[237] Habermas (n 235), *Faktizität und Geltung*, pp. 78–90.

[238] The accusation of circularity is tempting. But the structure seems to owe to the insight that, in reconstructing the justifying measure, we are always already performatively making a contribution to the altering of the justified object, in turn contributing to changing the measure. We can only begin with the practices in which we are already immersed and toward which we already take up a normative stance. We change them when we observe and reflect on them.

of participants but rather what they would have to presume if they were to live up to them. "The reconstruction of *implicitly presumed, counter-factual preconditions* provides an objective measure of evaluation, which is grounded in the observed practices themselves."[239] But where, exactly, in this scheme is a place for empirics if normative constructs are found at both ends of the reconstruction? The risk of this model lies precisely at this point, which Theunissen criticized in the context of Hegel's logic. According to him this logic grants no independent place and being to reality itself vis-à-vis the realm of concepts. Conceptuality thus encroaches upon reality, the material of reality losing its power of resistance, because it lacks the materiality constitutive of "being there," and it lacks the "externality of space and time."[240]

Now, this kind of critique, even if it is justified, is of limited value as the methodical reflection only incompletely determines what actually happens in the course of analysis. From this perspective, Habermas' considerations on constitutionalism and European integration seem a great deal more concrete than those of many other political philosophers, especially of those who criticize him for his normative stance. However, specificity is something other than openness to empiricism. If one considers the reconstruction in *Between Facts and Norms* (*Faktizität und Geltung*), it is striking how little room there is for variance. The immense differences, such as those between the French and American traditions of constitutionalism,[241] or between the German and American understandings of freedom of expression, are sidelined, or more specifically: they are decided in a theory-immanent fashion, for example as in Habermas' ultimately Rousseauian reconstruction of subjective rights.[242] Of course there are reasons for this route, but there remains too little room for empiricism regarding the self-understanding of the participants. Empirics only seem to be accounted for in that Habermas takes self-understandings as his starting point, even if their particularities vanish in the reconstruction's normative rationalizing filter. While the concept of rational reconstruction may be theoretically open to divergent self-understandings, its application cannot always be distinguished from a natural-law-like top-down approach. That could probably only be avoided by explicitly allowing empirical room

[239] Jürgen Habermas, "Hat die Demokratie noch eine epistemische Dimension? Empirische Forschung und normative Theorie" in: Id., *Ach, Europa. Kleine Politische Schriften VI*, Frankfurt/M. 2008, pp. 138–91, here p. 151. The concept of a problem here is—just as it was in the so-called conceptual jurisprudence of the nineteenth century—that of "construction." When does it take, when does it give?

[240] Michael Theunissen, "Begriff und Realität" in: Rolf-Peter Horstmann (ed.), Seminar: *Dialektik in der Philosophie Hegels*, Frankfurt/M. 1978, pp. 324–59, here p. 348.

[241] These are worked through by Hannah Arendt, *Über die Revolution*, München 1974.

[242] This claim refers, on the one hand, to the fact that Habermas rejects a protection of subjective rights which would be separate from the democratic process, and on the other hand, that he does not provide a procedural model that does justice to court procedures. On both, see Christoph Möllers, "Demokratie und Recht" in: Hauke Brunkhorst, Regina Kreide, and Cristina Lafont (eds), *Habermas-Handbuch*, Stuttgart 2009, pp. 254–63, here pp. 257–60.

for contingency of social and institutional developments, and such a space could probably only become visible if one were to argue with more than one possibility, that is if one worked *comparatively* or with alternatives from the outset. A political philosophy, which claims to be open to empirical observation, will thus have to descend into the lowlands of social, systemic, and constitutional comparison. It will, moreover, have to do so at the risk of leaving open the big political questions. That is, in the name of integrity and good procedure, it must refrain from making too far-reaching claims on the substance matter in question. If it does not do the former, the charge of normativism will always catch up with it; if it neglects the latter, then it runs risk that the endeavor at rational reconstruction, from being an element of autonomy, will devolve into a piece of heteronomy due to the theoretical assumptions.

And to what degree does this version of rational reconstruction operate as an *explanation* of social practices? This brings us back to the question of what can be recognized when examining *normative* self-descriptions. Of course, we do not only see mere appearances or illusions. It is both a cognitive deficit and a paternalistic trait of many social theories to dismiss normative self-descriptions as exercises at deluding or deceiving oneself or others. Yet, at times such deception or delusion indeed is present. There also are normative self-descriptions that deviate from Habermas, such as religious or naturalistic ones. As we have seen, both circumstances lead empirical research inspired by Habermas to problems which are then supposedly being solved by lowering the highly demanding criteria of communicative rationality down to very meager expectations of changing preferences. These, however, are clearly insufficient for justifying any political or juridical practice.[243] This radical move is likely due to the ambivalence of the generalizability requirement, against which objections are raised that, for good reason, are diametrically opposed to each other: one side of the critique claims that the requirement yields overly-determined answers, the other side claims the criterion to ultimately remain empty; that is, one side claims that it says too much the other that it says too little.

In the normative practice, generalization only works in an institutional context that sets limits to it. This is no necessary evil but rather the only means for the generalization to become practically relevant. But if the connection between normatively reconstructed self-understanding and actual practice is as multiply mediated as on this model, then its explanatory power becomes uncertain and unreliable for good reasons. For if the strength of this rational-reconstructive model lies in not putting assumptions under the pressure of operative success, then its weakness must lie in merely supplying limited explanatory value in its description of social developments. The normative pretense's gain in autonomy from the actual practice

[243] See above, pp. 33–37.

has to obstruct the description of said practice. This is just another way of stating the dilemma of world-distance and world-immanence of normative standards. It is thus no coincidence that, as a reconstruction of an explicit normative form, the constitutional theory in *Between Facts and Norms* is more consistent and coherent than the social theory developed in the *Theory of Communicative Action*, which presents its own version of the problem through the dichotomy of life world and systemic imperative. In sociological literature, we find the self-critical insight that a theory loses its descriptive value when both the project of modern society's description and its object, namely said society itself, are normatively constituted.[244] Similar skepticism is absent in the realm of social philosophy, when it claims to sharply see certain things by the aid of normatively impregnated concepts.

6.8 An Outlook with Kant

In his legal philosophy and in his writing on perpetual peace, Kant employs the concept of "the permissive norm" (*Erlaubnisgesetz*).[245] It enables a view of the relationship between normative standards and reality, embracing the distinction without ignoring the practical preconditions of realizing norms.[246] This notion of a permissive norm belongs in the realm of law and politics, not morality. It operates under empirical conditions, that is, within the limitations of order brought on by time and space. Permissive norms are rules that allow an otherwise prohibited behavior. In Kant's theory, they are to solve the problem of transitioning into a legal state of affairs, that is one regulated by general laws. Under the conditions of limited *space*, the appropriation of objects can only be of a *preliminarily nature*.[247] Even though the seizure of objects and territories as such does not establish rights, it cannot immediately be brought into question by the legal order without risking a violent conflict, or leading to the disputed object to be unavailable for any use. Even the unlawful status quo thus deserves the preliminary protection of a nascent legal order. For that matter, the legal order cannot establish itself if it does not provisionally protect the current allocation of rights and goods, as it is, in order to

[244] See the analysis by Armin Nassehi, *Der soziologische Diskurs der Moderne*, Frankfurt/M. 2006, pp. 335–42.

[245] Immanuel Kant, (n 109) § 2; Id., "Zum ewigen Frieden. Ein philosophischer Entwurf" in: Id., *Schriften zur Anthropologie, Geschichtsphilosophie, Politik und Pädagogik I*, Frankfurt/M. 1977, pp. 195–251, here p. 201, fn. (BA 16).

[246] The decisive breakthrough to this understanding, despite many contested interpretive questions concerning details, is found in Reinhard Brandt, "Das Erlaubnisgesetz, oder: Vernunft und Geschichte in Kants Rechtslehre" in: Id. (ed), *Rechtsphilosophie der Aufklärung*, Berlin 1982, pp. 233–85, here pp. 244–9. On the prehistory of the concept, Matthias Kaufmann, "Was erlaubt das Erlaubnisgesetz—und wozu braucht man es Kant?" in: *Jahrbuch für Recht und Ethik* 13 (2005), pp. 195–219.

[247] Kant, *Metaphysik der Sitten/Rechtslehre*, § 7. This interpretation is found in Katrin Flikschuh, *Kant and Modern Political Philosophy*, Cambridge 2000, pp. 121–34. Differently in Wolfgang Kersting, *Wohlgeordnete Freiheit*, Frankfurt/M. 1993, pp. 233–41.

then normatively examine this order of things after its establishment on the basis of general legal principles.[248] In another context, and following the theoretical model of preliminary judgment, Kant develops a program for a reform-minded, incremental application of normative principles.[249] The question of what follows in political practice from the principle of law, that is from an order constituted by general rules, is thus subject to an additional line of investigation with uncertain outcome.

From the practical contingencies under which social norms such as the law must operate, Kant thereby draws a twofold conclusion. He does so by placing the application of the legal principles under a caveat without modifying the standards to be applied. The permissive norm adds a further level to the distinction between legal norm and reality, however leaving the norm itself untouched. Instances of unlawfulness remain recognizable under real conditions, even if they at the same time are to be practically tolerated. This new level owes its existence to the factual conditions of legal enforceability by the aid of resources that are limited and thus prone to conflict. This construction comes significantly closer to our view of things than do the other approaches examined in this section. For Kant acknowledges the real conditions of a normative practice as relevant without thereby allowing the normative standard to become unrecognizable. Despite all their differences not only in their approaches but also concerning the problems being approached, Kant and Habermas share an approach to the relationship between normative and factual aspects that is able to navigate between two challenging cliffs: the task of on the one hand keeping up the distinction, and on the other avoiding its hypostatization into a strict separation.

[248] Regarding the degree to which Kant seriously envisioned such an examination, see Kaufmann (n 246), "Was erlaubt das Erlaubnisgesetz" pp. 217–19.

[249] Thus runs the thesis of Brandt (n 246), "Erlaubnisgesetz" pp. 247 ff., 249–55.

Interlude II: Do the Esthetics of Art Fall within the Realm of the Normative?

1. *Esthetic Norms—Normative Esthetics*

Up until this point in the book, examples from art and esthetic theory have accompanied our argumentation, yet without further justification.[1] But does art as a practice, and esthetics as its theoretical reflection even belong in an investigation of the normative? For one, the normativization of art certainly seems to have played a role in the history of esthetic theory. In an initial approach, we can distinguish internal and external esthetic norms. Internal norms refer to immanent esthetic criteria; they define the success of an esthetic product. External norms refer to a normative content within art, which extends beyond it, for example toward social utility or individual pleasure: *prodesse et delectare*. Even at first sight, it is not easy to say whether this normative excess, which is external to art, can be grasped in esthetic categories, or whether it needs to be expressed in other terms, such as political or moral categories. Neither kind of normativity are self-evident for esthetic theory, they have rather been viewed with suspicion and their meaning is frequently denied. And yet, esthetic practice and its theory cannot get by without norms. This will be argued in what follows.

But art-esthetic phenomena aren't only of interest because norms are of import for them but rather because social norms share commonalities with esthetic manifestations. These share with social norms a distance to the factual, the pretense of a degree of independence from the world. As such, esthetic theory gets entangled in ontological challenges that are meaningful for a theory of norms as well. The investigation of this specific constellation common to both these practices could also speak against a widespread intuition which, in taking up a—probably misunderstood—early Romantic heritage,[2] ties norms to duty and bondage and art to creativity and freedom. Comparing and contrasting these two practices could thus help to mark more precisely the difference in their normative pretenses and import. Whenever we distinguish between esthetic products and social norms in the following, this is not meant as an exclusionary distinction. An esthetic product can serve as a social norm, and vice versa. The reference of the terms I use will

[1] In its meaning and origin, "esthetics" denotes a theory of sensory perception, not necessarily a theory of art. In this sense, art theory does not necessarily have to be esthetics in the narrow sense but it is often generally described as such. In the following, we are interested in the theory of art.

[2] On early Romantic poets' love of normative institutions, see Theodore Ziolkowski, German Romanticism and its Institutions, Princeton 1990, pp. 64–137.

The Possibility of Norms. Christoph Möllers, Published by Oxford University Press (2020) under licence; © this translation, Alex Holznienkemper; © the original German edition, Suhrkamp Verlag Berlin.
DOI: 10.1093/oso/9780198827399.001.0001

be the respective object in question, but in their specific function (as either social norm or esthetic product).

2. *Between Representation and Intervention*

A norm is the affirmation of the realization of a possibility. The category of the possible is not foreign to art theory. Artistic production can be understood as the measuring of a realm of possibility. Admittedly, with the opening up of the concept of art, this realm orients itself less and less toward a reference to reality but instead presents the possible through the artistic product itself.

In his Poetics, Aristotle remarks that it is not the task of the poet to describe what really happened but rather that which could happen according to the criteria of the probable and the possible. This, according to Aristotle, distinguishes the poet who, like the philosopher, has to engage with the things that are general, from the historical chronologist.[3] For Aristotle, a poetic product's form commands a certain composition according to criteria of possibility, which has a higher truth value—one freed from the contingency of the factual—than does historiography. As a reference to possibility, this insight remains of interest under changed circumstances,[4] even if we have both a different concept of reality[5] and altered notions of how an artwork is to engage with reality.[6]

Earlier on, we introduced the concept of a norm by means of the idea of the *direction of fit*. We adjust descriptions to the world, but we adjust our world to norms. In contrast to descriptions, normative and artistic practices explicitly conjure up alternative worlds that draw their appropriateness neither from their correspondence to the world nor from the claim that the world should correspond to them. Using an expression from Niklas Luhmann, we can say that both operate with a "doubling of reality."[7]

[3] Aristotle, *Poetics*, 1451a37–1452a11. On this, Dorothea Frede, "Die Einheit der Handlung" in: Ottfried Höffe (ed.), *Aristoteles' Poetik*, Berlin 2009, pp. 105–21, here pp. 114–19. On the role of the figure as carrier of possibilities: Arbogast Schmitt, "Teleologie und Geschichte bei Aristoteles oder: Wie kommen nach Aristoteles Anfang, Mitte und Ende in die Geschichte?" in: Karlheinz Stierle and Rainer Warning (eds), *Das Ende. Figuren einer Denkform*, Poetik und Hermeneutik XVI, Munich 1996, pp. 528–63, here pp. 531–6.

[4] Niklas Luhmann even employs it as the ultimate determiner of art's function: as the "proof of order's compulsion in the realm of the merely possible" (*Die Kunst der Gesellschaft*, Frankfurt/M. 1995, p. 238).

[5] Hans Blumenberg, "Wirklichkeitsbegriff und Möglichkeit des Romans" in: Id., *Ästhetische und metaphorologische Schriften*, Frankfurt/M. 2001, pp. 47–73, here pp. 49–55.

[6] An information-theoretical esthetics that applies to all art forms operating with internal probabilities is provided by Umberto Eco, *The Open Work*, Cambridge, Mass. 1989, pp. 45–58.

[7] Niklas Luhmann, *Die Religion der Gesellschaft*, Frankfurt/M. 2000, pp. 58–64; Joachim Ritter speaks of the "double-tracked nature" (*Zweigleisigkeit*) of interpreting the world: *Vorlesungen zur philosophischen Ästhetik*, Göttingen 2010, p. 33.

Neither in the realm of esthetics nor in the realm of social norms does the doubling of reality depend on an aspiration to change the world. In as far as an esthetic practice—according to Aristotle—doesn't have to be limited to describing the world as it is,[8] so social norms needn't only be oriented toward intervening in the world. They can aim at mere conservation, at maintaining or reproducing ordered conditions, that is not at changing the world but at holding up an esthetically corrective mirror: a gesture that is ambivalent when the mirror is used to correct reality.[9] We can see a comparable principle expressed in the idea of corrective justice, from which natural law rules of justice, social norms, the law of damages, and criminal law have been developed. The course of events in the world becomes doubled under certain conditions,[10] at which point we imagine an alternative course of events in which the damaging event would not have arisen. Even though it is impossible to undo the damaging event, and we therefore must resort to substitutes such as money, the command of corrective justice fulfills a meaningful function. It is the normative foundation for measures of restitution that, even if they cannot rectify anything as it was, take the deviation of events from the norm seriously and endow it with sanctions that are oriented toward the content of the breached norm.[11] Here, with an old and ambiguous concept of esthetic theory, we can speak of a *mimetic understanding of norms*.[12]

At the same time, it is not only social norms but also esthetic products that can be understood as means of intervention in the world. For social norms, this is rather obvious. They can serve to change behavior or aim at constituting and shaping institutions. But esthetic products can also claim to function as an intervention into the world, such as when they become "politically relevant." And parallel to the invention of interventionary politics at the end of the eighteenth century, this is nothing new in art-esthetic practices.

This highlights two things. For one, the esthetic realm of possibilities can also have a normative side. The possibilities presented in works of art, that don't have to be of a cognitive nature, can transport preferences for certain possibilities, and in a way that could not adequately be viewed as representing reasons.[13] We will

[8] Aristotle, *Poetics*, 1454b9-12: "Since tragedy is the imitation of humans that are better than ourselves, we must also proceed like the good portrait painters. For these, too, reproduce individual traits and render them similar, yet more beautifully." (Original German translation by Manfred Fuhrmann.)

[9] On the twofold meaning of "holding the mirror up to nature" in Hamlet's speech: Franco Moretti, *Signs Taken for Wonders*, London 1988, pp. 66 f.

[10] On an understanding of possible worlds, which takes a starting point at a certain branching point: Jon Elster, *Logik und Gesellschaft*, Frankfurt/M. 1981, pp. 82–107.

[11] On the preconditions and problems of historical restitutions, and quite nuanced: Marc Galanter, "Righting Old Wrongs" in: Martha Minow (ed.), *Breaking the Cycles of Hatred*, Princeton 2002, pp. 107–31), whose considerations could be generalized for all forms of restitution. Compensation for damage is arguably the most plausible connection of a sanction to the content of a transgressed norm. On the problem of justifying these connections, see above, pp. 103–05.

[12] See above, p. 88.

[13] Lydia Goehr, "Art and Politics" in: Jerrold Levinson (ed.), *The Oxford Handbook of Aesthetics*, Oxford 2004, pp. 471–85, here pp. 479–84.

show later that such a normative claim tends to come into conflict with notions of esthetic autonomy. Secondly, what at first appears as an obvious difference between esthetics and normative practices actually does not lead much further. They cannot be sufficiently distinguished from each other by the distinction between esthetic description and normative intervention. Both can make use of either means, or limit themselves to one of them.

3. *Excursion on Fictionality*

A tradition dating back to Jeremy Bentham describes norms as fictions and criticizes their usage. In one of his examples, he states that it is actually not "the legal order" or "the court" that makes a decision, but rather an actual person, the judge.[14] The construction of fictitious subjects leads to the vanishing of the power relations encoded in the law. An analysis of fictions brings them back to light. But if it is true that norms and esthetic practices both operate with forms of reality-doubling, does it lead any further to understand them as fictions?

Fiction is not a concept that runs counter to reality.[15] They are part of the world and internally contain the world—"the so-called possible worlds of fiction lie within actual worlds."[16] Fictions refer to the real, and in some circumstances rely on the recipient's supplementation of the fiction with their world knowledge,[17] as fictions are always incomplete. On the flipside, we have to resort to fiction in portraying our own experience, since experience cannot be fully captured in its portrayal.[18]

Fictions thus also draw their content from reality, though not exclusively, and reality completes the fiction. In line with Wolfgang Iser, fictions can be understood as operations that combine reality and imagination, and that carry over elements of both into the mode of fiction that follows other rules. Fictions share this

[14] Charles K. Ogden, *Bentham's Theory of Fictions*, London 1932, pp. 118–21.

[15] Wolfgang Iser, *Das Fiktive und das Imaginäre*, Frankfurt/M. 1993, pp. 18–24; Thomas Pavel, "'Possible Worlds' in Literary Semantics" in: *The Journal of Aesthetics and Art Criticism* 34 (1975), pp. 165–76, here pp. 169–73. On the historical causes behind the liberation of *res factae* and *res fictae* from a pure antagonism: Reinhart Koselleck, "Terror und Traum" in: *Vergangene Zukunft*, Frankfurt/M. 1979, pp. 278–99, here pp. 278–84; radicalizing such an argument: Albrecht Koschorke, *Wahrheit und Erfindung. Grundzüge einer Allgemeinen Erzähltheorie*, Frankfurt/M. 2012, pp. 224–9.

[16] Nelson Goodman, *Ways of Worldmaking*, Indianapolis 1978, pp. 102 ff; see also the observation by Heinz Schlaffer quoted above, pp. 131 ff.

[17] Of course, and here the problems of the theory of the fictional arise, such supplementation operates according to fiction's conditions. See also the wonderful formulation by Clifford Geertz, "Local Knowledge: Fact and Law in Comparative Perspective" in: Id., *Local Knowledge*, New York 2000, pp. 167–234, here p. 184: law as a "distinct way to imagine reality."

[18] It is thus that the notion of "fiction of the factual" is invoked by Reinhart Koselleck, "Fiktion und geschichtliche Wirklichkeit" in: Id., *Vom Sinn und Unsinn der Geschichte*, Berlin 2010, pp. 80–95, here p. 91. Vividly regarding the ambiguity of a practice that strives to correspond to facts but must feign in order to reach its recipients: John D'Agata and Jim Fingal, *The Lifespan of a Fact*, New York 2012.

transcendence of reality with norms. Fictionalization is thus a cultural technique that does not squarely relate to processes of social differentiation. The same is true for norms. Is there thus a fiction at the heart of any norm? And what would be the descriptive gain of this claim?

For a concept of normativity, two elements of the fictional are of interest:[19] its ambivalent relation to reality, and its recourse to procedures of transforming reality and imagination into a new mode.[20] Both aspects evoke the genesis of norms. Because of their ambiguous relationship to facticity, fictions and norms rely on markings which make them recognizable as such. At the same time, there is no solid convention for such markings. The theory of fiction failed to establish clear criteria that would enable us to always recognize a fiction. The same goes for the theory of norms. The realizing marker of the norm concept developed here is an analytical criterion that does not correspond to any clear convention, which would define when a norm is present, and when not.

But because norms and fictions occupy an interstice between the real and the possible, the critique of certain norms, or of norms in general, as being merely "fictitious," which has appeared in theory ever since Bentham,[21] is moot. It is precisely part of their concept that norms do not simply correspond to some reality. The critique aims at a misuse of norms, but attacks the whole and thereby misses its point. The observation, going back to Bentham, that "in reality" decisions aren't made by normatively constituted fictitious entities, but rather by real persons, misses the complexity of the problem; this is because, for one, even the observation that a given person takes an action is the result of an ascriptive practice that itself relies on norms. For another, the conditions of action of individuals can change by their being incorporated into an organization itself constituted by norms.

The kind of norms that we view as having been "posited" operate similarly to fictions. Due to this, the theory of fiction is an unexploited resource for the theory of norm genesis. Yet this precisely rules out the option of referring to a norm's fictitious character as a means of debunking it, by highlighting the supposedly deficient, because of the reality-denying content of normativity.

Despite these parallels, and despite the anti-critical implications, which the comparison between norm and fiction yielded, the explanatory potential of this comparison has limits. This also has to do with fictions requiring a stronger notion of authorship than norms. Societies treat some of their normative material as products of a natural growth process, without imagining a creator. If I argued earlier

[19] This needs to be distinguished from the protection of fictions by norms, which presumes a separate normative theory of fiction. See Mareike Riedel, *Vermutung des Künstlerischen*, Tübingen 2011, pp. 125–32.

[20] Iser (n 15), *Das Fiktive*, pp. 19–51.

[21] See, for example, regarding the critique of the fictional construction of the State as a legal person: Ernst-Wolfgang Böckenförde, "Organ, Organisation, juristische Person" in: Christian-Friedrich Menger (ed.), *Fortschritte des Verwaltungsrechts*, Munich 1973, pp. 269–305.

that we should not endure a forced choice between making and finding in the theory of social norms, then we now see a difference between norms and fictions.

We encounter similar doubts as to whether other categories of esthetics, such as appearance and illusion, provide anything for a theory of norms, even if such questions yield ever greater interest.[22] Of course, normative practices can be investigated with regards to their staging—just as all other practices can. But on the one hand, it can be presumed that nothing specific will follow from it, and on the other hand, such forms of esthetic analysis—similar to the critique of fictitious norms—tend to present the observed patterns as what is actual in the practice, and to presume a debunking attitude. Obviously, just as is the case with fiction, sensory perception can play a role in the construction of norms, especially when the transition from the cognitive to the normative proceeds gradually and unnoticed. Norms that are presented as signs or images play a large role for some normative practices.[23] They then become of interest because creating an illusion isn't confused with deception, but rather with a particular coexistence of the consciousness of appearance and an embrace of this appearance, which could serve as a model for the point where cognitive "norms" turn into norms. For many remaining questions concerning normative practices result from their operation between mere description and normative support. Nonetheless, normative practices are strongly drawn into the conceptual-verbal once they are made explicit, which sets limits to such approaches.

4. *Norm and Artworks as Artefacts*

Just like artistic practices, normative practices depend on entities as concrete reference points. Let us call one group "norms," and the other "works," such as in artworks. For now, it can remain unclear whether "works" are normative entities. One might see in an artwork the ideal of being exemplary for imitation, or to displace other works, but this is not of immediate concern here. Just as it is not of pertinent interest, which is frequently debated, whether the notion of a work is still appropriate in contemporary art. Aside from the change in esthetic forms, such as in phenomena like *objets trouvés* or conceptual art, this discussion negotiates the status of sensory, subjective reception of art. Even if one admits the relevance of these discussions and thus refuses to presume the "primacy of the object,"[24] or to

[22] See, for example, Cornelia Vismann, *Medien der Rechtsprechung*, Frankfurt/M. 2011; Id., *Das Recht und seine Mittel*, Frankfurt/M. 2012.

[23] In this sense, legal and norm theory also had its own *iconic turn*: Klaus F. Röhl and Stefan Ulbrich, "Visuelle Rechtskommunikation" in: *Zeitschrift für Rechtssoziologie* 21 (2000), pp. 355–85; Klaus F. Röhl, "Das Recht nach der visuellen Zeitenwende" in: *Juristenzeitung* 2003, pp. 339–44.

[24] Theodor W. Adorno, *Ästhetische Theorie*, Frankfurt/M. 1970, p. 66 and more frequently. Appropriately critical in this regard: Georg W. Bertram, *Kunst als menschliche Praxis. Eine Ästhetik*, Berlin 2014, p. 131.

stylize the artwork into an actor in its own right,[25] works prove to be remarkably stable reference points for a starting point, even in more recent debates.

Artworks aren't simply objects. For some genres, artworks can be tied to an object, such as a painting or a sculpture. This form of the concrete object provides the work with an external border and makes it easier to be identified. But even these kinds of artworks are not to be equated with the object itself. They are not sufficiently described by referencing when they were found and where. They are more precisely understood as artefacts, as objects that were imbued with a certain intention,[26] which docks on to existing notions of art and work. An object, an intention, and a concept have to converge in order to be able to speak of an artefact.[27] Without an object, the esthetic intention of a producer, and a certain conceptual framework that assigns the object to a genre, and in turn said genre to art as a whole, we cannot understand the object as an artwork.[28]

Could we reconstruct social norms as artefacts?[29] Earlier here, we had argued that it is misleading to have to decide between the alternative of norms being either made or found. For some norms, it seems plausible that they were made, for others less so.[30] We had gone one step further in the observation of norm application. It is not authorized by virtue of itself but always depends on the self-authorization of a person applying it. This is also the case for positing norms, in as far as it refers to other norms, which is practically always the case. In this way, even social norms, which we treat as found, can be understood as artefacts. We can compare them with *objets trouvés*. In both cases, something found is intentionally transmitted to a different conceptual framework and thereby imbued with a new meaning. In the case of norms that are found, this content is generally not an object, it is a moral argument, such as the recourse to the nature of humanity or a stabilized practice.

[25] As is the case with Horst Bredekamp, *Theorie des Bildaktes*, Berlin 2010, pp. 48–56, who—with respect to the figure of the picture act—makes the picture itself into an actor. The power of the picture can also arise from the characteristics of the observer, for example out of her sexuality: David Freeberg, *The Power of Images*, Chicago 1991, pp. 338–44. Of course, these kinds of mechanisms can also be used for norms: Richard Thaler and Cass Sunstein, *Nudge*, New Haven 2008.

[26] A consistent Platonic view would deny as much and hold the work to be independent of its materialization. But in doing so, it must also deny that the work was made at all. It is no longer an artefact, but was found by its creator, it cannot even be destroyed. The practically decisive difference between actual and possible work thereby vanishes, as works are types of norms. See Nicholas Wolterstorff, *Worlds and Works of Art*, Oxford 1980, pp. 45–57.

[27] Empirical research suggests that the conceptual categorization of artefacts is practically and largely examined with recourse to the intentions of the creator: H. Clark Barrett, Stephen Lawrence, and Eric Margolis, "Artifacts and Original Intent: A Cross-Cultural Perspective on the Design Stance" in: *Journal of Cognition and Culture* 8 (2008), pp. 1–22, here pp. 15–19.

[28] In an unwieldy discussion, I here follow this trifecta as invoked by Amie L. Thomasson, "Artifacts and Human Concepts" in: Eric Margolis and Stephen Laurence (eds), *Creations of the Mind*, Oxford 2007, pp. 52–73. Artefacts do not have to manifest themselves in an object, see, for example, the examples in Richard E. Grandy, "Artifacts: Parts and Principles" in: Margolis and Lawrence (eds) (n 28), *Creations*, pp. 18–32, here p. 19.

[29] This needs to be distinguished from the insight into the meaning of artefacts for social norms. On this, Annelise Riles (ed.), *Documents: Artifacts of Modern Knowledge*, Ann Arbor 2006.

[30] Above, pp. 110–15.

Even though neither the object nor the natural predisposition depend on social practice, it is the practice that makes them into what they then are: art-esthetic products or social norms.

In both cases, there is a need for authorization. In both cases, the authorization isn't brought about via "production." After all, in these cases we're concerned with what is found, not with what is made, and the marking thereof. It is only the authorization of the one who finds that makes a work and a social norm into what they are. Without the ability to name an author in the sense of a producer, who might be someone at a conveyor belt in the case of the *objet trouvé*, or might be God in the case of human nature, we need self-authorizing agents in both cases who perform the authorizing marking. The fact that we distinguish between these kinds of authorization, when we accord the esthetic content to the artist, but not the normative content to the applier, may very well have to do with the divergent claims to obligation of the two genres. More on this at the end.

Just as with other artefacts, such as a city, norms generally cannot be identified with a single object, even if it were practically possible. For an individual norm, we could simply designate an object.[31] As we will see in the investigation of norm texts, in such a case it would seem short-sighted to view this object as a mere likeness of a norm. For entire normative orders, on the other hand, such an ascription of a norm and an object is practically inconceivable. In normative orders, even the question of which units are taken as an individual norm is a question of convention. That kind of determination then runs counter to a field of concepts and objects with which the normative practice operates and whose reference to the world of objects orients itself toward practical criteria, such as recognizability, ability to emulate, or simple applicability. Just like works, norms can then only be understood as *relations* between original intentions, conceptual contexts, and objects, in which the latter can be affirmed and gain substance.[32] This will become more clear and gain a further dimension when we consider structural analogies with artworks that do not manifest themselves in a unique object, but in a plurality.[33]

[31] See, for example, Bruno Latour, " The Berlin Key or How to do Words with Things" in: P. M. Graves-Brown (ed.), *Matter, Materiality and Modern Culture*, London 2000, pp. 10–21, here pp. 18 f.), where Latour identifies the title-giving object with an "action program" which commands to lock the main door from the inside during night-time, among other things. This would only constitute a norm, though, if one could digress from it.

[32] It is no coincidence that conceptual imprecisions inherent to this are more likely embraced by sociologists and literary critics that philosophers. Consider the thoughts on quasi-objects by Bruno Latour, *We Have Never Been Modern*, Cambridge, Mass. 1993, pp. 51 f., as well as those on the notion of object in Luhmann, *Die Kunst der Gesellschaft*, pp. 80–2, and those on concerning the concept of art's dependence on norms and objects by Miguel Tamen, *Friends of Interpretable Objects*, Cambridge, Mass. 2001, p. 66.

[33] On this distinction Stephen Davies, "Ontology of Art" in: Jerrold Levinson (ed.), *The Oxford Handbook of Aesthetics*, Oxford 2004, pp. 155–80, here pp. 156–70, for a different angle see the distinction between autographic and allographic art in Nelson Goodman, *Languages of Art*, Indianapolis 1976, p. 113, which may well be insufficiently specific regarding context.

5. *Esthetic Performance and Norm Application*

The normative character of esthetic processes emerges clearly in art forms that rely on performance.[34] Drama texts and sheet music share with written norms the relationship between authorized script and its application. They also have in common the fact that it would be wrong to reduce the work or norm to an original formatting of this script, or to a legal or esthetic notation. The notation gains its function not as a singular object, but as a model, the foundation of which allows transcriptions to be made without a loss of authority. Such transcriptions are functionally identical with an original, with an autograph of a composer, or the product of a formalized law-maker, who creates originals with the signature of authorized persons. The possibility of performance is inherent to such works. It even seems impossible for such works to exist without a perspective of being performed. We encounter something analogous in formalized normative orders struggling to locate "norms" somewhere between their formalized production, their materialization and multiplication, and their application.

We can best describe the need for performance or application of works and norms if we distinguish three levels. One is the *original level.* Esthetic and normative artefacts must make it through a process that certifies them as unique. Readymades and forms of multiplied art create unique challenges for the concept of work used here, even if the distinction between original and copy has largely been unproblematic to this day. One might even narrate the modernization of law as the history of the gradual, if not complete vanishing of legal objects' materialization: from the rock of the *Codex Hammurapi* to the parchment certificate with seal and signature on to automatically generated copies of administrative acts which are "valid without signature." But all forms of materialization serve to safeguard an authoritative claim that derives from an original. Thus the technique of forgery is of equal import for artistic and normatively relevant objects. Normative forgery can be found from the command issued by the Captain of Köpenick to the counterfeiting of official currency. Even informal social norms can be forged, for example when one declares the wearing of a certain shoe type at a certain time of the day as "English," thereby presenting it as an option worth imitating. This explains the need to secure originals for norms as well, even if these originals—through the continued practice of a norm—may become of interest for conservatory and philological purposes only, the originals having become obsolete for identifying the norm or the artwork.

Thus, at a second level, norms and works become *objects capable of reproduction* whose identification is no longer put into question by the loss of the original. The work becomes one with the abstraction, which may be reproduced yet no longer

[34] This normative character is worked out by Nicholas Wolterstorff (n 26), *Worlds of Art*, but at the price of ontologically degrading the application level.

can be spacio-temporally located, and can neither be described as an object nor as an event. As a phenomenon, this second level has its own right. It makes perfect sense to talk of an opera whose autograph has been destroyed and was never staged, or of a statute whose finalized version has been lost, was never completed, or which no-one obeys. But it would be equally misguided to declare this level to be the actual one, while treating social development and application as secondary phenomena.[35] Work and norm can only be understood within the context of these levels.

This second level is conceptually necessary as a reference point for the *third* level of artistic or normative execution, the performance or application. The execution has temporal and spatial coordinates, it is an event that can be documented by texts, images, and films, and yet it is fleeting. Moments of artistic execution can determine their own documentation. In formalized norm systems, the "performance" of a legal text in a court proceeding produces the new, likewise authorized text of the legal verdict. In contrast to art, a legal order relies on the coexistence of performance and authorized documentation of this performance. The documentation of the application procedure is an element of its conclusion, which is treated as the actual product of the application. Formalized orders conclude the application with a decision. In social normative systems, this selection of an endpoint in contrast to its coming to be probably arises from a heightened claim to obligation, whereas in esthetics, the same process is treated as open-ended and incapable of conclusion.[36] It is an endpoint at least in the self-description of a normative system, all the while, as seen from an external viewpoint, other events can follow and latch on to it. Esthetic and normative practices both have to make use of specific instruments in order to safeguard the authorization necessary in their execution.

Similarities between the two also rely on the fact that in both cases, authorization refers to an afactual object. For this reason, many challenges arising when trying properly to portray and describe normative orders can be seen as genuinely esthetic problems, even if the normative order in question has nothing to do with the realm of art. Norms and works are thus not only to be understood as *relations*, but also as *processes*. They extend over periods of time with more or less clearly defined beginning and endpoints.

In both cases, this process fulfills similar functions: At first, both procedures must be arranged such that their original authorization remains intact. However, this is expressly not about the solving of any hermeneutical problems, that is, to determine a specific meaning. On the contrary, arrangements such as judicial independence in a legal order, as well as granting the status of artist to a musical or theater performer, seem to run directly counter such notions of preserving a

[35] It is important to emphasize this, as both artworks and legal norms are often reduced to their performance or application aspects. For a critique, see below pp. 154–56.
[36] Eco (n 6), *The Open Work*, pp. 1–23.

certain (original) meaning. On the flipside, because of the significant degree of freedom in dealing with a reference, it is particularly imperative to secure a formal reference point which shields its identity from any interpretation in the form of an application or performance. Norms and works are expected to both converge in a concrete application or performance context, which is the only way for them to be actualized and remain relevant, *and at the same time* to remain distinct from these procedures of actualization, in order not to exhaust themselves in their application, thereby excluding further applications.

The comparison with art-esthetic works can help to inspire the theory of norms, and vice versa. Neither as abstract entities nor as texts or objects, nor as mere executions are norms appropriately described. As artefacts geared toward execution, they develop when intentions within a given conceptual framework are merged with objects of the exterior world, and when these linkages are multiplied and executed without thereby dissolving. The need to locate works within a conceptual context simultaneously blurs the distinction between autographical art, that refers to an original object, and autographical art, that can be reproduced. For in both types, the recognizability of a work as a work of art hinges on an interpretive process which can change the conceptual framework that determines what is to be taken as a work. Both types of art are thus of a procedural nature.[37]

This is crucial for the proper observation of norms because the predominant ontology of the social conceives of norms as products of coordinating or cooperating individual subjects.[38] Admittedly, these theories have developed highly elaborate models of how normative orders come to be through coordinated individual contributions; however, they are not interested in other forms of dealing with norms, just as if every normative practice were a perpetuated foundational situation. If I take norms to be the medium of an individual's guide to action, and if I orient my description of norms along models of moral normativity, this may seem an obvious view. If, however, I presume that norms do not only operate in terms of guiding action but that they also determine what an action is, if I distinguish between methodological and normative individualism and cannot simply deduce the latter from the former, and if I finally realize how much the practice of social norms depends on their treatment of artefacts, which are difficult to portray and are to be perpetuated in their meaning, then such a purely intersubjectively sustained ontology of norms loses its plausibility. One lesson from esthetic theory for the theory of social norms may consist in gaining insight into the meaning of objects for the perpetuation of a normative practice. That is, it leads us to realize that norms cannot be reduced to shared intentions alone. Instead we must understand how norms gain a certain autonomous existence of their own through being

[37] See also the formulation by Juliane Rebentisch, *Theorien der Gegenwartskunst*, Hamburg 2013, p. 49.

[38] See references and discussion below, pp. 376–81.

embedded in objects and concepts. A norm cannot permanently be reinvented or re-planned. The perpetuation of normative practices requires specific connecting points that are provided by objects and concepts.[39] In many instances, a practice begins with an original act, in which an artefact is designated as the expression of a norm or as an esthetic product.[40] In the perpetuation of norms, subjects fulfill a necessary function, but this function also consists in the designation of objects as norms or as norm indicators, to which other subjects can then make reference.[41] We will explore this in greater depth by examining constitutional texts, where we will see that the linguistic form of portraying a norm cannot simply be replaced by another form, that in some cases, norm texts are better understood as norm-constituting artefacts than as mere verbal representation of norms.

6. *Canon, Canonization, Esthetic Success*

In addition to the problem regarding cognitive commonalities of esthetic products and social norms, the question arises as to the normative claim of both. Esthetic practices operate with different normative forms, such as canonization, or by means of the esthetic evaluation of works. On the one hand, the need for evaluation seems inappropriate to large segments within esthetic theory, but on the other hand, it is practically indispensable in order to uphold the autonomy claims of art. Esthetic canons offer an entry into these considerations. These canons assemble works that *ought to* be remembered and studied. Nowadays, explicit canons, lists of "great works," come across as dated. Even if they have not completely gone extinct,[42] they tend to be part of a popular culture that doesn't want to be one, and that serves to ease an insecure audience in their selection process—akin to "100 masterpieces of world literature"—or as instruments of pedagogical self-affirmation.[43] At the same time, the institutionalized art scene is permanently working on a canonizing project by drawing on pre-existing canons and developing them further. It does so by selecting works which are presented in exhibits, sold in galleries, published by publishing houses, performed in opera houses, and interpreted by scholars. Art institutions collect works and inevitably draw distinctions between those that are worthy of such treatment, and the rest. There are differences between this

[39] In this discussion thread, John Searle is an exception, as he explicitly draws attention to the meaning of both in his theory. As a lucid sketch of his model, see: John R. Searle, "Social Ontology and the Philosophy of Society", in: Margolis and Laurence (eds) (n 28), *Creations*, pp. 3–17.

[40] Regarding esthetic objects, see Catherine Lord, "A Kripkean Approach to the Identity of a Work of Art" in: *The Journal of Aesthetics and Art Criticism*, 36, pp. 147–53.

[41] This is also the case with the esthetic counterpart to the moral norm, which purports to discard materialization, namely conceptual art. On its material necessity, see Rebentisch (n 37), *Theorien der Gegenwartskunst*, pp. 135–50.

[42] Harold Bloom, *The Western Canon*, New York 1994.

[43] The American debate about the canon is very much characterized by college education; it is functionalized from the outset.

selection process and the codification of an explicit canon. The modern art world's selection only represents one decentralized and factually open variation of classical canon formation, although the degree to which the two converge is empirically unresolved. Titian exhibitions and Titian research, for one, will certainly continue to exist. Both forms of canonization have esthetic preconditions that are not self-evident. They rely on a strong notion of "the artwork" and an esthetic of truth.[44] It is plausible to assemble and hand on collections of works only as long as art is thought to manifest itself in works and as long as some objective content is thought to result from these works.

Who authorizes canons and whom do they address? Even though any canon factually has one author—the one who selects and assembles—they remain authorless in their aspiration. The works themselves are supposed to manifest themselves in the canon, for the criterion of canonization is inherent to esthetics.[45] Conceptually, neither the number of copies sold nor a record sale can replace an esthetic criterion, even if both actually do. The belief in the existence of criteria inherent to esthetics draws its plausibility from the historically observable insistence on a core of generally cherished artworks that even prompted Marx to doubt his model of base and superstructure in the realm of art.[46] It moreover becomes plausible e contrario in light of the difficulties one encounters when trying to develop a convincing inventory of criteria themselves external to esthetics that could explain an esthetic canon.[47] For this reason, even if they are only treated with a sense of shame, canons fulfill an irreplaceable function for art discourse: the conditions of possibility for canonization are at the same time the conditions of possibility for an independent formation of esthetic criteria, and vice versa. If the faith in the possibility of canonization were to fade away, it would be unclear why art should lay claim to its own sphere. Canons are authorless norms whose successful authorization relies on esthetic criteria being independently formed—an assumption rich in preconditions that nevertheless stubbornly persists.[48]

Canons address an audience. Do they also address the producers of art? We will have to distinguish between the necessity to refer to art in order to produce artworks, and the aspiration of an artwork to influence other works. The former is inevitable, the latter however only the case when works function as role models, even as negative ones,[49] for future art. Is a work a norm? Does a work posit a norm?

[44] Rüdiger Bubner, "Über einige Bedingungen gegenwärtiger Ästhetik" in: Id. (n 44), *Ästhetische Erfahrung*, Frankfurt/M. 1989, pp. 7–51, here pp. 32 ff.

[45] Bloom (n 42), *Western Canon*, pp. 22–41.

[46] Karl Marx, *Grundrisse der Kritik der politischen Ökonomie*, Berlin 1953, pp. 29 ff.

[47] On the other hand, there may be esthetic criteria that simultaneously explain why the canonization of an artist failed, and why it would be inappropriate. For the case of Carl Phillip Emanuel Bach: Wolfgang Fuhrmann, "Gescheiterte Kanonisierungen" in: Klaus Pietschmann and Melanie Wald-Fuhrmann (eds), *Der Kanon der Musik*, Munich 2013, pp. 160–96, here pp. 190–5, esp. p. 194.

[48] See the observation by Adorno (n 24), *Ästhetische Theorie*, p. 35, that it could be advisable to act as though art were simply "given" while its justification and defense remain common.

[49] Not by chance, from the same author: Harold Bloom, *The Anxiety of Influence*, New York 1997, pp. 5–16.

Possibly so, even if this means to severely water down the concept of a norm, due to the "normative material" consisting in a plethora of esthetically incongruous works, and because it is perfectly permissible to refer to an uncanonized work in hopes of creating a work to be canonized. We can ascribe to a work the pretense of excluding the pretense of other works, if the former isn't going so far as to try to physically overwrite the latter.[50]

Currently, the situation for esthetic canonization appears rather different from the situation before the end of rule esthetics and the sweeping success of the notion of taste in the eighteenth century.[51] Before the latter, esthetic theory was still able to see itself as a systematic norm for the creation of successful artworks. Today, works of art are no longer seen as exemplary in following an esthetic norm, but their success is still implicitly or explicitly judged after the fact.[52] But the scope of the transformation should not be overestimated.[53] Of course, in the course of the nineteenth and twentieth centuries, a number of esthetic theories were developed, which formulated criteria for the success of art, some in light of Hegel's lectures[54]—even if only in shape of the normative expectation that a work of art has to do justice to its own present time, depict social conditions, or help us view the world with a different set of eyes.

The difference to other systems of social norms is clearly visible, but not categorical. The formulation of such esthetic norms frequently remains informal and contains a high degree of openness. But this is nothing special for normative orders.[55] The truth esthetic inspired by the philosophy of history and the canonization by market pricing have in common that it remains doubtful whether they are driven by art-immanent criteria.[56] Maybe it is actually quite the opposite: just as law in the late eighteenth century did not gain in autonomy with the invention of a modern constitution and a stabilized connection to politics. The irony might well be that with the end of rule esthetics, art no longer takes care of its own criteria formation but rather leaves that to others, such as the audience or the market. Even

[50] An example of the latter in Beatriz Colomina, *Privacy and Publicity. Modern Architecture as Mass Media*, Cambridge, Mass. 1996, pp. 84–90.

[51] Alfred Bäumler, *Das Irrationalitätsproblem in der Ästhetik und Logik des 18. Jahrhunderts bis zur Kritik der Urteilskraft*, Tübingen 1967, pp. 65–82 and more frequently.

[52] One could also view this judgment as an action for the future, thus in Christoph Menke, *Die Kraft der Kunst*, Berlin 2012, p. 58.

[53] See the observation by Moretti (n 9), *Signs Taken for Wonders*, p. 13 (and p. 40), that writing on literary history has never been able to ascertain the difference between a normal and a masterful work of art, suggesting that the masterful may be the particularly normal.

[54] In them, persistently trying to deny his own thesis of substitution of art by philosophy. On this claim, Dieter Henrich, "Kunst und Kunstphilosophie der Gegenwart (Überlegungen mit Rücksicht auf Hegel)" in: Wolfgang Iser (Ed.), *Immanente Ästhetik, Ästhetische Reflexion*, Munich 1966, pp. 11–32, here pp. 13–17.

[55] On the systematic differentiation of an independent notion of esthetic truth, see Ritter (n 7), *Vorlesungen zur philosophischen Ästhetik*, pp. 36–47.

[56] For examples on the connection between economic success and esthetic canonization, see Maren Polte, *Klasse Bilder. Die Fotografieästhetik der "Becher-Schule"*, Berlin 2012, pp. 9–13, and within it, the reference in fn. 20 to Isabelle Graw, *Der große Preis*, Köln 2008.

theories that want to view art as a depiction of social reality cannot get by without a theory of this reality external to esthetics, one which selects the relevant subjects.[57]

Besides notions of the esthetics of a work of art, we thus also have an esthetic canonization whose criteria, however, may not necessarily be inherent to esthetics. Here, just as in other contexts, the autonomy of art might be a demand that is upheld despite an awareness of its shortcomings,[58] thereby turning into a norm in its own right.[59] If the concept of a work disappears—an event that esthetic theory has seemed to anticipate for some time now, without it actually happening[60]—then the normative aspiration of autonomy would likely fade along with it. And yet, the esthetic description of art, as well as the need to evaluate art, calls for the format of a work. On this view, we could imagine art without its normative evaluation. It is, however, everything but clear that the urge to classify and engage with art in an evaluative manner is actually diminishing. Canonization as the normative self-description of the art system—although operating covertly due to the uncertainty in establishing criteria, and in theoretical contexts even bashfully—seems to remain inevitable, as long as art as a practice is making a claim to autonomy.

7. *Esthetic Judgment*

Despite its legal connotation—*judicium*—judgment is not a genuinely normative practice. Factual correctness, which is claimed in a judgment, raises no normative claim. On Kant's reading, esthetic judgments do not refer to an object but to the sentiment of a subject,[61] they say nothing about the esthetic objec, and nonetheless appear to transmit an impression of a judged object's success.[62] A whole string of esthetic theories uses this approach as a starting point, assessing art by the intensity of its sensory perception.[63] But what is the predicate of esthetic judgments understood in this way? For Kant, it is still the judgment as "beautiful" (*schön*), a predicate for which esthetic theory throughout the nineteenth century loses interest. In addition to ever more sub-predications,[64] nowadays the classification of an artefact

[57] This is Bubner's important insight into the tragedy of Marxist esthetics: Bubner (n 44), "Bedingungen," p. 26.

[58] This dilemma becomes apparent in the thoughts of Rebentisch (n 37), *Theorien der Gegenwartskunst*, pp. 168–79.

[59] Explicitly recommended as a normative concept in Rainer Schützeichel, "Autonomie als Programm" in: Martina Franzen (ed.), *Autonomie Revisited* (= 2nd special volume of *Zeitschrift für theoretische Soziologie*), Weinheim 2014, pp. 166–87.

[60] An attempt to rehabilitate the concept of a work can be found in Gunnar Hindrichs, *Die Autonomie des Klangs. Eine Philosophie der Musik*, Berlin 2014, pp. 12–17, 36–43.

[61] Immanuel Kant, *Kritik der Urteilskraft*, Frankfurt/M. 1977, pp. 127–31 (§ 8); more precisely, the following is concerned with the esthetic reflection judgment.

[62] Martin Seel, *Die Kunst der Entzweiung*, Frankfurt/M. 1997, p. 180.

[63] This allows other skillsets outside art to tie into esthetic dimension, see Winfried Menninghaus, *Wozu Kunst? Ästhetik nach Darwin*, Berlin 2011, pp. 195–259.

[64] See Sianne Ngai, *Our Aesthetic Categories: Zany, Cute, Interesting*, Cambridge, Mass. 2012.

as "art" seems to be the most important predication. This places a descriptive generic term in place of an evaluative predicate, while at the same time preserving the normative aspiration of the judgment expressed.[65] This is implausible because, with our expectations of art expressed in such a manner, we cannot think of these expectations other than in light of the idea of "bad art" as in the unacknowledged expansion of the family to include its wayward children.[66] It would lead to curious results if this generic concept were short-circuited with other applications of the concept of art, for example when dealing with the constitutional protection of the freedom of art. On the one hand, this legal guarantee is supposed to protect the autonomy of art, on the other, this autonomy is exercised to exclude bad art from the concept of art, which would lead to the legal system itself having to judge art for its quality before being able to protect it. In the end, the law would have to intervene in the socially relevant autonomy of art. The practical protection of art-esthetic practices is only possible if we avoid normativizing the generic concept. Only a radically consistent conception of autonomous art could disregard this problem, as even conceptually, it cannot rely on any protections provided from the outside through institutional measures—alas, this seems to be a theory for good times.[67]

Both the somewhat outdated judgment of an artwork as "beautiful" and its classification as belonging to the realm of art command esteem, and to the audience, affirm the possibility of engaging with the object at hand.[68] It is not just in the expectation that others share in the judgment, but in said possibility of engagement, that we recognize the normative content of the predicate. This might be claiming too much and too little at the same time: too much, because such an evaluation cannot justify its own aspiration—it remains unclear why others should make it their own, especially when it cannot be justified, as is the case according to Kant;[69] too little, because nothing of substance is said about the work with this predication.

In terms of the normativity of esthetic judgment, Kant remains guarded. It is inaccessible to justification, as it remains non-conceptual; on the other hand, it is supposed to come across to others as an "idealist norm."[70] The judgment thus calls for intersubjective agreement. Due to the impossibility to justify esthetic judgments,

[65] That this is problematic, as esthetic relevance is equated with esthetic accomplishment, is shown by Seel (n 62), *Kunst der Entzweiung*, pp. 182–7, 196 ff.

[66] On the problems posed by normatively charged category concepts, see above pp. 132–34.

[67] On the critique of an autonomy concept thus understood: Bertram (n 24), *Kunst als menschliche Praxis*, pp. 31–6.

[68] That is why it is difficult to do without the category of the beautiful or similar concepts, Adorno (n 24), *Ästhetische Theorie*, pp. 82 ff.

[69] Sianne Ngai, "Mere Interesting", in: *Critical Inquiry* 34 (2008), pp. 777–817, here p. 780, shows that the predicate "interesting" does not work by mere indication of sensory characteristics, but always remains in need of justification.

[70] Kant (n 56), *Kritik der Urteilskraft*, p. 159 (§ 22); Adorno (n 24), (*Ästhetische Theorie*, p. 247) remarks that such a judgment ultimately expresses the need for others to also be pleased by a work; On the normativity of judgments of taste, Andrea Kern, "Ästhetischer und philosophischer Gemeinsinn" in: Andrea Kern and Ruth Sonderegger (eds) *Falsche Gegensätze. Zeitgenössische Positionen zur philosophischen Ästhetik*, Frankfurt/M. 2002, pp. 81–111, here pp. 85 ff.

however, this agreement can only be achieved by sharing the experience with others and drawing their attention to it.[71] But the presumption that a true judgment also be shared by others does not justify a specifically normative claim, for it is contained in any descriptive expression whatsoever. Normativity arises when an affirmatively qualifying predicate is tied to the judgment.

In Christoph Menke's critical reconstruction of esthetic judgment, the success of an artwork reveals itself *via negationis* in the impossibility to judge it. The engagement with the work of art leads to no end that could produce a judgment, but remains in permanent flux.[72] If, however, I come to a judgment, then this is a sign of the observed work's flaw since it does not satisfy the boundlessly aspiring character of art.[73] But in this manner, reading Menke against Menke and other judgment-critical authors, we not only make a judgment call about a failed work but also about the successful work which does not allow for the cessation of pondering contained in the very act of judging. This judgment may not arise in the process of the engagement with the work of art, it lies outside of it. But nonetheless, this judgment remains possible, it is actually concretely made, when Menke accords that a work does not permit a judgment. With this, Menke would actually be providing what he wanted to avoid: a formalized criterion for a normative, esthetic judgment.

If a truth esthetic theory, one that judges artworks by their relevance to the present or their quality in social depiction, gets entangled in the pitfalls of criteria formation, if it philosophically or politically colonizes art, then an esthetics leaning on Kant can process what is specific to dealing with art. It does so by bringing the sensory experience of art observation to the foreground. However, the sensory side of this must also be complemented by a reflexive element. Yet even subjective esthetics cannot get around taking a stance toward the success of their object. Such theories should not refuse predication in order not to conceal the practice of judging art behind its inevitable selection mechanisms. For every theory remains dependent on these mechanisms, even if this is only due to the processes of selecting its examples. An esthetic judgment that does not simply want to retell reception history has to provide reasons, or at least impressions, why a predominant taste

[71] Frank Sibley, "Ästhetisch und nicht-ästhetisch" in: Rüdiger Bittner (ed.), *Das ästhetische Urteil*, Köln 1977, pp. 134–55, here pp. 140–2.

[72] Menke (n 52), *Kraft der Kunst*, pp. 77 ff. And from judgment-critical literature: Gilles Deleuze, " To Have Done with Judgment" in: Id., *Essays Critical and Clinical*, London 1998, pp. 126–35; Daniel Loick, "Creation, not Judgement. Response to Christoph Menke" in: Daniel Birnbaum and Isabelle Graw (eds), *The Power of Judgment. A Debate on Aesthetic Critique*, Berlin/New York 2010, pp. 30–5, here p. 31. The anti-critique, which cannot recognize how the theoretical presumption of philosophers can be historically observed, Isabelle Graw, *Judging, yes—but how?*, in: Birnbaum and Graw (eds) (n 72), *The Power*, pp. 36–43, here p. 37. One important inspiration for the critique of judgment is probably Benjamin's distinction between name and judgment, on this: Eli Friedländer, *Walter Benjamin—A Philosophical Portrait*, Cambridge, Mass. 2012, pp. 16 ff.; see also ibid., pp. 49 f., on the problem of reflection's cessation.

[73] This is expressed in the context of a painting by Neo Rauch in Menke (n 52), *Kraft der Kunst*, pp. 72–8. Menke's reference for the not-yet-characteristic of art is Hegel.

should be maintained or overcome.[74] If, however, the judgment simply remains a mere "symptom of the encounter with an artwork,"[75] then it does not fulfill this internal, normative function.

The impression that esthetic judgment raises a normative claim beyond the realm of esthetic accomplishment could also result from the tendency of modern societies to overestimate art in their self-description. For the assumption is made and passed on that what is recognized as art deserves attention, but this claim is usually made without any specific justification. Whereas other social spheres, such as economics, politics, or science are seen as indispensable yet quite contested and ambivalent with regard to their effects on society, the opposite seems to hold true for art. Explaining which purpose art serves is taken as an unseemly functionalization. But it will be likely to be difficult to identify a possible utility of a practice if we do not also hold this practice to be capable of causing any damage. Highlighting autonomy in art certainly leaves the normative pretense of an esthetic judgment unresolved and in limbo.

8. *Authorship and Liability*

As long as we tie art to works, we tie them to authorship. Thinking art without an author, despite all theoretical challenges, seems to be even more difficult than questioning the concept of a work, even if we do not tie authorship to the concrete creation issued by a free person, but rather functionalize the notion of authorship as something that is being presumed.[76] Even art that tries to rid itself from its character as a work of art is incessantly attributed to artists, and without such attribution the determination of a thing as art would actually seem hardly possible. The distancing from the production process, such as in the form of readymades, has neither avoided objects to be understood as works and conserved, nor to be accorded to a single author.[77] Even a readymade can be forged, which demonstrates quite well the continuing dominance of an author-centered work esthetics.

The rampant doubt that nonetheless persists concerning the concept of the author may have been ignited by the insight that the reference to an author entails a

[74] Stanley Cavell, "Aesthetic Problems of Modern Philosophy" in: Id., *Must We Mean What We Say?*, Cambridge, Mass. 2002, pp. 73–96, here p. 78. It might not be coincidence that this is a remark from the Anglo-Saxon context. In German esthetic theory, a certain shame tied to making judgments is partially responsible for there being no discipline of judgment comparable to the American literary criticism.

[75] Fittingly, and just as it is here, critically, in Bertram (n 24), *Kunst als menschliche Praxis*, p. 193, in fn. 41.

[76] This is how I read Carlos Spoerhase, *Autorschaft und Interpretation*, Berlin 2007.

[77] On the question of which characteristics allow for this attribution: Arthur C. Danto, *The Transfiguration of the Commonplace*, Cambridge Mass. 1981, pp. 90–114; to read complementarily on the critique of leaving out the sensory side: Martin Seel, *Ästhetik des Erscheinens*, Frankfurt/M. 2003, pp. 192–7.

normative structure, and that not only the author but the one who speaks of the author, lays claim to a questionable authority. Not least of all, it is the history of authorship that reveals the dependency of esthetic authorization practice from legal authorization practice.[78] A critique of the concept of authorship then becomes a critique of the claim to privileged access to a work. In literary theory, equivalencies for the notion of norm, such as the construction of an "author function" confirm the insight that neither one's own production is of concern, nor securing a certain intended meaning. Rather, the concern is with securing an authorizing context that cannot be disposed of without bringing into question the entire construction of artistic objects.

The need to name an author for an art-esthetic product stems from our treatment of artworks as artefacts, as something that has been made but for which we cannot identify a maker, yet absolutely need to present a godparent. "However, no interpretive theory denies the causal fact that every esthetic artefact was caused by an empirical author."[79] The naturally beautiful knew neither work nor author, yet it did know a creator of nature.[80] As we have seen, there is no immediate categorical difference to social norms, and yet the character of an artwork as an artefact certainly seems to be self-evident beyond the art-ontological discussions, whereas the character of norms as artefacts raises discontent. If even the social practice requires an authorization then at least the content of norms should not simply lie in the hands of creators. A work of art has to be created in order for it to be able to claim its aspiration as art.[81] The sculpture that is revealed to be a dripstone does not necessarily lose its esthetic content, but it does lose its classification as art. In turn, the character of a norm as an artefact raises doubts about its normative value, as it is the expression of a contingency, which we do not like to attach to social norms. The idea that norms develop by virtue of nature or reason, which is anathema for works of art, seems obvious for social norms. The idea of a natural good and something naturally right has not fallen out of favor to the same degree that the idea of the naturally beautiful has. This distinction also finds expression in the different function that commentaries fulfill. It is expected of some norms that they are motivated, i.e. justified, whereas works are merely to be explained or interpreted. But even if they are not already taken to be superfluous, these kinds of explanations contribute nothing to the authority or quality of an esthetic work, whereas justifications for some social norms convey the actual normative content. Certainly, works could be found that drift into their own commentating, similar to the notion of critique in

[78] Heinrich Bosse, *Autorschaft ist Werkherrschaft*, new edition, Paderborn 2014.

[79] Spoerhase (n 76), *Autorschaft und Interpretation*, p. 59.

[80] In as far as beauty stems from the relationship between work and nature, which it depicts, the reference to a human creator becomes an esthetic problem. See Ritter (n 7), *Vorlesungen zur philosophischen Ästhetik*, p. 21.

[81] However, in a discussion, Helmut Lachenmann described how attentive listening to and imitation of the sounds of a train become a piece of music, which Albrecht Wellmer expressly rejects in the same discussion (talk at Wissenschaftskolleg zu Berlin on 4 May 2011).

early German Romanticism,[82] but the comment thereby becomes part of the work. The difference between works of art and social norms with regard to their claims to bindingness and obligation is better explained by these factual differences in the respective practices than by purely conceptual operations. At least for some social norms, we expect a different justification for their coming to be because we estimate their obligation higher. What lies behind the obviousness with which we take works of arts to be made is a relativization of art's claim to obligation.

This difference in their claim to obligation decidedly does not stem from interpretive problems, neither does it stem from the ambiguity of the esthetic in comparison to the precision of the legal or the social-moral. Who wants to claim that a painting by Matisse allows for more interpretations than the command to honor mother and father? The question that is widespread in esthetic theory, and which traces its way back to Szondi, of whether the pretense to "understanding" is at all appropriate for a work of art, helps to determine distinctions more precisely.[83] For in our dealing with norms, the possibility of doing without understanding is not an option.[84] In as far as norms aim for the realization of possibilities, this does not diminish their ambiguity, but it does rule out dwelling in the ambiguity during diagnosis and leaving open—due to the openness of the norm—its pretense for realization. Whoever would do that would miss the normative aspect of the norm. Normative elements of esthetic practice, however, can remain inherent to esthetics, they can simply treat possibilities as possibilities. Thus, the claim that esthetic norms lack normative obligation,[85] especially when taken seriously, applies here, even if it irritates adherents of art-religious convictions.[86]

If art's strength consists in its open engagement with possibilities, then this strength needs to steer clear of the realization impetus of social norms.[87] Art will

[82] Walter Benjamin, "Der Begriff der Kunstkritik in der deutschen Romantik" in: Id., *Gesammelte Schriften*, Hermann Schweppenhäuser and Rolf Tiedemann (eds), Frankfurt/M. 1991, Vol. I/1, pp. 7–122, here p. 69.

[83] On the presumptuousness of the hermeneutic ideal of understanding, see Jochen Hörisch, *Die Wut des Verstehens*, extended new editions, Frankfurt/M. 1988, pp. 71–81; see also, pp. 301–4.

[84] See also the careful distancing of theological and legal treatment of texts from esthetic use, in: Michael Moxter, "Schrift als Grund und Grenze von Interpretation" in: *Zeitschrift für Theologie und Kirche* 105 (2008), pp. 146–69, here pp. 166 ff.

[85] Rüdiger Bubner, "Moderne Ersatzfunktionen des Ästhetischen", in: Id. (n 44), *Ästhetische Erfahrung*, pp. 99–120.

[86] Just how differently obligations are treated becomes obvious in social philosophy's treatment of art on the one hand, and religion on the other hand, as it seeks objective forms of obligation (for Habermas and Critical Theory: Jan-Phillip Kruse, *Normative Verbindlichkeit*, Magister Thesis at the Institut für Philosophie der Humboldt Universität zu Berlin 2014). While the analysis of art rests on the meticulous analysis of works, references to "religion" often remain much less specific. A profession to "religion" as such cannot exist, as very many—though not all—religious creeds mutually exclude each other. Thus, it only appears as a sedimented cultural practice, or in the form of a translation adequate for reason—no longer as religion. An immediate confrontation with religious elements, ones not ennobled or sublimated in this form, appears to dangerous—an indication that the obligation of religious motives is clearly estimated much higher than artistic ones.

[87] But even this is contentious in modernity, see the famous justification for the significance of Dante, which points toward his embeddedness in the Christian norm order, in: Thomas S. Eliot, "Dante" in: Id.,

rather secure something more simulative and, in this sense, remain non-binding. This lack of finality distinguishes it.[88] However, this deficit then disallows for connections being made to any further promises. Esthetic achievement's internal normativity cannot be linked with any external normativity of a non-artistic production. On the one hand, this sounds conventional, particularly since the autonomy of art is still held in high esteem. On the other hand, esthetic practices rarely give up on a normative promise beyond esthetics, they rather justify it indirectly, such as when claiming that engagement with art fine-tunes the senses, or opens up new perspectives on alternative developments, or shows the rationality of the irrational.[89] This might all be the case, it might even fulfill a function from an evolutionary perspective but it does not thereby have a normative content. The latter would only be able to be expressed as a loss of autonomy in art.

Can art's openness not develop its own obligatory nature by irritating that which already exists? Adorno sees it as the task of art to bring chaos into the social order.[90] Does not the complete opposite apply to social norms, which we frequently—for good reasons—view as part of normative "orders"? Here, too, caution is necessary. Just as social norms can and should bring disquiet and change into a society, so too does Adorno's observation apply to certain art periods at most, of which he certainly was himself aware. Of course, art can also stabilize social orders, and many practices, such as the collection of works in museums, seem to serve precisely such ends. Today, the opposite seems true. Museums indicate that there is an immanent esthetic value, which is also perceived as external and as extending beyond art. It is likely to be unjustifiable to react to this in a defensive manner and claim by way of reflex that this practice is no longer a proper way of engaging with art. This is particularly the case for an esthetic theory that, in contrast to Adorno, contains no more social theory that could justify such a defense. Rather, this reveals the dilemma which all normative claims are facing, that is they have to engage with the world if they are to change it. The paradox of esthetic-political Romanticism of wanting to be "fully free from the world, in order to be able to change it," cannot even be solved in theory by taking recourse to said dictum.

The Sacred Wood, London 1983, pp. 159–71, on the world view behind this reading, Moretti (n 9), *Signs Taken for Wonders*, pp. 222–39.

[88] Cavell, "Aesthetic Problems," p. 86.

[89] Exemplarily, Rebentisch, *Theorien der Gegenwartskunst*, p. 55. It is particularly the esthetics that emphasize subjectivity that appear as reflective truth esthetics.

[90] Adorno (n 24), *Ästhetische Theorie*, p. 144; concisely and lucidly on this: Seel (n 62), *Ästhetik des Erscheinens*, pp. 33–7.

4

The Reality of Norms

The Operating Conditions of the Normative

1. *Formalization, Authorization, and Written Fixation*

1.1 Formalization

I take formalization to be the techniques by which a normative order defines its own elements and thereby makes them distinguishable from each other, and from elements of other orders.[1] Formalizations initially attempt to solve cognitive questions. When is a norm present? How is it posited or discovered? Who is authorized to deal with it? Formalization techniques are supposed to bring about clarity, and with clarity, repeatability. But they can also be brought into connection with procedures of justification, that is procedures of democratic legislation, proclamation of dogma, or competent assessment. The concept of formalization evokes numerous kinds of mechanisms that complement each other: putting into writing, defining the conclusion of a proceeding as a "decision," defining functions such as the "author" or "norm addressee."

Formalization should not be conflated with bureaucratization or organization. It is concerned with mechanisms that make conceptual distinctions pragmatically manageable. For example, in ascribing something, I mark an event as an action, and I ascribe it to an author. In order to fulfil this task repeatedly, we have seen that there is a need for rules, and the formalization of these rules provides mechanisms to keep the application of the authorship concept consistent and practically simple. Thus, we formally ascribe decisions by seeing a person's signature at the

[1] Compare this conception with Arthur L. Stinchcombe, *When Formality Works*, Chicago 2001, pp. 18–27, 41–54, who works with the concept of abstraction. Niklas Luhmann, *Funktionen und Folgen formaler Organisation*, Berlin 1995, p. 38, defines formality by means of rules of membership, this too allows for repeatability. A different definition by Geoffrey Brennan, Lina Eriksson, Robert E. Goodin, and Nicholas Southwood, *Explaining Norms*, Oxford 2013, pp. 46–50, who differentiate between formal normative attitudes *de dicto* and informal ones *de re*. Informal norms refer to an existing language usage, formal ones to objects constituted by the normative order. This, however, draws a categorical boundary between formality and informality, where it is particularly transit zones that are of interest, as they can be observed in the (almost) natural language use of many formalized norms, such as law. The differences are correspondingly drawn too categorically, such as with the claim that formal norms only refer to actions, see ibid., p. 51.

The Possibility of Norms. Christoph Möllers, Published by Oxford University Press (2020) under licence; © this translation, Alex Holznienkemper; © the original German edition, Suhrkamp Verlag Berlin.
DOI: 10.1093/oso/9780198827399.001.0001

bottom of a document, or on the book cover. The question of whether that person actually signed the document, or wrote the book, does not concern us as long as there are no indicators to doubt the act of ascription. Sometimes we go on to immunize the form even further with the help of additional formalizations against doubts, such as when the Church sanctifies a person or when we set a time-limit for appeals.

Formalization always operates in light of an informal social practice. A normative order can make do without formalizations, even if this seems to happen only rarely. In a practice that operates with implicit, ritualized rules, one doesn't need a formalization, but once the order is made explicit, a need for formalization arises, for example, by putting into writing what "the norm" is. Formalization is not necessary wherever repeatability is not a desired outcome. Many one-off, mundane norm transgressions are sanctioned by a mere shake of the head or raised eyebrows without the need for formalization arising. But at first sight, informal norms frequently seem to depend on formalized procedures. Thus, most esthetic judgments are preceded by an organized preselection. This unfolds in educational paths through art institutions or delegation to professional critics, by mechanisms of curating museums or through the art market.

Formalized judgments can be revised. In every normative order, there are informal counter-authorities who work against the form, or can be integrated into it. The newly discovered artist alters the canon as much as the newly discovered proof of guilt may alter the verdict of guilt. Informality and form can mutually revise each other. It would thus be wrong to construe a hierarchy between formalized and non-formalized norms, in which formalization were understood as "mere form" vis-à-vis the real content, or in which, vice versa, formalized norms were taken to be the real norms. Furthermore, the transition from formalized to non-formalized norms is fluid. The oracle is an example. Its words have a normative content, it speaks with an authoritative voice. Formalization is at play because there is a determined place at which this authority expresses itself. Nevertheless, the oracle remains dark and ambiguous. There is no available hermeneutics to help make it comprehensible.

1.2 Form and Reality

Formality cannot be played out against the reality of normative practices; it belongs to the latter. Let us assume an administrative apparatus within a State marked by an established practice of corruption such that the formalized legal order, which defines and sanctions a certain kind of behavior by its public servants, were faced with a practice according to which a building permit will only be granted after the transfer of a "small present." According to a widespread formulation in social sciences, this kind of practice represents a social norm[2] that is "real" as opposed to the formalized legal rule forbidding corruption.

First, such an interpretation seems amiss because nothing speaks for reading the practice of bribery as the expression of a social norm. Although the social mechanism follows a regularity, not every regularity is an indicator of a normative structure.[3] For a permit applicant, it is useful to know what has to be done to obtain a permit, just as one should know which switch to flip in order to turn on a light. But this does not establish a normative context.

Furthermore, the claim that such bribery constitutes a normative practice insufficiently captures what is happening. That is because many elements of the way in which this practice is being upheld may be due to the fact that its participants are fully aware that this practice *contradicts* an existing normative precept. Bribes are not handed over in public. There are no price lists in public offices, neither are there any written agreements between the participants. The practice takes place in secret, in the shadow of possible sanctions,[4] and with an awareness that one cannot rely on certain mechanisms of enforcement, which are otherwise available to legal transactions. Within this secrecy, the normativity of the prohibition on bribery finds its recognition. The fact that it is under threat—be it only by the legal, symbolic prosecution of individual cases by an otherwise powerless State—must figure in any complete description of this practice. This shows how misplaced it would be to deny the reality of formalized norms because of a lacking adherence to them. What is more, formalized norms always serve as negative for capturing and describing divergent informal practices.

1.3 Source and Self-Authorization

In the last chapter, the question of the relationship between "is" and "ought" led to the concept of authorization, which can now be brought into connection with the concept of formalization. This is appropriate because it is among the most important tasks of formalization to ensure the certain and comprehensible authorization of a norm. In order to be able to distinguish between spaces where norms can be reliably discovered and other spaces, the practice of the normative often relies on the metaphor of the source. Taking a look at this metaphor will guide us into the relationship between informality and formality of norm authorization.

[2] See the determination of a norm as a constitutive element of a situation perceived to be real, in John Heritage, *Garfinkel and Ethnomethodology*, Cambridge 1984, pp. 101 ff., according to which every well-oiled social practice is to be taken as normative.

[3] On this, see above pp. 65 ff.

[4] This picks up on the well-known formulation from Fritz W. Scharpf about the "shadow of hierarchy": "Die Handlungsfähigkeit des Staates am Ende des zwanzigsten Jahrhunderts" in: *Politische Vierteljahresschrift* 32 (1991), pp. 621–34, here p. 629.

Unlike in historical writing, normative sources are not so much concerned with an undistorted access to historical truth but rather with securing the order against the risk of illicitly posited norms, sneaking into a normative practice. Whether we are dealing with a norm, then, hinges on whether or not it stems from a recognized normative source. The metaphor of the source thereby fulfils two tasks: it distinguishes between authorized and unauthorized contributions, and it completes the act of authorization, so that the latter does not drift into an infinite regress.[5]

"Rules for the producing of norms"[6] can rule out, or at least limit, other procedures or the mere invocation of certain origins from having a norm-producing effect. Such a procedure can free the question of sources from practical problems attached to it.[7] Herein lies the difference between the "parliamentary statutes" being a normative source for a legal order and the uncertain source of rules of etiquette. Admittedly, one could certainly further investigate and find out something about the latter, for example how, why, and toward what end such rules of etiquette were developed; one might even be able to agree on a person who "made up" the rule. But to describe this person as a normative source ultimately only leads us to being wrapped up in the problems concerning the historical-scientific notion of sources, among which one is that, lacking any formalization, the course of events leading to a given event cannot simply be abruptly concluded by making reference to one source.[8]

Sources are the result of a formalization that defines what counts as a source, at the same time presuming such a formalized rule in order for the definition itself to count as being authorized. Because of this, constitutions do not recount the history of their own genesis in a "realistic fashion" as a complex result of social, religious, political, and cultural relations, but they instead normatively stipulate their own genesis to be the act of a source authorized for this very purpose, a "constituent power,"[9] that only expresses itself in moments of constitutional enactment. This raises the suspicion that the authorization is being ascribed to a subject created ad hoc. Therefore, when the establishment of a constitution fails, we do not consider the failed political actors as unsuccessful constitution drafters; instead they simply vanish from the normative stage. However, when they succeed in their project, the success then elevates the political actors in the self-understanding of the established order to the status of a "constituent power," which had not previously existed when the drafting of the constitution began. Who has authorized whom in

[5] On the origin of the metaphor in law, Niklas Luhmann, *Das Recht der Gesellschaft*, Frankfurt/M. 1993, pp. 523 ff.

[6] As a variation from Hans Kelsen, *Allgemeine Staatslehre*, Wien 1993, pp. 233 ff.

[7] Brennan (n 1), among others, *Explaining Norms*, p. 43, show that informal orders know no defined agent that can posit the norm.

[8] On this, Hans Blumenberg, "Quellen" in: Id., *Quellen, Ströme, Eisberge*, Berlin 2012, pp. 9–93.

[9] Generalizing such figures, Albrecht Koschorke, "Zur Logik kultureller Gründungserzählungen" in: *Zeitschrift für Ideengeschichte* 1 (2007), pp. 5–12.

this scenario? An existing order has established itself. The enactment of a constitution operated as a self-authorization. As remains to be shown, this is no coincidence. The search for normative "sources," for select locations or texts in which a normative order expresses itself, leads to an authorization structure. But without exception, this authorization proves to be a self-authorization.

Before I argue in more detail for this consequence, one last word on the figure of a normative source. Does it also fit well with informal normative practices? Sources are a consequence of formalization. We cannot name a person or a procedure—no source—to whom or which we could attribute a rule of etiquette. And yet such a rule is not conceivable without any kind of authorization, for example arising from specific forms of inequality, between educator and educated, or between people who are not on the same level of a social hierarchy. Under such conditions, norms do arise without a discernible source. The context from of which the norm arises is diffuse. This causes ambiguity with regard to the inventory and meaning of norms, but it can also make them more persistent and sticky. The identification of their origin made impossible through their informality, these kinds of norms give rise to the impression of being the result of a natural process of growth. They simply and somehow "exist." and this can make them much more difficult to being amended or repealed. These kinds of norms may well be externally stabilized, for example by the aid of guidebooks on social etiquette, explicating what counts as "good manners"; however, this does not authorize them.[10] Instead, as will be shown, these forms of social normativity as well work by means of self-authorization.

1.4 The Normal Case of Self-Authorization

The image of the source led us to the phenomenon of self-authorization by aid of the example of a constituent power. Many theorists of constituent power have noted its self-authorizing structure, sometimes going as far as to stylize the phenomenon into a paradox.[11] As stated, the problem arises from the following mechanism: a political movement rebels against an existing order, overthrows it, and establishes a new one. Its foundational principles are codified into a constitution. The constitution also makes reference to its own genesis by presenting itself as the result of a democratic act of the constituent power. The successful side legitimizes its own success. Of course, the legitimacy of a constitution can be brought into question, just as that of any other norm.

[10] Just as in Asfa-Wossen Asserate, *Manieren*, Frankfurt/M. 2003, pp. 30–2.

[11] Naturally, the concept of paradox, which commands logical rigor, is employed rather loosely by these authors, such as with Luhmann: Christoph Möllers, "Zweifel am Zweifel—Antikritische Überlegungen zur Figur des paradoxen Rechts" in: *Zeitschrift für international Strafrechtsdogmatik* 5 (2010), pp. 2–7.

Upon closer inspection, the example of giving oneself a constitution proves to simply be a dramatic version of *every* form of norm genesis, for every social authorization requires an act of self-authorization. This can be shown by taking a closer look at the two sides of every authorization structure. Let us imagine a police officer arresting a person. The officer derives his authorization from a law, the law-maker derives his authorization from an act of voting. At the end of such a chain, there must be an act of self-authorization, in which an individual or collective agent must take a decision. From this vantage point, the situation of giving a constitution appears as nothing special.

However, *from the police officer's point of view*, we could still be dealing with a case of external authorization, be it by the law-maker or by an agent behind the latter. But we have already seen that the application of a norm is never fully authorized by the norm itself. This is why every application needs its own authorization.[12] Our police officer has to take the authorizing norm and operate with it. The norm cannot make this decision for him. If it could force him, it would no longer be a norm. For that reason, every process of creating a norm must always be the product of a self-authorization on the side of its participants. Even the act of recognizing a norm presumes an act of self-authorization. This is obvious when, in recognizing this norm, I also obligate others than just myself. But it also holds for situations in which the norm only addresses me alone, as long as I as part of a community cannot be thought of as simply being the master of my own obligations.[13]

1.5 Norm and Norm Text

The written word is one of the important techniques through which norms are portrayed and formalized. Norms appear as texts in legal codes, in court decisions, in catechisms, and in esthetic treatises. How does a norm relate to its textual fixation?

In his groundbreaking norm theory, Georg Henrik von Wright distinguishes between the norm and its linguistic formulation.[14] This distinction marks a prerequisite for the deontic logic which he helped establish, in which logical relationships between different kinds of norms are analyzed independently of their linguistic form. In the norm-theoretical debate stemming from Wright, the distinction has

[12] A structurally similar argument, yet with different epistemic interest, is found in Allan Gibbard, *Wise Choices, Apt Feelings*, Oxford 1990, pp. 177 ff.

[13] Lea Ypi, "Self-Ownership and the State: a Democratic Critique" in: *Ratio* 24 (2011), pp. 91–106. The determination of individual rights, claimed by virtue of the essence of the individual, has tangible political and legal consequences: Ulrich K. Preuβ, *Die Internalisierung des Subjekts*, Frankfurt/M. 1979, pp. 115–210.

[14] Georg Henrik von Wright, *Norm and Action*, London 1963, pp. 93 ff. On the practical advantages of written rules: James G. March, Martin Schulz, and Xueguang Zhou, *The Dynamics of Rules*, Palo Alto 2000, pp. 190 ff. Also on the critique of the distinction, Jochen Bung, *Subsumtion und Interpretation*, Baden-Baden 2004, pp. 95 ff., 107.

found broad recognition. But its descriptive value for certain social norms probably yields less than for others.[15]

Let us begin with a legal example. Article 1, paragraph 1 of the German Basic Law states: *Die Würde des Menschen ist unantastbar.* Is this the guarantee of human dignity or merely its linguistic formulation? To answer this questions, let us take a look at the English translation: "Human dignity is inviolable." Is this the norm, or is it its linguistic formulation? Most philosophers would presumably object to the identification of the norm with its norm formulation. The norm cannot be identified with either of the two texts but should be identified with the *concept* of human dignity. Lawyers, on the other hand, would mostly be content to identify the German text with the norm, but not in its English translation. For it is only the German text that was laid out by the thus-authorized entity, the constituent power. No translation can claim this authorization for itself. The translation of a national norm into a different language thus leads to a loss in authority of the text. This finding is also relevant in practice. For it has repercussions on the debate on whether the German Basic Law codifies a universal concept of human dignity or rather one that is particular to this constitution.

This close relationship between the norm and its concrete linguistic makeup is not only found in law, but in literary texts as well. In this realm, too, we take a text in the language originally intended by its author as enjoying a different degree of authority from that of any translation thereof, however accomplished it may be.[16] The act of translating is *intransitive*. We can produce a translation of a text, but we cannot get to the original by way of a translation. This asymmetry helps explain the difference in authority between the translated text and the text to be translated. The claim of a translation to be more accomplished than its original would seem inappropriate even if in and of itself it were justified due to the translation exhibiting certain qualities such as comprehensibility or humor that were missing in the original. We would take an improving translation to be the text of a new author. This commonality among legal and esthetic texts separates both from a norm-theoretical reconstruction that lays a strong focus on the distinction between a norm and norm text. For when translations into other textual versions are

[15] We also come across a distancing from the categorical separation of norm and norm formulation in the Jewish tradition: "In the Jewish tradition the centrality of the text takes the place of theological consistency" notes Moshe Halbertal, *People of the Book*, Cambridge, Mass. 1997, p. 1. But also see the observations that make relative the distinctions in Frederick Schauer, *Playing by the Rules*, Oxford 2002, pp. 62 ff.

[16] Ever since Walter Benjamin's essay "Die Aufgabe des Übersetzers" (in: Id., *Gesammelte Schriften*, Hermann Schweppenhäuser and Rolf Tiedemann (eds), Frankfurt/M. 1991, Vol. IV/1, pp. 7–21), the idea of a translation loyal to its text has encountered significant criticism, which ultimately, however—despite all recognition of the aporias revealed by Benjamin—has been unable to change translation from being an intransitive act that has to maintain a connection to that which is translated. Remarkably, for Benjamin this leads to a normativization, if not a moralization of the problem's formulation, that is, to the "duty" of the translator. On this, Alfred Hirsch, "Die Aufgabe des Übersetzers" in: Burkhardt Lindner (ed.), *Benjamin-Handbuch*, Stuttgart 2011, pp. 609–25, here pp. 619–22.

impossible without thus changing their authorizing structure, and when the latter is crucial for the practice of norms, then the connection between the norm and its linguistic form is more intimate than implied in these models. Norms are thus not identical with their linguistic expressions. Nevertheless, in certain cases and for certain purposes, norms can only be properly expressed in a specific linguistic form.[17]

1.6 Securing a Text and Citation

This is aptly illustrated for the legal, esthetic, or religious engagement with texts by the efforts being made in these practices in order to secure textual integrity and in the significance which they accord to citations. For modern legal orders, the integrity of their inventory of norm texts is crucial. Legal systems also operate as authorized agents of reproducing certain texts. They devise procedures in which the texts of constitutions, statutes, ordinances, court decisions, and administrative orders are kept identifiable by official gazettes, authorized production, and formalized correction procedures. Scholarly summaries of contents or systematic paraphrasing do not suffice to reach this goal. In the language of philology, one could speak of *techniques to avoid conjecture*. No matter how politically or legally contentious the meaning of a legal norm may be, the text that we identify with this norm should remain free of such doubts.

The attempt to stabilize norms by maintaining the identity of a text can also be found in the treatment of literary and religious texts, even if by other means. The practice of editing literary works has no formalization techniques at hand that are comparable to those of a legal system. It must proceed on a more case-specific basis, because it has to deal with a multitude of authors with different approaches, not merely with one authority positing law. It has to work with historiographical means if the literary production in question is not contemporary. The legal system can already tackle questions of editing in the process of production, which is not possible for either literary or religious texts. Nonetheless, all of these cases are concerned with the integrity of texts.[18]

[17] Max Black, "The Analysis of Rules" in: Id., *Models and Metaphors*, Ithaca 1962, pp. 95–139, here pp. 100–2.

[18] Furthermore, the differences in technique were not always so pronounced. In the early stages of the German Historical School, philology and legal sciences were methodically interwoven. Archaeological discovery and legal scientific progress, such as the discovery of the Gaius fragment by Niebuhr and its interpretation by Savigny, belonged together. For the legal source was not the product of a political production process, but rather of a historical discovery process, one whose own character of scientific creation is freely recognized. On this, see James Q. Whitman, *The Legacy of Roman Law in the German Romantic Era*, Princeton 1990, pp. 79–91; Friedrich Carl von Savigny, *Vorlesungen über die juristische Methodologie 1802–1842*, Frankfurt/M. 2004, pp. 207 ff.

Of course, philology also knows critiques of the notion of an original text. The notion of the "original" can be contrasted with the idea of a multitude of versions that do not necessarily relate to each other in a hierarchical way.[19] Many periods of literary production are unfamiliar with the concept of the original.[20] Can we gain anything from this for our theory of the normative? Well, there are heterarchical practices of continuing and passing on norm texts in the rabbinical tradition, or in a judiciary system without unifying appellate bodies that are vested with supreme authority. Norms do not have to be fixed in written form, and normative orders are even less held to produce any "original" norms. This is why the observation that norm and norm text cannot neatly be separated only applies to certain kinds of norms. It also highlights the more general insight that the relationship between norm and norm text can take various shapes. What is more, even a practice that can do without original texts cannot completely evade the need for an authorization. An editor may well publish a work as a variety of equally valid versions;[21] nevertheless an authorizing criterion remains necessary for that which is published to form a unity. This may by the identity of the sequence of signs used in the edition with that of a given textual object or manuscript or the fact that the different versions were written in the identical hand writing.[22]

The specific and independent relevance of text as a form for normative orders also shows itself in the way in which they treat citations. In the various texts produced by legal practice, in court verdicts, in legal complaints and indictments, and in expert opinions, literal verbatim citations assume a central role.[23] The same goes for references in authorized texts that readers themselves are supposed to track.[24] To quote an anonymous judge who described her work to an anthropologist: "Most verdicts are citations."[25] A large part of what is considered legal argumentation in practice turns out to consist in the copying of other texts into one's own text. Verbatim quotes, particularly from legal precedents, take on much of the burden that a legal reasoning has to carry. It appears as though the repeated sign carries its own authority over into another text.

[19] Thus, an authorization problem can arise by the lack of a manuscript (Shakespeare), or by there only being manuscripts (Hölderlin). I thank Luca Giuliani for this insight.

[20] Roger Chartier, "Macht der Schrift. Macht über die Schrift" in: Hans Ulrich Gumbrecht and K. Ludwig Pfeiffer (eds), *Schrift*, Munich 1993, pp. 147–58.

[21] Compare with Ernst Jünger, *In Stahlgewittern*, Helmut Kiesel (ed.), Stuttgart 2013.

[22] A critical historicization of the archiving of manuscripts after 1750 is found in Roger Chartier, "Die Hand des Autors" in: *Jahrbuch der Deutschen Schillergesellschaft* 54 (2010), pp. 496–511, here pp. 505–7.

[23] It is just as astonishing as it is characteristic that in certain established legal methodology teachings of various legal cultures, quotations play no role even though they make up the most frequent method of legalistic argumentation.

[24] On this phenomenon, which is probably not coincidentally rarely made explicit, Elisabeth Holzleithner and Viktor Mayer-Schönberger, "Das Zitat als grundloser Grund rechtlicher Legitimität" in: Birgit Feldner and Nikolaus Forgó (eds), *Norm und Entscheidun. Prolegomena zu einer Theorie des Falls*, Wien/New York 2000, pp. 318–51, here pp. 325–34.

[25] Peter Stegmaier, *Wissen, was Recht ist*, Wiesbaden 2009, p. 119.

Of course, citations always stand in a context and cannot be randomly transported into a different context. There is a technique of successful citation which distinguishes itself from the mere copying of signs. Just as rarely as other texts speak for themselves, so do citations. This doesn't change the fact that citations in legal texts represent an indispensable and hence widespread technique. In citations, a legal source seems to be incorporated in its entirety into an argument, or the appeal to the authority of the norm setting entity is used in place of an argument. Instead of the person citing the norm, the norm itself seems to have its say. The point of stressing this is less to criticize this invocation as illusory than to realize that the practical relationship between literal citation and authority can hardly be shaken by such a critique.

Similar observations can be made regarding the treatment of literary texts.[26] The practice of analyzing literary texts rarely makes do with merely paraphrasing the objects of its analysis. Instead, it must also reproduce the text in order to keep its object well-defined.[27] The same goes for religious texts.[28] In Catholic liturgy, the Gospel is a formalized literal quotation, which may not be replaced by a theological argument or any other form of paraphrasing, and it is not always easy to fulfil this requirement and all the while do justice to the audience attending the service.[29] The preceding reading from the Old Testament and the Epistles, and the ensuing sermon brings the citation into a further context, makes it comprehensible, and comments on it.[30] Of course, even the Gospel cannot speak for itself but it can only be expressed in the form of a citation and serves as the indispensable reference point of all contextualization. In a formulation to be found in Catholic theology, the sacrament cannot be identified with God because it remains inevitably symbolic. The word however can be thus identified.[31] Paraphrasing the text would bring into question its literary character or sacredness, as authorized and vouched for by literal citation.

It is no coincidence that the relevance of citations is recognized in the literary-esthetic and theological context, but not in legal practice. In literary-esthetic

[26] On the normative pretense of esthetic practices, see Interlude II, pp. 146–66.

[27] Stanley Cavell, "Aesthetic Problems of Modern Philosophy" in: Id., *Must We Mean What We Say?*, Cambridge 2002, pp. 73–96, here pp. 74–80, shows that it neither suffices to simply treat literary texts as "not paraphrasable" nor to paraphrase them. Literal usage, in contrast to metaphoric usage, cannot be paraphrased. We add that even the metaphor has to be quoted at least once in order to then be able to be gainfully paraphrased.

[28] Augustine underscores that the sacred texts are also written with human, conventional symbols: *Die christliche Bildung*, Karla Pollmann (ed.), Stuttgart 2002, p. 47. Of course, this is only possible because the church takes over the interpretation. On this, see Gerhard Strauss, *Schriftgebrauch, Schriftauslegung und Schriftbeweis bei Augustin*, Tübingen 1959, pp. 63–8.

[29] Josef Andreas Jungmann, *Missarum Sollemnia*, Freiburg i. Br. 1962, Vol. 1, pp. 517–35. Connected to the sacralization of the text is the special decoration of the book from which the Gospel is read, and the position of the reader in the church hierarchy, see ibid., pp. 566–8.

[30] Reinhard Meßner, *Einführung in die Liturgiewissenschaft*, Paderborn 2001, pp. 188–90.

[31] Henri de Lubac, *Histoire et Esprit*, Paris 1950, p. 366, quoted here by Hans Urs von Balthasar, *Henri de Lubac*, Einsiedeln 1976, pp. 63 f.

discourse, the status of a text as artefact is clear. Dealing with a literary text requires quoting from it. In Christian theology, the revelatory character of religion serves to accord a value of its own to the literal invocation of the text.[32] By contrast, citations in law seem call into question the independent claim to rationality of legal argument. In the law, citation remains a practice that is equally omnipresent as it is methodically shunned.

1.7 Authorization through Transporting of Signs

We have seen that the identification of norm and norm text helps us to approach the phenomenon of norm authorization. Equating a given text with a certain norm solves a pragmatic problem. It makes the authorization of the norm discernible. Now one could ask whether it is the norm or whether it rather is its author that is being made present in the norm text. This however would only be the case if "the norm" could be sufficiently distinguished from the authorized form of its textual manifestation, which is precisely not the case for many formalized normative orders. Thus, the parliamentary law-maker only appears in the form of statutes; in a legal order that has instituted a certain procedure of law-making, the author only becomes visible in the form attributed to him. Indeed, there is a parliament, a head of State, and other actors that participate in the act of legislation, but these agents are not to be equated with the author of the law, the law-maker. They are only part of the law-maker if they pass a law together. The distinction between an author and narrator is comparable, even if it cannot be formalized in the same manner. That is why there are borderline cases, such as the novel in which the first-person narrator shares the same first name as well as other features of the author. It would be wrong to equate such a narrating figure with the author. On the other hand, we would miss the very point of playing with this distinction if we weren't allowing for some lack of clarity and transition between the two, which alone lets us catch glimpses of the author through the spectrum of the narrator.[33] In these cases, the clear-cut distinction between norm and norm authorization is just as unhelpful as a strong distinction between norm and norm text. However, we can usefully speak of *text norms* in cases in which the norm can best be captured by reference to the text, that

[32] The fact that text integrity and citation are so central for normative discourses casts doubt on the thesis that the development of a primitive literalism toward a differentiated hermeneutics is characteristic of modernity. We should at least differentiate: it may be the case in ascertaining the meaning of texts, and it may also be the case that the cultic veneration of texts does not play a big role in modern legal orders or in the literary scene. But that does not alter the fact that upholding a certain *chain of symbols* remains of immense importance for both social practices. The digitalization of writing may well increase its significance for legal argumentation even more, seeing that all authorized texts are now immediately available and no-one relies on their memory or secondary texts anymore in order to reconstruct their content.

[33] Matías Martínez and Michael Scheffel, *Einführung in die Erzähltheorie*, Munich 2012, pp. 86 ff.

is whenever a reference to the norm text through direct citation becomes the best possible or only proper description of the norm.

The cases discussed here have in common that social practice each time refers to an artefact, a legal text or a literary work, whose observation is not independent from the knowledge of their production process. Even if the concept "artefact" initially seems out of place, the same can be claimed for sacred texts of a revelatory religion, in as far as they are taken to be the conscious product of a decision by God, and not an expression of any universal rationality to which God, too, is subject.

1.8 Countercheck

Conversely, the fact that norms can only manifest themselves in a certain text does not entail that the written form of a norm alone did suffice to ascertain its character as a norm. Let us take another look at the freedom of opinion as guaranteed in article 67 of the North Korean constitution. Is this a norm? What speaks against this is that it is not treated as such by anyone, neither by its creators nor by its readers. No-one counts on it to be realized to the end that political opinions in North Korea might be openly expressed. This does not preclude article 67 from developing into a proper norm: following a political revolution that would result in a reinterpretation of the non-normative texts into norms. Does this contradict our thoughts on the relationship between norm and norm text? This is not the case, as our observations on the ways in which modern legal orders formalize authorization through text do not imply this institutionalized practice that identifies norms with norm texts to be something that is immanent to the text as such. Of course, one and the same text can operate as a norm or not, depending on which practices predominate in a given society. Even the identification of a text as a text presumes more than a "text."[34] It suffices to realize that there are important normative practices for which the distinction between a norm and a norm text has no relevant meaning.

1.9 The Written Form and its Consequences as Illustrated by the Example of a Constitution

If we understand a "constitution" as being a set of rules for the organization and limitation of a political community, then it would seem to be common sense to treat the question of whether or not it is encoded in writing as merely secondary. By aid of the distinction between constitution and constitutional text, it would

[34] See Stanley Fish, *Is There a Text in this Class?*, Cambridge, Mass. 1980.

even be consistent to claim that there can be no "written constitution"[35] but only a transcript or protocol of the constitution. Political orders with a parliamentary structure of government, free elections, an independent judiciary, and a certain standard of basic rights protections can either—like Germany or Japan—choose to write down in a uniform document the rules which shape these orders or do without a written form, such as the United Kingdom or New Zealand. Of course, all these orders differ from each other, but is the written form a relevant distinguishing feature?

If this were not the case, would it be appropriate to take the written form as something secondary, as a coincidence, as an embodiment of a bundle of reasons?[36] Conversely, one would have to show that the written form, as an innovation of the late eighteenth century, has dramatically changed the ways in which constitutions operate.[37] The assumption that the written form merely represents a contingent medium fails to recognize its inseparable relationship to the normativity of modern constitutional law. Unwritten constitutions provide a collection of official practices, thus representing how the system of government has operated to date, or how it was shaped by the political process,[38] as is the case until today with English constitutionalism.[39] Written constitutions, on the other hand, assert a claim to reform which expressly distances itself from political reality. It remains to be shown that it is only by recourse to an integral text which claims to fixate the entirety of constitutional law that a number of mechanisms can be put in place which allow the normative pretense of the constitution to take great effect.[40]

Political orders without written constitutions also draw on the written form in order to regulate their political system. But they get by without a document from which the order *as a whole* is to be organized. Instead, they document individual practices in a multitude of documents, in written and unwritten conventions at a lower level of abstraction.[41] In a system with a written constitutional order that

[35] John Gardner, "Can There Be a Written Constitution?" in: *Oxford Studies in Philosophy of Law* 1 (2011), pp. 162–94.

[36] Consistently in regards to law on this, Joseph Raz, *Practical Reason and Norms*, Oxford 1990, pp. 58–84, 149–62, who identifies legal orders with a certain form of reasons, as *mandatory exclusionary reasons* which rule out all other reasons regardless of their content. But does this exclusion actually take place in the realm of reasons, or is it much rather in an institutional reality? And are there kinds of reasons without content in the realm of reasons?

[37] On this, also see Edward S. Corwin, "The Constitution as Instrument and as Symbol" in: *American Political Science Review* XXX (1936), pp. 1071–85, here pp. 1072 ff. I intentionally leave the sizeable differences between the American and French constitutional tradition aside for the time being.

[38] On the practice before the Atlantic revolutions, see John W. Gough, *Fundamental Law in English Constitutional History*, Oxford 1955, pp. 174–91.

[39] Ivor Jennings, *The Law and the Constitution*, London 1959, p. 136.

[40] James R. Zink, "The Language of Liberty and Law: James Wilson on America's Written Constitution" in: *American Political Science Review* 103 (2009), pp. 442–55, has already shown for James Wilson that this was common for the drafters of the constitution.

[41] Albert V. Dicey, *Introduction to the Study of the Law of the Constitution*, London 1920 (reprint 1923), pp. 27–9. For an overview of the objects and development of constitutional conventions, see Geoffrey Marshall, *Constitutional Conventions*, Oxford 1984.

claims general applicability and relevance, all questions of a certain normative dignity are integrated into the document.[42]

For one, this allows for a specific treatment of time. By entering the world as a concrete spatio-temporal object, the constitution receives a beginning. The drafting and proclamation of the constitutional text becomes the beginning of a new order, which is to be measured by different standards than the old one. Hannah Arendt's description of discontinuity's significance for the political theory of the late eighteenth century takes its departing point here.[43] Monarchies of preconstitutional times do not know any such originating moments. Since they draw on divine appointment, it is meaningless to search for a starting point; they are concerned with continuity, not with marking a break. But marking a break requires an event that defines it. Raising a document to the level of a constitution is such an event; and the possibility to connect this event with an object, the concrete text of the norm, materializes this break, and thereby allows to preserve it.

By becoming a written document, the constitution also turns into a concrete object that can be exhibited as an original and that can also be reproduced. Both possibilities foster its particular normative aspiration. The original copy of the constitution can turn into an object fit for museum display; it can become an elevated, revered object.[44] The authorized reproduction of the constitution permits for its widespread distribution and reading. For citizens that read the document, it becomes possible to compare the pretense and aspirations laid out in the constitution with political reality. The reproduction also allows for its becoming an object and reference point of political debate in a mass democracy.

The existence of a constitutional document not only enables the copying of the entire text, but also the selection of individual parts of the document, that is, its citation. The practice of citation, as we have seen, allows for the transfer of authorization by means of passing on certain signs. They also play a large role for legal argumentation, especially for the function that courts assume in interpreting the constitution. The practical relevance of the text and its citation do not imply any naïve literalism of meaning. Rather, reference to the text lets us address ambiguity in an authorized manner. The text secures the unity of the object, the ambiguity of which is debated. At the same time, this reference to the text legitimizes the dispute itself.

A similar doubling arises with regard to the alterability and permanence of the constitutional norm.[45] The written form simultaneously enables the text to be

[42] Ulrich K. Preuß, "Die Verfassung als Gegenstand allen Sehnens" in: Id., *Revolution, Fortschritt und Verfassung*, Frankfurt/M. 1994, pp. 13–28; Heinz Mohnhaupt/Dieter Grimm, *Verfassung*, Berlin 2002, pp. 116 f.

[43] Hannah Arendt, *Über die Revolution*, Munich 1974, pp. 31–5, 260–75.

[44] Halbertal (n 15), *People of the Book*, p. 14 ff, outlines the development from an external treatment with sacred texts in Judaism to one striving for understanding.

[45] Luhmann (n 5), *Das Recht der Gesellschaft*, p. 94.

altered and to keep it unchanged. On the one hand, a conglomerate of written-down traditions cannot be altered at will in any conscious and straightforward way. In the English constitutional tradition, there is no procedure for constitutional change, only steady evolution powered by practice. On the other hand, it is only the identification of the text with the constitutional norm that allows it to be left *unchanged*. We have seen how norms change in the process of their application. This also holds true for all types of constitutions. Only for written constitutions, however, is it possible to juxtapose this permanently changing practice with the immutability of the signs which make up the written document, thereby stabilizing the constitution's normative aspirations. This does not imply that the written form would allow us to permanently preserve a certain constitutional meaning and transport it over time. It is a truism of hermeneutics that we cannot but understand the same text differently now than we did earlier on. It also does not imply that political orders that chose to write down their constitutions are thereby subject to slower political or social change than those with unwritten constitutions.[46] Quite to the contrary, the reference to constitutional norms can even accelerate this change. One example of this would be the legal guarantee of equal protection and its consequences for the political order.

For this reason as well, speaking of stabilizing expectations by norms is misleading.[47] The possibility to leave the text, and thus "the constitution" unchanged strengthens its autonomy vis-à-vis other processes of social change. It does so even in cases in which the social change is brought about by making reference to constitutional norms. The permanence of the text does not imply the permanence of its meaning, but rather the unchanged potential to draw on the constitutional text as a standard for political reality. The text persists, even if it changes its meaning. But the reference to it continues to stand in for alternative possibilities that have not been realized in light of social change and the changed readings of the text.

At the same time, only written constitutions can devise mechanisms of their conscious and deliberate change. This, too, is an institutional innovation of the late eighteenth century.[48] Not every change to a text, however, entails the intended or even any consequences. What is more, practices regulated by the constitution may well change without the text being changed. In Germany, this phenomenon is referred to with the misleading term of "constitutional evolution."[49] However, by formalizing procedures for changing a constitution, both developments—changes to the text and evolving practice or meaning—can be

[46] Regarding this assumption, see Reinhart Koselleck, "Geschichte, Recht und Gerechtigkeit" in: Id., *Zeitschichten*, Frankfurt/M. 2003, pp. 336–58, here pp. 353–8. A history that proceeds slower than others, however, would intermittently have to "make up" time.

[47] See above, pp. 73–75.

[48] Also regarding the American prehistory: Horst Dreier, *Gilt das Grundgesetz ewig?* Munich 2009, pp. 35–47, who thus does not address the change-resistant point of the form.

[49] Literary critics, even if they were enlightened regarding reception history, would hardly speak of a Hamlet change.

kept distinct and the normative aspiration of the constitution can thus be better secured. This aspiration materializes both in the constancy of the text under conditions of amorphous evolution and in the direct access to the text despite the uncertainty as to which consequences a change to the text will have. In procedures of amendment, the authorizing situation of constitutional enactment is extended into the present because, with amendments to the constitution, norms are created that have the same priority as the original norms in the constitution, even though the foundational situation lying at its origin has passed and cannot be invoked anew.[50] Here, too, the comparison with unwritten constitutions is instructive. The possibility of changing a constitutional text enables us to update the entire constitution. Furthermore, every change to the constitutional text presupposes an application of the constitution, more specifically the application of its rules of change. In as far as all the provisions of the constitution are subject to these rules of change, any specific constitutional change does not only provide renewed authorization to the norms that are actually being changed, but to all other norms of the constitution as well, for these, too, could have been altered.[51] Unwritten constitutions, too, can be updated, they also know procedures like parliamentary legislation that perpetually re-enact and recall the unwritten doctrine of parliamentary sovereignty. In this respect, this model, too, does not operate purely by way of tradition. But what is missing is the autonomous character of the results created by these procedures vis-à-vis the process that created them. There is no means for someone outside the procedure, say a citizen, an outvoted minority, or a court, of calling into question this practice by taking reference to or invoking the constitution.

From among the vast number of possible formats in which constitutional change can take shape let us distinguish between three types according to their normative pretense. Among the first group, we can count constitutional rules that leave the original text untouched, such that changes only appear as addendums to the original text. This is the case in the United States. Every change is an *amendment*, an addition. Procedures of constitutional change of a second kind constantly change and update the text of the constitution, thereby allowing the original text to fade. This approach thus keeps with a formal identity of constitution and the constitutional text. There is no constitution outside the text, even if this text does no longer correspond to the original text.[52] In a third kind of procedure, however,

[50] In this way, however, regarding the American constitutional history, Bruce Ackerman, *We, the People*, Vol. 1: *Foundations*, Cambridge, Mass. 1993, pp. 92–4.

[51] For this reason, unalterable norms are comparatively weak in their legitimation (Luhmann (n 5), *Das Recht der Gesellschaft*, p. 93), they rather have the status of a natural event. Thus, regarding the prohibition on incest, Claude Lévi-Strauss, *Die elementaren Strukturen der Verwandtschaft*, Frankfurt/M. 1993, pp. 57–74, 198 f., 648–50; on the problem of the unavailability of norms, see below, pp. 265 f.

[52] David E. Kyvig, *Explicit and Authentic Acts: Amending U.S. Constitution 1776–1995*, Lawrence 1996, pp. 100–2.

provisions of formal constitutional change can also be enacted outside the constitutional document. The constitution-altering majority can enact a law that has constitutional status and authority but does not alter the text of the constitutional document.[53]

In the first type of procedure of change, every new constitutional provision is confronted with the constitution's original version. The moment in which the constitution was enacted remains present in the original version. In the third type of procedure, the document no longer offers reliable information regarding the current inventory of valid constitutional law. This variety of constitutional change procedure thus allows, for example, for a majority authorized to alter the constitution to enact a rule that makes it a punishable crime to spread negative views of pragmatic philosophers, without making any changes to the *text* of the guarantee of freedom of speech upon which this rule would infringe. In contrast, according to the second type of procedure, the law-maker altering the constitution would have to supplant the guarantee of freedom of opinion by a clause along the lines of "this rule may be suspended in order to protect the honor of pragmatic philosophers." In this case, the specific interest of regulating a particular case would have to be inscribed into the general rules of the constitution and be confronted with them.

The way in which these three types of procedures treat the written form expresses a differing measure of distinction of the constitution's normative pretense against the political and social processes that it seeks to regulate. In the first type, the moment of giving oneself a constitution gets preserved in the original text and cannot be unmade by any political process. A constitution perpetuates the moment of its own enactment by means of the constitutional text, and thereby remains distinct from its subsequent political practice. In the third kind of procedure, in contrast, it is possible to completely detach the state of valid constitutional law from the content of the text of the constitutional document. The constitution is thus found in a plethora of individual rules that no longer appear in one "constitutional document." In a strict sense, then, we are no longer dealing with a written constitution. As the uniformity enabled by official documentation vanishes, so does the pretense of a unified regulatory complex that confronts the political reality as its standard and measure. The rules diffuse along with the political practice in an unwritten constitutional order. The normative potential of a constitution, its distance to political practice, is thus mainly enabled by the unity of the written form. Without the fixation of the constitution in a document, "the constitution" remains a mere state of affairs. It is only due to the written form that it becomes a distinguishable norm. The written form is thus not merely external to the normative pretense of a

[53] Ewald Wiederin, "Über Inkorporationsgebote und andere Strategien zur Sicherung der Einheit der Verfassung" in: *Zeitschrift für öffentliches Recht* 59 (2004), pp. 175–212, here pp. 183 f.

constitution; it is not a medium that merely transports normativity, it creates its own mechanisms of normativization.[54]

And finally, the written form makes it easier to establish a hierarchy between the norms of the constitution and other norms. The substantive differences between the English political system and continental European political orders with parliamentary systems and written constitutions are hardly dramatic. In contrast, the normative pretense of the respective constitutions—that which we call "constitutional primacy," that is, the idea that all other norms in the legal order have to abide by the constitution if they want to maintain their validity—operates completely differently in these systems.[55] Traditionally, the English system does not know this "primacy of the constitution" over decisions of the parliamentary majority. The notion that the political process might be denied a certain decision due to reasons of constitutional law thus makes no sense in the English system.[56] What remains just as senseless in this kind of system is the reference to the constitution, familiar to other orders, as an expression of a basic normative orientation of the State: as an inviolable promise of a community in freedom, such as in the United States, as a model of republicanism in France, or as the post-totalitarian, moralized community of values, such as in the Federal Republic of Germany.[57]

Manifesting the constitution in a single constitutional document thus is an instrument to institutionalize a constitution's claim to primacy,[58] albeit not a sufficient condition for it.[59] France's history shows that written constitutions were able to bring about the normativity of a political republicanism but, for a long time, certainly not a strict primacy in a juridical sense. But even in cases such as these an understanding of a constitution as a political standard can hardly be imagined without a written fixation in a document. Such written fixation provides mechanisms in which normative contents can become autonomous from political and legal practice. It enables the individual reading of a text, with which the existing conditions can be compared; it enables the generalizing compilation of the contents of a political practice, as well as the application and citation of the constitution as a norm by courts.

[54] In this regard, it can remain open as to how far one takes the development of modern constitutions as a victory of certain ideas. The reliance of such ideas on structures of dispersal is even recognized by Jonathan Israel, *Revolutionary Ideas*, Princeton 2014, pp. 33–52.

[55] Here, juridical differentiations such as primacy of application and validity are not of concern.

[56] Particularities in implementing the European Human Rights Convention with the Human Rights Act can be left aside.

[57] Comparatively, Christoph Möllers, *The Three Branches. A Comparative Model of Separation of Powers*, Oxford 2013, Chapter 1.

[58] On its novelty in the late eighteenth century with the emergence of written constitutions: Gerald Stourzh, "Constitution: Changing Meanings of the Term from the Early Seventeenth to the Late Eighteenth Centruy" in: Id., *From Vienna to Chicago and Back*, Chicago 2007, pp. 80–99, here pp. 97–9.

[59] Christoph Schönberger, "Der Vorrang der Verfassung" in: Ivo Appel, et al. (eds), *Öffentliches Recht im offenen Staat*, Berlin 2011, pp. 385–403, here pp. 386–90.

1.10 A Counterargument from Ronald Dworkin

The practical relevance of texts for normative practices depends on whether norms can be understood as social artefacts—an assumption that, as we have seen, is by no means self-evident, and which cannot be upheld in the same way for all practices. Ronald Dworkin, for example, challenges the claim that the validity of law depends on social facts. With numerous examples, he tries to illustrate that the question of what a legal norm means for a case inevitably leads the participants to the question of why they recognize this legal norm, that is, to the question of what morally justifies it in substance. According to Dworkin, in legal practice, we thus can observe that participants not only disagree on the content, but also on the reasons for a legal norm's validity.[60] In his words, the practice of law does not apply a notion of law based on set criteria,[61] it contains no set of rules that conclusively define what belongs to a legal order. Thus, every legal dispute potentially leaves the realm of social facts and turns toward the *moral* question of its justification.[62] For Dworkin, it is only this kind of reconstruction that can explain that, in a legal dispute, we are arguing about one and the same object and that we not simply talk past each other with different words taken from our legal vocabulary.

By no means should it be denied that a legal dispute can move away from the question of a legal norm's meaning to one of its justification. Many types of legal argument aim in this direction. However, in many cases, this is not so much a moral justification in the sense of Dworkin but rather a purely functional justification. And in many cases, even this kind of a justification might not be resorted to. Norm texts are put in place precisely in order to relieve legal discourse from the burden of such justificatory problems, and it is all but obvious why the cases in which this in fact succeeds should be untypical for law. It is no coincidence that Dworkin in his analyses only treats cases turning on fundamental rights or other cases that pose unusual moral problems, and never the legions of cases that deal with legal-technical questions. His approach is tailored to norms for which neither the textual version nor the social authorization are decisive. This is namely the case for fundamental rights, at least in so far as these are taken to be pre-political moral entities, the pretense of which does not hinge on any positing or writing.[63] No-one would

[60] Ronald Dworkin, *Law's Empire*, Cambridge, Mass. 1986, Chapter 1, especially pp. 43 f. Good analysis of this argument, as well as other weaker ones, is provided by Scott J. Shapiro, "The 'Hart–Dworkin' Debate, A Short Guide for the Perplexed" in: Arthur Ripstein (ed.), *Ronald Dworkin*, New York 2007, pp. 22–55, here pp. 35–9, and Dale Smith, "Theoretical Disagreement and the Semantic Sting" in: *Oxford Journal of Legal Studies* 30 (2010), pp. 635–61, here pp. 637–41.

[61] Ronald Dworkin, *Taking Rights Seriously*, Cambridge, Mass 1987, pp. 39–45.

[62] The most famous case that he uses is *TVA v Hill*, 437 US 153 (1978). On this, see the critique by Brian Leiter, "Explaining Theoretical Disagreement" in: *The University of Chicago Law Review* 76 (2009), pp. 1215–50.

[63] On this exchange, simply see Christoph Menke and Arnd Pollmann, *Philosophie der Menschenrechte*, Hamburg 2007, pp. 25–42. On the problem that a value-based understanding of fundamental rights misses the actual point of the legal protection of freedom, see Alon Harel, *Why Law Matters*, Oxford 2014, pp. 25–48.

claim the same for a statute regarding legal remedies, or for a set of house rules, nor would we claim as much for the constitutional rules delineating federal and State powers, or a provision regarding the law of accounting, enforced by criminal sanctions. Whether fundamental rights are appropriately described by Dworkin is not of further interest here, though one can certainly understand the foundations of fundamental rights quite differently from him, namely politically or in a purely legal way.[64] What is important for us is that Dworkin's model remains far off from a general theory of law, not even to speak of a theory of social norms, as it is derived from a rather specific understanding of a specific type of norm.

Furthermore, one has to doubt whether the dispute about the foundations of the validity of a legal norm indeed presuppose any implicitly shared understanding of the foundations of law, which would establish the very unity of the dispute. It, to the contrary, seems more plausible to assume that we are arguing about which of the different concepts of law is appropriate for our practice. This is precisely what happens in the discussion that Dworkin leads with positivist legal theory. He shares with it an object of dispute, but not a notion of law. The unity of such a dispute does not require a shared notion of law.[65] What is more, in legal practice, these kinds of disputes are not led by moral arguments only. Instead we might also fundamentally disagree about certain cognitive questions regarding the epistemic possibilities of legal knowledge, such as when we dispute the meaning of "text" for the practice of law. What is more, legal procedures make use of quite tangible mechanisms of formalization, in order to determine both the factual and the normative side of a legal dispute: they lead parties of a dispute into a room at the same time, they define a spatio-temporally determinate object of dispute—an accident, for example—they use land registers, file and item numbers, and they work with legal texts that can be cited. These are all techniques for which legal philosophy shows suspiciously little interest.[66]

This helps to clarify the scope of the argument presented here: texts are artefacts. The distinction between a norm and a norm text, as shown, has greater value for some normative practices than for others. Many normative practices largely get by without a text—rules of etiquette or customary law—although, upon closer inspection, some traditions that supposedly arose out of orally passed-on practice, in fact, have arisen out of written traditions that were only later passed on orally.[67]

[64] One should at least note that in the realm of fundamental rights, on the one hand there are also very different interpretive practices, and on the other hand strongly formalized ones that hardly fit with Dworkin's model. Such diversity shows itself even within legal orders that interpret basic rights moralistically: James Fowkes and Michaela Hailbronner, "Courts as the Nation's Consience" in: Silja Vöneky, et al. (eds), *Ethics and Law. The Ethicalization of Law*, Heidelberg 2013, pp. 395–420.

[65] On this, David Plunkett and Timothy Sundell, "Dworkin's Interpretivism and the Pragmatics of Legal Dispute" in: *Legal Theory* 19 (2013), pp. 242–81, here pp. 261–6.

[66] For an exception to this, see the considerations in Thomas Vesting, *Die Medien des Rechts: Schrift*, Weilerswist 2011, §2, and Id., *Die Medien des Rechts: Buchdruck*, Weilerswist 2013, pp. 47–71, as well as the contributions in Annelise Riles (ed.), *Documents: Artifacts of Modern Knowledge*, Ann Arbor 2006.

[67] The idea of an original oral foundation that then becomes written down has encountered critique in many fields. With an eye toward late-medieval legal practices, see Simon Teuscher, *Erzähltes Recht*,

Considerations about the specific normative value of written fixation thus concern many normative practices, not only those that operate with formalized procedures of norm creation.

This leads to one last point, namely the practical implications which theoretical doubts about the meaning of norm texts can have. The equating of norms with "reasons" produces claims of authorization that run counter to the logic of the formalized production of norm texts. Claiming that a norm does not "merely consist" in the norm's text questions the authority of the formalized procedures of norm production. If the text does not contain the norm, but is merely seen as its means of transmission, then the institutions that are charged to interpret the text's meaning gain in authority at the expense of those institutions which produced the text and can change it, as well as with regard to readers who make use of copies of the text. This kind of understanding thus empowers constitutional courts and constitutional lawyers over and against law-makers and ordinary readers as well as theologians over and against reading believers. It is no coincidence that Dworkin favors a morally armed constitutional court as a check on the democratic law-makers. The claim that the norm is always something other than the norm's text is not institutionally innocent or meaningless.

1.11 Understanding Norm Texts?

The question of what a norm means needs to be distinguished from the question of which norm is of concern, even if the two often converge. It is the response to the second question, to which the textual fixation of a norm can contribute. Putting into writing cannot overcome vagueness, it only makes something recognizable, the norm text, around which this vagueness can crystallize. The character of the text as something "external" thus does not so much serve to destabilize meaning[68] but rather to stabilize a given practice.[69]

Now, one can certainly doubt whether texts can be understood at all, and these doubts have constituted a large topic in the scientific treatment of and theory on texts.[70] The aspiration to "understanding" is frequently brought into connection

Frankfurt/M. 2007, pp. 302 ff; and regarding the case of Indian law in its colonial reconstruction as a law of commands (not laws) Mahmood Mamdani, *Define and Rule*, Cambridge, Mass. 2012, pp. 21–6.

[68] Thus, drawing on Derrida, David Wellbery, "Die Äußerlichkeit der Schrift" in: H. U. Gumbrecht and K. Ludwig Pfeiffer (eds), *Schrift*, pp. 337–48.

[69] Put another way, the concern is not a return to the text as such (as with de Man's return to philology) but rather the meaning that preserving chains of symbols can have for extra-textual practices. On the critique of a return program, see Sheldon Pollock, "Future Philology? The Fate of a Soft Science in a Hard World" in: *Critical Inquiry* 35 (2009), pp. 931–61, here pp. 947 ff.

[70] See the reading of Schleiermacher that leads from text interpretation to critique by Peter Szondi, "Schleiermachers Hermeneutik heute" in: Id., *Schriften*, Vol. 2, Frankfurt/M. 1978, pp. 106–30, here pp. 129 ff. For an anti-hermeneutical paradigm, see Hans Ulrich Gumbrecht, "Ein Abschiedsgruß an die Interpretation" in: Id., *Präsenz*, Berlin 2012, pp. 171–89, see also above, pp. 165–66.

with the existence of an author. For many social norms, however, we do not even know whether there is an author. Whoever claims to know him or her thereby authorizes themselves and their interpretation of the norm.[71] For an influential segment of literary criticism, it is misplaced to even aim at understanding a text; at most, one can strive to process them for the present day and age. Norm texts that aim at being applied would then be entities that need to be presented, as in making something present, without being able to say anything about the rightness of such presentation.[72]

However, negating the possibility of proper understanding is not as easily done in a practice that aims at *applying* norms than it is in a practice that only seeks to *interpret* them. This has nothing to do with the immanent characteristics of the different texts. A traffic rule, as such, is no easier to understand that a symbolist poem. The difference between the two lies in what is meant by "application" in these cases. While it is inevitable in both cases for questions of meaning to be tied into questions of authorization, that is, to respond to the question of what the meaning of the text is by also considering the question of who the author of the texts is, it is only the application of norms that adds a perspective toward realization. Peter Szondi highlights that the engagement with a poem is not marked by a finalizing interpretation but rather by the insisting on further interpretations to be possible.[73] This applies, in the same way, to our engagement with a norm text, as far as this concerns a legal scholar who engages with a norm in an academic context.[74] A legal scholar interprets a text without applying it.[75] This, in contrast, does not hold in the same way for a judge or a guardian of public morals who deals with a norm text, that is, in *applying* the norm text in the sense outlined here, by drawing on the norm text with a unique normative aspiration. For these forms of authorized realization of the normative content, insisting on further interpretive options is not an option. The norm content cannot be simultaneously implemented in two different manners. This difference arises less from the differences between an esthetic and legalistic treatment of social norms than it does from the meaning of "application." A poem's interpreter does not apply a poem. A theater director, even if this sounds a bit unusual, applies a dramatic text and cannot simultaneously stage it in two different ways. The decisive difference in obligation is found in the pretense of norms to be *realized*, which finds no correlate in pure

[71] On the author function, Michel Foucault, What Is an Author?" in: Id., *Language, Counter-Memory, Practice*, New York 1977, pp. 113–38, here pp. 121 ff.

[72] This is embedded in a more general theory of judgment by Florian Klinger, *Urteilen*, Zürich/Berlin 2011, pp. 359–64.

[73] Peter Szondi, "Über philologische Erkenntnis" in: Id., *Schriften*, Vol. I, pp. 263–86, here p. 266.

[74] Of course, different legal cultures differ widely in how they treat contradicting interpretations and the question of whether law only envisions one solution for a problem. Comparatively, see James Q. Whitman, "No Right Answer?" in: John Jackson et al. (eds), *Crime, Procedure and Evidence in a Comparative and International Perspective*, Oxford 2008, pp. 371–92.

[75] On this distinction, Jochen Bung, *Subsumtion und Interpretation*, Baden-Baden 2004.

text interpretation and which does not allow for multiple readings of a text to coexist alongside each other. Of course, there are multiple possibilities for understanding how a certain norm can be applied, again: nothing speaks for norm texts to be unambiguous. But the possibilities that are to be realized cannot simply stand alongside each other like different interpretations of a poem; in an emphatic way, they exclude each other since the application in one situation only grants for one version of realization.

This does not yield any guidelines as to the question how the appropriate understanding of a norm is to be reached. With a distinction that Seldon Pollock developed for philology,[76] we can distinguish between three types of dealing with a norm text: a historicizing one that looks for an original meaning of a text; one with a focus on reception history, which draws attention to the multitude of traditions that have arisen from engaging the text; and a "presentist" one that makes the text fruitful for the present.[77] One might think that the third variation is of particular interest for norms, as norms aim toward realization, that is, qua their normativity, they are made for a future present. The first variation would then only be pertinent for past, and no longer valid norms. The following shall show that this is indeed the case, as we examine the temporal structure of norms.

For the aporias of textual hermeneutics, the possibility of changing a norm's text, revealed through formalization, offers a noticeable option. The interpretation of a literary or religious text faces the problem of how it should approach the intentions of an author, with whom, on the one hand, it cannot completely do away, but whose invocation, on the other hand, remains speculative.[78] The possibility of *writing over* the text with the same authority is not an option for such a hermeneutic endeavor.[79] This is different in formalized legal orders. Of course, a new text also cannot evade the challenge of interpretation. Its content might be less clear than that of its predecessor. As something posited in a certain situation, a change to a text updates the meaning of the norm text, yet in a way that is not available to the endeavor of pure interpretation, since the old text is de-authorized at the same time that the new one is authorized. The old text can then no longer coexist as coequal alongside the new one.

[76] Lecture at the Forum on Transregional Studies in Berlin, October 2013, apparently unpublished, but also see Pollock (n 69), "Future of Philology" pp. 950 ff.

[77] However, there are two ways of dealing with the second approach. Observing reception can serve the renewal or ossification. See the considerations by Eberhard Jüngel, "Das Entstehen von Neuem" in: Id., *Wertlose Wahrheit. Zur Identität und Relevanz des christlichen Glaubens*, Tübingen ^{2}2003, pp. 132–50, here pp. 137 f.

[78] This dilemma cannot be changed by the presence of the author who could then comment on the autonomized text because such commenting does not have the same authority as the text itself. On this dilemma, see Carlos Spoerhase, *Autorschaft und Interpretation*, Berlin 2007, pp. 442–7; see also Daniel Boyarin, *Intertextuality and the Reading of Misrash*, Bloomington 1994, pp. 33–8.

[79] In Halbertal (n 15), *People of the Book*, p. 16, the distinction between open and closed canons does not help to explicate the possibility of removing something from the canon.

2. *Time*

2.1 The Temporal Asymmetry of Normative Practices

"The relationship of meaning and intention to future action is *normative*, and not *descriptive*."[80] Just like the common parlance of normative expectations, this observation by Saul Kripke seems to imply that normativity operates *toward the future*.[81] Norms have an aspirational pretense. They aim at, by marking that something ought to become, is made possible to in fact *come to be*.[82] This, at least, follows from the notion of norm developed in the preceding sections; if one takes norms to be possibilities whose realization is affirmed. The concept of realization can only be thought of in a perspective oriented toward the future.[83] Whatever can still become might also not materialize. It lies in the future. If norms require authorization and point toward the realization of a possibility, a familiar scheme emerges. A norm authorized in the past affirms a possible condition in the future. The norm thus points toward the future and the past. Its authorization lies behind it, its object can only lie ahead of it.

While the figure of realization can be applied both prospectively and retrospectively, analytically speaking, it always remains oriented toward the future. One could say: it would have been better had God on the sixth day only created woman. Wouldn't this be a normative expression that simultaneously points toward the past and something impossible, thereby missing two aspects of our notion of a norm? No, as this claim remains meaningful in reference to God's possibility to act differently than he did, that is, from the perspective of his past future. As a social norm, it is furthermore only relevant if something *can* follow from its expression, such as how we treat men and women. This does not change anything about the scheme of the future orientation of a norm, which can only serve as a departure point, however. For this is where problems arise.

2.2 Past

The claim is that norms consistently operate in a way that is oriented toward the future. This does not preclude the possibility to also assume a normative disposition

[80] Saul Kripke, *Wittgenstein on Rules and Private Language*, Cambridge, Mass. 1984, p. 37.

[81] John McDowell, "Wittgenstein on Following a Rule" in: Id., *Mind, Value and Reality*, Cambridge, Mass. 1998, pp. 221–62, here p. 235.

[82] Even that which is viewed as characteristic *direction of fit* of normative practices, leading back to Anscombe (see above, pp. 71 ff.), denotes a temporal phenomenon, since the normative measure precedes its object, whereas the descriptive one follows it.

[83] If we could affect the past, it would also not be clear how we could take notice of such an effect: Douglas Kutach, "The Asymmetry of Influence" in: Craig Callender (ed.), *The Oxford Handbook of Philosophy of Time*, Oxford 2011, pp. 247–75, here p. 266. A dense history of the problem is found in Huw Price, "The Flow of Time" in: *Oxford Handbook*, pp. 276–311.

toward past events, but it helps us to specify what is thereby meant. To start with, we should distinguish between the future orientation of norms and the description of past normative practices. The description of these practices can yield insights into the subjective realm of possibility of past actors, insights into what, in their own experience and perspective, could have gone differently, into what seemed possible, and what didn't. The question of what was held to be imperative at one point, and what was held to be possible, is also of interest for the description of what actually happened.[84] For this, no counterfactual assumptions are necessary.

At a different level, historical events can be normatively evaluated. But this only seems meaningful to the extent that there were alternatives to the actual historical record. We may indeed, after the fact, speculate about alternative historical developments. In historiography, this however is methodically precarious, as the question "What would have happened if... ?" is speculative and methodically impenetrable. It certainly has to be embedded in a well-defined, factual context which denotes concrete alternative strings of events, which in turn orient themselves along lines of what actually happened and what contemporaries took into consideration.[85] But even if one were to do without such normative positioning and its correlated speculation, the progression of past events can hardly be claimed to have been necessary and without alternatives, without taking either a deterministic or a teleological outlook on this course of events. The portrayal of alternative possibilities of progression thus remains methodically challenging for historiography and simultaneously difficult to avoid.

Within and outside historiography, it nonetheless is not unusual to evaluate past events normatively. Some forms of normativity can actually best be sorted according to their temporal orientation. It would be unusual to devise a rule that applied to the past, but it would be equally curious to want to judge something that has not yet occurred. The form of a court judgment refers to a past event. Maybe these intuitions with regard to their temporal structure are the best conceptual points of departure for distinguishing between rules and judgments.[86]

Even if it refers to past events, the practice of legal judgment does not lose sight of the principal future orientation of the norm which is being updated in the

[84] I thank Jonas Grethlein for this, and for many other helpful pointers.

[85] Niall Ferguson, "Introduction. Virtual History: Towards a ›Chaotic‹ Theory of the Past" in: Id. (ed.), *Virtual History*, London 1997, pp. 1–90, here p. 86. It remains questionable for the outside observer whether the discussion of historical methodology has substantially progressed since its multifarious twists and turns concerning narrativity and fiction than with Max Weber, even if Weber's formula of "objective possibility" seems too strong: Max Weber, "Kritische Studien auf dem Gebiet der kulturwissenschaftlichen Logik" in: *Gesammelte Aufsätze zur Wissenschaftslehre*, Johannes Winckelmann (ed.), Tübingen [7]1988, pp. 215–90, here pp. 266–77.

[86] If one looks more closely, however, there might yet be rules that concern the past, for example a law that treats an old legal State as unjust, but this too is a historical judgment in the form of a legal rule. Compare with the law for establishing the "Stiftung zur Aufbearbeitung der SED-Diktatur" (*Federal Foundation for the Reappraisal of the SED Dictatorship*) from 5 June 1998, *Bundesgesetzblatt* 1998 I,

judgment. This is because the judgment of a past state of affairs occurs from the past horizon of action and the future-oriented vantage point of those who are now participating in the proceedings. The recourse to the participants' past possibility is taken seriously. At the same time, the application of the norm brings about a further norm. As such, a legal judgment about past circumstances also creates a new normative guideline oriented toward the future.

Is this also the case for political-moral judgments? How do we judge the fact that women in the French Revolution had no right to vote? If we were to apply the standard of current political orders, the judgment would not only be ahistorical, it would be nonsensical. We would be transplanting something into the past that cannot be found there. Here, too, a normative pretense can only be meaningfully formulated in one of two ways: either one tries to discover the normative standard in the historic situation to which it should apply. Olympe de Gouges, who was executed because of her fight for women's rights in 1793,[87] stands in for a normative standard that already existed at her time, which could be reconstrued as future-oriented in this past situation. Or we use a past situation as illustration of a given normative positioning in the present. In this way, slavery in antiquity can illustrate what positively distinguishes a democratic political order nowadays. But this is not a statement about the past but rather a depiction of the present that operates with historical means. It thus remains that the use of normative figures is only meaningful if the standards which they set could already be formulated at the time for which they are being used.

2.3 Normative Retroactivity

Normativity's temporal structure can also be unpacked in the phenomenon of retroactivity. At first sight, retroactivity is an impossibility. Nothing can act upon or have an effect on the past. The expression, taken literally, denotes the temporal reversal of a causal link. Its usage in a normative context confirms our finding that norms are not entities concerned with making causal claims. What we take a retroactive effect to be is extending a norm to an object that is older than the norm itself. We have seen that normative statements about the past are possible, even if they frequently become ahistorical in the sense that they apply a standard that was unavailable at the time to which it is being applied. Retroactive effects then are nothing other than the judgment of the past with categories of

p. 1226, with which, in the cloak of founding an organization, a past political order is morally judged by a subsequent political actor. In such a case, who wants to still differentiate between politics, morality, and law?

[87] Olympe de Gouges, *Declaration of the Rights of Woman and of the Female Citizen*, 1791.

the present. But doesn't the phenomenon of a retroactive norm refute our assumption that norms are oriented toward the future? Even a retroactive norm only regulates the past for the future. It aims at a possible treatment of the past in the future. The object being regulated temporally precedes the rule, but the latter only applies after its own enactment.

This phenomenon becomes clearer when we consider the reasons why some forms of retroactive norming are viewed as problematic in normative orders. Formalized legal orders are familiar with the prohibition on retroactive legislation. This does not apply to all kinds of laws but only for laws infringing on certain rights. In modern legal orders, it is permissible to retroactively introduce positive legal consequences, for example when applying a tax exemption to a set of facts concluded when no such exemption was in place, thus resulting in a repaying of taxes already paid. Retroactivity becomes problematic only when tied to norms to which negative sanctions are attached.[88] Norms that may not to be introduced retroactively sanction an illegal action in awareness of its illegality, that is, under the precondition that the addressees of the norm were aware of the prohibition and were able to integrate it into their frame of action one way or another. The prohibition on retroactive legislation thus implements a concept of freedom to act. It is not the action as such that is being sanctioned, but rather the action in light of its pre-existing disapproval by a community. The prohibition on retroactive legislation solves a specific problem tied to the freedom of action, while the possibility of retroactive legislation is implied in the concept of a norm. The investigation into the phenomenon of retroactivity demonstrates that we treat norms differently than causes, by norming that which we can no longer change.

And finally, the prohibition on retroactive legislation expresses an understanding of norms which takes these to be posited artefacts that can only operate in a certain temporal context. Whoever places the criminal sanction of a killing under the condition that this behavior had been prohibited at the time at which it occurred treats this sanctioning norm, which is to be distinguished from the actual prohibition on killing someone, as a legal artefact and not as a moral universal. The prohibition on retroactive criminal legislation thus cannot be reconciled with theories that view law as an expression of timeless models of justice.[89]

[88] Günther Jakobs, *Strafrecht Allgemeiner Teil. Die Grundlagen und die Zurechnungslehre*, Berlin 1991, pp. 64 f.

[89] This conflict becomes clear in the debate surrounding the retroactive prosecution of criminal acts in totalitarian systems, the judgment of which noticeably depends on a norm-theoretical pre-understanding: on the one hand, Robert Alexy, "Mauerschützen. Zum Verhältnis von Recht, Moral und Strafbarkeit" in: Id., et al., *Elemente einer juristischen Begründungslehre*, Baden-Baden 2003, pp. 469–92; on the other hand, Günther Jakobs, "Vergangenheitsbewältigung durch Strafrecht?" in: Josef Isensee (ed.), *Vergangenheitsbewältigung durch Recht*, Berlin 1992, pp. 37–64.

2.4 Temporality of Universal Norms?

The assumption that norms have particular orientation toward time thus cannot be reconciled with certain moralist conceptions of norms. One could claim that the norms violated by slave holding societies are neither of a juridical nor of a social nature, but that they instead are moral norms that claim timeless validity. From this angle, speaking of the future orientation of every norm would be miss something, as this would also take away a part of such moral norms' temporally universal pretense.

But even if one were to take the existence of "timelessly" valid norms as one's starting point, the question would remain as to what these could mean for a certain historical situation. A slave-holding society, for which the moral assessment of slave-holding is inconsequential, might be measured against a universal, moral prohibition on slave-holding. At least for a theory of normativity that is interested in observable normative social practices, however, this is irrelevant. It can treat the norm as though it didn't exist. As soon as any elements of a critical engagement emerge in a society, as with the critique of slavery in the philosophy of the Stoics,[90] the norm begins to become contemporary to this society. As far as the normative evaluation of historical events is concerned, the considerations made above will then once more come to play. Every treatment of moral reasons will inevitably refer and be tied to its own historical context, even if these reasons are employed with the pretense of resting on truths that are independent of a given context.[91]

2.5 The Problem of Empirics seen Temporally

Not all norms strive for causal effects, but for those which do, particular problem arise in their empirical observation. Norms are oriented toward the future. The concern from the vantage point of a norm is prospectively to mark a possible, and thus uncertain future, whereas the empirical investigation of normative practices seeks retroactively to attribute an event to a certain norm. The plausibility of such an attribution depends on how the norm was materialized, that is, which means were employed in order to depict the norm and apply it. The spoken command of a military superior toward a present subordinate, demanding a certain action, quickly followed by a corresponding action, can be interpreted in the following manner. We observe an action that can be explained by a normative act, the command. But in many cases, this identification turns out to be more complex, which

[90] On the context of this critique, Peter Garnsey, *Ideas of Slavery from Aristotle to Augustine*, Cambridge 1996, Ch. 1.

[91] Also compare the observation by Robert E. Goodin, "An Epistemic Case for Legal Moralism" in: *Oxford Journal of Legal Studies* 30 (2010), pp. 615–33, here pp. 631 ff.

shows itself not least of all in the methodical difficulties in the empirical investigation of social norms, from criminology all the way to the sociology of religion, because the ex post description of normative practices requires the establishment of a relationship between a normative claim that allows the possibility of deviation, and an actual event that precludes such deviation. This relationship makes the empirical description of normative practices all the more difficult. Something is supposed to be described that can both enable this relationship, yet cannot force it.[92]

This problem is related to expectations that have with regard to social norms. Bear in mind, norms that are ignored are difficult to describe, and norms that are universally followed provoke the question if this practice has anything to do with the norm. In a library, where a sign demands people to speak quietly, everyone speaks quietly. Does the practice of speaking quietly constitute a norm, or is the sign a consequence of the undisputed practice of speaking quietly in a library? The recognizability of normativity, to which a given event is to be attributed, decreases the more the course of events approaches the norm.[93] The attribution of a course of events to a norm becomes a speculative enterprise. The normative pretense to be realized in the future makes it difficult to establish any reliable relationship between an event to be normed, the actual event, and the norm. Not only do we not know why it came to this and not to a different course of events, but we also do not know whether this particular course of events wouldn't have unfolded regardless of the norm's existence.

The empirical investigation of a norm's effects proves to be the ex post reconstruction of a social practice, which at one point made a pretense toward a future which now lies in the past. This pretense does not vanish because of its not being upheld. Neither can we safely deduce that it has been fulfilled from the brute fact that the aspired course of events has in fact materialized. The empirical investigation must account for this fundamental uncertainty. It is for this reason, for example, that the relationship between social practices and criminal law remains so tenuous. The possibility to arrange for experiments with control groups is quite limited in this context. Furthermore, comparison between different countries becomes methodically difficult due to the diversity of social contexts in which formally similar legal provisions operate. The practice of normativity, as something that is directed toward the future and open to divergence, remains very difficult to

[92] This was astutely seen by Friedrich Nietzsche in "Der Beweis einer Vorschrift." See "*Morgenröthe*" in: Id., *Sämtliche Werke: Kritische Studienausgabe*, Giorgio Colli and Mazzino Montinari (eds), Munich 1999, Vol. 3, p. 35.

[93] In Brandom's explication of following rules, this is captured as follows: Regulism, which believes that there "are" solid, clearly defined norms, is too assured of the identification of the normative, regularism, which views norms as the expression of social norms' repetition, lets these norms vanish in the social practice (Robert B. Brandom, *Making It Explicit. Reasoning, Representing, and Discursive Commitment*, Cambridge, Mass. 1994, pp. 18–30). But it is less than obvious whether the temporal incommensurability of the two models—the prospect of regulism, and the retrospective nature of regularism—allow for a solution to be formulated that integrates both.

observe. This might well be a reason against a purely instrumentalist conception of norms. A norm may reveal a lot about who we are or want to be; taking them as means toward an end quickly runs up against cognitive limitations.

2.6 The Challenge of the Notion of Performativity

The problem would take care of itself if we could entirely rule out the future to be bound by a norm in practice. This is how theories of performativity argue, more specifically following Jacques Derrida's critique of the concept of intentionality.[94]

Strong theories of performativity begin with the claim that the practice of spoken and written language is precisely that: a practice, a relationship of actions, and thus an intervention into the world.[95] For institutionalized normative practices, this is an important observation, and one that is hard to challenge—my saying "yes" can create a marriage. But it appears doubtful whether this applies to all linguistic practices.[96] For radical theories of performativity, language actualizes itself in its execution, and this execution simultaneously changes what is being actualized. The referencing of linguistic actions always operates retrospectively and punctually. Meaning arises as a series of referencing events that each accord a content to a linguistic sign. It doesn't operate by way of extending a previously fixed meaning of given signs into the future.

If meaning had to be taken as a series of retrospective references, our assumption about norms to be oriented toward the future would become untenable. It would be impossible to accord any meaning to a text or other sign that could limit its future use. And under such conditions, one moreover could argue that any notion of an obligation extending into the future would have to introduce into the description of a course of events a level beyond causality and chance, one for which there is no ontological room. For a normative obligation can neither be taken to be a causal effect nor can it occur completely by chance. Finally, the theory of performativity describes practices as a series of events. This could also result in the distinction between norm and norm application becoming completely redundant. For according to such a reading, norms would not already just be there in order to be applied but they would only develop as a norm by their application, which accords them a normative content. It would be the application that makes a norm a norm.

[94] Jacques Derrida, " Signature Event Context" in: Id., *Limited Inc.*, Evanston 1988, pp. 1–25; for the case of law, Sabine Müller-Mall, *Performative Rechtserzeugung*, Weilerswist 2012, pp. 173–210.

[95] On the idea of a creative word of God, also see: Eberhard Jüngel, *Das Evangelium von der Rechtfertigung des Gottlosen als Zentrum des christlichen Glaubens*, Tübingen 2011, pp. 172 f.

[96] In as far as he distinguishes between locutionary, illocutionary, and perlocutionary acts, Austin does not represent this viewpoint: John L. Austin, *How to do Things with Words*, Oxford 1975, pp. 94–108.

The systematic weak spot of this model lies in the uncertain identity of the sign to which one is making reference. The theory relies on a distinction between sign and meaning of the sign, and it at least has to ascertain that it is the self-same sign that first comes into the world and to which then a reference is made.[97] Under the model's own presuppositions, it would be more consistent to deny the existence of a sign, and to view its existence as being the result of an act of making reference, an attribution extending backwards and after the fact. But this would completely tear apart the course of events. It would no longer be clear how a referencing event at the interval n, and one at the interval n+1 were related to each other. Nonetheless, the distinction between a sign and the meaning attributed to it would be difficult to grasp under these theoretical conditions. For there is no such thing as *the* sign, at most there are individual signs whose relationship to each other can only be ascertained by a model of meaning, which is precisely excluded by a theory of performativity. Why is this a the same as this a—and why might it even be the same as this a. According to a theory of performativity, these cannot consistently be viewed as being identical.

One central assumption of the performative argument concerns temporality. The proceeding of time generally enables reference to something in the past, but it does not permit the capturing of the future. A norm cannot be tossed about like a lariat to capture the future. On this view, every normative pretense pointing toward the future proves to be illusory and is only put forward about by institutions or actors in order to rationalize and justify a course of events that would have happened anyway. But why should we deny the aspiration to future realization of a norm which is expressed in the form of a rule or command? The performative model, which wants to wait for a symbol to become a norm via reference, confuses the norm with a certain success of the norm, namely that it is treated like a norm. The performative notion of norm equates the norm with its continued adherence and thereby misses its afactual character.

This might have to do with the theory's roots in the philosophy of language which suggests the assumption that everything that is carried out in language operates like language. And indeed, linguistic rules can only be identified when they are being followed in a linguistic practice. However, it is already questionable whether these rules are actually norms, or whether they might simply be the description of a natural language that needs to adapt when the language changes. Furthermore, we treat rather differently explicit social norms such as traffic signs or the behavioral rules laid out in a catechism.

Theories of performativity, by contrast, insist that a traffic sign can only be identified by an iterative process. According to them, it is hopeless to take recourse to the *intention* of someone positing a norm. The subject that makes a normatively

[97] Compare with the distinction between pre-norm and norm in Müller-Mall (n 94), *Performative Rechtserzeugung*, pp. 220–2.

intended utterance, for example, a command, only recognizes their intention after the fact.[98] This however raises the question of what exactly is being ascribed after the fact to a sign when we treat it as normative, as opposed to non-normative. We ascribe a future-oriented meaning to it, even when this ascription only takes place after the fact. Even if it is futile for a theory of performativity to search for the intention of a person positing a norm, at least the meaning that I ascribe after the fact to a sequence of signs still reveals a future orientation whenever I treat this sequence as normative. Otherwise, it would remain unclear how I could be able to distinguish a normative from any other social practice. In this way, our claim that norms are a form of reference to the future, and the doubts raised by theories of performativity regarding the binding effect of norms, are located at different levels. Even if normative practices could only iteratively be identified as such, they would nonetheless distinguish themselves by virtue of their referring to the future. "The persistent question concerning the relationship between concept and judgement, on the one hand, and *perception* and *experience* on the other hand obscure the fact that, in forming concepts, we largely are not dealing with the present, but rather with that which is missing, distant, past or future."[99] This observation holds true for norms as well.

In the end, the critique of traditional conceptions of normativity by performative theories proves to be of little consequence. Either normative practices are indeed capable of a "performative" reconstruction. But in this case claims about normativity to only arise "in its performance" remain without consequence. For in this case even the enactment of a law, more than everything else that is conventionally understood by the term "application." would then be a form of performance. Or one takes performance to merely mean the application of a rule. Then the concept misses the point of normative practices, which consists in also capturing the possibility of norm transgression without the practices losing their normative character.

Let us once more consider an example. A conventional norm theorist would claim that sheet music or the text of a law put forward an intention which the applicants in an orchestra or a court will have to consider when they execute the law or perform the musical piece. This claim is denied by theories of performativity, according to which there are no texts that can be understood as norms *as such*. On their view, normativity only arises in the execution of the court's decision or the musical performance, both of which refer to a sequence of signs and thereby turn this sequence into something normative. Norms always need to be actualized anew as norms. Normativity is an iterative practice. But this is just as much the case for the process that is conventionally considered as the positing of norms as for the

[98] Derrida (n 94), "Signature Event Context" pp. 13–21.
[99] Hans Blumenberg, *Theorie der Unbegrifflichkeit*, Frankfurt/M. 2007, p. 33.

application of norms. Even the writing down of the musical score falls under this broad notion of performance, and yet it is unproblematic to take this act as referring to the future, even if the author can only recognize this aspirational dimension after the fact. Even the iterative, retrospective reconstruction of norms has to accord a future reference to them.

Finally, I would like to highlight two problems. The first concerns the subject-centered character of a notion of norm that presumes an iterating subject. In theories of this kind, neither institutions nor organizations are ever considered, and in this regard, they mirror other approaches that view norms as reflexes of subjective dispositions.[100] The iterative performance occurs within the subject.[101] This makes the description of social institutions all the more difficult.[102] A second problem consists in the fact that this performative deconstruction and critique of intentions only applies to an objectified understanding of intentions. However, hardly anyone believes that a text expresses and transports an intention that the author really "had." What is of concern is that our engagement with a text has to presuppose authorship and intention in order to distinguish itself from dealing with causally determined events.

2.7 Brandom's Common Law Model

But doesn't it remain the case that norms from the past cannot obligate the future to anything? Current practice always and inevitably will remain the master over the norm stemming from the past. In this context, Robert Brandom suggested the model of a judge in a common law legal order for whom no legal text is available but merely the legal precedents decided by her predecessors.[103] The judge's decisions depend both on whether she believes that the case she is currently deciding has relevant similarity to any precedent, and on whether she thinks that the pertinent case has previously been decided correctly. The normative power of precedent thus lies completely in the hand of the judge. There is no trace of an obligation stemming from the past. But Brandom points out that this judge is also part of a historic succession, that she, too, can become a past norm provider for a *future* judge. Therefore, her approach to the old precedents is also shaped by the aspiration of herself being able to count as an authority. Just like her predecessors and

[100] See above, pp. 42 ff.

[101] One exception in this regard is Luhmann's Systems Theory, in which the social system admittedly seems constructed according to a model of the subject.

[102] A well-intended view could compare theories of performativity with quantum mechanics, which, at a micro-level, might be the best theory, but cannot render classical mechanics (here: a rule theory for describing social norm phenomena) obsolete.

[103] Robert B. Brandom, "Some Pragmatist Themes in Hegel's Idealism" in: Id., *Tales of the Mighty Dead*, Cambridge, Mass. 2002, pp. 210–34, here pp. 230–33.

successors, she cannot bring the interpretation of the norm to a conclusion. Thus, according to Brandom, the asymmetrical relationship seems to become a symmetrical one,[104] in which every participant shares a potentially equal part in an interpretive project.

Really? In this argument, normative and factual aspects are curiously merged with each other. At first, Brandom's reconstruction is unaware of any point at which the success or failure of such practice could be determined. Success is rather presumed based on the construction of the relationship's symmetry. But at the moment in which the judge willfully employs different standards than those she herself deems appropriate, or than those of which she knows everyone else to deem appropriate, a branching-off of the interpretive chain can result, one which other judges may follow. We would have a chain of misinterpretations, one whose flawed character might at some point be lost from sight. Brandom is correct in claiming that even in this case, it would be possible for each judge to return to an appropriate interpretation, just as much as it would be possible for each judge to arrive at an inappropriate interpretation from an appropriate one.[105] But the possibility of self-correction does not rule out that a certain generation of judges might have taken this route, and that the thus ensuing damage could not be undone. It also is not obvious why the success of a practice should depend on the most current state of this practice, that is, to what degree past misinterpretations can be redeemed by future ones. Brandom furthermore presumes that the judge, who wants to exert an influence over the future by way of her decision, is better off orienting herself according to how influence was exerted in the past. According to this view, those who seek to draw a dividing line and to distinguish themselves from the lines of the existing practice thereby risk their influence. This brings to mind the empirical insight that judges are primarily interested in recognition by their peers, and that orientation along the lines of factually operative legal standards thereby is strengthened.[106] As correct as that is, two things need to be added. On the one hand, Brandom makes use of a concept of normativity which is distinct from the one he employs elsewhere.[107] Here, he is not concerned with reasons recognized by an interpretive community, but rather the effects of this recognition, as well as the consequences of a participant denying these reasons. On the other hand, Brandom's presumption is certainly not right in the generality that is assumed in his philosophical argumentation. All experience indicates that normative reasoning that is revolutionary and

[104] Ibid., p. 233.

[105] What is left aside completely is that tradition can also carry over contradictions and interpretive disputes. If it does, then there can also be debate about why it does so—in order to conclusively exclude divergent opinions, or to secure them for future usage. On this, see Halbertal (n 15), *People of the Book*, pp. 51 f.

[106] This idea is found in Richard A. Posner, *How Judges Think*, Cambridge, Mass. 2010.

[107] On this, see above pp. 26–28.

normatively "unfaithful" can at times be successful. They can ring in a new paradigm which future judges follow.

For this reason, the claim of a symmetry existing between predecessors and successors in the role as judge is misleading, even if it is clear that the practice of applying legal concepts takes the future into view.[108] Beyond legal restrictions, a judge is limited in her possibilities in many ways. She is subject to political and social pressure, just as her predecessors were and successors will be. Whether they are all equally limited across time remains an open question. It would be an astonishing historical coincidence if US judges of the same status in the years 1850, 1900, and 1950 were subject to the same political and societal pressures. Even the structural comparability of the situation of judges from different periods does not change anything about the asymmetry of the constellation. The later judge can deal with the decisions of her predecessor, but the opposite does not hold true. It also does not alter the fact that the factual limitations to which a judge is or believes to be liable, do not need to be interpreted as being of a normative character. This does not imply a denial of such restrictions, but at the level of abstraction at which Brandom argues by invoking a legal example without concerning himself with any actual legal institutions, and in making the typical hermeneutical move of declaring the judge a reader, he cannot explain these restrictions.[109] From the drills of a lawyer's education over the justificatory burden brought about by the availability of an appeal, to the hearing of parties, the doctrine of precedent and the scientific critique of inconsistent decisions, much could be highlighted that indicates that legal practices can keep the meanings of legal norms within certain parameters. But all of this does not correspond to Brandom's notion of normative restrictions.

Our observation of theories of performativity on the one hand, and of the common-law model on the other hand, make it easier to describe the way in which norms operate into the future. In contrast to Brandom's claim, there is no symmetry between past and present norm application. The norm is oriented toward the future, but it lies in the hand of the one applying it, who has influence over what her predecessor did, whereas the temporally opposite relationship does not exist. But this does not mean that the normativity of the norm is simply a product of the person applying it. Those applying it are not free in their treatment of norms, and a normative meaning posited into the world is not simply the product of an ex post ascription.

[108] Ludwig Wittgenstein, *Philosophische Untersuchungen*, Frankfurt/M. 2003, § 195 (p. 131), and the critique of Kripke in McDowell (n 81), "Wittgenstein" pp. 226–8.

[109] In this regard, Brandom's point mirrors Gadamer's. See Hans-Georg Gadamer, *Wahrheit und Methode*, Tübingen ^{6}1986, where a juridical approach (pp. 330–46) is marked as an exemplary one, although one learns nothing more specific about the juridical other than that its texts are applied.

2.8 Aspiration Gap: Build-up of Tensions and the Updating of Norms

If norms affirmatively point toward a possible state of affairs, then they can also determine *when* to expect their realization. In their moment of enactment, or with a delay, norms make possible their own adherence or violation. This aspiration of realization can be conceived as unlimited, or as temporally limited. It can be made explicit, such as by a deadline ahead of which I can fulfill but not violate an obligation. In many cases, the temporal limit of the normative aspiration remains nebulous. The normative aspiration for a birthday present can be met a day before, or even a day after the birthday, but it would hardly do so if the gift only were received after half a year. I will call the timespan between the moment in which we can count on the realization, adherence, or violation of a norm, and the expiration of the norm as the *aspirational gap*. The size of this gap is practically meaningful for every social practice.

If a norm consists in the portrayal of a possible state of the world and the affirmation of this state of affairs being realized, then it can construct different temporal perspectives on its realization. A skeptical look into the eyes of my counterpart can express a strong, morally charged expectation for a concrete action, one which should have followed *immediately* but did not. The aspiration gap only lasts a short while, then the normative communication dissolves, as it has lost its meaning in the passing of this moment.

Despite the fleeting brevity, a norm was at work here. In an evaluative manner, the look pointed toward the possibility, or more precisely to the holding-to-be-possible of a divergent unfolding of events by my counterpart. The twitching drew attention to an alternative unfolding, in which the addressee would have fulfilled the mimicked command. This communication changed the meaning of the actual course of events for the participants.[110] The actual course of events proceeds in light of a divergent idea of one of the participants, and under certain conditions, this gravely changes the meaning of the events, just as the fleeting encounter with a stranger changed the life of the passerby in Baudelaire.[111] In the fitting formulation by Heinrich Popitz, the norm has "burdened the situation with an alternative."[112]

The fact that we hesitate to accord a normative content to such a moment within a moment has less to do with its meaning than with its fleeting nature. The norm is tailored to a unique course of events, something it shares with every verbal command; at the same time, the time frame that we classify as an aspiration gap is so short that it is difficult to measure. This is why it is easy to overlook the

[110] See also the observation by Jeremy Waldron, "A Right to Do Wrong" in: *Ethics* 92 (1981), pp. 21–39, here p. 30.

[111] Charles Baudelaire in: Id., "Les fleurs du mal" Boston 1982, pp. 275 f.

[112] Heinrich Popitz, *Soziale Normen*, Frankfurt/M. 2006, p. 61. A differing view in Brennan et al. (n 1), *Explaining Norms*, pp. 102 ff., who tie the relevance of social norms to a certain permanence.

gesture—and thereby also overlook its normative content. Nonetheless, it fulfills all the requirements of a social norm.

But we can also make out practices in which the end of an aspiration gap remains indeterminate. The most dramatic examples are eschatological expectations that concretely portray an imagined future, the kingdom of God, and expressly affirm its arrival. The problem now lies in how such a completely different and distant course of events can be portrayed.[113] Not least of all, this is owed to an undefined time frame. In the case of the Christian concept of the delay of Parousia,[114] the expectation of the early Christian community for the coming of God's kingdom was set on the lifetimes of its adult community members. But the coming could not be clearly dated, thus the moment of transition of the aspiration into its disappointment, remained unclear.[115] This distinguishes this constellation from the situation which prompted Leon Festinger to develop the notion of cognitive dissonance. In a sect observed by Festinger, the expected end of the world was precisely dated for a specific day, and it lay within the biographical framework of the sect's members. The absence of the end of the world could not be explained with the normative expectation's temporal uncertainty. The moment passed—and nothing happened. At first, this did nothing to shake the conviction of the believers, but rather led to an even stronger missionary effort.[116]

The perception of historic change[117] and the general treatment of time in a certain community has effects on how long an aspiration gap can endure before the norm is no longer accepted and the tension created by it dissipates. Up until this day, the tradition of the political notion of constitutions, from the period of the eighteenth-century revolutions onward, brings about norms that are more easily read as practically unfulfillable promises rather than as applicable rules. The aspirational politics which ensued from these revolutions, such as in socialist orders, operates with uncertain normative expectations for large time frames. The arrival of communism is a normative promise whose date of fulfillment is unknown.[118]

[113] On this problem, from the perspective of a theological dispute with Kant's esthetics of the notion of symbol, see Petra Bahr, *Darstellung des Undarstellbaren*, Tübingen 2004, pp. 269–92; more generally on the ability of portrayal: Eberhard Jüngel, *Gott als Geheimnis der Welt*, Tübingen 2001, pp. 307–15.

[114] Georg Strecker, *Theologie des neuen Testaments*, Berlin 1996, pp. 224–9; Rudolf Bultmann, *Theologie des neuen Testaments*, Tübingen 1984, p. 535. See also the interpretation by Martin Heidegger, "Einleitung in die Phänomenologie der Religion" in: Id., *Gesamtausgabe*, Vol. 60, Frankfurt/M. 1995, pp. 1–156, here pp. 98–105. For Heidegger, the expectation of parousia is a command to more concentrated expectation, not to enthusiasm.

[115] Concisely on the missing proof for a crisis, see Christopher Rowland, "Parusie, II. Neues Testament" in: *Religion in Geschichte und Gegenwart*, Tübingen [4]2003, Vol. 6, cols 962–964, here 964.

[116] Leon Festinger, *Theorie der kognitiven Dissonanz*, Bern 1978, pp. 242–52. On this, also see Popitz (n 112), *Soziale Normen*, pp. 175–86.

[117] This perception is in turn historically not self-evident. On this, see Reinhart Kosseleck, "Geschichte, Geschichten und formale Zeitstrukturen" in: Id., *Vergangene Zukunft*, Frankfurt/M. 1979, pp. 130–43.

[118] See, e.g. the analysis of Karl Kautsky by Leszek Kołakowski, *Main Currents of Marxism*, New York 2005, pp. 388–94.

Because of this aspiration, as remains to be shown, the order in place is held to perpetually justify itself anew. The normative tension can be sustained both by the updating of the norm and by factual developments that draw attention to the norm.

The esthetic canon and modern clothing fashion are two extreme cases. Both are scarcely formalized, and there are no defined procedures or recognizable originary events. There are significant distinctions between the two regarding the temporal disposition, distinguishing themselves both from each other and from the practices already discussed. An esthetic canon only develops due to its aspiration to permanence. Canonization means stabilization. Practically speaking, in the historic development of any receptive community works of historical development may fall out of their canon, that is, out of that which one "has to" read or see. But if one accepts the canon, the "official fiction of authority of literature"[119] as a norm, then this falling out can only be read as the correction of an error. The work in question either never belonged to the canon or wrongfully fell out of it. From this internal perspective, the canon cannot change, it can only grow, but never shrink, otherwise it would have been faulty. An esthetic canon thus presumes timelessness; it raises a claim that brings to mind the aspiration of some moral arguments. Its claim to validity is limitless, its aspiration gap is boundless. Its endlessness creates no tension.

Fashions arise from variations that don't necessarily have to be esthetically motivated. A soldier begins to wear his camouflage uniform in his leisure time; a cohort of migrants that becomes visible introduces a certain look, or someone combines whatever is at hand, since their luggage has gone missing. Under certain circumstances, a look that thus arisen can be picked up by fashion designers, legitimized, and made popular by others. The forerunner of a given fashion, just as with the canon, is rather short-lived. We become unfashionable the moment a new fashion looms on the horizon.[120] The aspiration gap is limited, however. It lasts until the breaking of the next fashion trend. The norm of fashion becomes noticeable, just as Simmel observed, through deviance: whatever everyone is wearing is no longer fashionable.[121] Reference points for the length of a fashion cycle arise from discovered, albeit ambiguous conditions of the lifeworld.[122] I should be able to experience a change in fashion more than once during a certain age span. And fashion can latch onto a "season" that picks up on the weather dependency of clothing and simultaneously allows for variations for a change of fashion. Certain fashion trends will generally last longer than one season, but if they last too long, they do not

[119] Manfred Schneider, "Der König im Text. Autorität in Recht und Literatur" in: *Zeitschrift für Ideengeschichte* III (2009), pp. 48–63, here p. 53.

[120] A critical insight into the social theory of fashion is found in Barbara Vinken, "What Fashion Strictly Divided" in: Id., *Fashion—Zeitgeist. Trends and Cycles in the Fashion Cycle System*, Oxford 2005, pp. 3–40, here pp. 5–19, and from the same volume: "Adorned in Zeitgeist" pp. 41–59.

[121] Georg Simmel, "Philosophie der Mode" in: *Georg Simmel Gesamtausgabe*, Otthein Rammstedt (ed.), Vol. 10, Frankfurt/M. 1995, pp. 7–39, here pp. 16 f.

[122] Hans Blumenberg, *Lebenszeit und Weltzeit*, Frankfurt/M. 1986, pp. 291–4.

provide enough possibility for a participant, who under certain circumstances has to adjust fashion to his age, to experience a change.

A canon cannot limit its time of validity without ceasing to operate as a canon. For fashion, the opposite is the case. Both contain concrete commands to action by determining what one should read or wear, which respectively take effect without any run-up. Such forms of the normative thus define specific expectations in terms of a point in time for their fulfillment. It is only after the passing of such point in time that one can recognize whether the norm was obeyed or violated. Others do without defining this moment. A socially relevant normative tension develops in the build-up and dissipation of normative aspirations, in the possibility of consciously following or violating the norm. One important instrument for building up this tension lies precisely in the temporal limitation of the norm.

The normativity of fashion is very specifically shaped by its temporal structure.[123] Fashionable is whatever seems particularly proximate to one's own present time and thereby seems to preclude what the future holds. We can cherish fashion as a special instrument for diagnosing the present, as Walter Benjamin did,[124] or dismiss it as the epitome of what is not relevant because it does *not* remain. On the first reading, fashion promises more than presence, namely contact with the future, a preamble to the realization of what is possible.

How norms operate, and how they can be justified, is thus substantially shaped by their temporal horizon. One decisive, if often only implied parameter of this temporal horizon is the duration of time in which a norm can be followed or violated, the aspiration gap. Leaving this distance uncertain or approximate provides an important technique for leaving open the question of whether the norm is followed or not, whether it raises its claim successfully or not. This also has an influence on the question of the norm's justification.

2.9 Actualization

The longer the aspiration gap, the more urgent it becomes a normative practice's need for actualization. The normative beginning can grow old and fade, the norm "dies down";[125] it requires to be re-actualized or is forgotten.[126]

[123] Elena Esposito, *Die Verbindlichkeit des Vorübergehenden: Paradoxien der Mode*, Frankfurt/M. 2004, pp. 154–60.

[124] "Whoever might understand how to read it would not only know in advance about currents in art, but also about new legal codes, wars, and revolutions." Walter Benjamin, "Das Passagen-Werk" in: Id., *Gesammlte Schriften*, Vol. V/1, p. 112.

[125] This expression found in Popitz (n 112), *Soziale Normen*, p. 72. (Note by translator: the German phrase here is much more poetic, evoking the imagery of a sound dying down, *abklingen*. This metaphoric quality is lost in the English translation).

[126] We need to distinguish between a reminder of a current norm and one of a past norm that is no longer in effect. Admittedly, this distinction does not always have to be practically relevant for a social

If a community had at one point outlawed putting a curse on someone, this rule might have intermittently been forgotten without ever officially being abolished. The prohibition is actualized by court proceedings and through convictions. But this formalized means of actualization only takes effect if someone has violated the prohibition. We have already seen that norm transgressions are an important means to remind participants of existing norms and to make them present in the minds of a community. Regardless of how we, politically or morally, justify the practice of criminal prosecution, it certainly fulfills the function of actualizing or re-enacting a set of norms and therefore reminding a community of their continued validity.[127]

Actualizing a norm can be facilitated by formalization, but formalization is not necessary for actualization. The only person, from a party of twenty invited guests, who is never again invited by the host thereby will at times experience a formless actualization of certain behavioral norms. If formalization is to secure repeatability it becomes a central technique for stabilizing normative practices.[128] Procedures define a time frame, at the end of which a decision is reached. Formalized procedures also serve to avoid an undesirable consequence of a norm's growing old because they allow us to keep "the norm" distinct from its actualizations, as the formalized actualization clings to a certain norm text as "the norm," which does not get changed by the process of actualizing. This allows us to bridge the aspiration gap without further harm.

A military command, or a statute enacted in a legal procedure are norm types whose production can be repeated. Repeatability changes the temporal horizon of a norm. Normative practices derived for repeatability define the size of the aspiration gap quite precisely, they thus formulate an expectation on whether and when one should expect adherence to a norm. This does not necessarily make adherence more likely. But it does make it easier to ascertain if the norm was adhered to. If a certain state of affairs envisioned in the norm materializes before the moment projected in the norm, then this event does not directly seem to have to do with the norm. We cannot properly speak of a "norm violation" if someone acts against a norm at a moment in time that lies before the moment starting from which the norm itself demands adherence. Repeatability of norm application and the precision with which the content of the norm can be determined are linked to each other. The repeatability of the norm application allows us to observe the norm's effect in practice and, if necessary, to react to such response with further specifications.

practice, especially if tradition itself serves as the source of current norms. On the fear within Judaism to forget the specific commandments after Moses' death: Halbertal (n 15), *People of the Book*, pp. 20–3.

[127] There are plenty of penal theories that recognize this and abstain from the seemingly pointless enterprise of justifying criminal law morally or constitutionally: for example, see Günther Jakobs, *System der strafrechtlichen Zurechnung*, Frankfurt/M. 2012.

[128] On the status of repeatability and normativity, see above pp. 100 ff.

Actualizations, however, do not depend on repeatability, and they are also not limited to applications, that is, the attempt to temporally synchronize norm and reality in a certain situation. Norms can be actualized without a normative pretense being made, by simply referring to them in a descriptive way. Under certain circumstances, a community will more easily embrace a norm if they do not know exactly which meaning it will have for a specific situation, and if there also is the option not to enforce it, for example when it encounters resistance. For this reason, actualizations can be more important for a norm's persistence than applications. It would be wrong to view them as something merely symbolic.

2.10 Contradictions in Temporal Disposition

Actualizing a norm can come into conflict with other normative cycles, just as much as with the conditions for the effectiveness of an actualized norm. This becomes obvious in the relationship between legislative periods and the factual effects of democratic legislation. For reasons of preserving their own legitimacy, all democratic systems know procedures that require periodic repetition, such as elections. But the periodic, regularly recurring nature of elections can sometimes hardly be squared with the expected effects of a given statute enacted after an election. It might take longer than four years for a certain measure to noticeably reduce unemployment, and it is possible that a parliamentary decision in another case solves what is perceived to be an urgent problem so rapidly after the legislature's commencement, that its success does not concern or impress anyone during the next election campaign. What is interesting is the temporal dissonance that arises from the juxtaposition of the expectations.[129] Regularly judging the legislator, namely at election time, is inevitable, and that also means measuring him according to his own aspirations and standards, even if everything points toward the conclusion that these aspirations could not possibly be fulfilled within such a time span. At the same time—and this has frequently been described and lamented—political aspiration tends to assimilate to the periodic nature of elections, something that is criticized as accounting for the structural disadvantage of policies directed toward sustainability in democratic politics. However, this critique should not neglect the normative claim raised by elections. For if the claim to legitimate political decision making is to flow from and be granted by the election, then its success cannot be determined independently of these elections, solely by the time frame set by the problems to be solved. From this angle, proclaiming the ideal of "sustainability," that is, a mode of solution that is oriented toward the actual duration of a substantive problem at issue, seems like an argument against the repeatability of the

[129] On the suspicion that this is regularly overestimated by the political process: Robert E. Goodin, "Keeping Political Time" in: *International Political Science Review* 19 (1998), pp. 39–54, here pp. 46–8.

legitimation procedure itself. It cannot be easily squared with this form of legitimation. Rather, in this constellation, not only are two legitimate normative temporal horizons overlapping, namely political legitimation and practical problem solution through politically legitimated action; what is more, both horizons have an effect on each other. For if one measure of political judgment lies in the solution of practical problems, but the time frame of this judgment makes this solution impossible, then this comes to be an internal deficit of the legitimation procedure as well. But this deficit cannot simply be solved by adjusting the time frame, so long as democratic politics are viewed as being a general solution for treating diverse problems with different time frames.

2.11 The Temporal Structure of Justifying Normative Orders

The justification of a normative order needs to be distinguished from its authorization. Considering the time structure, it is helpful to distinguish between originary, prospective, and actualizing forms of justification, that is, between justification via reference to a past event, a possible future, or a repeatable, justifying, and re-enacting procedure.[130] This distinction upholds that the act of norm authorization lies in the past. The norm development is past, even if the present or future are taken up in its justification.

Democratic constitutional orders combine originary justification, which draws on the moment of constitutional enactment, with a perspective on the future. Constitutions are full of explicit and implicit promises, and they rely on the impression that we are approaching the fulfillment of these promises—that there is progress.[131] It is for this reason, too, that constitutions include actualizing justificatory techniques, such as elections and legislative procedures, whose reference to the origins is weaker than the immediate reference to a constitutional text. This does not imply a rejection of, but an enhancement of the authorization scheme, as these procedures themselves arise out of the constitution. With their help, the old original approaches the present, without the ties to the origin of constitutional enactment being cut.

Even orders based on tradition cannot get by without a moment of actualization, such as with the birth of a successor to the throne, which both renews and maintains the order. However, orders whose justification cannot be tied to any mechanism of actualization get into practical difficulties. A revolutionary beginning

[130] The interest in temporality might be so minimal because political philosophy operates with an idealized notion of procedure, in which the temporal unfolding, that which actually marks a procedure, is abstracted from. On this, see above pp. 16–19.

[131] Ulrich K. Preuß, "Sozialer Fortschritt oder politische Freiheit?" in: Ibid., *Revolution, Fortschritt und Verfassung*, pp. 29–45.

can accord a high measure of authorization to an order, but as such it provides no link for future practices of actualization. In actual socialist systems, revolutions serve as both authorizing origin and empirical confirmation of their historical-philosophical foundation. Theoretically, these revolutions bring the order closer to the politically "proper" condition. But neither does any relevant procedure follow from these revolutions, nor is there any other actualizing mechanism inherent in the order that could keep fresh its claim to legitimacy. The contentious question of whether Marxism can be understood as a moral theory[132] certainly seems to become evident on this reading insofar as Marxism takes social development not as something *possible* but as something *necessary*, a future condition from which deviation in the long run is factually impossible. The revolution, then, is merely a moment in which the insight into something asserts itself, something that is inevitable and, lacking the possibility of deviation, can have no normative moral content. This also does away with the need to arrange for procedures of norm actualization. In this way, typical problems arise for these orders such as acceptance deficits, or uncertainties regarding the procedures in which official positions are to be filled.

From the perspective of time, this can be carefully generalized. An order that does not justify itself based on the past or its actualization, but rather from the promise of a certain future, has a difficult time stabilizing its own justification *because that which lies in the future—other than that which lies in the past—cannot be actualized.* Justification thus relies on the observation and evaluation of factual societal development, which, admittedly, is also of relevance in other political orders, but in this case is the only justificatory element. If, in contrast to the kingdom of God, communism can only be realized step by step and not in one instant, then successfully making this order plausible requires an experience of progress. In the end, this requirement then turns on its head the schema of justification. The expectation of a coming communism does not justify the socialist present; rather, the presence of progress justifies the expectation of communism. This reversal makes the system susceptible to practical setbacks. It enters into a crisis of finality.[133]

Norms can be more easily stabilized if they avoid defining their justification with an eye toward the future. For the early Christian experience of disappointed messianic expectation, it was easier to cope with the kingdom of God not materializing than it was for the sect that Leon Feistinger investigated. One reason for this might be that there neither was nor is a concrete date for the coming of the Messiah.[134]

[132] Daniel Brudney, *Marx's Attempt to Leave Philosophy*, Cambridge, Mass. 1998, pp. 325–59; Allen W. Wood, *Karl Marx*, New York 2004, pp. 127–42.

[133] This expression, and the analysis of the German Democratic Republic from the 1970s onward can be found in Sigrid Meuschel, *Legitimation und Parteiherrschaft*, Frankfurt/M. 1992, pp. 221, 229–41.

[134] Leon Feistinger (*Theorie der kognitiven Dissonanz Theorie der Kognitiven Dissonanz*, Huber Verlag Bern 2012, pp. 25–8) classified the lack of a specifically set end of the world by his investigated sect as a "cognitive dissonance." The term was accurately chosen, even though the vision of the end of the world was normatively charged for the sect. The sect judged everything that occurred *sub specie finis mundi*. But the vision of the end of the world also had a cognitive function, namely making the existence of the norm system plausible in the first place. The missing end of the world thus did not figure as

Either way, it was important for Christians to develop a horizon of aspirations that allowed them not to read the continuingly absent judgment day as a rebuttal of their own faith. This is not meant in a religiously skeptical manner, as if religious communities could control their dogmas at will and make them immune to the course of events. The example of the sect shows that they cannot. But the early Christians had a constitutive situation *in their past*, namely the crucifixion and ascension of Christ, which made the entrance of a further event possibly less urgent. Even for them, a purely future-oriented structure of justification would have been fragile. For the practice of justifying norms, these considerations also show that the question of how a norm is justified recedes into the background behind the question of how much time is accorded to it in order for it to establish itself. Structures of justification can thus—with more or less success—be directed by different time structures. This also has repercussions for how the norms of these orders are to be applied.

2.12 Application and Justification in Time

A normative order can justify itself by virtue of its origins alone. The corresponding model of justification can be called *originalism*, as authorizing origin and justification merge in it. Furthermore, in the search for the original intentions of constitutional authors, in the demand to stage a musical work in its original sound, or in the recognition of philological imperatives for the understanding of a religion, these two—authorizing origin and justification—also converge. But the question arises as to why something from the past can justify current restrictions. Methodically, we face the problem of whether any application inevitably represents an actualization, which brings about something completely different from the supposedly "original" norm.

We need to distinguish models that treat such fidelity to the origin as a justificatory element from those that only want to see a justification in the current meaning of a norm for those applying it. It is in this sense that originalist and functionalists dispute the proper reading of the constitution in the United States.[135] Is it to be read

a norm violation, but rather as an act of deconstituting the order. Imagine a group that worships a holy receptacle, which no-one may touch because it has carried within it a script with all the commands honored by the group. At some point, someone might knock over the receptacle by accident, it opens, and everyone realizes that it is empty. This brings about a cognitive dissonance. However, it is one that draws on a cognition, which is the precondition of the norm. The anticipation of the salvific act may have had normative effects, that is, it might have been open for disappointment. For the entrance of salvation itself, this is not the case.

[135] Overview in Steven G. Calabresi (ed.), *Originalism: A Quarter-Century of Debate*, Washington, D.C. 2007.

as it would have been in the late eighteenth century, the moment of its genesis? Or is it to be read through the eyes of a contemporary? These questions are practically relevant, for example, when concerned with what *cruel and unusual punishment* means, which is prohibited by the American Constitution.[136] Originalists claim that neglecting fidelity to the origin would translate into a neglect of the constitution as a whole,[137] since the criteria for adapting the constitution's meaning did not stem from the constitution itself, but rather from the present day. The presentists take this to be a misunderstanding.[138] A constitution, so runs their argument, cannot be understood other than as constantly evolving. The object thereby evolving was still the constitution. Comparable discursive frontlines can be found in various practices. Am I still playing Monteverdi if I use a large symphonic orchestra to perform his score? On the flipside, what does it mean to twenty-first-century musicians stage a musical piece from early modernity with old instruments and philologically attested notes in front of a contemporary audience?[139]

Three observations should help us assess this discussion. For one, both sides treat the same problem, namely the question of how a norm stemming from the past is to be appropriately applied in the present. It thus seems pointless to have to decide between the normative origin and its actualization. This observation is not as trivial as it sounds. In opting for one side over the other on this issue, and stylizing it as the "actual" one, many contributions seem more vested in dissolving the problem than in actually solving it, as if the problem could be done away with by ignoring either the fact that the application takes place in the present or the fact that it is something from the past that is being applied.

Secondly, the different conceptions have divergent practical consequences. They operate with their own specific techniques of norm interpretation and actualization, and this leads to different results. It is important to see that *in this* they do not go wrong. From the point of view of philosophical hermeneutics, for a given situation—this goes for our initial observation as well—there should likely be only *one* appropriate interpretation, namely the one that makes something from the past fruitful for a certain present and a certain context. In the end result, this would dissolve the differences between an originalist and a presentist interpretation.[140]

136 Concisely on this development, Colin Dayan, *The Story of Cruel and Unusual*, Cambridge, Mass. 2007.

137 Antonin Scalia, *A Matter of Interpretation*, Princeton 1997.

138 One reference from a tremendous debate may currently suffice: Cass R. Sunstein, *The Partial Constitution*, Cambridge, Mass. 1993, pp. 93–122.

139 In music theory, these questions appear less frequently examined, but on the inevitable contradictions of original staging practices, see the instructive work by Laurenz Lüttken, "Neuer Wein in alten Schläuchen? Alte Musik in historischer Aufführungspraxis" in: *Musik & Gottesdienst* 67 (2013), pp. 8–13, here pp. 10 f.

140 In this sense, a critique of the distinction between *de dicto* and *de re* following Gadamer: Cristina Lafont, "Meaning and Interpretation: Can Brandomian Scorekeepers be Gadamerian Hermeneuts?" in: *Philosophy Compass* 3 (2008), pp. 17–29.

This does not seem very convincing, for it is difficult to deny that we understand "cruel" quite differently today than did the American founding fathers. The question is not whether there is a historical difference, but rather whether this difference is meaningful for the *current* treatment of a norm from *this* time.[141] Neither an invocation of a past meaning nor of a current meaning can provide us with an answer to this, and this leads us to the third observation.

We cannot deduce an appropriate engagement of norms from any notion of fidelity to the norm, no matter how it is understood. To act according to a norm can mean to make the best of it for the present, but it can also mean not abiding by its idiosyncrasies that are no longer convincing. Fidelity to a norm can be taken to be historical-voluntaristic or presentist-rationalistic.[142] Neither understanding, however, can be deduced from the norm itself.

At most, I can deduce a criterion for the appropriate interpretation of a norm from the way it was authorized.[143] Does the norm justify itself by virtue of its origin, or of its appropriateness for the present? We have just seen that a norm does not need to justify itself by recourse to the past simply because of its character as a norm, just as little as it must be justified by the present simply because it is being applied in the present. Rather, we have to confront the question of how we view the norm's authorization in order to be able to appropriately interpret it. Are the norms supposed to uphold something, or change something? Do they express a foundational situation or a history of progress? The situation surrounding the US Constitution, the difficulty of changing it, and how each change leaves unaffected the original text, might point toward its justification structure to be drawing more forcefully on its originary moment than other constitutions, and thus more heavily drawing on the past.[144] By contrast, a normative order that is easily changed, in its interpretive battles is less held to recall its foundational moments, moments that anyway tend to fade away over the course of the order's continued practice. In shifting the perspective from immanent meaning to the temporal orientation of authorization as a criterion for the understanding of norms, the problem of appropriate application certainly is more precisely framed, but certainly no easier to solve, if only because the conditions for justifying a norm will likely remain highly contentious themselves, particularly when the meaning is contentious.

[141] In order to describe this problem, we have to know the difference. For this reason, philology is necessary but not sufficient for solving such problems, see Pollock (n 69), "Future Philology" pp. 931–61, here p. 956.

[142] For the Jewish tradition, these contrasting interpretations are made vivid by Halbertal (n 15), *People of the Book*, pp. 27–32.

[143] See ibid., pp. 47 f., on the distinction between authorship and authority. God created the law, but maybe he recused himself of its authoritative interpretation?

[144] On this, see above, pp. 181 292 ff.

2.13 Real Time and Social Variance

If norms aim for possible states of the world, then this will manifest itself in an aspiration gap. The future orientation of a norm demands a time frame in which the possibility can become realized, but does not have to. This aspiration gap, as we have seen, can be quite small, even a short instant suffices, in which a branching-off of a chain of events can appear and be viewed affirmatively or negatively. Are there also social techniques that make do without an aspiration gap and nevertheless formulate a normative pretense?

An initial such example are political polls that serve the investigation and analysis of preferences among a population. Even if meant to have a merely descriptive role, the results of such polls can enter into a competition with elections regarding their legitimizing role. If the duration of a mandate is defined for an elective act, then the justification of the person elected should ideally remain unchanged for this time frame. We can view it, for example, a legislative period as an aspiration gap in which the political-programmatic realm of possibilities for a normative decision can realize itself. Poll results, however, question the meaning of this form by contrasting this mandate with an informal mandate toward which political processes are held to orient themselves. Polls have the effect of factually shortening the aspiration gaps formalized for the political system. In the words of a politician: "We're going into a world where there's an instant referendum on everything before it even starts."[145]

Such shortening is sometimes taken as an improvement as it accelerates what is taken to be too slow of a legitimation rhythm. While there are supposedly technical reasons for only electing a parliament every four years, these reasons supposedly undermine the normative ideal of permanent self-determination. In the model presented here, however, the length of the aspiration gap is not the result of a practical limitation, but rather the expression of a *normative* aspiration, which is claimed by the political electoral procedure. If an election sets up to shape a society according to a certain political program, then it is this aspiration that helps to define the length of a legislature, since such a goal cannot be achieved in an arbitrarily short time. Expressed differently, a shortening of legitimation cycles would also have to minimize the political aspirations for action, which would then have to be oriented toward what one could sensibly claim to be able to accomplish. Formulating this relationship implies neither a claim that there are no other criteria for the length of legislatures, nor that the currently predominant length of four to five years is best-suited to live up to aspirations of political reform. What is crucial is the connection between the normative

[145] Michael Bloomberg, quoted by Ken Auletta, "After Bloomberg" in: *The New Yorker* from 26 August 2013.

pretense of a political decision-making procedure and its temporal rhythm and implementation.

What follows is that procedures which depict political convictions in real time, can make *no* normative claim *whatsoever*, as they are not referring to anything in particular that could be realized. Due to the lack of an aspiration persisting over time, there is no possibility to organize the kind of tension between a norm and its realization that is distinctive of normative practices.

A second example is found in digital surveillance technology. Under the project name "Indect," the European Union has, for some years now, been supporting the development of technology for the automatic detection of threats.[146] These kinds of programs aim to enable an automatic digital analysis of monitor movements and Internet activity detected by camera so as to thwart imminent criminal acts. Fighting crime is thus antedated so far that behavior detected to deviate from certain programmed standards is automatically noticed and can then be subject to closer examination or "treatment" by law enforcement. These procedures do not capture rule violations, but rather permissible behavior which indicate a rule violation that will occur with significant probability in the future. This project is but one example for a general development in security regulation, one that could also be referred to as de-normativization or cognitivization.[147] Behavior is not measured by a standard whose violation is normed, but it is rather guided onto the right tracks ex ante, via invisible incentives,[148] or by organizing surveillance in cities.[149] What I called cognitive norms above[150] is succinctly deployed in these contexts in order to bring about or avoid a certain behavior.

This example also operates with a closure of the aspiration gap. A certain behavior is certainly expected, but this preference is to be realized by means of excluding alternative possibilities. Expressed in temporal terms, the realm of possibility for realization and transgression is closed in favor of a regulating scheme that no longer provides a time frame for the possibility of deviance. According to our understanding, this is no longer a normative practice, but rather a causalist approach toward shaping society. The fact that the incompatibility of such practices with our conception of normativity could also result in a specific normative deficit will be of concern toward the end of the book.

[146] See http://www.indect-project.eu/, see also Christoph Berens, *Süddeutsche Zeitung* from 1 December 2011, online at http://www.sueddeutsche.de/wissen/europaeische-ueberwachungstechnologie-werkzeug-fuer-diktatoren-1.1223440 (last accessed 15 September 2014).

[147] In this context, the analyses by Foucault seem inspiring, but also excessive, as the generalized internalization of power phenomena diagnosed by him cannot describe certain developments.

[148] Richard Thaler and Cass Sunstein, *Nudge*, New Haven 2008; Ids., "Libertarian Paternalism" in: *American Economic Review* 93 (2003), pp. 175–9.

[149] Roger Brownsword, "Code, Control, and Choice: Why East is East and West is West" in: *Legal Studies* 25 (2005), pp. 1–21, here pp. 4–8.

[150] See pp. 137 f.

3. *Space*

3.1 Spatial Constructivism and its Limits

The philosophical "realm of reasons" is only a space in a metaphoric sense.[151] Reasons have no determinable space, and they cannot move. This distinguishes them from social norms, which arise in a space and apply to a space, be it the formalized validity space of a State's legal order, be it in a house, or in a locally rooted community of individuals. The pretense of a norm can restrict itself to a delimited space, the engagement with the norm can shift from center to periphery, or it can change due to shifting geography.[152] Spatiality plays a large role for social norms. At the same time, social theory has long highlighted that "spaces" should be taken not so much as a given condition, but as alterable consequence of social practices.[153] This is also the case for normative practices that do not simply find themselves at one space or location but rather help define these spaces and locations, opening and limiting them. The conceptual connection between normativity and space, however, is not as strong as the one between normativity and time. Concerning the realization of possibilities, our notion of a norm dictates a certain temporal structure, whereas norms are linked to certain spaces and affect these in turn, yet they are not necessarily conceptually tied to a spatial concept.

Since the time of Georg Simmel, who took space as a function of social relations, spatial theory has turned toward a constructivist understanding,[154] according to which the social relevance of the spatial is not something primordial or "natural." The assumption is that one cannot speak of "natural limits" or "middle positions" without naturalizing social relationships. Of course, many constructivist theories of social "space" are not vested in locations or physical spaces,[155] but rather employ the term "space" as a metaphor,[156] as conceptual backdrop upon which social-theoretical categories are projected.

[151] The oft-quoted expression from Wilfrid Sellars, *Empiricism and the Philosophy of Mind*, Cambridge, Mass. 1997, p. 76.

[152] In early cultural theory, this has been frequently described, and at times lamented, such as by Blaise Pascal, *Pensées and Other Writings*, Oxford 1999, pp. 23 ff. (Lafuma No. 60; Brunschvicg No. 294). The connection appears more inevitable in Charles de Montesquieu *The Spirit of the Laws*, Cambridge 1989, Books 14–18.

[153] A short overview of currently shared convictions of sociological space theory found in Martina Löw, "The Constitution of Space" in: *European Journal of Social Theory* 11 (2008), ppp. 25–49, here pp. 26 f.

[154] Georg Simmel, "Über räumliche Projektionen socialer Formen" in: *Georg Simmel Gesamtausgabe*, Vol. 7, Frankfurt/M. 1995, pp. 201–20.

[155] As an example, Pierre Bourdieu "Social Space and Symbolic Space" in: Id., *Practical Reason. On the Theory of Action*, Stanford 1998, 1–13), where the term "space" is employed so metaphorically that it scarcely adds any value to social analysis; quite to the contrary in Martina Löw, *Raumsoziologie*, Frankfurt/M. 2001, pp. 179–83.

[156] Poignantly, the observation by Sabine Müller-Mall, *Legal Spaces*, Heidelberg et al. (eds), 2013, p. 65.

Frequently, these metaphors lead astray. The existence of "norm-free spaces" is as imprecisely formulated as spatializing notions of norm contradictions as "collisions." What appears behind these formulations is the notion that there are two- or three-dimensionally defined gaps in which there is "room" for a norm. Since this notion is wrong,[157] a theory of normativity's relation to "space" inevitably becomes a critique of spatializing metaphors, whether they are naturalizing or constructivist.

In the theory of social spaces, the transition from naturally given locations to socially constructed spaces does not simply reflect a theoretical progression. Behind this change in theory lies a dispute concerning the value of societal modernization, in which, among other things, a substantialist, static notion of location is viewed as conservative, and a model that reads space as a social construction is read as progressive. But even a constructivist spatial theory should remain open for asynchrony and take social practices seriously, for which locations are normatively meaningful. Just as insensible it is to treat all norms as "made," so it is of little descriptive help to reduce the spatial rootedness of the normative to social constructions for every normative practice. Just as the construction of norms builds on the social preconditions, so too does the construction of spaces. These preconditions are not completely accessible to them.

3.2 Normative Proximity?

Norms are frequently described in categories of proximity and distance. A locally rooted order is close to its community, and highlighting this is supposed to express something positive. So should norms ideally operate not too far from their addressees?[158] This idea is powerfully and exemplarily expressed in the principle of subsidiarity in Catholic social teaching: "so also it is an injustice and at the same time a grave evil and disturbance of right order to assign to a greater and higher association what lesser and subordinate organizations can do."[159]

Here, too, proximity is employed metaphorically. It is not concerned with closeness that can be measured in distances. Proximity and distance rather operate as metaphors for the numerical membership size of a community, and for the measure of formalization and abstraction of its inventory of norms. Norms that are considered "close" are specific and informal, maybe even non-verbalized, "distant" norms are abstract and formalized. Of course, abstraction

[157] See below, pp. 219–21.

[158] A rare critique of this idea is provided by Roman Schnur, "Politische Entscheidung und räumliche Interessen" in: *Die Verwaltung* 3 (1970), pp. 257–81.

[159] *Quadragesimo Anno*, No. 79 (1931), concerning the extended use of this principle in constitutional and European law: Josef Isensee, *Subsidiaritätsprinzip und Verfassungsrecht*, Berlin 2001; Christian Calliess, *Subsidiaritäts- und Solidaritätsprinzip in der Europäischen Union*, Baden-Baden 1999.

and formalization are means to conceptually account for social differences, be they spatially mediated or not.

This becomes clear in democratic theory, in which debates persist until today about what is preferable: a small, compact republic "close" to its citizens, in which alone egalitarian rule can be organized,[160] or the large, "distant" democracy, in which the plurality of the population and the cacophony of interests are institutionally checked and balanced in such a way that they can successfully fend off the capture of democratic will formation by individual social actors.[161] Both models illustrate how spatial metaphors connote contradictory criteria for a normative order's success. Informal proximity can be burdensome, abstracting distance can appear liberating; abstracting distance can miss its object, normative proximity is more adept at processing insights about the regulated object. At this point, the *dilemma of norm realization* plays an important role. The more similar a norm is to the practices to which it appeals, the more likely it becomes that it will be absorbed by them, that the normative *direction of fit* is reversed and the norm adapts to its surrounding conditions.[162] Small communities and their dense and short-distanced norm structure are frequently indistinguishable from the practices they aim to direct, the latter dissolve in and become identical with the former. A form, in turn, that abstracts from concrete realities can account for the better recognizability and enforceability of a norm.

One example for such relationships is found in norms that outlaw discrimination, understood as the unjustified differential treatment of persons. These kinds of antidiscrimination statutes contain a prohibition on discrimination, which relies on an abstract formulation. They require the conceptual distancing from a social practice. It is therefore not surprising that, in federal orders, antidiscrimination rules are posited by the highest level of multi-level government, that is by the federal level in the United States, and by the EU legislation in Europe.[163] The prohibition on discrimination, as prohibition to make a certain distinction, is a command for abstract formalization, one which intervenes in the social interactions of a community, as when they prescribe not to exclude potential contractual partners, such as women or black citizens, but rather to recognize them as legal persons. From the perspective of the spatial metaphor they are norms that make use of their distance to social practices in order to change society. They draw their very effectiveness

[160] Montesquieu adhered to this model. On this, see Jacob T. Levy, "Beyond Publius: Montesquieu, Liberal Republicanism, and the Small-Republic Thesis" in: *History of Political Thought* 1 (2006), pp. 50–90.

[161] We initially encounter this idea in David Hume, "Idea of a Perfect Commonwealth" in: Knud Haakonssen (ed.), *Political Essays*, Cambridge 1994, pp. 221–33; also see the *Federalist Papers*, No. 10 (Madison); and applied to India by Sunil Khilnani, *The Idea of India*, London 2012.

[162] See above, pp. 71 ff.

[163] On this idea: Christoph Möllers, "Demokratische Ebenengliederung" in: Ivo Appel et al. (eds), *Öffentliches Recht im offenen Staat*, Berlin 2011, pp. 759–78, here pp. 772 ff. Upon closer examination, one would presumably realize that these kinds of models are spread from certain federal members via the center to other Member States.

from their abstractness. The latter ensures that norms better correspond to their own particular justificatory background, for the more specific the norm becomes, the less it could be understood as a regulation that promotes "equality." A highly specified norm would lose this legitimating connection just as much as its high measure of clarity stemming from the lack of exceptions. Accordingly, the application of such a norm frequently suffers from incompletely taking account of concrete contexts, such as when an antidiscrimination rule ultimately continues to put a certain minority at a disadvantage. Nonetheless, the example of such rules shows that the broad emphasis on "proximity" does not provide a useful criterion for the justification of normative orders, just as sweeping praise of the small, spatially compact political community[164] prompts scrutiny from a norm-theoretical perspective. This kind of praise is aimed to deflect formalized normative impositions in the name of a proximity that can have quite ambivalent effects: at times serving to provide protection and safety, at times promoting informal power and harassment against pluralist elements of society. Conversely, in the sense of a "normin" technique that abstracts from circumstances, "distance" creates other problems. In this regard, theory can only try to put normative connotations, transported by such metaphors, in their proper place.

3.3 Realization in Space

Even if it is characteristic for norms to leave open the possibility of their own transgression, the conditions of possibility for their realization can differ from one location to another. Thus, it seems that norms created at the center of a large empire encounter different treatment at its periphery, and that they are relativized by the norms pre-existing there.[165] However, such observations are methodically subject to scrutiny because without further assumptions it is not clear how variations in the ways of application can be distinguished from instances of deviance. Maybe it is only the periphery that "properly" understands what is meant by the norms created at the center. We need to be on guard that an empirical observation does not automatically assume the center's internal perspective, which is already implicit in the asymmetrical distinction between center and periphery. Furthermore,

[164] Such praise can be located on the left or right, politically speaking, and even serve as an argument for certain forms of centralization. For one, see Carl Schmitt, *Der Nomos der Erde*, Berlin 1997, pp. 13–20; for another, see Robert Menasse, *Der europäische Landbote*, Vienna, 2012, p. 88. See also the portrayal of tightly-knit communities by Robert Cover, "Foreword: Nomos and Narrative" in: *Harvard Law Review* 97 (1983), pp. 4–68, here, pp. 20–5.

[165] Paradigmatically for the Habsburg monarchy, Eugen Ehrlich, "Das lebende Recht der Völker der Bukowina" in: Id., *Recht und Leben*, Berlin 1967, pp. 43–60; for early modern law in Europa and the Spanish colonies in Latin America: Thomas Duve, *Sonderrecht in der Frühen Neuzeit*, Frankfurt/M. 2008, pp. 29–38; on research strategies to free oneself from the distinction between core and periphery: Id., "Von der Europäischen Rechtsgeschichte zu einer Rechtsgeschichte Europas in globalhistorischer Perspektive" in: *Rechtsgeschichte* 20 (2012), pp. 18–71, here pp. 34–9.

the root cause for spatially divergent application practices often does not lie in the spatial distance from the norm's source. The measure of variation in application does not simply increase in linear fashion the further away one gets from the location of the norm's positing. It is also difficult to determine whether variations in application—understood from the point of view of the center as more or less correct applications—have something to do with "distance" to the norm-positing institutions, given that the location of the norm-positing institutions cannot simply be understood as the "center" of the normative order. For example, if Brussels is the location of European law-making, then this location should not be understood as the center in any substantial meaning if simply because the content of European legislation should not be dependent on the location at which it takes place. We would think no differently of it if it took place in Madrid or Vilnius; quite to the contrary, we would view repercussions from the concrete local conditions on the procedures of norm-positing as illegitimate. And one simply cannot observe that norms from Brussels are applied more accurately in one location than another due to the former being closer to Brussels.[166]

Nevertheless, it *is possible* that the application of norms is made difficult due to geographical distance between norm-positing and application, particularly if the spread of norms relies on spatially fixated media, when a norm text has to travel from one location to another. This applies to both the integrity of the text and the impossibility of also transporting the context along with the norm. Formalization can more or less guarantee textual integrity—this is a further constellation in which it would thus be amiss to view norm texts as mere depictions of norms. Norms that are fixated and transported in texts gain a new context, and thus a different meaning and another perspective on realization. In light of the Internet, the optimization of techniques for transporting norms has the seemingly ironic implication that they work in the same manner for the most diverse kinds of norms. Now these compete with other omnipresent norm texts, and choosing between these will be oriented along criteria that are locally mediated. The mediation of norm texts does not have to lead to the homogenization of application.

3.4 Norm Collisions?

Different norms can point to possibilities, the simultaneous realization of which is practically impossible. In this way, the possibility of realizing a norm depends on the realization of another norm. In this sense, if a norm is physically enforceable it

[166] Corresponding research seems rare, but concerning the political circumstances in American Member States, see the relativizing take on geographical distance: Wendy K. Tam Cho and Erinn P. Nicely, "Geographic Proximity versus Institutions" in: *American Politics Research* 36 (2008), pp. 803–23.

can collide with another enforceable norm.[167] This kind of possible collision has a spatial reference. In civil law, for example, this can concern a plot of land or an article.[168]

We can only imagine these kinds of collisions in application contexts, in which two norms are spatially and temporally specified, and this specification is realized. These are demanding conditions. And with the possibility of realization, they do not question the applied norm.[169] A norm that could not be followed in a certain application context because of its contradiction to another norm can be applied again in a later constellation. The norm outlasts the contradiction with the other one in a concrete application context and continues to be in place. Its violation persists.[170] In this way, speaking of norm collisions is misleading as it treats norms as temporally and spatially defined events. Contradictions between norm contents can only be described from the vantage point of an applying subject.

This should also give pause to consider how many social norms provide those applying them with wriggle room in order to avoid collisions. Thanks to this maneuvering room collisions rarely seem inevitable. But such flexibility does not only result from indeterminacy of norm meanings, but also from the fact that two norms of a given normative order, which appear to provide contradictory orientations for action, can only be interpreted in the context of each other. There is a necessity inherent to normative orders to avoid collisions, not systematic contradictions, if only because the identification of a norm is only possible with knowledge of all the other norms within this order, and because social norms often call for individual application decisions to be made. If norms refer to what is possible, then this is imperative for norm-immanent reasons. For "collision" is then simply another expression for the impossibility of a certain norm application in light of another one. Thus, we can analytically imagine an order that formulates colliding obligations, but it is unlikely, if only because the interpretive application of one of

[167] On Kant's legal theory in this context: Marcus Willaschek, "Right and Coercion: Can Kant's Conception of Moral Right be Derived from his Moral Theory?" in: *International Journal of Philosophical Studies* 17 (2009), pp. 49–70, here pp. 59–65.

[168] This spatial aspect is highlighted by Katrin Flikschuh, *Kant and Modern Political Philosophy*, Cambridge 2000, pp. 132 ff., and by Arthur Ripstein, *Force and Freedom*, Cambridge, Mass. 2009, pp. 368–72.

[169] Unless there is a hierarchical relationship between them. Those kinds of conflicts can certainly also arise in the application of ethical commands for Kant: Jens Timmermann, "Kantian Dilemmas? Moral Conflict in Kant's Ethical Theory" in: *Archiv für Geschichte der Philosophie* 95 (2013), pp. 36–64, here pp. 53 ff.

[170] Accordingly, for moral norms the following questions arises: if I am obliged to do A and B, yet these mutually exclude each other, and it is thus impossible to do A *and* B, do both of these obligations lapse because of impossibility? Bernard Williams argues that no-one would feel obliged to do both, but merely one or the other. For him, though, this does not preclude that both appear obligating for the situation; see Bernard Williams, "Ethical Consistency" in: *Proceedings of the Aristotelian Society* 39 (1965), pp. 103–24, here pp. 118–22.

the obligations always has to unfold in light of the other, in order to do justice to the order as a whole.

This is not to deny the practical dilemmas or tragic situations in dealing with norms, but it does indicate two things. For one, it highlights that contradictory norms can have the consequence of *enlarging* the maneuvering space for the addressee of a norm. Unlike in the casuistry of practical philosophy, these kinds of norms rarely appear as tragic alternatives; and secondly, they show how the applicant's responsibility increases along with the growing maneuvering room opening up by virtue of the contradiction. While the seemingly fatalistic image of a collision seems to insinuate that the norms themselves bring about a possibly violent conflict, a different impression arises. Norm contradictions do not necessarily produce a collision of obligations, or even of applications. It is rather that existing conflicts are portrayed as norm collisions by applicant, in part to obfuscate their own responsibility in application, which arises from their reference to the norm.

3.4 Enforceability as the Distinctive Criterion Separating Social and Moral Norms?

Does the reference to space offer a criterion for distinguishing social and moral norms? While social norms could conflict with each other, such as in law, supposedly this would not be the case of moral norms, at least on a Kantian reading. For example, for two people, it would be equally morally permissible to eat the only apple hanging from a tree, even if only one of them can actually eat it. But it would not be possible for each to have a right to eat this apple, as only one of them can eat it.[171]

This argument suffers from its ambiguous notion of a right. The more precisely I specify a right, such as if I determine that it is to be exercised at a certain time, the greater the possibility that only one person can exercise the right thus specified. Frequently, there is an instance of specification first. Whoever claims the right in a specified way obtains the right thus specified.[172] Whoever exercises his right of assembly first at a certain place at a certain time enjoys a right that is no longer accorded to those who also want to stage a political assembly at the same place and time, yet arrived later, even though they enjoy the same legal status. This has nothing to do with the moral or legal nature of the right in

[171] Willaschek (n 167), "Right and Coercion" pp. 62–4.

[172] However, concerning the practical problems of this form, see Andreas Voßkuhle, "'Wer zuerst kommt, mahlt zuerst!' Das Prioritätsprinzip als antiquierter Verteilungsmodus einer modernen Rechtsordnung" in: *Die Verwaltung* 32 (1999), pp. 21–41.

question. In their collectively owned garden, both partners in marriage could, for instance, have the right, guaranteed by the State, to eat the apple, and whoever of the two does so and beats the other to it does not thereby violate the right of the other.

For Kant, moral norms are not enforceable, as they presuppose an internal achievement that is not enforceable. If a morally imperative action comes up against physical limitations of realization, then the obligation thereby ceases, without the norm as a whole becoming extinct. *All kinds* of norms, once they have been issued into the world, can escalate into conflicts in which only one of multiple norms can be realized. But this does not apply to *all norms*, as not all norms refer to scarce goods. The possibility for conflict has to do with the structure—permission or command—and spatial and temporal specification of the norm, but not with the origin of a legal, moral, or other authoritative kind of pretense.

By contrast, and for this reason, not all social norms can be enforced. In his reconstruction of the relation between legal and moral norms in Kant, Arthur Ripstein has defined the legal sphere as one focused on objects, and the moral sphere as one focused on concepts.[173] As elegantly as such a construction can be incorporated into the architecture of Kant's oeuvre, drawing parallels with practical and theoretical philosophy, it is just as doubtful whether this can hold true for social norms. Drawing once more on an example from law, a parliament's obligation, determined by a court, to enact a statute, does not concern an external object, but rather a process within the normative order. Under certain circumstances, this judgment can be "enforced," but this enforcement does not operate physically. The court itself might stipulate the content of the statute in a judgment. But there is no court officer that comes around to make the parliamentarians lift their arm at the right point in time. Even in criminal law, obligations such as not killing other persons[174] are rarely enforced. The only thing that is always enforced is the sanction after the legal transgression.

The criterion of enforceability presumes a strong distinction between interior and exterior world, as well as a causal notion of the social, external world. These two presumptions are not fitting. Social norms can have effects in the interior world; they can prompt a revision of preferences. By contrast, many legal obligations are not enforceable, because they are not oriented toward a causal context. Coercive enforceability in space is not a necessary characteristic of social norms. It is precisely their physical implementation that pushes them to their limits. Social norms are located in the gap between noumenal and phenomenal world opened up by Kantian philosophy.

[173] Ripstein (n 168), *Force and Freedom*, pp. 366–87, esp. 370 f., 373–87. He is concerned with the solidity of objects in space, which leads to only one being able to also occupy one space.

[174] I leave it up for debate as to whether such an obligation exists at all, and whom it would apply to, the victim or community, or whether criminal law limits itself to sanctioning the act in question.

3.5 The Boundaries of Normative Orders

Norms refer to what is possible. This is the fundamental boundary to their scope, a boundary which admittedly in many cases isn't clearly defined. Norms can also help in dealing with one's own ignorance regarding the boundaries of the possible. In terms of norm theory, spatial boundaries are not to be taken as physical barriers but rather as a bundle of spatially defined reference points for defining a normative order's field of application and validity. Physical barriers which do not allow anything or anyone to pass are not boundaries in this sense because boundaries understood thus will only fulfill their role if they can be crossed. Boundaries themselves are not norms. In and of themselves, they neither prohibit nor permit their own transgression. They merely mark a norm's field of application, even that of the prohibition to transgress them, which in some cases might not be in legal force on the other side of that boundary.

The opening and closing of a normative order can be particularly well studied at the example of modern States, as State boundaries are both highly formalized and sanctioned by means of coercion.[175] The situation of modern States also lends itself to highlight the limited possibility to define a normative order merely spatially and territorially.[176] Even at the height of modern nation-States' claim to sovereignty, the application of foreign legal norms by State courts was nothing exceptional.[177] It seems to always have been quite practical to also make use of the normative inventory stemming from other State legal orders, or from other social norm orders, and to define the applicability of a norm not only territorially but also with respect to persons. Certainly, these kinds of phenomena can hardly be squared with the State's pretense to sovereignty. For in this case, another authority is shaping the rules in one's own territory. In order to uphold the claim that the State legal order is nonetheless closed, attempts are frequently made to territorially reconstruct this kind of norm usage.[178] Thus, one could argue the applicability of a foreign norm to one's own territory to result only from this norm being admitted into the legal order by another norm internal to this legal order. The transnational use of norms would thus be capable of being brought into harmony with the pretense of a territorially enclosed dominion. The problem would then become, that under these conditions, the State can decide on opening and

[175] On the nationalization of borders, see Wolfgang Reinhard, *Geschichte der Staatsgewalt*, Munich 1999, pp. 351–4.

[176] For a differentiated account, see Michael Zürn, "Globalization and Global Governance" in: Walter Carlsnaes et al., *Handbook of International Relations*, London 2003, pp. 402–5.

[177] For a landmark work on international private law, which regulated such relations, see: Friedrich Carl von Savigny, *System des heutigen römischen Rechts*, Vol. VIII, Berlin 1849, Third Book, First Chapter.

[178] One example for many is the way national laws engage international influences, such as in the German engagement of European law, the metaphor of a state "bridge guard," Paul Kirchhof, "Der deutsche Staat im Prozeß der europäischen Integration" in: Josef Isensee and Paul Kirchhof (eds), *Handbuch des Staatsrechts*, Vol. VII, Heidelberg 1992, § 183, para. 65.

closing as such, but only in a very limited way could it decide about the content of norms thus introduced. The solution—as always when notions of sovereignty are at stake—only becomes plausible with a high measure of formalization and abstraction. But tendencies toward greater autonomy always remain possible for the norm inventories thus entering the State.[179] The more people cross-national boundaries, and the more they are accompanied by religious, moral, and legal norms, the more these norms gain in relevance at their final destination. These are frequent side effects of perfectly legal behavior, of crossing borders, such that it would be imprecise to see this as a problem of preserving the "identity" of the national norm order. since part of said identity precisely consists in its opening up. If one at all wants to employ the notion of a normative order's "identity," and this may well be no great idea in light of its unclear boundaries as well as the mutual overlapping of identities, then this rather reveals how incompletely defined, if not ambivalent, these kinds of identities can be.

For one, most orders of social norms are not precisely delimited, and secondly, they overlap with other normative orders.[180] It is doubtful that this is a historically new development, it is more likely that the opposing claim of State sovereignty makes it particularly visible. Normative orders tend to lose their form, and in many respects, they leave the extent of their own reach open. Boundaries aim to formalize this reach territorially without it being possible to always clearly locate these boundaries. They are found wherever the order applies distinctions such as that between citizens and foreigners.[181] At first sight, a territorial connection entails cognitive advantages, for it allows for a response to the question of the order's applicability: there is a measurable criterion. The territorial connection also fits well with the norm-setters' claim to political legitimacy, as a spatially defined application criterion can be nicely combined with the demands of democratic generality and equality. Thus, assuming the lack of another norm order, coherent democratic link can develop between the legitimizing subject and the positing of the norm.[182] This becomes all the more difficult the more the order's addressees themselves become mobile or desire external mobility. Then the border creates a territorial condition that has meaning for many, or even most norms of a norm order, and it can be used as a fall-back rule on all kinds of normative questions. At the same time, however, the boundary is less and less able to assign elements of a norm order to a territory, or a territory to an entire normative order. At a territorial level,

[179] This is displayed exemplarily in the seemingly futile attempt to view the effects of European law in Germany as the mere result of German agreement to European contracts, thereby upholding German sovereignty.

[180] Saskia Sassen, *Territory, Authority, Rights*, Princeton 2006, pp. 378–90.

[181] Rainer Bauböck, "Migration and the Porous Boundaries of Democratic States" in: Stephan Leibfried u.a. (eds), *Oxford Handbook of Transformations of the State*, Oxford 2015, pp. 516–31, here p. 518; Lena Laube, "Wohin mit der Grenze? Die räumliche Flexibilisierung von Grenzkontrollen in vergleichender Perspektive" in: *TranState Working Paper* 112, Bremen 2010, pp. 31–5.

[182] Michael Zürn, *Regieren jenseits des Nationalstaates*, Frankfurt/M. 1998, pp. 237 ff.

borders operate similar to the status of citizenship at the personal level. As a bundle of reference points for the validity of a norm, without thereby monopolizing the reference.[183] Mobility does not make borders lose in relevance, the borders actually only carry relevance for those who desire to move. But they change their function. Borders change from being instruments of limiting mobility to ones of observing this mobility.[184]

The presumption of a sovereign order that enjoys precedence over and contains all other orders on a certain territory loses convincing power due to the mobility of people and objects, but even taken in and of itself, it is hardly plausible.[185] Ultimately, as we shall see, concepts such as the "monopoly on norm creation" can only themselves be understood as normative propositions. They formulate a claim but cannot rule out the practical possibility of other norms being posited. We can describe this insight as norm pluralism without thereby gaining anything on a conceptual level.

Thus, even formalized and physically established territorial boundaries are incapable of fully fencing in and containing a norm order. What is more, fencing in is not the only or even the most important function of a border. Of course, borders serve to restrict mobility, in light of the victims of border regimes, this function is not a trivial one. But the relationship between a normative order and coercive or violent border enforcement merits a closer look. It cannot simply be viewed as the neutral application of a norm. For one, the application here as elsewhere carries repercussions for the order. It is doubtful whether the coercive or violent prevention of border crossing can only contribute to maintaining the identity of the spatially delimited order, since this violent practice inevitably becomes part of this identity. For this reason, it is trivializing to interpret the German Democratic Republic as an order that was normatively tied to certain fundamental rights, one in which the killing of fleeing persons could be treated as a transgression of the order's own norms.[186] Instead, these killing were part of its political order whose normative inventory would be insufficiently described without also including these killings. The borders of the European Union, too, are protected through coercion and violence. As it concerns immigration, not emigration, and since the border runs through water, the death of migrants can more easily be accorded to themselves, as opposed to the border agents or a community lacking in solidarity. At the same time, the European "community of values" would be insufficiently described, if done without including the willingness to tolerate a system

[183] The concept crucial for this insight was coined by Philip C. Jessup, *Transnational Law*, New Haven 1956.

[184] Concerning this twofold function, Bauböck (n 181), "Migration and the Porous Boundaries" p. 517.

[185] On this, Kenneth C. Culver and Michael Giudice, *Legality's Border*, Oxford 2010.

[186] This interpretation helped to justify the retroactive punishment of border agents; countering this, once more, Jakobs (n 89), "Vergangenheitsbewältigung durch Strafrecht?" pp. 52–9.

that prefers letting many people die to spending more money for their rescue. For a highly formalized order such as the European Union, an additional phenomenon comes to play. The physical borders also serve to avoid the legal scrutiny of the situation, that is, they physically keep people from applying for asylum. Due to practices that *themselves are normatively guided*, one's own normative order remains unapplied.[187]

Both examples show that borders cannot simply be understood as formal, spatially defined, physically enforceable limits of a normative order. In the case of the German Democratic Republic, it is precisely the use of force that expresses the core of the order, its spatial enclosure. In the case of the European Union, the extraterritoriality of procedures shows a normative distancing from its own normative inventory and commitments.

Despite these kinds of phenomena, borders highlight the proximity of the one side to the other, which is also made clear by the curiosities of "zone edges" even in the most isolationist of regimes. As Hegel notes, natural borders such as rivers, as connecting points of two sides, can become centers.[188] This idea can be generalized. These considerations also show that the talk of "blurring boundaries," widespread throughout the social sciences, and of instead "transitions" being the relevant object of investigation, is imprecise.[189] Just as borders do not become blurred because they are crossed, so too norms are not vague because they are violated. It is less that we are observing transition phenomena, normative grey areas, than a layering and overlapping of diverse orders with different reference points, among these also spatial ones. The notion of a third space, popular in cultural studies, a space in which one is neither in nor outside an order, itself might still be too indebted to the idea that, at least at some point, it was normal to be part of a certain order at a certain place. Regardless of whether this is the historical case,[190] the concern here is with analyzing the plenitude of informal and formalized, moral, religious, legal, and other norm orders, between which and within whose boundaries stark conflicts may arise, without these orders explicitly colliding; orders whose boundaries, however, do not need to be imprecise. As a constituent element of a norm order in this sense, boundaries, however, only work if they are porous.

[187] For an observation of this in Australia, where you can only apply for asylum outside the State, Bauböck (n 181), "Migration and the Porous Boundaries" p. 518.

[188] Georg Friedrich Wilhelm Hegel, *Vorlesungen über die Philosophie der Geschichte*, Frankfurt/M. 1986, pp. 118 ff. Concerning border-crossing identities, Tam Cho and Nicely (n 166), "Geographic Proximity versus Institutions" p. 817.

[189] The examples in Bauböck (n 181), "Migration and the Porous Boundaries" p. 519) are less about intermediary conditions as they are for the layering of various yet clearer belongings, or for an increasing rift between clear legal belonging and a divergent, yet also clear spatial residency.

[190] The critique from within cultural studies often underestimates the richness of the Western constitutional-theoretical tradition. Exemplarily, see the influential, yet consistently general reflections offered by James Tully, *Strange Multiplicity: Constitutionalism in an Age of Diversity*, Cambridge 1995, pp. 58–98.

3.6 Norm-Free Spaces?

If spatial boundaries cannot define the purview of norms in an absolute sense, then speaking of norm-free spaces loses its meaning. Even in concentration camps and in urban centers with high crime rates, norms are at play,[191] one might even say that such areas are frequently and even obsessively shaped by norms.[192] Aside from an overestimation of norms' determining power, it is the apparent coexistence of extremely dense norming and utter arbitrariness of norm application which leads to nevertheless speaking of norm-free or lawless spaces. But we have to be cautious with the assumption of arbitrariness. For behind any supposed arbitrariness might lurk a perverse normative logic, which, in its apparent lack of criteria, seeks to deny one final form of recognition to victims, such as when victims deliberately are being selected in a random fashion. Here, too, the experience of normlessness is embedded in a stable normative horizon. In light of the strained effort to classify systematically, identify meticulously, and persecute tirelessly its victims, all in turn out of normative considerations, terms such as "arbitrary rule"[193] miss the point.[194] For National Socialism, Ernst Fraenkel developed the distinction between a state of norms and a state of measures, in order to describe a practice in which a legalistic and highly formalized legal practice and an informal practice of political persecution did not contradict each other, but rather functionally complimented each other.[195] The fact that informal practice does not proceed according to rules precisely does not mean that it does not follow a normative logic, one which simply does not want to allow itself to be completely tied down in formalization. By contrast, the fact that a constitutive informal practice exists does not mean that the formality in place is a mere empty shell. It fulfills its role precisely because its realm of application is limited. It also supports the legitimacy of the persecuting regime and apparatus by providing an alternative norm program whose realm of application is externally determined, but whose mere existence also shapes the entire order because relevant parts of the people subjected to these norms are only addressed by this formalized part of the order.[196]

[191] In the second case, the phenomenon can only be described with recourse to norms.

[192] Here, an exemplary legal analysis of Guantánamo, wrestling with Giorgio Agamben's theory of camps, helps us further: Fleur Johns, "Guantánamo Bay and the Annihilation of the Exception" in: *European Journal of International Law* 6 (2005), pp. 613–35.

[193] Note by translator: in English, we would most frequently translate this as tyranny; however, the choice of "arbitrary rule" translates more literally from the original German "*Willkürherrschaft*."

[194] On the concept of arbitrariness as the opposite term of order, see below, pp. 242 ff.

[195] Ernst Fraenkel, *Der Doppelstaat*, Frankfurt/M. 1984, pp. 88–96; more precisely concerning the distinction: Horst Dreier's afterword "Was ist doppelt am 'Doppelstaat'?" for the new editions of Fraenkel's classic study *Der Doppelstaat*, Hamburg 2012, pp. 274–300.

[196] The case of Soviet law (pre-1960) might provide a different example, in as far as family law was consistently reconstrued for a socialist notion of education and formation: Harold J. Berman, *Justice in the U.S.S.R.*, Cambridge, Mass. 1963, Part III.

4. *From the Normative Disposition to the Normative Order—and Back*

4.1 Hart versus Kant

"To qualify as a norm, a rule must be used normatively by a subject."[197] According to a thesis from Kant, we can only speak of norms where a subject takes a certain disposition toward a norm, such that both the adherence to and the rejection of the norm represent a possibility.

It seems that norms presume subjects that walk through life with a certain attitude. Does this necessarily mean it is a moral attitude? H. L. A. Hart doubted this. On his reading, it is necessary for a norm to have a staff of people who would assume an internally normative disposition toward the order. However, this normative disposition would not necessarily have to be a moral one. According to him, a normative disposition consists in a measure-taking attitude toward the behavior of others by a certain, yet not necessarily moral standard.[198] On this view, Hart recognizes normativity in the sense of its providing a standard against which certain objects are being measured, but simultaneously and explicitly denies that such recognition would have to entail a moral condoning of this standard. Hart is thinking of a judge who acknowledges the validity of a legal order and applies it without morally condoning it; he also could have thought of a guest who is aware of the customs in a host's home and heeds them, even though he thinks them to be ridiculous. According to Hart, there can be plenty of non-moral reasons to follow these standards, even if only to copy others. He calls this disposition an internal point of view.

Hart's view of things was mostly rejected by his readers from moral philosophy.[199] The critique maintains that it is impossible to assume an internal and recognizing disposition toward a normative order, without this disposition thereby necessarily being of a moral kind. The person either recognizes the order, and this would be understood as a moral deduction and grounding of this order, or that person switches to a non-normative and an external point of view. Many critics

[197] Patricia Kitcher, *Kant's Thinker*, Oxford 2011, p. 218.

[198] H. L. A. Hart, *The Concept of Law*, New York 2012, pp. 88–91. On the critique discussed in what follows: Scott J. Shapiro, *Legality*, Cambridge, Mass. 2011, pp. 113 f.; Richard Holton, "Positivism and the Internal Point of View" in: *Law and Philosophy* 17 (1998), pp. 597–625, here pp. 600–6.

[199] Shapiro (n 198), *Legality*, pp. 114 ff., 213–17, highlights that law is concerned with more grave things than a game, and that these can only be justified with moral ends. For a critique, see Plunkett, who highlights that the determination of an order could also depend on *claiming* to follow such ends: David Plunkett, "Legal Positivism and the Moral Aim Thesis" in: *Oxford Journal of Legal Studies* 33 (2013), pp. 563–605. It is doubtful, however, whether we can understand legal orders as ends-oriented, as they are marked by many institutional mechanisms that certainly inhibit a direct pursuit of ends: Rights, judicial independence, and separate procedures for implementation and execution. More complex: Holton (n 198), "Positivism" pp. 603–6; Joseph Raz, "Incorporation by Law" in: *Legal Theory* 10 (2004), pp. 1–17, here pp. 4–7.

shift their objections to the question of what might count as a reason for recognition. On their reading, a normative reason would be one that draws on a justification and thereby is indistinguishable from a moral reason. Whoever accepts something out of pure habit, by contrast, does not have a normative reason, but rather acts without a normative foundation.

We may very well doubt whether every form of justification is necessarily a moral justification, but either way, Hart does not mean a justifying normative reason, but a cognitive reason that refers to something normative. For Hart, *recognition* denotes the finding or awareness of a norm, not its acceptance.[200] This is not a normative effort, but it does refer to a norm. Whoever observes that a practice operates with certain norms has reason to believe that a norm order exists. All who participate in this practice—as a well-born guest critical of social etiquette or as a law-skeptical judge—assume an internal perspective since they participate in the order and are aware that others participate in it. Hart observes a social world in which a judge decides a rent dispute in favor of the tenant even though his moral intuition falls to the landlord's side. His theoretical conception rests on the idea that many social practices can be *explained* by looking at normative orders, which can be achieved without examining the moral reasons that lie behind these norms. For Hart, "justification" denotes justifying a non-moral norm by reference to the very order to which it belongs.[201]

But what might in this case still be meant by speaking of an *internal* point of view?[202] If I only relate justification to a certain order as a hypothetical imperative, for example, if I claim that the justification of a certain action solely depends on certain behavioral rules, then the question arises as to what distinguishes an internal attitude from an external one. Couldn't anyone claim that, under the condition of a certain order's existence certain actions are justified, without assuming a perspective to this order? Yes, this is possible. But I can only assume an internal perspective if I believe—of myself or of others—this justification to also become relevant for my or their actions. The internal perspective finds its distinction in my taking the norm order seriously for my own actions, as opposed to simply contemplating the order. This distinguishes a cynical judge who applies legal norms according to his own understanding, from a legal sociologist who looks for the economic basis behind the juridical superstructure. The judge assumes his role as a judge in the moment in which the fact that something is done by other judges, for

[200] Similarly in the German translation by Alexander von Baeyer: p. 122 and more frequently.

[201] Holton consistently muddies this by viewing moral justification as the only possible form of justification. See, however, "Positivism" (n 198) p. 606, fn. 21 and the rebuttal in the following section.

[202] Another objection at this point is that Hart commits the is/ought fallacy in his argumentation. Representative for many, Marco Iorio, *Regel und Grund*, Berlin 2011, p. 130. Shapiro (n 198), *Legality*, pp. 102–5, however, sees a categorical mistake at work, as Hart deduces rules, i.e. abstract objects, from practices. But the question arises as to what these objections precisely could mean for social norms, particularly as Hart does not limit himself to observation of regularities, but rather to an attitude toward them, which is not irritated by a norm transgression.

him, turns into a reason to also behave in this way.[203] This does not necessarily entail an inner affirmation, and certainly not a moral sanctioning of the legal order, at the moment at which he is judging. For Hart, "internal" means internal to the order, not to the subject. An internal disposition to behavioral rules claims that these are necessary for describing my behavior. An external perspective, by contrast, could claim that this is false, and that I am in fact concerned with something else, such as not endangering my career options by bad behavior, the consequence being that I only adhere to these rules whenever such a threat arises, but not otherwise. It is an empirical question as to which description is more appropriate for my actions; but the concern is always with how my actions are best described, not with what I make of them. What is decisive for Hart is that people have to take on this kind of internal perspective in order to establish a norm order. As we have seen, there is a grey zone between explicit affirmation and mere observation. With the help of Hart's theory, this problem can be reformulated and made more precise. An order that explicitly marks itself as normative can be established more firmly by participants recognizing the relevance of the order without substantively affirming the order.

4.2 A Thought Experiment: The Imagined Norm

Does a norm that is recognized as relevant for action have to actually exist? And what does "actual" even mean here? Let us take a look at the following case. A socially insecure man falsely believes that there is a social norm which prescribes that men wear a tie to an evening event at a certain house. He shares this false assessment with some friends who believe him, and they too arrive with ties, along with another group of men who succumb to the same false belief, and a further group whose members do not care what is expected of them, but nonetheless like wearing ties without expecting it of others. In the end, more than half of the male attendees are wearing ties at this event. And in all of this, not a single tie-wearer holds an affirmative disposition to a social norm that prescribes dressing up in such manner. The only thing that is widespread is the false assumption that such a norm exists, and for some, the personal preference for ties.

Does the misconception about a norm thereby create a norm? Can I equate the false assumption of recognition by some with real recognition? As a comparison, a widespread misconception about a fact cannot make this fact true, as long as we can provide a workable criterion that can test its truth. Does the same hold for norms? It does insofar as our supposed norm has the possibility of correcting the misconception, such as by inquiring about the customs of the house and finding

[203] See Michael I. Hardimon, "Role Obligations" in: *The Journal of Philosophy* 91 (1994), pp. 333–63, here p. 338.

out that the hosts do not care about their guests' wardrobe. Formalizing techniques also exist in order to rule out such misunderstandings, as well as false and falsified norms. Furthermore, let us take a look at the norm that might develop in this way: more and more guests might observe the number of tie-wearers, then other guests would arrive who make the supposed norm their own, and ultimately other guests, arriving without ties, would become subject to criticism. This, however, would be a different norm from the one which the initial guests had imagined: it would be a norm created by custom, not by the hosts.

Nevertheless, the possibility of such a norm arising out of error helps to illustrate three things. For one, it makes clear that the development of norms not only does not presume a moral, not even a normative disposition, but rather a cognitive one about a social relationship which is interpreted as a norm.[204] If wearing a tie establishes itself even though no-one wants it to but simply because a growing majority believes such a norm to exist, then there is more at play than simply a practice of wearing ties. The possibility to deviate from and to critique this practice marks it as normative, whereas the fact that about the same number of persons are showing up with and without a tie would not provide any answer as to whether a norm exists.

Secondly, this kind of norm development is insufficiently described by referring to its focus on intentions and plans of its participating individuals, even if the idea of intention is frequently used so broadly in such contexts that anything would fit within it. The participants refer to an existing clothing practice and an authority structure that they themselves did not develop, but simply misinterpreted. This error would not have been possible if one could not presume the hosts' authority to posit certain norms. The idea that a host can make commands for behavior at their house is not an idiosyncratic one, though. The error is linked to pre-existing norm structures, even if it misinterprets them at a decisive point.

Finally, the example demonstrates that norms are capable of being projected very differently than facts. This brings back to mind their commonality with fictions. Just as with fictions, norms do not operate independently of the factual world, one could even say that imagined norms are more dependent on facts and existing normative contexts than other norms since the error rests on a misinterpretation of given conditions, making it impossible for imagined norms, unlike other norms, to be posited in willful ignorance or conscious opposition to the status quo. In the end, a norm indeed presumes a subjective disposition, but a cognitively subjective disposition is sufficient, and even the mistaken assumption of a norm can suffice.

Cases of falsely imagined norms are rare, and the real norms that arise from them are fragile. Those who reject the norm in its substance can thereby also be motivated to probe its origins, to see through its development, and thus chip away at its foundation. At the same time, however, the practice provoked by the supposed

[204] See also the conclusion by Brennan et al. (n 1), *Explaining Norms*, p. 183.

norm can also attract people who want to adhere to this rule in particular—according to Nietzsche, those who are creative in order to adhere to the law.[205] A social norm can also bring about the motivation to subject oneself to it.

4.3 Expectation, Disappointment—and Free Will?

Let us go one step further and ask which achievement must be expected from a person in order for norms to develop, and what kind of "disposition"[206] must be expected of subjects in order to contribute to a norm order. In responding to this, let us begin with the phenomenon of disappointment.[207] As such, expectations are not norms. It is only disappointed expectations that set free a "sense of possibility"[208] which is necessary for any normative practice. This means that there is no normative practice without the capacity for expectation and disappointment. Furthermore, we have to be able to remember disappointments and imagine other courses of events.[209] Social normativity begins with the identification of alternatives, with a two-pronged worldview, by a remembered and stabilized experience of disappointment. The presumption of a twofold course of events also is at work, but possibly does not entail the demanding condition of subjective freedom. We encountered this reversed relationship above, when we investigated the relationship between action and norm. If it is true that norms do not only refer to actions, do not only prescribe them, prohibit them, or evaluate them, then this might confirm that the subjective achievements which are needed in order to establish norms do not have to reach the demanding threshold of free will.

Peter Strawson has tried to show that the practice of normatively judging actions of others does not have to coincide with the assumption of its members' free will: in response to the behavior of others, we assume a reactive disposition, which is distinct from an objective disposition toward things. According to Strawson, practices of this kind of reactive attitude, such as holding others accountable for their actions, or such as our frustration about them, are so deeply entrenched in our emotional economy that even if we knew that the other was not free to choose his action, but rather determined in his behavior, we still *could* not set them aside.[210]

[205] Nietzsche (n 92), "*Morgenröthe*" p. 23 (No. 9)

[206] For example, Nicholas Southwood, "The Authority of Social Norms" in: Michael Brady (ed.), *New Waves in Metaethics*, London 2011, pp. 234–48, here pp. 204 f.

[207] For a countering point of view, see Christine Korsgaard, *The Sources of Normativity*, Cambridge, 1996, pp. 46 ff., who, concerning *moral* norms, demands self-consciousness as necessary and sufficient condition for normativity. This seems too internal and demanding for *social* norms.

[208] This expression stems from Robert Musil, *Der Mann ohne Eigenschaften*, Reinbek 1978, Vol. I, p. 16. On its context, Niklaus Largier, "Mystik als Medium. Robert Musils ›Möglichkeitssinn‹ im Kontext" in: Andrea Kleihues et al. (eds), *Intermedien*, Zürich 2010, pp. 401–11.

[209] Merely concerning expectations, see above, pp. 73–75; concerning remembering and imagination, above, pp. 76 ff.; on disappointment, above, pp. 116, 118, and 123–25.

[210] Peter Strawson, "Freedom and Resentment" in: Id., *Freedom and Resentment and Other Essays*, London 2008, pp. 1–28, here pp. 22–7. Consequently, the question arises as to which standards should

For Strawson, it is even doubtful whether we should give up this reactive practice if we had this knowledge. After all, it has served us quite well so far, and there is no reason for which the theoretical insight into determinism should lead us to change ourselves.

Strawson's considerations met with significant pushback, and two points are of further interest for us.[211] For one, it is questionable whether Strawson might not underestimate the measure to which our reactions to others' behavior is socially mediated and historically alterable. Why should we rule out that our feelings toward some behavior can change, such that we could also make do without the reactive attitude described by Strawson? And could the insight into our lack of free will possibly lead us to treat each other as objects after all?[212] This objection is worth noting, as much would indicate that emotional reactions are subject to historical change.[213] This gives us reason to assume that our normative practices depend on what we know, or think we know, about our capacities as subjects. In this sense, the critique of Strawson is convincing. But it neither shows that normative practices depend on our free will per se, nor that our free will depends on the knowledge of our will being free. This strong relationship is certainly not implied by our critique of Strawson. We can take seriously the problematic consequences which positive knowledge of our *lacking* free will could have, without thereby having to claim that our free will in any way depends on the positive knowledge of our free will.

This leads to the second objection, which concerns the distinction between free will as such and a reactive practice that presumes said will. This distinction seems to collapse in Strawson's contribution, as he is only concerned with participants' reaction to a certain behavior, and not in turn with the question of whether those reactions are also justified. Against this, claims are made that it is very much possible for a community to misjudge the question of responsibility of one person, that they can react inappropriately.[214] According to this critique, Strawson therefore fails to demonstrate the compatibility of free will and determinism. Setting aside whether Strawson wants to demonstrate this,[215] it is indeed true that the distinction between the empirically observable, real accountability of a person and the

be applied to a free decision for the punishment of perpetrators: Tatjana Hörnle, *Kriminalstrafe ohne Schuldvorwurf?*, Baden-Baden 2013, pp. 49–57.

[211] Here, I follow the clear overview in Michael McKenna and Paul Russell, "Introduction: Perspectives on P.F. Strawson's ›Freedom and Resentment‹" in: Id. (ed.), *Free Will and Reactive Attitudes*, London 2012, pp. 1–17, here pp. 10–14.

[212] Dierk Peereboom, "Revising the Reactive Attitudes" in: M. McKenna and P. Russell (eds), *Free Will*, pp. 219–34, here pp. 223–8.

[213] Simply see the overview by Jan Plamper, *Geschichte und Gefühl*, München 2012.

[214] This point is developed along the lines of McKenna and Russell (n 212), "Introduction" pp. 12 ff. See also Thomas Nagel, *The View from Nowhere*, Oxford 1989, Chapter 6.

[215] In Strawson's contribution, Richard Holton recognizes the assumption that claiming a person to have free will can be taken to be a normative claim in its own right, one which serves to sustain the normative practice. Lecture manuscript at web.mit.edu/holton/www/edin/introfw/introfw3.pdf, (last accessed 16 August 2019).

social practice of attribution of responsibilities dissolves in Strawson's argument. This, however, is quite compatible with our considerations, because social norm orders experiment with standards of attribution and accountability. They presume that certain classes of people can indeed control their behavior in certain contexts, adjust these presumptions according to new experiences with this behavior, and orient them toward normative expectations without there being any defined determination of what accountability "as such" is. Of course, a community can miss its own standards of accountability in a concrete scenario, it can misapply it; but it is very difficult to imagine that it could systematically do this again and again without these standards thereby changing.[216] And how should responsibility for actions even be able to be determined independent of the community that demands it? If we criticize a community for its practice of attribution, we tend to do this in light of experiences we made with another community. After all, the idea of accountability used here is more tightly aligned with certain practices than with any philosophical notion of free will. It is not grounded in a fact of the matter, but rather in the continual new determination of that which can be possibly expected of an agent. Toward this end, Strawson is incorrect in trying to immunize the existing reactive practice against presumably external rational insights.[217] But the criticism can also be turned around. The internal practice is not without repercussions for what can count as rational insight into the capacity for responsible action.

In this, and despite the objections to it, Strawson's considerations confirm our suspicion that we do not have to assume a social practice of normativity only under the condition that its participants have free will, even if the presumption of free will supports the practice.[218] We can limit ourselves to thinking of subjects as capable of disappointment, that is, of being able to remember expectations and imagine alternative courses of events.[219] On this basis, we might be able to flip around this idea and describe subjectivity as an epiphenomenon of a practice in which courses of events are confronted and evaluated with other expected, imagined, or remembered courses of events.

4.4 Ordered Norms and Normative Orders

Attitudes can become norms, and norms can become normative orders. "Order," however, is no more of an exclusively normative category than "rule." Both can

[216] See above, pp. 8 ff.

[217] Nagel (n 214), *The View from Nowhere*, pp. 214–17.

[218] In this sense, and with an eye toward law as a form that supports this presumption, see: Christoph Möllers, "Willensfreiheit durch Verfassungsrecht" in: Ernst-Joachim Lampe and Michael Pauen (eds), *Willensfreiheit und rechtliche Ordnung*, Frankfurt/M. 2008, pp. 250–75.

[219] See the attempt to relativize the demands of subjectivity by Philip Pettit, "The Reality of Rule-Following" in: Id., *Rules, Reasons, and Norms*, Oxford 2002, pp. 26–48.

denote cognitive or normative phenomena. The concept of a rule can express either a repetitive regularity or a general directive. With the concept of order, we cognitively connect a pattern, a structure without which recognizing a relationship becomes impossible. Order is a condition of cognition. Individual norms can form patterns and merge into an order, be it rigidly structured, be it more loosely. If this is the case, then not only can we describe these as individual norms, but as part of a relationship of cohesion. This relationship of cohesion can provide an indication that its various norms have a common source, and that they claim a similar kind of authority, though this need not be the case. Initially, the relationship between these norms remains a cognitive one.

For this reason, we need to distinguish between a set of norms ordered by a recognizable pattern and a normative order. In a normative order, the element of order itself is normative. Here, norms are brought about which stem from a common authoritative source, and which thereby stand in relationship to one another. While the cognitive order of norms does not contain normative implications, the existence of a normative order has cognitive implications, as it increases the recognizability of individual norms as norms. The common form of the authority invoked leads to the order's individual norms exhibiting a certain similarity and makes them recognizable as being related to each other. This kind of relationship does not have to arise from the top down. It can also exist as a decentral coexistence of certain processes of norm development, such as through the institution of several adjudicative bodies on the same hierarchical level that all follow similar procedures. Nevertheless, normative orders are only conceivable with some form of secondary rule, with a norm that defines the process of norm creation.[220]

Practically speaking, we are faced with vague transitions between the two meanings of a notion of order. For if norm and norm application bring together the more general with the more specific—and if it is possible to not only infer the specific from the general, but also to infer the general from the specific—then normative orders can develop from the patterns of cognitive orders, such as by tying individual norms to systematizing meta-rules like the freedom from contradiction. Freedom from contradiction is initially a precondition for rationality, it is cognitive. Normative orders have to be free of contradictions, in as far as they should not make factually mutually exclusive commands, which would entail something impossible. But in another sense, normative orders may well contain contradictions, such as when successive setting authorities have pursued contradictory goals with norms, without them getting in the way of each other concretely. Rectifying such contradictions in the name of an "order" means to commit the same kind of fallacy as when one infers a norm from a regularity. The conclusion is wrong, but in a way,

[220] Formulated for law, but generalizable: Hart (n 199), *The Concept of Law*, pp. 91–110.

the cognitive order invites this conclusion,[221] even if the order as such does not justify it.

Different kinds of social norms to differing degrees hinge on the existence of a normative order. A legal norm is inconceivable without a legal order, other social norms can arise from further norms in relative isolation from each other. A norm can be brought about from within an order, and by contrast, individual norms can amalgamate into an order. Toward that end, we can distinguish between ascending order developments and descending norm development.[222] Individual norms can condense into patterns, from which normative orders—with the aforementioned challenges—arise, or an existing order produces its own norms.

Frequently, both processes unfold simultaneously. Occasionally, the action constellations within a group of persons are mould into a stable, effective normative order without any norm-positing authority intervening.[223] In other cases, a community constitutionally agrees to a new order and establishes further norms upon this foundation. Both phenomena need to be distinguished from each other, but likely they rarely appear in isolation. Even the most dramatic revolutionary break will resort to traditional norm inventories that do not hinder its political project, simply equipping them with a different foundational validity.[224] On the other hand, every spontaneous rise of an order "from below" depends on other established orders that shield or support its development. Neighbor relations in the American "Western frontier," or the development of a privately regulated trade law among transnationally acting enterprises, the so-called *Lex mercatoria*, need other orders, namely States that guarantee them safety and sometimes even positive standards to which they can at times resort.[225] The choice of perspective from which to describe these relationships itself then often appears to be normatively guided. It is shaped, for example, by the question of whether one wants to describe the French Revolution as a turning point of bourgeois self-liberation, like Michelet, or as a continuity of administrative centralization, like de Tocqueville.

The coexistence of ascendant and descendant norm development structures is nothing other than the formulation of the difference between norm and norm application on a macro-perspective. Just as specific acts of application can be the starting point for more general norms, so orders can be established by means of the

[221] See above, p. 100.

[222] Following Walter Ullmann, *Principles of Government and Politics in the Middle Ages*, London 1961, who distinguishes between ascending and descending legitimacy.

[223] Such as in the case of the territorial regime of ranchers in the American West: Robert C. Ellickson, *Order without Law. How Neighbors Settle Disputes*, Cambridge, Mass. 1994. This could correspond to the—admittedly difficult to observe—spontaneous arising of order in Hayek, even if it is likely a rare phenomenon.

[224] Thus, there is no revolution without the transgression of norms: Horst Dreier, "Revolution und Recht" in: *Zeitschrift für öffentliches Recht* 69 (2014), pp. 805–53, especially p. 839.

[225] Christoph Möllers, "Globalisierte Jurisprudenz—Einflüsse relativierter Nationalstaatlichkeit auf das Konzept des Rechts und die Funktion seiner Theorie" in: *Archiv für Rechts- und Sozialphilosophie*, Vol. 79 (2001), pp. 41–60.

concentration of individual norms. Just as norms require for their perpetuation an actualization through application, so normative orders have to prove themselves in individual norms. Just as norms change in their application and can only be held distinguishable by particular formalization techniques, so normative orders are simultaneously solidified and changed by its individual norms. The question concerning the proper starting point of these kinds of processes is the wrong question, insofar as one wants to *describe* norms and normative orders, whereas it remains appropriate when addressing the problem of conceptual clarification and justification in the sense of a normative priority.

4.5 The Problem of Methodically Individualist Models of Norm Development

For this reason, theories of social ontology, which read norms purely as the result of common intentions of individual subjects, might not do justice to the complexity of normative relationships[226]—regardless of whether they are taken as a collective subject, a "we," or as the relationship of individual, subjective intentions, operating based on a division of labor.[227] In as far as these theories already presume that a normative structure exists among the participants, they cannot offer anything in terms of the concept of normativity.[228] Without this precondition, social facts such as norms are supposed to arise under the condition of mutual knowledge and adaptation of different individual intentions.[229] In these kinds of models, normative orders present themselves as chains of intersubjective originary moments and new beginnings.

Yet the puzzle of social norms consists in their independence from the actual stock of actors making up the normative practice.[230] Individuals are born into a normative order.[231] By contrast, models that operate with common intentions

[226] One should certainly acknowledge the claim that the theory merely serves "modest sociality" as Michael E. Bratmann (in *Shared Agency. A Planning Theory of Acting Together*, Oxford 2014) reminds us, even if it is not obvious how I could still make use of it in light of the reduced presumptions of subjectivity, in order to describe relationship pairs?

[227] Margaret Gilbert, "Shared Intention and Personal Intentions" in: *Philosophical Studies* 144 (2009), pp. 167–87; John Searle, *Wie wir die soziale Welt machen*, Frankfurt/M. 2012, pp. 153–207; differing, Michael Bratmann, "Shared Agency" in: Chrysostomos Mantzavinos (ed.), *Philosophy of the Social Sciences*, Cambridge 2009, pp. 41–59. See also the reference in Bratman, *Shared Agency*, pp. 126–31, which emphasizes the distinction between actors and intentions: It is easier to presume a group agent (e.g. a swarm) than a common intentionality.

[228] Thus in Gilbert (n 227), "Shared Intention" pp. 175–9. The same could go for the social ontology of Searle, who emphasizes the deontic power of constitutive concepts, yet does not clarify what he means by deontic.

[229] Michael E. Bratman, *Intention, Plans, and Practical Reason*, Cambridge, Mass. 1987, pp. 28–49.

[230] See also the critical observations by Frederick Stoutland, "Why are Philosophers of Action so Anti-Social?" in: Lilli Alanen et al. (eds), *Commonality and Particularity in Ethics*, New York 1997, pp. 45–74, here pp. 66–71.

[231] Hardimon (n 203), "Role Obligations" pp. 347 ff. In light of a methodical problem, Max Weber also highlights this: Max Weber, "R. Stammlers ›Überwindung‹ der materialistischen Geschichtsauffassung"

bring to mind social contract constructions and share their weaknesses.[232] An initial problem of such approaches could lie in the fact that even the entities who are supposed to produce norms in these orders cannot be understood without recourse to the normative order that they purportedly are constituting. A second problem might consist in the concept of intention having to be conceived so broadly as to almost become meaningless. Even if I consciously break a norm, I thereby still confirm its existence.[233] Intentions, then, only serve the purpose of fitting actions into a normative context that can be external to, formalized and independent of any present individual intentions. They are not produced in the subject in order to then collide with a normative order. Instead, from the outset, they are oriented toward a practice and are articulated along its lines. For example, political opinions can only be expressed within the framework of an existing realm of preferences in a political system, such as "right" or "left." Compensation claims against another person have to be conceived of as "rights" in a legal order. These precepts are not unalterable, but these kinds of intentions cannot be explained other than in relation to a malleable, yet not easily accessible stock of previously formatted norms. The example of the merely imaginary rule regarding clothing showed that a normative order can operate as such as long as, from the outside, it can be understood as the affirmation of a possibility without thereby necessitating an inner affirmation by the participants. The question of their justification can become troublesome for these kinds of orders, yet at the same time, routinization can also succeed at displacing this question. To view a normative order, one that has its own set of procedures, its construction of accountable subjects, and its own formalized decision structures, as the sum of intentions of those subjects who are currently participating in the order, does not always appear as the most fruitful possibility and is likely to be all the less helpful, the more complex the order becomes.

There are two systematic problems, despite all these difficulties, that invite a reconstruction of social norms based on individual intentions. For one, the insight that the world of the normative is dependent on subjective attitudes, that is that they have to play a constitutive role for a theory of social norms. Secondly, the fear of having to face ontologically obscure entities if one's descriptions extend beyond subjective attitudes. The question is how far both aspects carry.

We already encountered the first problem in considering the degree to which norms are artefacts. Without delegating normative meanings to objects, normative practices are just as difficult to stabilize as esthetic ones. Even if subjective

in: Id., *Gesammelte Aufsätze zur Wissenschaftslehre*, Johannes Winckelmann (ed.), Tübingen 1988, pp. 291–359, here p. 330. See also the observations in Michael A. Tomasello, *Origins of Human Communication*, Cambridge, Mass. 2008, pp. 220–5, esp. p. 225.

[232] John W. Gough, *The Social Contract*, Oxford 1957, pp. 244–55. It is here that Durkheim's motif of the extra-contractual preconditions of the contract arise.

[233] See also Brennan et al. (n 1), *Explaining Norms*, pp. 240–4.

dispositions are a necessary condition for social norms, a perspective limited to them does not thereby provide a sufficient description.[234] Normatively designated artefacts serve an important end for normative orders in that they are less easily available than intentions. A traffic sign was available to a community in the moment it was produced, mounted, and identified with a norm, but it is not easy, in some cases even more demanding, to repeat such a moment of availability to the collective in order to take the sign back down again.[235] Even if the common inventory of intentions had turned away from the norm, or even from the procedure of designating the sign, this would not simply lead to a replacement of the norm. A description of social norms has to acknowledge and account for the features of those objects that play a role in a normative practice, and it cannot simply describe them in the mirror of the participating subjects.[236]

Normative practices can oftentimes be pinned down to objects, which we tried to show earlier with reference to texts whose meaning can only be described if they are understood as text-objects that cannot be reduced to a meaning merely transported by the text. We should perform similar analyses for traffic signs, uniforms, or fences. Taking objects seriously does not mean to hypostatize them to actors or sources of power, but it very well means not taking them as mere copies of something that can only find its "true" expression and form in a concept.[237] A normative practice can only be appropriately described by investigating the way in which intentions, concepts, and objects are tied to each other.

There is a second argument that supports a reconstruction of social norms limited to subjective intentions. It has the advantage of not having to deal with and to accord agency to ontologically obscure entities. Here, the same problem arises that Bentham faced with regards to some kinds of normative fictions.[238] Who is actually acting when the "legal order" is acting? This objection should be taken seriously, but the ontological level needs to be distinguished from the epistemological one.[239] As long as we cannot describe the practice of social norms by

[234] As far as I can tell, Searle is the only representative of this school of theory, which emphasizes the meaning of objects: John R. Searle, "Social Ontology and the Philosophy of Society" in: Eric Margolis/ Stephen Laurence (eds), *Creations of the Mind*, Oxford 2007, pp. 3–17, here p. 8.

[235] See also the remark by Gerald A. Cohen, "Reason, Humanity, and the Moral Law" in: Korsgaard, *The Sources of Normativity*, pp. 167–88, here pp. 169 f.

[236] Tim Ingold, "Materials against Materiality" in: *Archaeological Dialogues* 14 (2007), pp. 1–16, here pp. 11 f., favorably quoted in Caroline Walker Bynum, *Christian Materiality*, New York 2011, p. 295, fn. 40; another person referring to traits is Lorraine Daston, "Introduction: Speechless" in: Id. (ed.), *Things That Talk*, New York 2004, pp. 9–24, here p. 15. If we go one step further and see traits simply as the result of practice, then of course, the risk arises of once more losing sight of the particularities of the object practice. This is expressed in Miguel Tamen, *Friends of Interpretable Objects*, Cambridge, Mass. 2001, pp. 140 ff.

[237] Jürgen Habermas, "Die Lebenswelt als Raum symbolisch verkörperter Gründe" in: Id., *Nachmetaphysisches Denken II*, Berlin 2012, pp. 54–76, here pp. 72–6.

[238] See above, pp. 149 f.

[239] The following argument is found in Christian List and Philip Pettit, *Group Agency*, Oxford 2011, pp. 75–8.

reducing them to individual contributions, we have to incorporate collective or institutional actors into the description. As long as we do not have a sufficient description of a "state" that can be broken down to individual action contributions, we have to speak of the "state," under methodically controlled conditions even of an actor.

This is not even always only the second best solution. A theory of normativity that presumes a carrier of intentions as the basic unit cannot capture the important, action-constituting aspect of social norms. If, by contrast, one presumes the existence of a normative order, then all actors are derived from this order, both individuals and collective entities. This may be plausible from a perspective internal to the order.[240] But it is also descriptively relevant if we insist that the character as an agent can never be understood as detached from the alterable normative expectations of certain action possibilities. If actions cannot be conceived of without norms that determine the demands of an action, then normative orders cannot be reduced to the contributions of individual intentions. In this case, norms prove not only to be the consequence of individual, albeit specific "we"-related normative attitudes, but these attitudes also prove to hinge on norms.

4.6 Beginning and End of Normative Orders

In spite of significant differences in their understanding of the concept of a norm, many definitions of normative orders have one thing in common. They determine orders by resorting to a pseudo-quantitative criterion. What is meant by this? A normative order is presumed to become established if and when a "sufficient number" of people share a certain normatively held attitude, or if it is "generally" followed.[241] I call this criterion pseudo-quantitative because it introduces a quantitative criterion that cannot quantify but is merely qualified in virtue of the condition to be defined, the order, establishing itself. Is it the "sufficient number" that defines the order, or the order that defines the "sufficient number"? This leaves the question open as to when an order becomes established. The definition extrapolates a notion of the individual norm to one of a critical mass, the size of which it cannot identify. Empirical research cannot take such a determination as its starting point.[242]

240 In accord with the distinction between legal and natural persons: Hans Kelsen, *Reine Rechtslehre* (1934), Tübingen 2010, pp. 63–71.

241 See, for example, Hart (n 199), *The Concept of Law*, p. 117; following up on this, Brennan et al. (n 1), *Explaining Norms*, pp. 28 ff.

242 As an additional criterion, Hart demands that official representatives of an order treat its norms as binding. This criterion also does not appear necessary or particularly capable of distinguishing, especially since all orders authorize persons to apply norms.

Other models do not differentiate orders quantitatively but qualitatively, with concepts such as the "basic norm" or "compelling reason."[243] It is no coincidence that such contributions tend to deal with legal theory, given that, due to their high degree of formalization, legal orders particularly rely on clearly distinguishing themselves from other orders. This is not the place for an immanent critique of these kinds of theories. Many of their strengths and weaknesses are likely to reveal themselves in light of a concrete legal order. In contrast to Hart's model, which is oriented toward the empiricism of social norms, such theories primarily serve to develop reasons for the internally closed character of a normative order, whereas they can contribute little to the external description of said order.

Qualitative and quantitative defining theories of norm orders, theories that seek to develop a clear criterion for when a certain kind of social norm is present and when not, run the risk of ignoring the gradual character—long familiar to the social sciences—of normative orders. In the practice of normative orders, conditions of norm condensation dominate, which can only be clearly identified as an order by means of formalizations internal to the order.[244] The genesis and disintegration of norm orders do not follow an either/or scheme in the way that models inspired by law or social contracts have to assume for legitimate theory-internal reasons.[245] For the empirical investigation of normative orders, the question of the coming to be, condensation, and dissolution of norms is decisive, and it is an access point that from the outset presumes the possibility of a "more or less," that is the gradual character, of order.

But in this regard, can we even speak of a norm order coming to be and dying away? The assumption that an order could be centrally instituted can likely only be upheld if one assumes what cannot be observed: that everything that is treated as a norm in a normative order is observed, ratified, or potentially corrected from a central institution. This makes an order being instituted extremely improbable. At the same time, norm systems do not simply dissolve by norms being broken or rejected. We can only speak of the disintegration of an order when the norm order has lost its recognizability, that is, when whatever could be described as a transgression of a norm can no longer be described as such.

It is difficult to say much of a general nature about how norm orders dissolve, aside from urging caution when speaking about generalities. Yet, in contrast to

[243] Kelsen (n 240), *Reine Rechtslehre*, 1st edn, pp. 78–81; Raz (n 36), *Practical Reasons and Norms*, pp. 149–54; for an interesting precursor of a model of basic norms employing this notion, see Edmund Husserl, *Logische Untersuchungen*, Vol. 1 (= *Gesammelte Schriften* 2), Hamburg 1975, p. 57.

[244] This internal perspective has its own right and can have meaning for the outside. It might even be relevant outside an order whether an organization understands itself as a State and a different one sees itself as a religious community. Yet criteria for responding to this question neither arise from the notion of a norm nor from that of an order. And it is equally doubtful whether they can develop for all religious communities out of a notion of religion, or, with a strong theoretical tradition, among which we can count authors such as Kelsen and Raz, whether it can develop for all legal orders from a notion of law.

[245] Christoph Möllers, *Staat als Argument*, Tübingen 2011, pp. 199–203.

what the concept of validity might suggest, there is no point at which the order simply shifts from validity to invalidity, there is only gradual decay. Furthermore, such dissolution probably does not progress in linear fashion, but rather decelerates or accelerates at certain thresholds.[246] We cannot empirically and clearly point to the decay of a normative order being fostered by neglectful persecution of smaller norm transgressions, as had long been claimed in criminology.[247] This, however, in turn means that the "varnish of civilization"[248] is not as thin as it is claimed going back to Freud's dictum; in other words, violence is not simply the return to a permanently latent condition, but itself for the most part normatively regulated and in need of its own explanation.

4.7 Civil War, Arbitrariness, and Exception: Opposing Concepts of Normative Order?

We have seen that the concept of order initially carries a cognitive meaning. The pattern alone does not make the order normative. For this reason, the descent of a State into a civil war is hardly a case of normlessness, it should not even be read as the lack of an order. If order generates recognizable patterns, then a civil war, often taken to be the quintessence of normative disorder, cannot proceed without such an order. For even the distinction between the fighting parties, between friend and foe, presumes a manageable cognitive order, without which the civil war would turn into a violent entropy. This then no longer represents the lack of an order, but rather the lack of an appropriate order, one that rules out violent means in the case of conflict, or at least pushes back against such means. But a criterion of appropriateness cannot be derived from the concept of order. If it is not disorder as such that is problematic, then order as such cannot be the solution. In particular, order cannot be identified with the one central power that is capable of deciding all imaginable conflicts. We will pick up on this idea again when investigating the concepts of the monopoly on violence and sovereignty.

When asking about the opposing concept to normative order, "arbitrariness" is frequently invoked. This concept has only more recently carried a negative connotation.[249] For Kant, arbitrariness (*Willkür*) marks the maneuvering room available to a subject in order to reach the proper practical decision. Without arbitrariness there is no freedom. By contrast, the conventional modern usage of the term seems

[246] Mark Granovetter, "Threshold Models of Collective Behaviour" in: *American Journal of Sociology* 83 (1978), pp. 1420–43.

[247] Bernard E. Harcourt and Jens Ludwig, "Broken Windows: New Evidence from New York City and a Five-City Social Experiment" in: *University of Chicago Law Review* 73 (2006), pp. 271–320.

[248] Not by Freud, but in Edgar Rice Burroughs, *The Return of Tarzan*, Chicago 1915, Chapter 2.

[249] Horst Dreier, "Recht und Willkür" in: Christian Starck (ed.), *Recht und Willkür*, Tübingen 2012, pp. 1–25; Juliane Rebentisch and Dirk Setton, "Freiheit ohne Gesetz, zur Einleitung" in: Id. (eds), *Willkür*, Berlin 2011, pp. 7–24, here pp. 17–24.

to aim at decisions that are not rational. But what is more likely meant is not so much cases of lacking criteria, but cases of applying wrong criteria. Pure lack of criteria is chance. We certainly don't wish for a judge that flips a coin, as opposed to offering reasoned judgment, but in other procedures, chance can be imagined. The decision of who takes which side in a football match is decided by the flip of a coin, and aleatoric moments can help ensure open access to political office required by democratic equality.[250] This raises issues with viewing arbitrariness as the counter-concept to normativity, just as calling dictatorships "arbitrary rule" belittles them. Here, too, the application of inappropriate norms is equated with the lack of any norms.

It is also misplaced to conceive of normativity as the counter-concept to the exception. We can begin to understand the fact that the exception affirms the rule when we call to mind that the transgression of norms fulfills a constitutive function for every normative order. "Rule and exception" do not need to be used normatively, but the insight from this saying can be read in a norm-theoretical manner.

In postmodern norm theory, and in line with Benjamin and Schmitt, the concept of the exception has been widely debated and investigated in recent years.[251] On Derrida's reading, it is the moment of application itself that amounts to suspending the norm. We have already encountered the vast insecurity in applying any norm. But we can only convincingly account for these if we do not loosen the connection between application and norm as far as Derrida does. In the application, he claims to recognize period of "*épokhè*" that brings the entire order into question.[252] This only turns the puzzle on its head, for if the dizzying openness of every act of application is now more recognizable, then its link to that which is being applied becomes all the more puzzling. Thought through to its logical end, this leads to a dissociation between norm and norm application, which then would not even serve as a proper object of deconstruction.[253]

For Schmitt, it is the moments of the instituting and suspension of the order that particularly characterize this order.[254] But, as we have seen, orders are not instituted or suspended at once, but always gradually. And we should not underestimate the exculpatory effect inherent in making accomplices, followers and rule addressees into mere objects of a an "imposition" by someone. In the reconstruction developed here, the systematic overestimation of regularity and strictness in a normative order and in the concept of the exception are two sides of the same conceptual

[250] Reasons for this in Hubertus Buchstein, *Demokratie und Lotterie*, Frankfurt/M. 2009, pp. 296–315.

[251] The canonized quotations in Carl Schmitt, *Politische Theologie*, Berlin 1934, p. 11; Walter Benjamin, "Über den Begriff der Geschichte" in: Id., *Gesammelte Schriften*, Vol. I/2, pp. 693–704, here p. 697.

[252] Jacques Derrida, "Force of Law: The Mystical Foundation of Authority" in: D. Cornell, et al. (eds), *Deconstruction and the Possibility of Justice*, New York 1992, pp. 3–68, here pp. 36 ff.

[253] See above, pp. 197 ff.

[254] Schmitt (n 251), *Politische Theologie*, p. 11.

coin. Once again, it is a curiously static conception of a centrally ordained validity of the order that enables the fixation on the concept of the exception. Our investigation, however, demonstrated something else to be the case: normative orders are more precarious, more clearly marked by transgressions and violations, and also more inert, that is, less easily vanished from the face of the earth, than is suggested by what is ultimately legalistic talk of exceptions and states of emergency being the foundation of an order.[255]

4.8 Monopoly on Violence and Sovereignty as the Epitome of Normative Order?

The concept of a monopoly on violence is imprecise, as even in a well-ordered system, the use of violence cannot be monopolized, not even the definition of the norms regulating when violence may be exerted.[256] And in every society, certain kinds of violence are permissible. So even conceptually, we are not dealing with the monopolization of violence, but with monopolizing the norming of violence. Weber rightly speaks of the monopoly on "legitimate" physical force.[257] But with this qualification, the concept not only gains in precision, it also becomesless tangible. In particular, the question arises as to why reference to violence is necessary in order to describe an order, especially if the concern is a monopoly of norming or legitimizing. For this could also exist for orders that do not generally deem private violence to be illegitimate and express this by privatizing criminal persecution and the execution of criminal sentences, by liberalizing rights of self-defense, and by guaranteeing a right to bear arms for all citizens. This kind of an order would not cease to be a normative order, yet at the same time it would not be characterized by a monopoly on legitimate physical force.

In light of this, we need to search for a different meaning. The concept denotes less a certain content of the order in question than the degree of its enforceability. What is meant, but not well expressed, by the concept of monopoly on legitimate violence is an order that either absolutely has a very high probability of enforcing its rules, or relatively has a higher chance than all other orders.[258]

Both questions—that of enforceability of the order, and that of the violence used as its means—are of great interest for the description of normative orders. But from our considerations, certain methodical precautionary measures

[255] Giorgio Agamben, *State of Exception,* Chicago 2005, pp. 1–40; differently in Frederick Schauer, *Playing by the Rules*, Oxford 2002, pp. 44 ff., fn. 7.

[256] Möllers (n 245), *Staat als Argument*, Chapter 13.

[257] Max Weber, *Wirtschaft und Gesellschaft*, Tübingen 1980, p. 29.

[258] What is also frequently presumed is the dubitable assumption that the most effective means for implementing norms is physical force. But it is also often a means for questioning the implementability of the order itself.

follow when we seek to answer these questions. First, an order can give particular attention and value to limiting its own enforcement. This is the case for continental understandings of the rule of law that, as Luhmann expressed so well, forbids deducing the means from the ends.[259] States abiding by the rule of law opt to limit the enforcement of their own rules. They prefer mechanisms in which some crimes stay unatoned and transgressions are tolerated, because enforcement could, factually and normatively, entail too high a price to be paid. Secondly, every form of execution by force is subject to all the uncertainties that we examined in the figure of application.[260] Whatever is executed by force is often subject to change during the process of enforcement. But then it becomes difficult to quantify the degree of enforcement, and to make it the criterion of success for the order. Thirdly, the influence of one normative order on another one can become effective in the most diverse levels of norm development and norm application. It may seem as if a certain order succeeds well at enforcing its demands on concrete addressees of certain obligations; but at closer sight, this norm-abidance might prove to be the product of another order—as is claimed to be the case for any State legal order from a Marxist legal-theoretical perspective. As such, the comparison of chances of enforcement becomes a necessarily holistic and methodically demanding project.

The same structural problems arise for the concept of sovereignty. Whereas it is often deployed as a building block for a robust and realistic understanding of order, on our view it becomes dependent on a formalizing view of the order which is to be described with its help. Since not only every establishment of an order, but also its sustainment depends on cooperation of participants, theories of sovereignty have to categorically distinguish between contributions from above and contributions from below. But this distinction is a normative one. The contribution by the sovereign is an expression of the legitimate order, the one by its subjects only conceived as occurring on occasion and by coincidence. But since so many things occur within every normative order, things that no single entity can know or want, the model of the all-powerful sovereign quickly changes into a highly formalized exercise at attributing certain "expressions" to an imagined "entity," an exercise that necessarily draws and depends on such presumptions.[261]

Furthermore, in theory, the concept of sovereignty does not point toward some kind of normative order, but more specifically to a political one. The victorious march of this notion of sovereignty began in the differentiation of political from religious powers.[262] Tied to it is a notion of a political order's own autonomous value,

[259] Niklas Luhmann, "Die Grenzen einer betriebswirtschaftlichen Verwaltungslehre" in: *Verwaltungs-Archiv* 56 (1965), pp. 303–13, here p. 308.

[260] Above, pp. 122–23.

[261] This critique, which has not received enough attention in political theory, is developed in Hart (n 199), *The Concept of Law*, pp. 50–78.

[262] Pierre Manent, *An Intellectual History of Liberalism*, Princeton 1995, pp. 3–10.

the establishment of which cannot wait for and should not make itself dependent on any indisputable religious or moral truths being available in order to provide the normative order with its content. Once more, the issue at hand is the intrinsic value of a cognitive notion of order, particularly when the sovereign is *not* only the one who ends the civil war, but also the one who starts it.[263] A political perspective is supposed to distinguish itself precisely by including the actual conditions of a normative order into the deduction of appropriate normative arguments.[264] In a rather peculiar way, this assumption brings together a descriptive thesis with a normative justification. Because politics is realistic, it can draw on a special justification, for politics or the political are also a cipher for the real conditions of norms and a justification of norms as appropriate for reality.

Taking the real conditions of social norms into consideration is one of the central concerns of this book. Nevertheless, this kind of understanding of sovereignty does not help us. For one, there are also real conditions of norms that are not appropriately described as political. For another, this kind of reconstruction exhausts the concept of politics and ultimately deflects the development of criteria for an appropriate order to other instances, such as religion or moral philosophy. For our perspective on the concept of sovereignty, it is important to see that these real conditions themselves often prove to be normative constructions, just as we have seen that the figure of the central norm setting entity is not helpful without certain formalizing assumptions.[265] In and of itself, this does not necessarily merit critique, but it does bring to mind that the relationship between sovereignty or political power on the one hand, and the aspiration of realistic description of normative orders on the other hand does not always hold true.

This critique of the concepts of the monopoly on violence and sovereignty does not aim to relativize the possible civilizational achievements of centralized normative orders such as the territorial State. It only clarifies that centralization is a relative phenomenon that cannot only be understood from the perspective of the center. Having to decide between centrality or decentrality in describing normative orders in turn means being subject to a false opposition. The concept of sovereignty seeks to single out one specific normative order from the conventional plenitude of orders as the actual one, the one from which all others are either factually derived or must be normatively justified. But first, sovereignty contains as little of a justificatory content as order, and secondly, the concept privileges a deductive or top-down description of norms, all without providing reasons for this preference.

[263] Concerning how this might not have been coincidental in the case of English drama: Franco Moretti, *Signs Taken for Wonders*, London 1988, p. 46.

[264] For a contemporary formulation of this idea: Andrea Sangiovanni, "Justice and the Priority of Politics to Morality" in: *The Journal of Political Philosophy* 2008, pp. 137–64, here pp. 158 ff.

[265] See above, pp. 56 f.

4.9 . . . And Back

One of the lessons to take from these considerations is that describing normative orders from the point of view of the order and from the viewpoint of the individual norm both have a justification since the one cannot be understood without the other. In other words, there is no methodical hierarchy between a micro- and a macro-perspective on normative practices, and every implicit privileging has to operate with formalizations or other presumptions. Nonetheless, norm and normative order are not symmetrical entities. We can imagine a norm without a normative order, but not a normative order without norms.

III

YIELDS

5
The Meaning and Function of Social Norms

1. Concept

A social norm affirms the realization of a possibility. This notion does without a justificatory element because the concept is supposed to be used to describe, not evaluate, social practice, including practices in which norms are not being justified and cannot be justified. The concept does without a criterion of success, a measure for a norm being established, because such criteria obfuscate the difference between a norm and its adherence. Finally, the concept does without the threat of sanctions. Every norm carries with it a specific sanction, because both an action that transgresses it and one that is in accord with it can receive a new meaning from the norm. Norms create a tension with reality, which they seek to bring into harmony with themselves. They can neither completely dissociate themselves from this reality nor completely converge with it if they are to keep operating as norms. The more successful a norm is in terms of being in accord with the course of events, the less obvious it becomes what *noticeably* distinguishes the norm from this very course of events. This is why normative orders deploy numerous instruments for securing their own distinguishability. It is only in this distinguishability from reality that norms find their achievement, thereby fulfilling a number of different functions. But social norms are just as irreducible to a certain function as appropriate descriptions are.[1] In particular, they do not depend on the moral acquiescence of participants. Conversely, the philosophical fixation on moral reasons might actually obscure the fact that stable orders should not depend on their being cherished, even if they were worthy of such appreciation.[2]

[1] Concerning the lack of any function for some social norms, see Lina Eriksson, "Rational Choice Explanations of Norms: What They Can and Cannot Tell Us" in: M. Baurmann et al. (eds), *Norms and Values*, Baden-Baden 2010, pp. 179–97, here pp. 188–92.
[2] For the case of democratic orders and open markets, see John Mueller, *Capitalism, Democracy, and Ralph's Pretty Good Grocery*, Princeton 1999, p. 253.

The Possibility of Norms. Christoph Möllers, Published by Oxford University Press (2020) under licence; © this translation, Alex Holznienkemper; © the original German edition, Suhrkamp Verlag Berlin.
DOI: 10.1093/oso/9780198827399.001.0001

2. *Ethical Implications?*

2.1 The—At Most—Indirect Relevance of the Concept of Norms

The development of a conceptual framework for the description of social norms requires no ethical presumptions. But once a concept is established, we can ask which models of moral action fit with practical formations of social norms, and how and why.[3] In this regard, the concept explicated here gains an indirect normative content to the degree to which it provides another perspective to the discourse on rightness, justice, and legitimacy; that is it adds a perspective which asks if and how a certain theory of justification can actually operate as a social normative practice. For example, if an ethics grounded in the generalizability rule cannot be reconciled with the principles of social division of labor,[4] then it might be the wrong rule for a society based on the division of labor.

Models of social normativity can provide and complement practical philosophy with a different kind of criterion formation, which should not be concerned with sociologically reducing models of moral justification, but rather with confronting these models with the contingent character of normative practices: Social norms have to be recognizable as norms. Norms follow a certain temporal structure, they depend upon a coexistence of formalization, deformalization, and informality. These kinds of factors could lead to a different assessment of discourses on moral justification, thereby serving as external aspects of their assessment without directly intervening in that discussion.

Various aspects have shown what this in practice means. If theories of moral realism treat normative reasons as objective facts, then they avoid an additional element that makes explicit the normative pretense. But if we distinguish between the authorization of a norm and its justification in social practice, then we will hardly be able to make do without an explicit distinction or marking of norms as norms. The fact that smoking hurts my health might provide a reason not to smoke. For a social practice though, this is meaningless, as it persistently requires authorization

[3] Practical philosophy itself almost never becomes socially normative in our sense but remains experimentally stimulating, as the realization of reflected possibilities is generally not intended. This might not be the case for philosophical practices that extend into political activism, and of course, philosophers are part of society. But philosophical reflection on norms should by no means be confused with social norms, just as a sociological experiment should not be confused with society. The pretense that practical philosophers are "guardians of the social order" (Christine M. Korsgaard, *The Sources of Normativity*, Cambridge, 1996, p. 54), does not only overestimate the relevance of the subject and misjudge its scientific claim, but—if true—would also entail a responsibility for the consequences of its own doctrine, which we would wish upon no-one. In contrast to philosophical discourse, the claim of "being misunderstood" would soon reach its limits in social orders.

[4] Edna Ullmann-Margalit, "The Generalization Argument: Where does the Obligation Lie?" in: *Journal of Philosophy* 73 (1976), pp. 511–22, here pp. 515, 517.

that goes beyond this fact, whether the friendly reprimand or the securing of a prohibitive sign.

In the analysis of theories that seek to sacrifice the distinction between norms and facts, similar problems arose. One was that the distinction itself is presumed by its critique. Another lay in the unfulfilled claim to be better able to describe social practices by giving up the distinction, because whenever the categorical distinction between the normative and the factual is postulated in the name of better approximating reality, we were able to observe how this claim in turn makes it more difficult to gain distance from factual developments.

At the same time, however, a model of social norms should not content itself with an idealization of moral reasons, which views every form of practical implementation as deficient. For example, if majority rule only represents an incomplete representation of an idealized public use of reason, which builds on the generalizability of arguments, then rightness and reality are played out against each other in a way that misses a social practice that aims for realization.[5] In addition, this kind of idealization rules out the empirical observation of normativity. What is sought after are "reasons" which are precisely marked by their eluding empirically observable causal relationships.

Finally, even an instrumental understanding of norms, in the context of social norms, leads nowhere. If norms are merely means to ends, then the question of why causes should not be used in place of norms remains unanswered. Norms contain the possibility of their own transgression. This characteristic makes them unsuitable as means of mere pursuit of given ends.

Concerning the question of whether normative statements are capable of being true or not, this book provides no answer, and it does not have to, as long as the question of whether a social norm is present or not in a given relationship readily proves to have a truth value.[6] As practical philosophy is looking for the proper theory, the theory of social norms is interested in the consequences which theoretical presumptions entail for the practice. For example, it has long been disputed in philosophy whether norms can be rationally justified. But in social practice, it is increasingly common to solve practical ethical problems by way of a scientific-like deliberation in expert committees. Implicitly, these institutions make a significant meta-ethical preliminary decision by presuming that we can rationally deliberate about ethical problems. Non-cognitivist models that doubt this to be possible are thereby relegated to the fringes, practically speaking.[7]

[5] See above, pp. 16–19.

[6] Concerning this perspective shift in the case of law, but generalizable in light of Davidson's reconstruction of indirect speech: Jochen Bung, *Subsumtion und Interpretation*, Baden-Baden 2004, pp. 100–9.

[7] Concisely, Christoph Möllers, "Ethische Beratung der Politik durch die Wissenschaft?" in: *GegenWorte* 27 (2012), pp. 20–3.

2.2 The Practical Necessity of Metaethical Promiscuity

The practice of social norms is meta-ethically promiscuous, and it appears difficult to imagine it otherwise. The paradoxical task that social norms demand of us, of distancing ourselves from our own practice in order to, in turn, draw on this distancing for this very practice, could hardly be dealt with if we had to opt for one meta-ethically consistent treatment of norms over another—deontic or consequentialist, cognitivist or non-cognitivist. Aside from this also being systematically difficult, a number of problems would arise. For in order to deal with norms, we have to both have command over norms and extract them from our command, to treat them as both made *and* discovered. In order to find appropriate criteria for norms, we have to rely on what we have *and* distance ourselves from it; we have to argue from within a situation *and* detach from it, keep the context in sight and look toward generalizability. This sounds dissatisfying, if not vain. But in normative orders, we have to rely on both the *connoisseurs of diversity* and the *guardians of universality*.[8] The history of practical philosophy can be read as a continuous, failed attempt to overcome this plurality and contradiction.

3. *Conceptual Distinctions*

3.1 Normative Order, Norm, Norm Application

The distinction between a normative order, a norm, and the application of a norm is nothing more than a heuristic instrument. The element of an order that we denote as "norm" depends on the customs of the entire order, just as the content of a norm can principally only be grasped if one knows the entire norm order. The *application* of a norm creates a new norm. The positing of a norm is also always the application of another norm, as the norm production draws on a pre-existing norm. The concept of application brings to mind the specification of something general. But a specific norm can also be used in a generalizing way. A reference to a norm does not necessarily have to entail a normative pretense. This reflects the distinction between application, representation, and execution of a norm. Whereas the *application* of a norm always denotes an authorized treatment thereof, the *representation* only indicates its existence without raising the pretense that its content be realized. This is the kind of attitude that sociologists or tourists can take with regard to a norm. The *execution* of a norm requires authorization, but itself is ultimately no longer a normative endeavor, as it rules out the possibility of deviation.

[8] Richard Rorty, "On Ethnocentrism: A Reply to Clifford Geertz" in: Id., *Objectivity, Relativism, and Truth*, Cambridge 1991, pp. 203–10, here p. 206.

3.2 Authorization, Authorship, and Justification

We need to distinguish between authorization, authorship, and justification of social norms. Social norms can be justified—or not—according to various kinds of criteria. But they certainly require an *authorization* that makes them recognizable as norms. To begin with, this means nothing more than the simple demand to mark their existence as norms. In the terminology employed here, this is the external side of the realizing marker. There is no unified form of authorization. Norms can have an *author*, a subject that has posited a norm. However, authorship of a norm is not self-evident but rather the result of formalization and attribution which point to other norms that constitute such subjects and empower them to produce norms. But norms do not require a determinable author. One example would be a custom that becomes a norm.

If every norm requires authorization, then every application of a norm requires its own authorization, which always operates as a self-authorization. Every normative practice relies on someone attending to it. How does this constitute a self-authorization? Because norms cannot be the cause of their own application if they contain the possibility of non-adherence within themselves. Thus, it is never enough to point toward a norm to explain what happens when someone applies it. Rather, in the act of application, there always lies a productive element that is not covered by the norm, and that does not only concern the content of the decision but also the question of who decides. Even a court imbued with comprehensive powers has to make its *own* decision about what it is allowed to decide. In this way, every act of application contains the applier's self-authorization. This sounds suspicious, but it is not. This isn't so much hubris as it is a necessary component in dealing with social norms.

The self-authorizing structure of application indirectly also has a moral implication: whoever applies a norm is responsible for this application, as their own contribution has to be considered in the notion of application, and because every norm in every situation allows for a different application.

3.3 Norms for Action and Identity Norms

The limitation of the notion of norm to actions, widespread in norm-theoretical discussions, proved itself as too narrow. Norms cannot only affirm the possibility of actions but also of certain identities of people, or of institutions. A lot of confusion has been brought about by the figure of the constitutive norm. In certain cases, identity norms can be taken as a subcategory of constitutive norms, namely when they actually affirm the possibility of the constituted object without having to then look for an affirming action. This distinguishes a constitutional notion of marriage from a norm setting standard for the size of a screw. Theories that only allow for action norms import—for no substantive reason—a methodological individualism into practical and political philosophy by treating action as the basic unit without justifying this preliminary decision in its own right. This too closely ties the theory of social norms to certain philosophical theories of subjectivity.

3.4 Norm and Value, Rule and Judgment, Rights and Obligation

The definition of normativity developed here contains kinds of norms that are frequently treated as categorically different: prescriptions and evaluations, rules or norms in a narrower sense, judgments, rights, and obligations. These are all norms in the sense developed here, whose distinguishing features from each other, in practical philosophy, generally result from the way in which they can be justified. The model developed here—along with the limitations undertaken at the outset—remains agnostic to this. This also has the advantage that certain kinds of social norms cannot be excluded from observation merely for reasons of a specific theory of justification.[9]

If the model developed here understands norms as possibilities whose realization is affirmatively marked, then valuations prove to be an elementary form of the normative. All kinds of norms are possibilities that—with various degrees of specificity—are denoted and evaluated with a realization marker.[10] Values refer to conditions such as "peace" or institutions like "family" or "democracy." Norms, in the narrower sense, refer to more or less specified actions. Judgments refer to past actions. Rights refer to actions, the exercise of which simultaneously excludes other people from interfering with these actions.

This reconstruction remains purely norm-theoretical. It provides an argument *against*, not for the categorical distinction between "values" and "ought."[11] It does not provide an argument in favor of a normative priority of unspecific over specific norms. Such arguments, for example in favor of a political order that legitimizes itself by means of individual rights, but not by objective values, are not up for debate here. A lot can be said for a normative individualism in political theory, but it cannot be deduced from the concept of the norm, and neither can the claim that the notion of action is the necessary basic unit of every normative theory. The only thing that is norm-theoretically relevant is that more specific norms make

[9] For example, the observation by Herbert Schnädelbach, "Rationalität und Normativität" in: Id., *Zur Rehabilitierung des* animal rationale, Frankfurt/M. 1992, pp. 79–103, here pp. 90 ff., in fn. 10: For reasons inherent in his theory, Habermas would have to reconstruct intersubjective claims of validity as disguised prescriptions. Another example for this kind of exclusion is offered by Marco Iorio, *Regel und Grund*, Berlin 2011, pp. 129 f., who conceptually deduces that prescriptive rules need to have an author, albeit without explaining how we should deal with phenomena such as customary law.

[10] On such unspecified obligations: Ralph Wedgwood, *The Nature of Normativity*, Oxford 2007, p. 91.

[11] See Dietmar von der Pfordten, *Deskription, Evaluation, Präskription*, Berlin 1993, pp. 264–79.

more specific offers for realization. This becomes particularly apparent in rights that define an action and put the possibility of carrying it out into the hands of the participants, who bring a possibility closer to realization in exercising their right. Rights as a legal form seem to have practical advantages,[12] as they specifically link together realization and local justification.[13] Generally, forms of normativity that tie themselves to subjectivity prove to be quite practicable as they guarantee a high level of recognizability of the norm and responsibility for its application. For a justification of the legal form as such, however, these observations are pointless. By contrast, philosophical hypotheses, such as the one that reasons are ontologically more stable than persons,[14] might be applicable and have implications for a philosophical theory of the relationship between rights and values, but for our dealing with social norms, they offer nothing. If the social norms of a community provide a perspective for realization, then the time horizon in question is always limited to the degree that stability across time, which is practical philosophy's concern, cannot provide any useful criteria for it. Even in the long term, norms that are only valid in the short term might prove themselves better at solving practical problems.

3.5 Interpretation and Meaning of Norms

Even if there are no norm-specific standards, it is of the utmost urgency to interpret norms as they aim toward realization. In dealing with norms, we cannot resort to the option at times considered in textual analysis, namely to do without the pretense of a proper understanding, as the practice of the normative cannot treat the coexistence of diverging interpretations of a norm in the same way that literary studies can treat multiple interpretations of a poem, even if the interpretation were to remain contested. This does not mean that norms are easier to interpret, but it implies that social norms rely on institutions that put an end to the interpretive play without always having a sufficient argument ready for doing so. Instead, such institutions can through their decisions produce reasons, which then find recognition. In Wittgensteinian terms, normative institutions are charged with organizing custom and repetitions; they do not string further interpretation on previous interpretations but rather formalize decisions once interpretations have exhausted themselves; they posit dogmas and condition appliers.[15]

[12] Without the political consequences having to be shared thereby, these cognitive achievements of rights are seen in Hayek: Friedrich August von Hayek, "The Use of Knowledge in Society" in: *American Economic Review* 35 (1945), pp. 519–30.

[13] Local justification denotes the circumstance that the concrete utilization of law cannot justify the general guarantee of law, but it can very well justify the perception of an individualized aspiration drawn from the law. In other words: rights make self-authorization explicit and justify themselves with it.

[14] Derek Parfit, *Reasons and Persons*, Oxford 1984, pp. 245–80.

[15] Ludwig Wittgenstein, *Philosophische Untersuchungen*, Frankfurt/M. 2003, §§ 198, 199, 201, 206, 217 (pp. 132–5, 139 ff.); Id., *Über Gewißheit*, Frankfurt/M. [12]2012, § 349 (p. 91).

Nevertheless, there is no satisfying solution to the basic challenge of interpreting norms. What are we to make of a norm, which has been authorized in the past, to be expected to exert authority in the present? In this context, it seems misplaced to pit original meaning and present understandings and challenges against each other. We cannot deduce from a norm whether it is to be understood in line with idiosyncrasies of a past creative process or in light of present developments. It depends on how we understand authorization. Social norms are neither simply accessible to a community by consensus, nor can their meaning be objectively and unambiguously determined. Recognizing the "middle way"[16] arising thus simply means leaving all practical problems open and giving up on the hope on grand theoretical solutions.

3.6 An Idealized Genealogy of Normativity's Autonomy

What is decisive in social norms becoming autonomous is not the degree to which they are viewed as appropriate for moral or other reasons but rather the degree to which they become independent in relation to the non-normative world. In trying to begin outlining this, an idealized genealogy of the normative could distinguish three levels of normative development. At the first level, normativity develops out of the disappointment of expectations and the generalization of the experience of disappointment. If I affectively imbue an expectation, which amounts to an affirmation of a possible future series of events, then the lack of its materialization is the basic form of normativity. At this level, the demands of the social capacity for reflection are minimal for the practice of normativity. In particular, it is not necessary to highlight the possibility of alternative developments, or to imagine elements of an alternate world, which is then systematically contrasted with one's own experiences.

At the second level, a perspective independent from experience comes into play. This can manifest itself as social imagination in politics or art, which itself is in turn normatively marked. Transcendence is an important means in the coming to be of the autonomy of the normative,[17] although we should state that transcendence should not be conflated with religion or with moral normativity. Objects are transcendent if a community treats them as neither accessible to experience nor available by practice, since they find themselves outside of their spatial and temporal context.[18] By invoking transcendence, a community can establish afactual

[16] John McDowell, "Non-Cognitivism and Rule-Following" in: Id., *Mind, Value, and Reality*, Cambridge, Mass. 1998, pp. 198–218, here p. 215; Id., "Wittgenstein on Following a Rule" in: Id., *Mind, Value, and Reality*, Cambridge, Mass. 1998, pp. 221–62, here p. 242.

[17] Ingolf Dalferth, "The Idea of Transcendence" in: Robert Bellah and Hans Joas (eds), *The Axial Age and Its Consequences*, Cambridge, Mass. 2012, pp. 146–90; Stephan Dreischer et al., "Transzendenz und Konkurrenz" in: Id. (eds), *Jenseits der Geltung*, Berlin 2013, pp. 1–28, here pp. 3–9.

[18] Dalferth, "Idea of Transcendence" pp. 153–60.

figures of thought and solidify these against experiences of disappointment. Now, *norms* can develop alongside the personal *experience of the normative* from disappointment. The norms' existence can more or less be detached from factual deviation. Even if such norms do not necessarily have to point toward a transcendent origin, the relationship between transcendence and normativity is likely to often be rather close. They are not in the hands of the community, they cannot be changed, and can only serve certain ends. These kinds of norms are better suited to serve as the foundation upon which to judge the condition of the world than they are at providing guidelines for changing it. Thus, long into modernity, law was rarely understood as an object one could shape or as an instrument of change. It is not by chance that one of the earliest examples of a normative order oriented toward alterability and change was the canonical law of the Catholic church of the late Middle Ages;[19] that is, a normative order that itself is not transcendent[20] but traces its validity to a transcendent order.[21]

This leads to the third level, in which norms become both malleable[22] and serve as a means of change. In the pretense to achieve change through norms, the orientation of the normative toward the future becomes explicit. It is no longer only its analytical element but rather explicitly serves the project of shaping the world, which, following Koselleck, is typical for the *Sattelzeit* ('saddle time') in European history.[23] This step is better understood as an *addition* to the other levels of normativity, rather than as their replacement. At this third level, that is, with the spreading assumption of "making" or "positing," norms are no longer viewed as primordial or the result of determined or contingent social processes but they rather become the object of decisions and thereby also become the object of social or individual processes of reflection.

At present there are no visible signs of a fourth level following these admittedly heavily idealized sequences to be developing. However, the awareness of the continued presence of the first two levels seems to have sharpened. This becomes obvious in the case of human rights. As universal guarantees operating outside of

[19] Harold Berman, *Recht und Revolution*, Frankfurt/M. 1995, pp. 144–98, 342–56; Hauke Brunkhorst, *Critical Theory of Legal Revolutions*, London 2014, pp. 99–101.

[20] In its own understanding, Catholic canon law both is and, to a large degree, is not divine law: Winfried Aymans and Klaus Mörsdorf, *Kanonisches Recht*, Paderborn 1991, pp. 32–7; fundamentally, also Ralf Dreier, "Der Rechtsbegriff des Kirchenrechts in juristisch-rechtstheoretischer Sicht" in: Gerhard Rau et al. (eds), *Das Recht der Kirche*, Vol. I, Gütersloh 1997, pp. 171–98, here pp. 176–9.

[21] On the fluid transitions between theological (ecclesiological) and church-legal argument: Andreas Thier, *Hierarchie und Autonomie*, Frankfurt/M. 2011, pp. 166–8, on the reception of Cyprian's theology for the church-legal understanding of the office of the papacy, ibid., pp. 351–65. On the twofold juridical and Christian source of papal power, see also Hauke Brunkhorst, *Legitimationskrisen*, Baden-Baden 2012, pp. 53 ff.

[22] To be distinguished from the realm of the contingent, which is well-known to authors such as Montesquieu or Pascal for social norms, even though there could be no control over contingency.

[23] Specifically for constitutional categories in Reinhart Koselleck, "'Erfahrungsraum' und 'Erwartungshorizont'—zwei historische Kategorien" in: Id., *Vergangene Zukunft*, Frankfurt/M. 1979, pp. 348–75, here pp. 368–75.

national legal spheres, they enjoy a rather brief history.[24] Their realization in legal procedures remains the exception; instead they mostly figure as moral grounds and titles to enable certain political claims. They are reaffirmed in international legal contracts but not treated as though they were brought into existence by these very contracts, but rather as though they are found in another source—not least of all in human "nature." By contrast, however, their moral pretense often only takes root because they can be understood as part of a legal order largely based on consensus.[25] The moral argument does not gain its authority from itself. Instead, the political process on occasion of dramatic experiences of disappointment produces, in its own forms, what it purports to discover and thereby reaches back to a normative understanding of levels 1 and 2. The world is not meant to be changed, but rather to be restored into an original condition because—using a formulation of international law—"disregard and contempt for human rights have resulted in barbarous acts which have outraged the conscience of mankind."[26]

4. *Heterogeneity and Hierarchy in Normative Orders*

4.1 Pluralism and Contradiction as Normal Condition

Every normative order points toward other normative orders and depends on these. The plurality of normativity is not a new phenomenon, neither is it a product of "globalization." Every normative order stands in a more or less antagonistic interplay with other normative orders.[27] If different relationships unfold within social groups—between individuals, in families, in pre-political, political, and religious communities—then different normative orders develop alongside these. They can contradict each other and yet depend on and refer to each other. The contradiction between normative directives is nothing unusual for a social practice, particularly since the cognitive preliminaries—How do I recognize a norm? How do I figure out what it means?—bring a measure of imprecision into the order, suggesting that in everyday disputes about the interpretation of a normative order, the consistency—even if indeed existent—would most likely go unnoticed

[24] They are assessed particularly late by Samuel Moyn, *The Last Utopia*, Cambridge, Mass. 2010, pp. 176–211.

[25] I am indebted to Chris McCrudden for this insight.

[26] This is the beginning of the Universal Declaration of Human Rights (emphases mine): "*Whereas* recognition of the inherent dignity and of the equal and inalienable rights of all members of the human family is the foundation of freedom, justice and peace in the world." What is also remarkable is that this is a declaration; that is, it is not a document that constitutes rights that did not previously exist. On this form Christine Fauré, *Ce que déclarer les droits veut dire: Histoires*, Paris 2011, pp. 13–34; Francesca Raimondi, "Einleitung" in: Christoph Menke and Francesca Raimondi (eds), *Die Revolution der Menschenrechte*, Berlin 2011, pp. 95–101.

[27] Albrecht Koschorke, *Wahrheit und Erfindung. Grundzüge einer Allgemeinen Erzähltheorie*, Frankfurt/M. 2012, pp. 371–6.

by everyone. Benjamin's critique of law as an institution that only applies force in order to sustain itself as an order,[28] may apply to legal orders that are kept homogenous by means of their procedures or contents, but less to those whose features and boundaries are blurred due to persistent politicization and moralization in procedures and arguments.

4.2 Norm-Hierarchical Reductionism

Among theories of the normative, we come across the tendency to look for what is "actual" within different norm orders. Thus, it is presumed that behind legal norms there "actually" lurk moral principles or social custom, and behind these there are "actually" religious commands or bare power relations at play. Such attempts at reduction yield little, as many normative practices cannot be explained independently of other normative practices. They ultimately end up defining social normativity out of the equation. The frequent treatment of formalized orders as mere surface phenomena of social norms, or the treatment of written rules that are frequently broken, such as house rules, as un-actual in favor of the behavior transgressing them, underestimates the meaning of the written rule and reduces what is formalized, not only to what is informal but ultimately to the non-normative. What counts when taking this outlook is merely that which can "smoothly" be observed, that is simply the practice without its corresponding social norm.

In his early theory of organization, Luhmann demonstrated how organizations are not only capable of incorporating parallel, informal structures, but how they actually remain dependent on such informality.[29] This relationship can also be reversed. Formal organizations and rule systems as well indirectly structure the informality that escapes or runs up against the formalization.[30] They convey a place or function to this informality, at times even one that deviates from the formalized order. Formalized orders build up a potential for resistance to themselves, which can have a stabilizing effect, yet cannot be controlled by the formalized order itself. Due to this reciprocity, disregarding formalization is not a solution. Most significantly, such disregard of form could not possibly be organized. No normative order remains entirely under control, but if one ever attempts to exercise control over a

[28] Walter Benjamin, "Zur Kritik der Gewalt" in: Id., *Gesammelte Schriften*, Hermann Schweppenhäuser and Rolf Tiedemann (eds), Frankfurt/M. 1977, Vol. II, pp. 179–203; on this, see the concise analysis in Christoph Menke, *Recht und Gewalt*, Berlin 2011, pp. 49–57.

[29] Niklas Luhmann, *Funktionen und Folgen formaler Organisation*, Berlin 1995, pp. 85–8.

[30] In the practice of filling offices in international organizations by certain States, we see a current, interesting example of informality that asserts itself against formal rules, and yet also has to justify itself toward those rules, and could become frail because of this justification: Jacob Katz Cogan, "Representation and Power in International Organizations" in: *American Journal of International Law* 103 (2009), pp. 209–63, here pp. 216–18.

normative order—and this can indeed succeed—then only by means of formalization. Furthermore, norms need to be given a distinct form, and access to them must be defined by this form. To gain control of a normative order means to formalize this order and to pay a price for this formalization, both in terms of content and in terms of its chances of implementation. Whatever occurs when I put up a sign that defines the norm, or when I charge someone with watching over the adherence to a norm, has to do with the form itself. Charging a watchdog can raise animosities or doubts concerning the authorization of the person charged, which would not arise in case of freely circulating, informal norms. Every attempt to control norms through forms develops a life of its own.

Yet the consequence of all this is not defeatism—neither in terms of what normativity achieves, nor in terms of its formalization. Rather, the achievements of norm formalization are currently quite underappreciated.[31] Nevertheless, it is still important to enumerate the costs of formalization in order to understand norms in a social practice.

4.3 Conditions and Limits of Normative Hierarchies

One way to come to terms with numerous diverging norms consists in establishing hierarchical structures. The legal orders of nation-States operate with norm hierarchies. But these do not simply become effective by themselves. One precondition for hierarchization to work is the practical comparability of the hierarchized norms. Of course, we can determine that moral norms are ranked higher than norms of a national legal order, but in order for this assumption to gain practical relevance, both have to be put into a comparable format, generally by means of formalization. It is also possible to strengthen formal hierarchies by presenting them to the public as being tied to a "political climate" or to notions of justice. For the form's stability, however, this strategy can become a threat even when formal and informal norms are similarly oriented in substance.

Every formalization has informal side effects. A formalized moral norm may well stand above a legal norm, but in said formalized state it looks much more like this legal norm than it previously did. If one opts against such a procedure, then the hierarchization will hardly succeed, just as it would be pointless to bring table manners and legal norms into a hierarchical relationship with each other. Both norm orders may well appeal to the same people at the same time in the same place, but their normative pretenses and fields of application stand in no relation to each other.

[31] One noteworthy exception are the thoughts by Arthur L. Stitchcombe, *When Formality Works*, Chicago 2001.

In addition to the formal assimilation of the normative material, the establishment of a norm hierarchy requires institutional protection. The hierarchy has to have consequences, and these have to become part of the order. The assertion alone that a norm of type A enjoys primacy over a norm of type B will likely lead the hierarchy to end up nowhere. In legal orders, norm hierarchies become effective when different political processes stand behind the norm complexes, as is the case in federal orders, or when the requirements for generating new norms are formalized with different levels of stringency, or when an authority is charged to watch over the adherence to the hierarchy.[32] Furthermore, for practical reasons, norm hierarchies frequently provide for the applicability of norms that run counter to higher-ranking norms.[33] That is, they do not consistently follow their model. In a social practice, a norm hierarchy can only be established by means of additional mechanisms that—being formalizations—have the potential to also bring about perverse effects.[34]

Problems also arise at the level of application. Norm hierarchies do not only operate by specifying a higher norm vis-à-vis a lower one whose content is to be defined, but also in the opposite direction by means of abstracting from a lower norm for determining the content of the higher one. This becomes necessary simply because higher-ranking norms are regularly less specifically expressed. In many cases, norm hierarchies develop out of the coexistence of norms that are formally equal, yet formulated to differing degrees of generality, among which the less specific ones are more pertinent when in doubt. This is the case for legal orders that carry fairness or loyalty clauses in their backgrounds in case certain rules fail. It is also the case for social norm systems in which a general command of "politeness" covers more specific rules, such as the normative expectation of not eating with a full mouth. More general rules take the role of summarizing and completing the entirety of existing norms. They intervene when a specific rule is missing but a norm transgression is presumed. But how do I know the meaning of the general, unspecific norm? For one, by the work on the concept of "politeness," and also by observing its applications. The treatment of norms suffers—unsurprisingly, yet also precariously, from the interior perspective of the normative order—from all the problems of norm application. Yet this does not mean that hierarchies are necessary to organize the coexistence of different normative orders.[35]

[32] Once more, concerning different types of hierarchy development, Christoph Schönberger, "Der Vorrang der Verfassung" in: Ivo Appel et al. (eds), *Öffentliches Recht im offenen Staat*, Berlin 2011, pp. 385–403, here pp. 386–90.

[33] Carlos Santiago Nino, *The Constitution of Deliberative Democracy*, New Haven 1996, pp. 193 f.

[34] It is arguably no coincidence that these effects have predominantly been discovered by organization theorists (see, e.g. Giuseppe Bonazzi, *Geschichte des organisatorischen Denkens*, Wiesbaden 2008, pp. 191–219, on Michel Crozier and Philip Selznick), whereas norm theory only ever seems interested in one particular type of norms.

[35] Thus for the Roman Republic: Christoph Lundgreen, *Regelkonflikte in der römischen Republik*, Stuttgart 2011, pp. 257–85.

4.4 Fundamental Norms?

The preceding considerations raise doubts about the idea of fundamental norms that are meant to serve as the basis for an entire normative order. Even the metaphor is misleading, albeit widespread both within and outside of the theory of norms.[36] It remains unclear what exactly is meant when norms are to serve as a "foundation," be it for other norms, be it for a social community. The image is static, which is why it cannot account for a number of characteristics of norms, such as their temporality and their relation to the forming of alternatives. What is more, the more fundamental a norm claims to be for a community, the less clear is its meaning, and all the more contentious it might be, as it is to serve as the epitome of all other norms. In German law, the guarantee of human dignity in Article 1, Paragraph 1 of the Basic Law stands atop the normative hierarchy, which is formally secured by the fact that it cannot be amended and that its adherence can be controlled in the courts. And yet the guarantee of human dignity is among the most contentious norms of the Basic Law, it is clearly more contentious than other fundamental rights at the constitutional level, or than ordinary legal norms.[37] This shows just how implausible the metaphor of "laying the foundation" is. Stabilization is much more likely to be achieved through more specific, lower-ranking norms that, if there is agreement on their meaning, can contribute to giving structure to the higher-ranking norm. This also sheds light on the way we have to imagine consensus as the normative foundation for a society. We can think of consensus as a goal that cannot be achieved yet nevertheless guides our thought process, but not as an existing foundation that is ingrained in a norm such as the guarantee of human dignity. The claim would be that consensus practically and continuously arises from solving small and concrete questions, not in great formulas. Questions of war and peace or basic standards of human rights, by contrast, are not capable of consensus if one takes consensus to mean more than the agreement to a compromise formula.[38] Finally, the question arises whether a normative order is not better served by the organization of dissent.[39] Fundamental norms would then merely be objects of a desired dispute. If this is the case, then we are no longer

[36] On critique from a comparative perspective that may well undermine the conceptual pretense of philosophical conceptualization: Felix Heidenreich, *Grund, Gründe, Begründen—architektonische Rationalitätsmetaphern im interkulturellen Vergleich*, Presentation at the XXII German Congress for Philosophy in Munich, 13 September 2011.

[37] Instead of an all-encompassing documentation, I here simply refer to the diagnosis by Horst Dreier, in: Id., *Grundgesetz*, Vol. I, Tübingen 2013, Article 1.I, paras 47–63.

[38] Viewed differently by Jürgen Habermas, "Das Konzept der Menschenwürde und die realistische Utopie der Menschenrechte" in: *Deutsche Zeitschrift für Philosophie* 58 (2010), pp. 343–57. What is realistic is that human rights can currently not be instituted in China and Russia, and that the promise that the current state of international human right protection will ultimately enjoy its implementation even in politically strong States appears unlikely.

[39] Concerning international legal order, see Isabelle Ley, *Opposition im Völkerrecht*, Heidelberg 2015, pp. 131–65.

dealing with the idea of a normative basis of an order, consisting in agreed-upon, fundamental norms.

Would it be better to do without normative hierarchies? No, for these are neither meaningless nor without consequences. As the worldwide success of constitutional review exercised by courts shows, they are capable of bringing about concrete institutional consequences, such as the shift of powers of definition from parliaments to courts. Norm hierarchies can be successful by keeping a certain normative practice within certain parameters. In analyzing these techniques, however, we need to keep an awareness of the hierarchy's operating mechanisms, their dependence on formalization, the price to be paid for this formalization, as well as the problems of their applicability.

Finally, we should only speak of a successful normative order—as measured by the degree of adherence the duration of its continued existence—when an order does not so much seek to displace other previously existing normative orders but rather to maintain them in their functional potential, that is, as long as the order does not try to superimpose itself hierarchically. The higher durability of liberal-democratic, constitutional States, in comparison with the States of real socialism, can arguably be explained by the former not trying to replace other normative orders, such as religiously inspired social practices, but rather treating them more or less indifferently. By contrast, real socialist orders tried to displace other orders such as religion, without being able to fill the void thereby created—in dealing with existentially and normatively demanding situations such as birth and death.[40] Orders that are too demanding in terms of their content, too heavily centralized, and too formalized thus run the risk of undermining the conditions of their own continuation.

4.5 Inalienable Norms?

Atop any normative hierarchy, there stand norms that cannot be changed, for it is only norms of this kind that cannot be subject to any other norms. Can we think of inalienable norms as social entities? Except maybe for the prohibition on incest, the universality of which is highly contentious, we cannot empirically identify any norms that have always been in place and still are. But what is then meant by "inalienability"?

Things that are alienable are available and alterable in a way that the person altering it can control. Inalienable things too are available but at the same time withdrawn from any altering access. What is necessary is inalienable, coincidence is as well. On this view, inalienability becomes a burden because it describes that

[40] I am grateful for this insight from Yuri Slezkine, presented at the Wissenschaftskolleg zu Berlin, Fall 2013.

which leaves us no choice, something with which we are confronted, whether we like it or not.

This is probably not what is meant when speaking of the inalienability of a norm. Rather, this way of speaking denotes inhibiting by means of a norm something that would be factually possible, but which, in virtue of this norm, is removed from our control. More to the point, the usage seems to fluctuate between the two meanings. If human dignity is inviolable, then no heinous act, no matter how gruesome, should be able to impair it—and indeed, we would scarcely claim that a victim of torture has lost their dignity. But how then do I recognize a transgression of this dignity, and why would I have to protect this dignity by means of a norm? The inviolability by itself does not seem to prompt a need for any norm. Inalienability thus denotes norms that I cannot posit or change because they are already present, as well as norms that I cannot violate. Yet in both readings, the norm loses its practical meaning. For either I cannot change anything about the norm or there is no need for a norm because its content is always and necessarily realized. This would speak in favor of doing without the concept of inalienability and recognizing what it actually is: a rhetorical means to strengthen the legitimacy of a normative pretense that is, in fact, quite alienable.[41]

5. *Social Integration through Norms?*

5.1 Norms as Instruments of Stabilization?

Do norms serve as means to integrate societies? This claim might over- and underestimate the relevance of norms because, on the one hand, a community that produces norms is distinguished by that very act. That means that norms are not a necessary condition for the existence of community, but rather that the production of norms can be the consequence of its existence. On the other hand, it is possible for communities to be destroyed or damaged by norms. Luhmann highlighted that this risk arises from moral norms that can undermine the functional differentiation of society due to their universal and unconditional claim to validity.[42]

We can take integration to mean the production of commonalities or commonality by means of a gradual suspension of differences. In this regard, the achievement of norms proves to be rather ambivalent. Norms can foster unity, for example

[41] This critique needs to be distinguished from Luhmann's claim that every norm in a society can be violated under certain circumstances. Niklas Luhmann, *Gibt es in unserer Gesellschaft noch unverzichtbare Normen?*, Heidelberg 1993, pp. 1–4. That may be the case, but it does not allow for deducing the dispensability of the norm, as this dispensability in turn can only be normatively grounded.

[42] Niklas Luhmann, *Paradigm Lost*, Frankfurt/M. 1990. This kind of risk certainly does not arise from all moral norms, and some norm-theoretical doubts are in order concerning the presumed sociological paradigm of a strong differentiation. See more carefully Judith Butler, *Giving an Account of Oneself*, New York 2005, pp. 41 ff.

by defining standards of membership in a group. On the other hand, one important function of norms is to maintain differences, namely the different identities of individuals, norms that serve to protect a kind of behavior that is repudiated by the majority. If norms succeed, be it as a rule of social distinction, be it as a fundamental rights guarantee, at protecting a kind of behavior dismissed by a majority, they thereby do not enable integration, but meaningful disintegration; that is, differentiation.

This same ambivalence is found in the claim that norms can stabilize expectations. Norms stipulate expectations. At the same time, they can contribute to expectations being disappointed. A norm can serve the purpose of adding new expectations to existing ones, thereby developing the stock of expectations. Many forms of law, for example civil rights, operate in this manner. Additionally, norms can make their own violation visible, thereby making disappointments explicit. A norm can constitute an expectation that it cannot live up to, it can even serve to highlight this disappointment, that is it can make a certain condition in the community visible by means of its ability to disappoint.

Simply associating norms with stabilization or stability sells their achievements short. Things that we think to be stable—solid objects, natural laws, or people without self-doubts—would appear not to need the sense of possibility that norms express. And the insight into the fact that conditions could be different, or should be different, can bring a destabilizing disquiet into a community. Of course, in a second step, the view of possible deviations can entail a stabilizing effect, which is why democratic orders have a longer life expectancy than authoritarian systems do. But the notion of stability thereby implied demands much more than what can simply be expected of norms.

It would be wrong, however, to draw from this that norms should be viewed as mere epiphenomena that a society could put on like a dress. Despite their significant differences, both a Marxist legal theory and Catholic teachings on natural law assume that there is a substratum of socialization—be it the distribution of the means of production, or human nature—to which every normative order must ultimately subject itself. The theoretical critique of formalized norms, according to which form merely represents a shell, the content of which is determined by "real" social processes, is one variation of this argument. Lasalle's distinction between the constitution and constitutional reality is one example.[43] Whereas the expectation that norms can integrate societies either overestimates, or at least mislocates their significance, the assumption that norms are something socially "un-actual" also misses their point. Norms serve the end of describing courses of events that do not necessarily materialize. If norms point to possibilities, but the measure of the

[43] Ferdinand Lasalle, *Ueber Verfassungswesen*, Berlin 1919; concerning this, please see the excellent critique of the specifically German preconditions of this distinction in Wilhelm Hennis, *Verfassung und Verfassungswirklichkeit: ein deutsches Problem*, Tübingen 1968.

possible itself remains unknown, if the figure of possibility itself is an expression of this uncertainty, then a critique of the normative as socially "un-actual" misses its object. The marking of alternative possibilities by way of norms is no self-evident achievement of a community.[44] The comparison with animal communities illustrates the fact that the complexity of human communities does not necessarily lead to greater stability. With heightened demands for functionality, the number of possibilities that do *not* live up to these demands also increases. In evaluating possibilities, norms enable the distinction between that which is and that which could be, which happens also to have destabilizing effects. By contrast, a social practice that does what it does without paying attention to alternative possibilities does not have to take recourse to norms. Thus, norms operate at a much more fundamental level than the claim about the normativity's stabilizing function presumes.

5.2 Internalized Norms

For Durkheim, and still for Parsons, internalized norms signified an important element of cohesion in societies. And to this day, many social theories presume that a critical mass of members of a community members need to share a basic stock of commonly expressed moral orientations relevant to action that. These are not simply mediated by solely rational insight, but also by affective attachment.

Of course, in social practice it is likely that it will often be unclear what exactly will constitute this commonality of moral orientations. The persistent fragility of normative practice arises from the ever-new interpretation of even the most minute normative contexts. This has been made convincingly clear by the ethnomethodological critique of Parsons.[45] Furthermore, even internalized moral norms can have both cohesive and disruptive effects. They can bind a community together or tear it apart.

Finally, it is up for debate how desirable shared action-relevant orientations are in the first place. For they would have to prove themselves in a society based on the division of labor. Edna Ullmann-Margalit has drawn attention to the following: tt does not follow from the insight that it would be bad if everyone carried out an action A that this action should be prohibited for everyone, or even for a specific individual.[46] Even though we do not want everyone to become a baker, we do not

[44] Thus, Michael Tomasello doubts that communities of apes that live in groups form such possibilities. Michael Tomasello, *Origins of Human Communication*, Cambridge, Mass. 2008, p. 213.

[45] John Heritage, *Garfinkel and Ethnomethodology*, Cambridge 1984, pp. 19–36. On the critique of ethnomethodological research, which is marked by many commonalities with models of performativity, it is important to continuously emphasize that social norms do not dissolve in a practice, that they do not merely concern the present, but also the future. On this, see Armin Nasehi, *Der soziologische Diskurs der Moderne*, Frankfurt/M. 2006, pp. 231 f.

[46] Ullmann-Margalit (n 4), "The Generalization Argument" pp. 515–17.

prohibit any single person from becoming one. Under these conditions, it is useful to work with norms that allow for great leeway under the auspices of a general rule.[47] With Kant, such leeway can be found for good reason in the realm of legal, not moral normativity, that is, not in common, internal moral orientation, but in differentiated, externally operating force.

5.3 Loyalty to Norms?

Another reason not to instil too much hope into the stabilizing effect of norms is because norms partake in the general uncertainty concerning the stability of meaning. We certainly are aware of norm-typical mechanisms for stabilizing meanings: formalization, sanctions, and the socialization of responsible personnel. But the meaning of norms is contested in principal in a particular way. If their content were obvious, we could frequently do without them. For the appropriate approach to norms, there are no reliable meta-rules. Treating a norm as an obstacle toward some end sometimes may be an indirect indication of loyalty to a normative order. Norms show their relevance most clearly when the engagement with them is not perceived as leading toward a goal, where ends are not achieved *with help of them* but only *in spite of them*. Even the willingness to disrupt certain courses of events already looming or social developments in their predictable unfolding, too, can indicate loyalty to a norm. For it is only when one is willing to confront reality that norms are taken seriously.

6. *Reality, Ideality, and the Effect of Norms*

6.1 Critique of the Ideal Norm

Norms can normativize circumstances that are already the realized, and norms can normativize contents that will likely never be realized. This they have in common with fictions.[48] The fact that norms can have effects and change the course of events might count as convincing proof of their reality. But the reality of the normative does not depend on their efficacy. Norms can still claim reality even when they are consciously violated, when their application is concealed, ultimately whenever traces of a presumed alternative course of events and its evaluation can be found in a social practice.

This led us to a critique of different conceptions of ideal norms. At a descriptive level, we saw the distorting influence of different norm theories that can only observe what they theoretically presume, namely reasons or preferences.

[47] See above, ppp. 220 f.
[48] See above, pp. 149–51 ff.

At a legitimizing level, another problem arose in examining the majority rule. Procedural norms play an important role for social practices because they define normative practices temporally and spatially. Political theories that emphasize rationality tests in favor of the majority rule do not achieve this. They are not actually dealing with procedural norms, as they operate within an ideal, timeless realm of reasoning. To declare them procedural norms does not only veil their ideal character but also their missing open-endedness, because in contrast to the majority rule, a generalization test only knows one right answer. As such, ideal procedures have either to miss their pretense to social relevance or neglect their own idealizing formation of criteria in order, when push comes to shove, to return to procedures such as the majority rule if it becomes necessary.

6.2 Cross-Check: Real Democracy

Our concept of a norm, however, cannot only be turned against the idealization of norms, but also against a "realist" critique of norms, for example in the diagnosis that democratic government only unfolds as an empty form, as a simulation.[49] In this regard, it is less of interest whether this observation is appropriate to the political reality of certain communities than how it can be substantiated.

Of course, it can make sense to speak of certain orders to exist "in appearance only." Political orders purport to be something different than what they are. Nevertheless, the pretense of a democratic order is normative. A democracy is not a mechanism for transferring and integrating wills or intentions, not a causal event, but a normative project that codifies procedural rules and conditions of success for democratic government such as freedom of opinion. In the course of this, the order has to define aspirations that cannot be completely fulfilled, the lack of fulfillment of which, however, does not necessarily make the order undemocratic. By contrast, whoever highlights that "the people" were would not "really" governing by doing so puts forward a causal model of representation when instead the only concern can be that a political order ought to demand of itself that it makes and seek to realize certain egalitarian, normative aspirations/demands of itself.[50] In the end, this means that a critique of normative orders always has to distinguish between the unavoidable deficits of the order and their complete failure. This heightens the complexity in describing and evaluating democratic orders immensely, as this not only requires being able to recognize individual norm transgressions but also has to evaluate whether the degree to which such transgressions operate within the

[49] For an affirmative turn of the concept, see Ingolfur Blühdorn, *Simulative Demokratie*, Berlin 2013.

[50] Christoph Möllers, "Expressive versus repräsentative Demokratie" in: Regina Kreide (ed.), *Transnationale Verrechtlichung*, Frankfurt/M. 2008, pp. 160–82.

limits of common, everyday deviance or whether they should be taken as the beginning of a different order.

6.3 Immanent Power of the Normative?

Can we ascribe a power to social norms that is particular to them, an immanent effect?[51] References such as the "curiously forceless force of the better argument"[52] serve to bring a conception of moral norms relegated to the realm of reasons back into a social, causal relationship—or, alternatively, to rid a binding social norm of its compulsory, forcible character. But first, highlighting the factual effects of norms is always speculative. The supposedly compulsory effect of a justificatory discursive situation can hardly be empirically captured.[53] If it were in fact *compulsory* in the literal sense of the term, we wouldn't be able to speak of it as a norm. Whether or not an effect emanates from norms per se is an open question. After all, even reasonable norms are broken, and breaking norms, as we have seen, does not have to be detrimental to their existence. The power of the normative can be described differently on the basis of our model.

An initial effect of norms can arise from the marking of a certain possibility making it factually more difficult to strive for other possibilities. This was described under the heading of "cognitive norms."[54] In distinguishing, preferencing, making explicit one certain possibility by means of a norm, I authoritatively lay claim to attention that is then no longer available for other possibilities. Many "soft" norms, which lack formal binding effects yet display a high degree of adherence, operate in this way.

A second kind of effect brought about by norms can arise from the fact that the identification of a norm presumes an insight into its authorization structure, even if I ultimately do not follow the norm. By perceiving the norm, I participate in the social context that authorized the norm which can even have an effect on me if I violate the norm. In other words, even if I do not follow the norm, I do not want to contest the authority that stands behind it, be it because it threatens me, be it because I recognize it despite my deviant behavior. For this reason, I secretly break the norm and thereby partially express its effectiveness.

A third effect of norms is tied to the mechanisms that enable their establishment. Norms and norm application need to be consistently distinguished from each other. If this is done, even fleeting events can be treated as norms. But very

[51] Most recently, Andreas Fischer-Lescano, *Rechtskraft*, Berlin 2013, pp. 61–103.

[52] Jürgen Habermas, "Wahrheitstheorien" in: Ibid., *Vorstudien und Ergänzungen zur Theorie des kommunikativen Handelns*, Frankfurt/M. 1984, pp. 127–83, here p. 161.

[53] See above, pp. 33–37.

[54] Above, pp. 79 ff.

transitory norms hardly develop social relevance.[55] However, if norms stabilize themselves and gain permanence, then this does not happen by means of, but *in* their effects. The norm has these effects *qua* its own establishment as a norm. If it is established, then we can routinely refer to it, or even have to.[56] Frequently, there is a self-fulfilling prophecy at play in practices of normativity, as for everyday norms of short or medium range, the practice of their establishment needs to be distinguished from adherence to them at an analytical level, but they cannot be separated at a phenomenological level.[57] Whoever posits an "ought," in many cases needs to incorporate social practices, thereby taking a first step toward realizing this "ought." This is not a natural law of the normative, but it is a common result of social norming.

John Austin's concept of the illocutionary speech act provides a conceptual framework for the description of the transitions between a norm its effects. These speech acts go beyond mere description without on the other hand directly producing effects,[58] thus evading the broad distinction between constative and performative speech acts.[59] For norms, the concept of the illocutionary is of particular import as it captures the transition from description to effecting, which is where normative practices operate. Austin distinguishes between the *force* of the illocutionary and the *effect* of the perlocutionary.[60] In this context, *force* should neither be equated with violence nor with compulsion. The illocutionary act can have an effect, but it does not need have one. In Austin's example: the expressing of a warning is illocutionary, however, linguistically convincing someone by way of speech is perlocutionary. Here, I am less interested in Austin's attempt to categorize the illocutionary, which frequently leads him to normative practices, but rather in how Austin understands a substantive part of our approach to language to be a practice through which possibilities are marked by bringing about a certain expectation without thereby necessitating its fulfillment. Whenever I pose a question,[61] I do not compel a response, but it is only in virtue of the question that an answer becomes possible. These mechanisms reveal something that resembles an immanent power of the normative. They allow us to explain what the "power" attributed to norms could consist in, something which is neither mystical[62] nor

[55] However, see Michael Reisman, *Law in Brief Encounters*, New Haven 1999, pp. 149–73.

[56] Wittgenstein, *Philosophische Untersuchungen*, § 231 (p. 142), and the well-known reference to blind following, ibid., § 219 (p. 140).

[57] Geoffrey Brennan/Lina Eriksson/Robert E. Goodin/Nicholas Southwood, *Explaining Norms*, Oxford 2013, pp. 105–7.

[58] Austin describes the former as locutionary, the latter as perlocutionary. The value of this distinction is also highlighted by Jeremy Waldron, "A Right to do Wrong" in: *Ethics* 92 (1981), pp. 21–39, here pp. 38 ff.

[59] Thus, it is the most interesting of the three kinds of speech acts for him: John L. Austin, *How to do Things with Words*, Oxford 1975, p. 103.

[60] Ibid., p. 121.

[61] Ibid., p. 99.

[62] Jacques Derrida, Force of Law: The "Mystical Foundation of Authority" in: D. Cornell, et al. (eds), *Deconstruction and the Possibility of Justice*, New York 1992, pp. 3–68 here pp. 11–16.

necessary, but rather something that can result from the everyday mechanics of social norms.

7. *Norm—Form—Freedom*

7.1 The Good, the Right—and the Formalized

Nothing speaks for communities being able to agree on a clearly defined sphere of the good in their normative practices. Yet very little speaks against the idea that there can be arguments for or against certain lifestyles in certain contexts. We certainly continuously participate all the time in practices that evaluate lifestyles and seek to give reasons for these valuations.[63] Once engagement of norms becomes explicit and reflexive, it also tend to be formalized. In order to be made a topic of thought, norms have to be made graspable, that is they must be brought into a certain form. This formalization is neither neutral to the norms' meaning nor to their effects. Formalization is not a form into which a normative content can be molded without thereby being affected. Instead, it is rather the disposition of the form toward identifiability, repeatability, and regular applicability that changes the norm.[64]

Against this background, we gain a new perspective on certain frontlines of debate in practical philosophy. For formalized normative orders, our criteria need to be accommodated to this background. The assumption that formalized normative orders like the law—*qua* formalization—destroy social relationships and the communal freedom expressed therein[65] comes across as too sweeping because, in light of this, a formalized normative order can also contribute to the dissolution of social relationships that had threatened the freedom of some of those who participated in them. However, formalization effects need to be observed individually, and the results of these observation must be used more precisely to calibrate the relationship between formal arguments that are aimed at generalization and "justice," and those focused on context and oriented toward the "good." The notion that liberal and communitarian concepts of normativity mutually exclude each other obviously goes well beyond every kind of normative practice. The observation of the

[63] Rahel Jaeggi, *Kritik von Lebensformen*, Berlin 2013, pp. 428–46. Whether this critique can be deduced from within its conceptual framework is a different question.

[64] This formalization problem is especially discussed under the rubric of the limits of law, going back to Mill, but especially British legal theory. See Patrick Devlin, *The Enforcement of Morals*, Oxford 1965; Gerald Dworkin, "Devlin was Right: Law and the Enforcement of Morality" in: *William and Mary Law Review* 40 (1999), pp. 927–46. Also Lon Fuller, *The Morality of Law*, New Haven 1969, pp. 106–18.

[65] Axel Honneth, *Das Recht der Freiheit. Grundriß einer demokratischen Sittlichkeit*, Berlin 2011, pp. 146–56. On the critique of this assumption, see Charles Larmore, "Besprechung" in: *Hegel-Studien* 47 (2013), pp. 145–51, here pp. 150 f.

effects of form is a promising way to enrich this general insight with more concrete observations.

7.2 Limiting and Enabling—A Freedom-Theoretical Addendum

Even the strictly sanctioned prohibition of a narrowly defined action is only normative because it points toward an alternative possibility, to the possibility of its neglect. That which appears as a possibility from a norm-theoretical perspective by contrast appears as a mere limitation from a freedom-theoretical perspective. Do norms thus operate as limitations on freedom? Considering the norm-logical, deontic operators, that might appear to be the case. To prohibit an action is to limit freedom; ordering an action does as well. Allowing an action only appears to expand action options, since an action has to already have been prohibited in order to be allowed.[66]

Once more, the problem with this argument lies in its limitation to the concept of action and the implicitly individualistic perspective on norms inherent to this limitation. This is because, of course, doing something with others can expand my possibilities, and such an expansion of the realm of action can be made possible with norms. If I want to discuss a certain topic with someone, then a social convention can keep me from doing so, but it can also make it easier for me to begin a conversation in the first place. A legal institution can enable me to bring a certain project to fruition, by means of a contract, for example. Formalized rules can contribute to freeing people from informal restraints—from ties within a village, or a family that refuses to treat them as normatively coequals.

Hegel saw that there is no natural realm of action for an individual, that individual freedom is in much greater need of a social and institutional context in order to be able to realize itself. Thus, for Hegel, law—and the concept of "law" should not be confused with a positive conception of law, but rather must be understood as a successful social norm order—is a "second nature,"[67] that is, a necessity inscribed into the natural freedom of action from the outset.[68] In this sense, norms certainly cannot only be understood as external limitations of a given sphere of freedom, they are just as enabling of freedom as they are limiting of it.[69]

[66] Georg Henrik von Wright, *Norm and Action*, New York 1963, pp. 85 ff.

[67] On remaining questions concerning this figure, see Christoph Halbig, "Varieties of Nature in Hegel and McDowell" in: *European Journal of Philosophy* 14 (2006), pp. 221–41, summarily pp. 230–7.

[68] At this point, it is no longer of interest what this means for political theory and the design of institutions. Concerning the narrow framework of certain constitutional institutions, see Christoph Möllers, *The Three Branches. A Comparative Model of Separation of Powers*, Oxford 2013, Chapter 2.

[69] Robert B. Brandom, "Freedom and Constraint by Norms" in: *American Philosophical Quarterly* 16 (1979), pp. 187–96, here pp. 190–2.

But is this also the case for institutionalized norms? A claim from the *Grundlinien* would seem to speak against that:

> With reference to *concrete* action and to moral and ethical relations, abstract right is only a *possibility* as compared with the rest of their content, and the determination of right is therefore only a *permission* or *warrant*. For the same reason [*Grund*] of its abstractness, the necessity of this right is limited to the negative—*not to violate* personality and what ensues from personality. Hence there are only *prohibitions of right*, and the positive form of commandments of right is, in its ultimate content, based on prohibition.[70]

Here, Hegel is not only speaking of abstract law and its relationship to concrete actions. Nonetheless, he is concerned with a generalizable idea.[71] Norms define possibilities, however they can ultimately be reduced to prohibitions. If this were the case, wouldn't norms just limit freedom after all? For example, if at first it appears that a norm which establishes the institution of "private property" creates new possibilities for action, then doesn't this institution turn out to simply be a prohibition on others to damage my property, that is, as a mere limitation of limitations, which grants me no new possibilities for action?

A false naturalism lies at the heart of this conclusion in its determination of what is possible.[72] It is only norms that can bring about the possibility to sell an object that is in my possession; they allow for this transaction to be protected by institutions, for this object to obtain a market value through a formalized currency, and for it to thereby be posited in relation to other objects. Here, the owner "does" something with the object that he could not do without a network of norms, even if his capacity for action were available aside from this network.

As such, the concept of a norm displays neither a positive nor a negative yield. If freedom manifests itself in social relationships, the norms can enlarge or shrink the leeway. In practice, both possibilities will overlap. The estheticization of clothing fashion can free me from other normative binds: from social rules of clothing, from accommodating a situation, a professional function, or a hierarchy. At the same time, these hierarchies forge ahead within fashion: like the economic possibility of being able to afford a certain kind of look. What is crucial is that different normative demands take position toward each other in these processes.

[70] Georg Friedrich Wilhelm Hegel, *Grundlinien der Philosophie des Rechts*, § 38 (pp. 96 ff.) (English translation by H. B. Nisbet, Cambridge 1991, pp. 60–1).

[71] Thus in Michael Quante, *Die Wirklichkeit des Geistes*, Berlin 2011, pp. 189–91.

[72] Concerning the structure of the *Grundlinien*, we need to bear in mind that Hegel's treatment of abstract law is to be understood in terms of theoretical justification, as opposed to theoretical validity. We need to see to it that abstract law is not robbed of its pretense, but rather that this pretense is placed within the broader context of what is ultimately its ethical justifiability. On this, Quante, ibid., p. 287.

These kinds of effects of norms can come into conflict with each other if that which is expensive and successful, because it is expensive and successful, does not pass an esthetic test, they can also mutually reinforce each other if an esthetic of wealth and power gains credence. But in no way are these kinds of possibilities of expression possible without norms.

8. *Dogmatics: On the Rehabilitation of Local Normativity*

8.1 Old and New Dogmas

Nelson Goodman's claim that, in practice, the truth of a statement is often irrelevant[73] corresponds with the suspicion that the justification of a norm is rarely practically relevant. As such, "rarely" is to be taken as a qualitative entity, not a quantitative one. Justification does not enter the scene from time to time in order to put the practice on the right path. Rather, claims of justification are chopped up and defined away in the realm of the normative. Communities often operate with justifications that have a minimal purview, with the communities accepting them as they are. They live with small dogmas, they use patterns of justification that they cannot share with other communities, and rarely do they use kinds that stake claims to generality.[74] Since Kant, dogmas have not enjoyed a very good reputation. Over and against the dogmatic disciplines, jurisprudence, theology, and medicine, which deduced their theses from scriptures alone, Kant presented the new faculty of philosophy, subject only to reason.[75] This approach was liberating, but along with its demand for rational examination, it empowered those who saw themselves fit to administer such examinations. For Kant, dogmas are unexamined propositions authorized from outside—and nothing speaks against distancing oneself from unjustified propositions, not only in sciences. Indeed, many social norms require justification, but the latter is subject to other rules than the justification of moral norms. Furthermore, for social norms we do not expect a substantive justification. There are morally indifferent norms that fulfill a function which they would not be able to if they were reduced to moral rules. As such, Kant's critique overshoots disciplines such as jurisprudence and theology, which consist in more than just a core that is to be morally and philosophically substantiated and an otherwise exchangeable amount of normative filler material.

[73] See above, p. x.

[74] On this, see the reconstruction by Allan Gibbard, *Wise Choices, Apt Feelings*, Oxford 1990, pp. 197–201, 204–18.

[75] Immanuel Kant, "Der Streit der Fakultäten" in: Id., *Schriften zur Anthropologie, Geschichtsphilosophie, Politik und Pädagogik I*, Frankfurt/M. 1977, pp. 265–393, here pp. 284 ff.

For normative discourses that are constituted by objectively and spatially specified rules, one could reintroduce the concept of dogmatics, while at the same time stripping it of the negative connotations stemming from philosophy, not so much from theology and jurisprudence.[76] Dogmatics does not rule out justification, but it also only minimally demands it, and if it does demand it, then it does so usually from within dogmatics. Thus, many norm orders operate without this coming across as a deficit. Norms point toward other norms. Only in certain cases do they point toward a justification, and very rarely are we tempted to say that, in a crisis situation, they do so, aiming for a generalizing justification that actually extends beyond the order at stake. To claim that it is only the search for such generalizable justifications that would provide practices with a foundation contradicts all plausibility, as we have seen in expounding upon norm hierarchies. Rather to the contrary: we only gain an idea of how generalizing justifications operate by means of the more compartmentalized practices of argumentation.

Formalized generalizing principles can be liberating. However, our engagement with them, practically speaking, is rather rare, and it inevitably takes place in a context that forges their meaning. For most cases with short-ranging and incompletely justified norms, dogmatics can be a means to make such applying practices explicit and to reflect on them. Conflicts surrounding norms are not simply the result of an epistemological deficit; rather, normative pretenses are frequently the cause of a conflict. Dogmatics is thus—here, Luhmann's critique of polemical moralizing and the Anglo-Saxon theory of compartmentalized norm justification work together—also a means to limit such conflicts.

8.2 Tradition and Community as Source of Norms?

This critique of Kant's critique, as well as the assessment that social orders operate "dogmatically" in our sense, neither leads to a communitarian understanding of social norms, nor to an idyllization of traditional orders. In justifying norms, invoking a "tradition"—aside from all methodological difficulties to even be able to prove its existence—does not appear to be sufficient anyway because traditions can never be taken over completely, but only select elements from them. As such, there is always a decisive step between tradition and claiming a norm. Regardless of what one holds to be normatively desirable, every aspect of a tradition can never be desirable.[77] This selection, however, is no longer part of the

[76] Also see Georg Essen and Nils Jansen (eds), *Dogmatisierungsprozesse in Recht und Religion*, Tübingen 2011.

[77] Walter Benjamin, "Über den Begriff der Geschichte" in: Id., *Gesammelte Schriften*, Vol. I/2, pp. 693–704, here p. 696.

tradition but follows different rules. This does not mean that normative practices can be reduced to this selection, that it would be plausible or even observable, or that communities would orient themselves along the lines of the consciously chosen standards. This is the case because the selection does not only presume the criterion of selection but also that which is to be selected from. Normative practices persistently chip away at that which is available to them and with which they already have experience. We have to treat the reference to communities and their practices of deducing a norm with the same prudence. Wherever such referencing becomes necessary, a problem is already at hand. For normative questions are only made explicit on the fringes of the practice, where not only the question of what justifies a practice is contested, but even what exactly a practice that represents the community consists in. Here, every normative argumentation has to extend beyond the practice in order to justify itself.

6
Research Perspectives

1. Empirics

1.1 Twofold Level of Observation

We have seen that empirical research stands in often remarkably direct dependency of its philosophical preconditions. Yet, social norms can neither be reduced to subjective preferences, nor to actually occurring practices, nor to convincing moral justifications. In order to be able empirically to describe them in an appropriate manner, we need a research design that is capable of both taking the normative self-description of a community by its word and capturing the social practice pertaining to it. Thus, in an observable social practice, we need to look for traces of recognition *and* of deviance in order not to reduce norms to factual effects. Otherwise, the normative practice would be robbed of its distinctive character and the description would remain incomplete.

1.2 Description of Forms as a Point of Departure?

Of course, in describing social practices it is not enough to limit oneself to the examination of just one particular norm inventory. Saying as much sounds trivial—but the significant role that legal forms and legal thought have played at times in historiography and political science shows that making this point is necessary. A description of "Roman constitutional law" not only is not a description of the Roman political system, let alone of Roman society, but it isn't even immediately obvious what is meant by "constitutional law," which it seeks to describe. This is because the relevance of a formalized legal order for its community is contingent and itself has to be addressed in order to make plausible its potential additional descriptive value.

Formalized normative orders can certainly be used as a first step in describing social practices, particularly since they are tangible and easily accessible. They can be read as models of reality whose descriptive value, in and of themselves, does not have to be smaller than that of other social-scientific models. It does not have to be a mistake to begin with the text of a constitution when describing a political system. Nevertheless, such an approach demands caution, as the description of the formal order as such cannot say anything about the meaning of form for the whole.

The Possibility of Norms. Christoph Möllers, Published by Oxford University Press (2020) under licence; © this translation, Alex Holznienkemper; © the original German edition, Suhrkamp Verlag Berlin.
DOI: 10.1093/oso/9780198827399.001.0001

In a legalistic culture such as the German one,[1] I presumably capture more of the political system than in a less legalistic one such as French culture. By examining the Catholic *Codex*, we do not learn much about Catholic theology and pastoral practice, and we do not even learn much about the formalized treatment of the *Codex* by church courts. The question of which relevance a formalized norm order has cannot be answered simply by means of investigating this norm order. Not only is this the case for its impact on the workings of society as a whole but even for the reality of its own formalized procedures.

The fact that the descriptive value of such an approach is limited does not mean that the search for what lies "behind" or "beneath" the form would necessarily yield more. Formal and informal norms cannot be reduced to each other so that the form would only be the incomplete image of a "real," informal normative practice, or vice versa, that what is informal would actually constitute the core of the norm order.

1.3 Observation of Social Norms

In communities with complex normative self-descriptions, it is not easy to work one's way into norm orders. If legal sociologists understand little of law, and religious anthropologists understand little of theology, then there is a risk that research will become one-dimensional. Then, descriptions of what can be observed in courtrooms will be completely identified with the normative side. The very point of normative practices, the doubling of perspectives, would disappear from view. In its place, this way of looking at normative practices generates predictable results in which norms "in reality" look like the practices themselves. It is no coincidence that significant amounts of norm-anthropological research reach the conclusion that norms were to be seen not as "rigid," but rather as "negotiated," that "in reality" they operate differently than the "norm texts" would envision, and that entirely different normative practices lie behind the respective forms.[2] This is not merely trivial; it often overlooks that not only the formal side depends on the informal side, but also the informal on the formal.

What is more, a curious tension arises regarding the question of a norm's proximity to realization. The further away a normative condition is defined as, then obviously the less likely its realization becomes, and the higher its recognizability

[1] M. Rainer Lepsius, »Institutional Structures and Political Culture" in: Herbert Döring and Gordon Smith (eds), *Party Government and Political Culture in Western Germany*, London 1982, pp. 116–29, here pp. 124–6.

[2] The problem with reducing norms to actual practices is clearly seen with an eye for the discipline by Clifford Geertz, "Local Knowledge: Fact and Law in Comparative Perspective" in: Id., *Local Knowledge*, New York 2000, pp. 167–234, here p. 208.

as normative. By the same token, the closer a normative content moves toward reality, the shorter is its step to realization, and the more difficult it is to recognize it as normative. Thus, it is inappropriate to equate the degree of normativity with the chance of and proximity to realization, as is sometimes done in empirical research.

The quantitative exploration of norms also has to account for these features. Arranging the judges of a court according to their political convictions, in order to construct an algorithm for predicting their decisions on this basis, skips the normative level.[3] In order quantitatively to investigate patterns of normative justification, we must first engage them qualitatively. For this, it is necessary to isolate normative contents. In this case, this entails nothing other than that which holds for quantitative literary studies:[4] it is only the knowledge of a program of forms, originating in juridical, esthetic, or courtly norm orders, that allows us to develop empirical questions that lend themselves to quantitative research. To take one's starting point right at the behavior of participants means to ignore the normative level by looking for explanatory models that do not include the possibility of their adherence or transgression. Trying to break down normativity to quantifiable parameters has to also account for the internal methodological problems of the described norm orders. For example, if we take "legalization" as a function of three scalable characteristics—the degree of a norm's binding effect, the precision of the norm, and the measure to which its interpretation is delegated[5]—then the question arises as to how the precision of a norm could be measured aside from comparatively observing its application, which in turn depends on the degree to which the norm claims a binding character and on the way delegation takes place; that is, how the norm is applied. Here, the taxonomy seems to presume results of research which it is seeking to enable in the first place.

It is probably more promising to begin the empirical investigation of norms with smaller phenomena. Thus, practices such as citation, which have proven to be meaningful for formalized norm orders, would seem to encourage empirical research designs. For this, it would be necessary to give an empirically graspable form to certain structures of argumentation.[6] The example of literary studies

[3] This could justify an objection to the research program of Christoph Engel, *Legal Experiments. Mission Impossible?*, Den Haag 2013, pp. 18–22, which ultimately reduces the norm to the behavior prompted by it. A similar objection holds against Cristina Bicchieri, *The Grammar of Society*, Cambridge 2005, who ultimately does not investigate social norms but rather the development of social behavior which corresponds to certain presumed normative standards such as fairness.

[4] Two different, quantitative research programs with demanding qualitative preconditions are: Franco Moretti, *Distant Reading*, London 2013; Winfried Menninghaus, *Kunst als "Beförderung des Lebens"* München 2008.

[5] Thus, Kenneth Abbott, Robert Keohane, Andre Moravcsik, Anne-Marie Slaughter, and Duncan Snidal, "The Concept of Legalization" in: *International Organization* 54 (2000), pp. 401–19, here pp. 402–4 and 408–18.

[6] Approaches of this kind, though admittedly with much qualitative friction, are presented in Arthur Dyevre and András Jakab, "Foreword: Understanding Constitutional Reasoning" in: *German Law Journal* 14 (2013), pp. 983–1015.

appears interesting in this context for two reasons: because literature is familiar with procedures of world formation and thus with levels of thought coming to be that are independent of mere world description, and because it contains a thorough canon of forms.

2. *Norms Beyond Functional Differentiation and Autonomy*

2.1 Luhmann's Model of the Pure Norm

Theories of functional differentiation have to draw a distinction between norms of different provenances. Rarely has this been carried through as consistently as in Luhmann's systems theory, even if his chosen strategy can be traced back to predecessors of classical modernity, and even to the legal theory of Kelsen.[7] However, Luhmann's approach pays the price of hybrid forms of normativity being defined away or suspected of dysfunctionality as they do not live up to the imperative of functional differentiation.[8] Furthermore, ascribing a practice to a certain normative order unfolds either in a purely nominalist fashion, or it produces curious results, as it obscures the fact that every normative practice extends beyond itself. Thus, it is not self-evident, as Luhmann's theory would have it, to accord to the legal system a court decision achieved through bribery, or an indictment that only invokes political or moral arguments.[9] Luhmann's distrust of moral arguments of a universalist kind is probably not simply due to his conviction that they can prompt dangerous conflicts but it is also tied to their incompatibility with his conception of functional differentiation and operative closure.

Of course, the simple fact that there are events in which different social functional relationships converge does not provide a convincing argument against the assumption of social differentiation.[10] Denying it is also not an option. Nevertheless, the disassembly of social events into functionally differentiated operations runs the risk of no longer being able to describe normative practices in an appropriately complex manner. As norms can rarely be neatly attributed according to their function, since law, morality, and efficiency orientations amalgamate in them, it is problematic to speak of the self-referential character of normative

[7] Horst Dreier, "Hans Kelsen und Niklas Luhmann. Positivität des Rechts aus rechtswissenschaftlicher und systemtheoretischer Perspektive" in: *Rechtstheorie* 14 (1983), pp. 419–58.

[8] This is actually a methodological imperative that claims not to be normative, but it does not hold up to this claim when it doubts human rights or solutions to negotiations.

[9] For this reason, attributing constitutional courts to the legal system without further ado is dubious without gaining much from the formula of the "structural coupling" of law and politics. On this, see Christoph Möllers, "Legalität, Legitimität und Legitimation des Bundesverfassungsgerichts" in: Matthias Jestaedt, Oliver Lepsius, Christoph Möllers, and /Christoph Schönberger, *Das entgrenzte Gericht*, Berlin 2011, pp. 283–419, here pp. 320–8.

[10] Armin Nassehi, *Der soziologische Diskurs der Moderne*, Frankfurt/M. 2006, p. 397.

operating systems. The claim that law decides what belongs to law, and that politics decides what belongs to politics, presumes a degree of mutual independency of operating systems that cannot be observed in many hybrid phenomena.

2.2 The Inevitable Hybrid Character of Social Norms

Thus, trying to decide whether human rights should be accorded to the realm of law, politics, or morals does not lead us anywhere: It could be the case that the moral authority of a human rights norm only unfolds because it is mediated by a legal form. We can only appropriately describe such a case with the help of the distinction between law and morality. But we cannot simply accord it to the legal system or rest content with the fact that the legal system incorporates moral or political contents. Not only can such contents severely change when being incorporated into a legal order. Conversely, juridical norms could also be adopted by other normative orders, such as civil-religious constitutional norms that are adopted as their own by a religious community. It is just as futile to accord religious-political movements *either* to politics *or* to religion—or to seek to ban religion from the realm of politics for reasons of discursive hygiene. A comparable critique applies to economic models that try to isolate their understanding of rational action from other forms of rationality, such that a simple view aimed at specifically economic rationality suffices to explain economic action.[11] A number of phenomena overlap and reinforce each other in those kinds of assumptions; an overestimation of the explanatory merit of grand theories in light of the plurality of normative practices, a modernizing-theoretical inflation of differentiation,[12] and an overestimation of the formalizing and positing achievements of modern normative orders. The investigation of social norms should duly take note of social differentiation, but it should not fear hybrid practices and ambiguous findings. It is precisely the point of a norm theory that proceeds in a comparative fashion not to only look for commonalities among functional differences, as does structural-functionalist sociology but also to look for phenomena in which the functional limits are in question.[13]

[11] For a critique of the theory of functional differentiation stemming from insight into the plurality of normative phenomena in the realm of the economy, see Jens Beckert, "Die sittliche Einbettung der Wirtschaft. Von der Effizienz- und Differenzierungstheorie zu einer Theorie wirtschaftlicher Felder" in: *Berliner Journal für Soziologie* 22 (2012), pp. 247–66.

[12] The inflation itself might well have its own religious provenance. See Hans Joas, "Modernisierung als kulturprotestantische Metaerzählung" in: Id., *Glaube als Option*, Freiburg 2012, pp. 86–105; Manuel Borutta, "Genealogie der Säkularisierungstheorie" in: *Geschichte und Gesellschaft* 36 (2010), pp. 347–76.

[13] Concerning the related problem of »autonomy«, see also: Martina Franzen et al., "Begriff und Wert der Autonomie in Wissenschaft, Kunst und Politik" in: Id. (eds), *Autonomie Revisited* (= 2nd special volume of *Zeitschrift für Theoretische Soziologie*), Weinheim 2014, pp. 5–28, here pp. 18 and 22, where a distinction is drawn between loss of autonomy and differentiation.

3. The Challenge of Historicism and the Project of a Comparison of Theories

3.1 Savigny and Troeltsch

In his well-known introduction to the first issue of the *Zeitschrift für geschichtliche Rechtswissenschaft*, in 1815, Friedrich von Savigny polemically contrasted historical legal thought with non-historical legal thought. According to him, only historical legal thought is capable of imbuing law with a degree of conceptual necessity, whereas non-historical natural law thought delivers itself up to the arbitrariness of political rulers.[14] Nearly a century later, theologian Ernst Troeltsch made almost the identical distinction between dogmatic and historical thought, and defined similar, if by then more humble, expectations for his scientific discipline.[15] According to Troeltsch, only a historical perspective allows for a scientific grounding of norms for a normative theology. Both thinkers faced the challenge of how norms can be justified in light of historical change and the modernization of scientific methods. Both found the solution—at the beginning and at the end of this historical epoch—in a respectively different understanding of the scientific treatment of history.

We face the same problem today.[16] However, it lurks behind the division of labor between an analytically practical philosophy, which forces the historical and the social into a clinical-like isolation of formalized arguments, and differentiated historical research that renounces all legitimizing pretenses. Between these two extremes, we encounter a number of political theories that are rich in context. But even models outside the bounds of analytical theory in a narrower sense, the conceptual framework of normative theories often appears like the result of ad hoc abstractions that expressly do not take note of historical or other contexts, even though they stem from highly specific historical and intellectual contexts. Does the distinction between liberalism and communitarianism fit within any other institutional landscape than that of the United States? From

[14] Friedrich Carl von Savigny, "Ueber den Zweck dieser Zeitschrift" in: *Zeitschrift für geschichtliche Rechtswissenschaft* 1 (1815), pp. 1–17. This marked the beginning of historical legal sciences displacing legal philosophy. Similarly, contemporary philology attempted to displace philosophy: Axel Horstmann, "'Erkenntnis des Erkannten'. Philologie und Philosophie bei August Boeckh" in: *Zeitschrift für Germanistik* 20 (2010), pp. 64–78, here pp. 68–70.

[15] Ernst Troeltsch, "Über historische und dogmatische Methode der Theologie" in: Friedmann Voigt (ed.), *Ernst Troeltsche Lesebuch*, Tübingen 2003, pp. 2–25, here pp. 12–17.

[16] One of the few authors who expressly recognize this, and in turn seek to solve this problem by drawing on Troeltsch, is Hans Joas. See his book *Die Sakralität der Person. Eine neue Genealogie der Menschenrechte*, Berlin 2011, pp. 147–203. The model of an "affirmative genealogy" naturally must distinguish affirmation and genealogy; that is, it has to find reasons beyond genealogy in order to justify why it is appropriate to protect people, otherwise it might face the accusation of affirming a genealogy of "abuse of the person."

examining the principle theories of law by Dworkin or Alexy, does one learn anything about legal orders other than those of the writers' home countries, the United States and Germany? Particularly in normative theory focused on institutions, which does not so much ponder an analytical conception of a norm but more specifically fundamental rights or democracy, regional findings are frequently described with a universal conceptual framework. This could be avoided if one were to compare and contrast one's theoretical inventory with its political and institutional context.

3.2 Ways out through Small Steps

If there are solutions to the problem of how normative justifications can be better embedded in historical and cultural contexts without simply disintegrating in them, then they are not going to operate in the vein of grand theory but rather in minute detail, for example by investigating the collision of different models of normative ordering—the democratization of politics, the juridification of certain social relations, the confrontation of politeness, willingness to help, or concrete religious doctrines with certain social realities. Thus, every model of the normative requires a *comparative* perspective from the outset, which brings the contextualizing element of historicization into a synchronous perspective. It should still be obvious that the question of how norm orders react to contact with society does not necessarily entail an answer that leaves the norm order unscathed. It is inevitable that every theory of a norm order's justification has to come to terms with its own relativization in its application. It is not obvious that this would ultimately leave us empty handed, a fear that clearly drove Troeltsch, whereas Savigny did not even conceive of it. But it could lead to normative theories becoming better at understanding what they actually plan to do with the world.

Despite our skepticism with regard to overly grand theorizing, the comparative side of theories in the vein of Luhmann's systems theory, or Foucault's discourse analysis, as it appears in *Les mots et les choses—Une archéologie des sciences humaines* or in *Die Gesellschaft der Gesellschaft*, deserves to be highlighted. Neither can we deny the danger of implicit "historical philosophizing" inherent in such endeavors, nor do such theories do always do justice to the historical circumstances which they seek to situate within a greater context.[17] But the discourse-comparative approach should be particularly attractive for the investigation of norms. At points, research on such questions already exists, concerning the relevance of the

[17] For an exemplary critical analysis: Otto Gerhard Oexle, "Luhmanns Mittelalter" in: *Rechtshistorisches Journal* 10 (1991), pp. 53–66.

invention of stochastics even for the development of fictional literature, regarding the critique of liberalism in German constitutional scholarship and in Protestant theology, regarding certain literary genres that are common to various disciplines, such as commentaries, and concerning hermeneutic techniques.[18] These kinds of investigations bring more specificity into ways of observing discourses and at the same time they can show just how much theoretical reconstructions hinge upon external constellations. We should certainly continue pursuing the idea of comparative studies of theory, a comparative field of study that not only compares French and Spanish novels, or Canadian and South African constitutions with each other, but rather one that compares French theory of the novel with German legal theory, *roman experimental* and naturalist criminology, or Protestant grace dogma and genius esthetics.

3.3 Normative Studies?

At this point, it might be opportune to offer an interdisciplinary program that integrates such questions under the heading of "normativity." Yet, despite all our interest in pursuing commonalities, the field of norms contains too many phenomena that operate too differently as to lead such meta-inquiry toward fruitful, overarching questions. Furthermore, even the commonalities to be described are insufficiently sketched out, and they are too thin for any substantive research framework. Once more, one would have to begin on a smaller scale and confront at most two normative disciplines with the descriptive methodology of a third—empirical—discipline. The two normative disciplines to be thus confronted would have to be equipped with a sturdy methodological identity, an openness toward methodological self-doubt and impartial comparison, and a certain resistance in light of empirical elucidation. Caution is advised, however. A scientific approach to normative phenomena with purely empirical and quantitative instruments could also let such phenomena dissolve: "As the sense of causality increases, so does the extent of the domain of morality decrease."[19]

[18] Regarding the listed questions in corresponding order: Elena Esposito, *Die Fiktion der wahrscheinlichen Realität*, Frankfurt/M. 2007; Klaus Tanner, *Die fromme Verstaatlichung des Gewissens*, Göttingen 1989; David Kästle and Nils Jansen (eds), *Kommentare in Recht und Religion*, Tübingen 2014; Jan Schröder (ed.), *Theorie der Interpretation vom Humanismus bis zur Romantik—Rechtswissenschaft, Philosophie, Theologie*, Stuttgart 2001.

[19] Friedrich Nietzsche, "*Morgenröthe*" in: Id., *Sämtliche Werke: Kritische Studienausgabe*, Giorgio Colli and Mazzino Montinari (eds), Munich 1999, Vol. 3, p. 24 (No. 10) (transl. J. M. Kennedy, London 1911, No. 10).

4. Over-normativization and Under-normativization—Two Perspectives on Normativity Succeeding

4.1 Apology of the Normative

Norms are not some form deficient in reality but rather a curious cultural achievement in which imagination and capacity for abstraction must come together with reality. Our intuition that views social norms as a weaker form of social reality does not help us. It is even doubtful whether substantive descriptive propositions can be conceived of without a counterfactual perspective. At least for natural scientific causal relationships, this is seriously discussed, and in social sciences and the science of history, counterfactual background assumptions are frequently revealed.[20] Given this, the supposed weak point of normative statements also applies to descriptive statements, losing its specific relevance for norms. "If there is a sense for reality, then there must also be a sense for possibility."[21]

One problem of social norms might be the fact that they exclude possibilities. As expectations imbued with a preference, they can diminish our perception's openness; as the social presence of constant evaluation, they can make life plans become joyless; as commands enforced by sanctions, they can stand in the way of desired actions. Presumably, this negative side of the normative came up too short in this book, it possibly remained too apologetic of norms. The book's approach emphasized the enabling side of the normative vis-à-vis its limiting side—in part because critique of the limiting side is so commonplace.

4.2 Successful Normativity

Based on our model, we can only speak of a norm or a normative order "succeeding" in an indirect sense. Normativity can only succeed in so far as it maintains an appropriate distance to the reality it seeks to realize. Norms are to build up and maintain a distanced tension with the world. Norms that only codify what will inevitably happen gain no distance; they can ultimately not be distinguished from the world as it is. Conversely, norms that remain so distant from the circumstances of the world that there can hardly be any talk of their affirming a "possibility" either remain meaningless, since that which is normed by them is so distant that it has no perspective for realization, or they aim for effects that no longer show any consideration for

[20] In Jon Elster, *Logik und Gesellschaft*, Frankfurt/M. 1981, Chapter 6, we find a comprehensive, albeit minimally received attempt at reasoning for this in the social sciences.

[21] Robert Musil, *Der Mann ohne Eigenschaften*, Reinbek 1978, Vol. 1, p. 16.

the state of social practice, thereby tearing apart the social fabric as Hegel described it in the context of the "Reign of Virtue" during the French Revolution.[22]

Norms do not serve as means to an end. If one were to limit oneself to the attainment of ends, it would be easier to resort to causes; that is, to bring about certain results without making use of norms. Norms can certainly be used for the attainment of goals, but that is not their point. In opening up *possibility*, norms open up the fulfillment of an end, but also the possibility of falling short of it, which takes away nothing of their normativity. The distinction between ends and effects, however, should not be taken as a sweeping plea for norms as a form of securing freedom over and against the automatism of causality. Of course, there are situations in which insight into causal relationships can improve norm orders. Thus, the Enlightenment critique of criminal law, by authors such as Beccaria, Bentham, or Feuerbach served as a reminder of how certain forms of punishment are tied to ends that they must inevitably fail to achieve. This insight into causal relationships was important in limiting criminal law, even if the consequence has been the persistence of the idea that criminal punishment is merely an instrument in a social engineer's toolbox. The penalty for murder, however, does not only serve the end of deterring future homicides, but also the normative reassurance of the penalizing community.[23] The question of where exactly to draw the line between identity affirmation and problem-solving remains a fundamental challenge for every normative order. Norms may well emancipate themselves from their ends without thereby burdening a community with any heavy costs. Eating with cutlery is not a requirement of hygiene as long as one thoroughly washes one's hands. But sometimes this emancipation of norms from their ends fails to keep the price at a reasonable size. It is not clear how many people have to die in the war on drugs in order for the expressive prohibition of a practice deemed immoral to lose its priority over the costs of the fight against it.

A second condition of success is intimately linked to the first one: If successful normativity has to maintain a certain distance to its envisioned realization, then it has to grant space to this reality and appropriately capture it. Thus, the major part of a court proceeding deals with the reconstruction of an event, whereas its normative evaluation often requires little effort. The justice of the court proceeding, one might solemnly put it, lies in doing justice to the facts of the case. This is not particular to legal procedures. Normativity presumes that there is something that can be properly described, for only then can the affirmation of the realization expressed by norms gain traction and bear fruit.

[22] For the present conception too narrow, but nevertheless structurally similar, Schauer observes that rules have their institutional strength where the norm positor and norm addressee have differing views of results, but share a common language: Frederick Schauer, *Playing by the Rules*, Oxford 2002, p. 139.

[23] On the indispensability of an expressive element inherent in punishment, see Tatjana Hörnle, *Straftheorien*, Tübingen 2011, pp. 29–43.

In light of this, and beyond the question of the internal justification of an inventory of norms, communities can be described as *under-normativized* or *over-normativized*. A community may count as over-normativized if its own positing of norms subjects itself to a level of expectations that it cannot live up to, but which it still attempts to live up to by deploying means which call into question the community itself. We can classify communities as under-normativized if they describe themselves as without alternative, and if they no longer want to react to disappointments by reflecting on alternative courses of events.

Various criteria come to mind with which to distinguish different shades on this spectrum of normativization. To begin with, norms need to be recognizable; that is, the community has to identify the demands it imposes upon itself. This recognizability often requires formalization, but it also has a substantive side. The more distant the content of a norm becomes from perceived social reality, the clearer the norm's aspiration becomes, and the more forcefully it will urge for an intervention in the community's status quo. If we want to distinguish degrees of normativity, two factors seem helpful: for one, the way in which norms are marked; that is, how recognizable the norm's character as a norm is made in its context. Secondly, the norm's proximity to realization; that is, how far the state favored by the norm is removed from reality.

4.3 Over-Normativization and Coercion

The difference between norms and physical coercion cannot be captured in moral categories. In terms of norm theory, the difference consists in coercion not granting space for any deviation. If norms have to be coercively enforced, then this is an indicator of problems that might also lie in the norm itself. This observation aims neither to justify organized resistance to democratic laws,[24] nor a naïve critique of the means of physical enforcement. The critique isn't trivial, though. The monopolization of violence by organized government has its own price in the maintenance of violence, which can overshadow its pacifying effects. In any case, established orders of government are well advised to avoid coercive enforcement[25] even when they are convinced of the legitimacy of the norms being enforced, because the use of force always pulls into the spotlight the fact that the order's means of enforcement are limited. Beyond all moral objections, the use of force indicates that the costs of the norm whose implementation is at stake are too high. This is a significantly weaker statement than Hannah Arendt's claim that violence always indicates

[24] At this point, some readers might think of peace demonstrations, others might think of banking federations, but the argument should not depend on the association.
[25] This should be distinguished from the sanction of a norm violation by physical means.

powerlessness.[26] The experience of calculated, successful deployment of violence contradicts her claim. The fact that there is still something norm-immanently wrong with any coercive enforcement of norms is due to the fact that by choosing a norm as one's means one always has already bought into the idea that deviations from the norm are possible. If norm adherence is enforced then this indicates a problem that extends beyond the individual norm transgression.

In order to investigate this, however, we need to distinguish between norm and coercion. Attempts to undercut this distinction by emphasizing the "violence at the foundation" of every normative order, by neglecting this distinction, thereby discard a helpful descriptive instrument. Of course, even democratic States under the rule of law did not come to exist by way of agreement, free of any violence, in the form of social contracts, and it also is true that violence cannot always be successfully reined in through norms. Yet these two considerations should not lead us to equate norms and violence.[27] In the preceding, it frequently became clear that the idea of a centralized norm-positing body overestimates both the possibilities for standardizing the positing of norms and the relevance of the deployment of coercive force for a normative order. If at all, a normative order only proves itself in physical enforcement as long as such force remains rare and irregular. By contrast, regimes that structurally rely on informal, violent terror in order to stay in power can only achieve this by creating a general willingness to tolerate norm transgressions, which in turn draws into question other means of their own power.

4.4 Under-Normativity and Digitalization

Democratic orders are normative orders in a very specific sense, for they not only posit norms as other political orders do, but they take themselves to be orders whose normative pretense is unfulfilled and ultimately cannot be fulfilled. In a democracy, it is commonplace to criticize the undemocratic conditions of one's own system, and if all goes well, this distinguishes these orders from authoritarian or traditionalist systems as well as from systems that are inspired by the philosophy of history. For in the latter case the actual condition cannot be viewed as lagging behind the system "as it ought to be." The expectation of the Communism to come does not allow for the critique of the current state of Socialism; to the contrary, it serves to rule it out. Self-criticism in this context only takes the form of a staging,

[26] Hannah Arendt, *Macht und Gewalt*, Munich 2005, pp. 36–58; critically, Michel Wieviorka, *Violence. a New Approach*, London 2009, pp. 145 ff.

[27] This tendency found in Walter Benjamin, "Zur Kritik der Gewalt" in: Id., *Gesammelte Schriften*, Hermann Schweppenhäuser and Rolf Tiedemann (eds), Frankfurt/M. 1977, Vol. II, pp. 179–203; Daniel Loick, "But Who Protects Us From You?" in: jour fixe initiative Berlin (eds), *Souveränitäten*, Münster 2010, pp. 159–78. More cautiously, Christoph Menke, *Recht und Gewalt*, Berlin 2011, pp. 49–69.

whereas the existence of an opposition, of institutionalized political criticism, can be seen as the practically decisive marker of democratic systems.

At the same time, the institution of an opposition reveals the ambivalent relationship of democracy toward its own norm order. A democracy affords itself an institution whose very task is to claim that, at least in part, there are wrong norms in place. If democracies are normative orders in this specific sense, then they hinge upon deviance in a particular way. Norms are not possible without the possibility of deviance, and without the possibility of deviance, democratic orders are not possible. Political theory is too concerned with commonality and cohesion. This is because certain threats to democratic orders also develop when possibilities for deviant behavior are factually eliminated.

These possibilities for deviation essentially arise for cognitive reasons. They concern our treatment of space, time, and objects. They operate—presumably just like collective, political identities—by means of shared perception and debate about its meaning.[28] The way in which these possibilities are treated can enable or eliminate a community's occasions for the self-distancing which finds its expression in the breach of norms. A community can observe behavior, analyze the statistical probability with which its inherent potential for deviance will materialize, and prevent this from the outset. A community that subtly pre-shapes decisions through inconspicuous hints, one that influences the use of space through traffic control, or precludes public debate through polls, from the outset pre-empts any confrontation of its normative demands with practices that deviate from them. In temporal terms, this closes the aspiration gap;[29] in spatial terms, it prevents self-distancing. With regard to facts, it follows a kind of constructivism that immunizes itself against any kind of disappointment, thereby also making normative practices impossible. It takes more for normativity to arise than a shared perception of objects alone, and yet there is a significant relationship between the serious treatment of norms and the willingness to be corrected by the perception of facts. The pretense of realization expressed by a norm cannot be imagined without the presumption of a reality that is not entirely available to the subject. Therefore, normativity would be a pointless enterprise not only when we were to believe that alternative courses of events were inconceivable, but also when we were to believe that everything were possible. The pretenses of norms, of evaluating, of maintaining, or of changing would become empty without a factual exterior world against which they could rub.

Instances of norm actualization provide us with a fresh perspective on the norm, be it that the actualization consists in upholding or in violating it. Adherence to a norm can show us what is wrong with the norm, just as the violation of another

[28] As I recall, during the summer semester of 1993 in Munich, Luhmann pointed out that even though everyone would leave his lecture through the self-same door, this arguably had little to do with consensus, and more with common perception of objects.

[29] See above, pp. 202 ff.

norm might increase its plausibility. This broadens the wealth of alternatives, the variance of social practices. Durkheim and sociology of classical modernity assumed that deviance was part of every society's normality.[30] Nowadays, the concern is a different one, namely the conditions of possibility for a society either to imagine alternatives to deviance, or to prevent such notions before they can take shape. The latter precludes a community from being able to recognize some of their own possibilities. Making possibilities visible thus might be one of the most important tasks of normative practices. In virtue of possibilities for deviance, a society has to take stock of how things could develop differently than they do.[31]

This problem is already envisioned in the critique of prevention, which—inspired by Foucault—is found in criminology.[32] If prevention is concerned with undermining deviant behavior, newer technology appears to aim at already undermining the cognitive preconditions of alternative action: paths are provided, behavioral patterns are extrapolated, and needs are fulfilled before they can even be articulated. This becomes especially apparent with digital tools which, by analyzing our past behavior, both thwart from the outset the envisioning of divergent behavior and feed with appropriate offers the preferences we have already expressed.

What might our insight into the variance-enabling character of norms imply for the design of digital media? What is obvious is that an algorithm rules out normativity. A community whose behavior is programmed has no room for norms. If, however, the development of the normative takes its origins in the disappointment of expectations, then it would seem imperative that we deliberately subvert the mechanical continuation of preferences derived from observing previous behavior. This could be done by using algorithms that oppose such mechanical continuation, thus creating a systematic resistance to it. But these, too, would be the result of the same mechanisms against which they are being deployed. For this reason, incorporating mechanisms of chance would be an important means for securing contingency, the precondition of normative practices. If the risk lies in behavior being directed along certain lines before it can even express itself, in social relations gaining an unlimited technological plasticity, then chance as a means for enabling variance is an option available from within the technology at hand. Encountering chance points us toward alternatives that allow for the formation of social norms.

At a second level, we have to strive to open up behavior-guiding forms to deviant behavior, and to incorporate structures for the selection of sanctions. Even if norm violations are foreseeable, the possibility must remain to let these violations occur. Therefore, a need arises for mechanisms in which the detection of deviance and the reaction to it are delayed, or even completely filtered out. Finally, at a third level, it

[30] Compare, for example, the considerations on the concept of anomy in Robert K. Merton, *Social Theory and Social Structure*, New York 1968, pp. 185–248.

[31] Roger Brownsword, *Rights, Regulation, and the Technological Revolution*, Oxford 2008, pp. 240–57.

[32] Bernard E. Harcourt, *Against Prediction*, Chicago 2007.

must be made practically possible for all participants of a practice to intervene in the programming of algorithms.

Digital structures could also operate as *implementation buffers*. Traditionally, norms played this role vis-à-vis other norms. Around here, it violates social norms to eat with one's hands, but it would arguably be an even greater *faux pas* to admonish a guest loudly in front of others and force silverware into their hands. Normative institutions, such as criminal trials, operate similarly, but they presume that there was a possibility to violate a norm. Paradoxically, an adequate approach to the practice of the normative going forward will not only have to accord for the prevention, but also the enabling—not the facilitation—of norm transgressions. For only where norms can be broken do they maintain their normativity. And only where norms operate can we overcome what we already are.

Acknowledgements

First, I need to thank the Wissenschaftskolleg zu Berlin (Berlin Institute for Advanced Study). Its stimulating silence, as well as the assistance from its wonderful library service allowed me to explore initial thoughts in my fellowship year 2006/2007, and I have been able to write the principal part of the text during my time as a permanent fellow since 2012. Furthermore, I am grateful for the Deutsche Forschungsgemeinschaft (German Research Foundation) granting me a research semester, and especially for the discussions on the theoretical framework that arose as a partial project within their "Sonderforschungsbereich 626."

Among the numerous people with whom I could expressly or occasionally discuss the text, or who provided council on individual questions, I would like to thank Johannes Bethge, Anja Breljak, Hubertus Buchstein, Jochen Bung, Lorraine Daston, Georg Essen, Jonas Grethlein, Rainer Forst, Luca Giuliani, Stefan Gosepath, Ulrich Haltern, Marco Iorio, Rahel Jaeggi, Gertrud Koch, Jan-Phillip Kruse, Laurenz Lüteken, Franco Moretti, Armin Nassehi, Sabine Müller-Mall, Hartmut Rosa, Marlene Teichmann, Alexander Tischbirek, Maike Voltmer, Hans Vorländer, Chris Volk, Anna von Notz, and Lara Zwiffelhoffer.

I extend special gratitude to readers of the entire manuscript, Hauke Brunkhorst, Marita Möllers, and Tim Wihl, as well as to Eva Gilmer for her rigorous and able editing. Finally, I thank Isabelle Ley. Her advice that there are more important things than the profession, albeit nothing more important within the profession than to write a book, was doubly successful. Firstly, the book was finished, and secondly, it took much longer than thought.

Responses, Corrections, Applications

Afterword for the Paperback Edition

> Our engagement with norms is never identical with their content, otherwise there would be no Pharisees or moralists, so towards that end, *no* normative speech is correct, not even in the case of reasoning for norms. The strict obligation in general nourishes an increasing randomness in particular.
>
> Bernhard Waldenfels[1]

1. *Questions and Line of Inquiry*

The present book arose from a perceived void: the lack of a comparative study of social norms. The investigation of social norms still largely follows their respective provenance from law, politics, religion, and other social fields, and accordingly is disciplinarily divided up among jurists, political scientists, theologians, art historians, and psychologists. At least in part, this division of labor can be attributed to the lack of a conceptual foundation for comparative research, namely a concept of the normative that is sufficiently broad, yet also clearly limited enough in scope, so as to enable commonality in the line of inquiry. It is from this intuition that the book takes its departure point in order to unfold in three steps.

In a *first* step, I seek to demonstrate that the gap caused by the lack of a general concept of norms is regularly filled by concepts that stem from practical philosophy. This is problematic for two reasons. For one, because these concepts are too narrow to capture the plurality of social norms. They select phenomena without justifying the selection process itself. For another, these concepts are vested in the kind of knowledge sought after by practical philosophy; that is, constructing criteria for the justification of norms or actions. In doing so, however, they also implicitly shape contributions that employ such concepts with merely descriptive aspiration. It is my suspicion that determining norms as

[1] Bernhard Waldenfels, "Begründete oder Beliebige Ordnung?" in: Id., *Ordnung im Zwielicht*, 2nd edn, Munich 2013.

The Possibility of Norms. Christoph Möllers, Published by Oxford University Press (2020) under licence; © this translation, Alex Holznienkemper; © the original German edition, Suhrkamp Verlag Berlin.
DOI: 10.1093/oso/9780198827399.001.0001

good reasons or necessarily rational obstructs the adequate description of normative practices.

In a *second* step, I develop my own conception of a social norm which I outline as the affirmation of a possibility's realization. The objective of this definition is to remain open to diverse forms of normativity and various kinds of justification, while simultaneously being able to draw a distinction between norms and other practices. As such, it is also necessary to detach the concept of a norm from the phenomena of its establishment and adherence: an attempt at establishing a norm can falter. Even an established norm can be dismissed on a large scale without affecting its status as a norm. The concept of a norm thus not only needs to be distinguished from that of justification but also from a notion of practice frequently tied to Wittgenstein in recent discussions. The latter has the advantage of not reducing practices to actions, but it cannot distinguish between normative and other practices.[2]

This outline of the concept of a norm has a number of implications. The presence of a norm thus does not hinge on a sanction (pp. 101–06),[3] which shows how rich in preconditions and complex the relationship between norm transgression and sanction is often structured. Speaking of implicit norms that only become visible at the point of their transgression is futile. In such a case, one is introducing a parameter which, by its very definition, cannot be observed as long as it holds meaning for the situation being observed (pp. 123–25). Ultimately, the use of norms always hinges on an element of self-authorization which cannot arise from the norm alone. Applying a norm always, at least partially, means to arrogate the power to apply the norm to oneself (pp. 169–71). The relationship between a norm and its implementation thus also gains a high degree of complexity and contingency: no application simply "follows" from the norm which is to be applied.

Outlining the concept of a norm in this way defines an orientation for the comparative analysis of norms and sharpens the awareness for common problems of diverse social practices. Norms posit realities as possibilities.[4] However, dealing with possibilities urgently hinges on permanent stabilization. The norm's recognizability, its current meaning for a given situation, and the question of who should apply it requires continuous affirmation. As such, a norm's relevance can be threatened both by its factual success and its failure. A norm that enjoys general

[2] A more nuanced notion of practice that exemplarily does not do this: Theodor R. Schatzki, *Social Practices*, Cambridge 1996, pp. 101–6.

[3] The page numbers listed in parentheses from here on denotes the respective page numbers within the book.

[4] For expressing it in this manner, I am grateful to Christoph Menke for his discussion: "Distanz und Urteil. Das Paradox der Normen"in: *Deutsche Zeitschrift für Philosophie* 64 (2016), pp. 299–306, here p. 302.

adherence can lose its counterfactual pretense based on this success. It becomes a routine whose possible alternative—deviance—is lost from sight. By the same token, a norm can withstand significant deviation under certain circumstances. In this sense, normative orders also have to distinguish between what is unruly in the sense of illegal, which falls under the qualification grid of the order, and that which is merely rule-less or not ordered at all.[5] That which is illegal confirms the norm. What distinguishes normative orders from norms without sustaining orders is that they can withstand substantial deviance precisely because they do not merely consist in individual norms.

In a *third* step, these considerations are made more concrete with an eye toward certain social structural relationships. The corresponding chapter—here one might recognize the juridical author—begins with the practice of formalization, which I view as being constituted by all attempts to stabilize normative practices by means of introducing techniques of ascription and identifiability (pp. 167–71). Formalization serves the purpose of dispersing the constitutive uncertainties of all normative practices and solidifying "the norm," its "author," and other parameters. While these attempts are frequently successful in practice, they also always raise unwanted questions. No formalization can completely overcome the fundamental uncertainty concerning where exactly a norm is located within a normative practice. We can already see this in constitutional law, which on the one hand is viewed as a tradition of written constitutions outside of England in post-revolutionary modernity, yet also demands the ability to distinguish between constitutional text and the "actual" constitutional norm. It is not quite clear how these two can operate in tandem, and this seems emblematic of the confusion[6] that stems from the reception of a philosophical notion of norms that makes normative practices immaterial. Certain social norms remain more intimately tied to texts than the talk of norms as reasons permit.

Envisioning norms as a realm of asymmetrically marked possibilities in no way denies their occasionally brutal harshness[7] but rather brings them into a single perspective. Enabling and limiting are inseparably tied together.[8] One might mark this as a paradoxical structure.[9] For me, qualifying it as such does not help, for one because the concept of paradox sounds appropriate in such cases,

[5] Helpfully, Bernhard Waldenfels, *Ordnung im Zwielicht*, Frankfurt/M. 1987, p. 20.

[6] On this, see also the fitting considerations which can also be generalized beyond the sphere of law, in Niklas Luhmann, *Das Recht der Gesellschaft*, Frankfurt/M. 1993, pp. 338–40.

[7] This is what Rainer Forst argues in his discussion of my book, "Wie utopisch sind Tischsitten?" in: *Die Zeit*, 14 January 2016, p. 43.

[8] On this point, I agree with Schatzki (n 2), see *Social Practices*, pp. 162 f.

[9] This is the observation by Menke (n 4), "Distanz und Urteil" pp. 304 f. Less clearly, but not extending beyond this scope: Andreas Fischer-Lescano, "Wozu Rechtsphilosophie? Kritik des Hyper-Juridismus bei Christoph Möllers und Rainer Forst" in: *JuristenZeitung* 73 (2018), pp. 161–70, here pp. 162–5.

but it is ultimately used metaphorically.[10] Furthermore, I do not know what is supposed to follow from a diagnosis from which nothing can follow according to classical logic.

Social norms need to be investigated in terms of their illustrative challenges, which result from their asymmetrical refence to possibilities. A further attempt at systematization cannot be tied to this. On the contrary. It is disconcerting when the normative phenomena are being adjusted and made fitting by using narrow and narrowing concepts.[11] On my view, by contrast, we gain more by first descriptively highlighting the plurality and disordered nature of many normative practices. It is at least not surprising when this is more difficult for legal scholars to understand, scholars who—at times for reasons of self-legitimation—try to impose rather unaspiring systemic fictions upon unordered structures, than it is for those from other disciplines[12] who were able to get more out of the book.[13]

At the same time, this does not mean that the directions taken in the book are not somehow connected to the thus developed notion, and that the thus determined practice could develop randomly.[14] A practice that aims for the realization of possibilities will have to operate differently than practices that do so without realization reference, or those that deal with realia and actualities. This insight guides the further construction of the argument.

The publication of this book was met with a pleasingly broad, mostly favorable reception. Starting with the most considerable critiques, the following seeks to pick up on select considerations and extend certain questions.[15] As such, I will begin by once more turning toward the concept itself, especially concerning the question of the relationship between action and justification (2). Then I will examine the phenomenon of regulating social practices (3), and finally consider more recent research perspectives (4). I want to close with reflections concerning the book's political content.[16]

[10] Christoph Möllers, "Zweifel am Zweifel: anti-kritische Überlegungen zur Figur des paradoxen Rechts" in: *Zeitschrift für Internationale Strafrechtsdogmatik* 1 (2010), pp. 2–7.

[11] As a remedy, see the portrayal of manifold figures of the normative by various cultures and in various periods in Laurent de Sutter, *Après la Loi*, Paris 2018, which is convincing even if one does not buy into Sutter's Lacanianism.

[12] See, however, Michael Pawlik, *Normbestätigung und Identitätsbalance*, Baden-Baden 2017.

[13] This discontent is noticeable for Robert Alexy, "Besprechung: Die Möglichkeit der Normen" in: *JuristenZeitung* 72 (2017), pp. 788–9, here p. 789, and Marietta Auer, "Hundert Klassiker der Weltliteratur" in: *Rechtsgeschichte* 24 (2016), pp. 430–3, here p. 433.

[14] This, and thus the whole point of the book, is missed in the juxtaposition of deontic and semantic norm conceptions: see Alexy, "Besprechung" p. 789.

[15] See also Christoph Möllers, "Replik von Christoph Möllers" in: *Soziopolis* from December 21, 2015 (= Möllers-Buchforum [5]), https://soziopolis.de/beobachten/recht/artikel/Moellers-buchforum-5-replik-von-christoph-moellers/ (last accessed: 21 August 2019).

[16] Aside from the foreword, this edition limits itself to the correction of formal mistakes, whereas the substantive questions raised in this afterword leave the text at hand unaltered.

2. *Norm—Justification—Action*

2.1 Norm and Justification

The distinction I highlighted in the book, between norms and their justification, encountered critique particularly from people in practical philosophy.[17] On such views, on the one hand, it would be pointless to want to understand a norm without the context of its justification. On the other, a justification-driven perspective would not lead to every norm being viewed as justified. As far as practical philosophy is concerned, of course unjustified norms exist. And indeed, one of the fundamental concerns of my book, from the outset, is to shake up the idea that norm and justification are inseparably bound up with each other. It is among the most common social practices to deal with norms whose justification is unclear or disputed, without this directly necessitating an impact on the norm's claim to recognition. Often it is easier to agree on the content of a norm than on its justification. Of course it can be of pertinent interest to observe justificatory practices. However, it must be done in light of their plurality and contradictions even when referencing one and the same norm. Normative practices can remain in place even if their justification changes; they can arise and dissipate for causes that can neither be described by examining their coinciding, concrete justification practice, nor by reconstructing possible reasons for their justification.

It is indisputable that we can also discuss unjustified norms under such conditions. The problem lies at another level. The remaining question is not whether there is space for unjustified norms in practical philosophy, but what practical philosophy can contribute to the description of these norms with its own conceptual instruments. It is my suspicion that they will ultimately tend to find the success of norms that they see as being justified easier to explain than that of unjustified norms, without any apparent reason why this should be so. In this sense, Rainer Forst expresses a critique of the book: "Rather, one has to identify an instrument to analyze, for example, sexist norms … which examines the justifications they rest on, and which explains why they remain so stubbornly and establish a hegemony."[18] But why is it particularly imperative to explain why "bad" norms establish themselves? This assumption presumes an empirically informed model of the relationship between justification and effectiveness, one which I cannot identify in the debate that is chiefly concerned with justifying its respective understanding of successful justification.

[17] Forst, »Tischsitten«; Jakob Huber, "Zwischen Beschreibung und Rechtfertigung«, in: *Soziopolis* 30 November 2015 (= Möllers-Buchforum [2]), https://soziopolis.de/beobachten/recht/artikel/moellers-buchforum-2-zwischen-beschreibung-und-rechtfertigung/ (last accessed: 21 August 2019).

[18] Forst, "Tischsitten."

Again, this does not mean that the question of how a norm is justified becomes socially irrelevant. This is not claimed at any point in the book,[19] only that the distinction between proper and false justification contributes nothing to the analysis of a norm's social relevance. Under certain circumstances, contexts can be convincingly explained in empirical fashion, both positively,[20] when justification practices prove themselves effective at increasing adherence to a norm, and negatively, when they reveal themselves to be the cause of diminished recognition.[21] It is worth noting, however, that these kinds of empirical observations are actually not interested in the content of the justified norm. The effectiveness of these mechanisms of justification can only be observed because they refer to the same norm or normative order. Thus, they have to analytically distinguish norm and justification. A comprehensive portrayal of the relationship between justification practices and the recognition of given social orders, which consequently should not privilege some form of justification over another, is still lacking. It is possible that the question is too large for an empirical approach. Max Weber's types of legitimate power are arguably the most famous example of such an approach.[22]

Thus, it has to be asked of those segments of practical philosophy that emphasize the distinction between the normative and descriptive what they can say about unjustified norms with their respective means. For the segments that doubt the distinction between the normative and descriptive, the question to be raised concerns the degree to which their patterns of normative justification can also serve as patterns of social explanation (pp. 131–34).

2.2 Reference to Action

The objection that the concept of norm which I develop was already anticipated in this book (pp. 97–100), but nevertheless encountered some criticism. In some remarks, the fact that the concept of a norm does not presume the presence of a normative order seems to have been overlooked. Interestingly, particularly for legal scholars, the idea that there are norms without a normative order is hard to imagine, as this observation does not apply to legal norms. But in many other contexts, norms arise that do not rest on a normative order. This does not mean that my decision to expand the notion of a norm to other objects than action, namely

[19] Inaccurate Auer, "Klassiker" p. 432.

[20] Tom R. Tyler, *Why People Obey the Law*, Princeton 2006, pp. 94 ff.

[21] Karen Stenner, *The Authoritarian Dynamic*, Cambridge 2005, pp. 69–72, concerning the provability of "normative threats"effectiveness.

[22] Max Weber, "Die drei reinen Typen der legitimen Herrschaft" in: *Max Weber Gesamtausgabe*, I/ 22, 4, Tübingen 2005, pp. 717–742. As far as application to sociological research are concerned, see the overview in Cathryn Johnson, Timothy J. Dowd, and Cecilia L. Ridgeway, "Legitimacy as a Social Process" in: *Annual Review of Sociology* 32 (2006), pp. 53–78.

identities or institutions, and thus to also deconstruct the differentiation between norms and values, is appropriate. Even though I made the case for it (pp. 256–57), I shall nevertheless back it up with considerations that have arisen from some discussions with readers.

For two reasons, norms cannot be limited to directions for action. For one, because we can find countless examples of norms whose content is not specific to actions but rather to institutions or group identities; secondly, because norms also determine which events count as instances of answerable action. Maybe the fixation on action as an analytical category has a normatively grounded reason: the assumption that subjective freedom is the decisive docking point for all forms of justification, and that it manifests itself in actions.

But how can one adhere to a norm other than by an action? Asked this way, the question itself, with its emphasis on adherence, points in the direction of an action. Some norms cannot be followed, but a given development of the state of affairs can still be in line with them. This leads us to a further objection to the action-reference of the concept of norm. I would like to make the case that with the action-reference, a methodical individualism is constructed unintentionally,[23] because the assumption that norms can only refer to actions quickly leads to the presumption that normative institutions could only be described as the aggregate of actions.[24]

Finally, this raises the question of whether there is a need for a strong form of subjectivity in order for normative practices to become established. Admittedly, my investigation took an—albeit elaborate—detour around this question (pp. 228–34). The concern is not so much with developing a theory of subject but rather to detach the demands for participation in normative practices from an overly rigid concept of personal freedom. This seems to also be a far more recent theoretical approach than dealing with norms themselves. In other words, whereas the philosophical discussion about free will distinguishes between functional and dualistic positions,[25] the social treatment of norms is always functionalist. Capabilities such as being able to make free decisions are not clarified by the order but are rather presumed, and if they prove to be too demanding or minimal, they are adjusted accordingly.

[23] Ultimately, then, I am interested in a critique of the deduction of methodical individualism from a normative one, not vice versa. This has been misunderstood by Auer, "Hundert Klassiker" p. 423, who assumes I am interested in a critique of methodical individualism as such. Her proclaimed independence of normative and methodical individualism is thus frequently undermined, as the book seeks to show with many examples (see, for example, pp.32–50).

[24] This reference becomes noticeable, even if only implicitly, in the debate about the relationship between possibility and obligation, see, for example Michael Kühler, *Sollen ohne Können*, Münster 2013, and the comments on it by Felix Koch, "Impliziert Sollen Können?" in: *Deutsche Zeitschrift für Philosophie* 62 (2014), pp. 150–9, here p. 154.

[25] Portrayed in Michael Pauen, *Grundprobleme der Philosophie des Geistes*, Frankfurt/M. 2015.

2.3 Norms, Values, and Obligation: A Self-Correction

Tied to these questions is the book's attempted leveling of the distinction between norms, which need to refer to actions according to widely held views, and values. If one thought the distinction were helpful, then the concept developed here would be evaluative at its core: the marking which privileges a given possibility is the evaluation of this possibility. But this has nothing to do with a preference for a certain form of ethics but only with the lacking specificity of values, as well as the implicit greater generality of the notion of values. Evaluations can be specified to the point that they refer to an action and become prescriptions, but they are also not limited to that. By contrast, the search for a specific difference between "It is good for you to undertake Action p" and "You should do p" for empirical ends yields nothing. As far as I can tell, the former should be used as the more general.

Discussions concerning questions of justification which tie themselves to these concepts remain untouched by this. Even if one wanted to concede more significance to the distinction between obligation and values than its neo-Kantian provenance would suggest,[26] for our purposes they serve no end. As I see them, prescription and evaluation are both norms. Correspondingly, evaluations and directions for action seamlessly merge with each other in many social practices.

Now one could ask what an evaluative statement such as "This ice-cream is delicious" should have to do with a norm.[27] But even this statement privileges the possibility of consuming the specified kind of ice-cream, as opposed to other kinds. We are dealing with the affirmation of a possibility's realization. Yet doesn't this show that the notion represented here is too broad since the observation says nothing about whether others should also eat this kind of ice-cream? In Kant's *Critique of Pure Reason*, the judgement of taste is presented as an "idealist norm" for others (p. 161). It expresses something that should also bear meaning for others. The practice is not only affirmed for the subject expressing itself but also for the others. On the flipside, one could also ask whether the determination of the ice-cream being delicious would still have to be viewed as evaluative, even if it were limited to individualist expression, merely stating: "*I* like this ice-cream, but *you* probably won't like it." A social norm presumes an intersubjective reference. It is distinguished from a mere exclamation by virtue of exhorting something of someone else—it does not, however, imply that this person were able or feel prompted to begin something with this request, or that she would even understand it correctly.

[26] This, too, Marietta Auer ("Hundert Klassiker" p. 431) misunderstands on my view, as—drawing on Kant—she curiously plays off the Is-Ought-dualism against the concept of possibility. However, the connection between Is and Ought that is of interest here can actually be found in Kant: Immanuel Kant, *Kritik der reinen Vernunft*, Frankfurt/M. 1977, pp. 678 ff. (A 807, B 83). The distinction between obligation and values remains secondary in nature.

[27] Thus runs the objection presented in person by Stefan Gosepath.

As I mulled over the critique, it became obvious that I had not fully fleshed out this distinction in the book. Rather, I imputed the distinction between mere intention and affirmation in the sense of my norm conception into the subject (pp. 94–95), instead of explicitly understanding affirmation intersubjectively in the sense of a demand on others. Furthermore, while the norm tied to an action has become redundant in the completion of the action according to my portrayal, my attempt to distinguish between actions as such and those that are held to be appropriate remains not only unnecessarily psychologizing, thus giving up on the subject-theoretical agnosticism in the investigation, but it primarily misses the aspiration toward a usable differentiation between normative and other practices.

The discontent with the broad conception of a norm might stem from another motif, namely the fact that my conception of norms lacks any criterion of established binding character of the aspiring norm. This is so because it is unclear what exactly is expected of a norm by stipulating such a criterion. In our conceptual engagement with norms, a curious doubling frequently arises. We speak of "positive" or "valid" law, or "binding" norms, even though the context does not grant any room for invalid or non-binding norms. Since they do not distinguish anything, such doublings entail no descriptive value. Of course, an isolated command—"eat that!"—has less social relevance than a legal norm enforced through sanctions. But the difference between the two does not lie in their normativity, rather—if at all—in the stability and relevance of this normativity. Classifying a norm as "binding" can mean different things: that the norm has been appropriately justified, is generally recognized, or regularlyobeyed. These are three different aspects that can be practically interwoven with each other, but they need not be. They do not all belong to the concept of the norm itself, otherwise one would sacrifice speaking of norms that are insufficiently justified, generally despised, and scarcely followed.

3. *New Forms of the Rule*

Quite possibly the most urgent practical problems of normative orders are tied to the automation and rule-bound determination of social practices, and toward the end of the book, I list some brief reflections on this topic (pp. 290–93). In the meantime, I have at least gained more clarity about directions in which this line of inquiry could be further pursued.

3.1 Algorithms and Application

In the book, I failed to build a bridge between the application of norms and the increasingly urgent question about the meaning of algorithms for normative practices. As such, algorithms are not norms but rather rules that determine a process.

A certain input becomes a certain output according to a certain algorithm. In other words, algorithms work as rules. Rules can be norms, but they need not be.

One important peculiarity of algorithms is that their application knows no room for variance. As the application of a rule, the algorithm contains no decision. That means that no contingencies or points of discussion can be cultivated by algorithms. Decision theories, whether taken more positively shaped by the concept of the power of judgement, or more aporetic in nature, gain no traction on algorithms, just as models of the hermeneutics of rules. One reason why the humanities and social sciences still contribute little to the challenges of digitalization might be that they have a lot to say about uncertainty and vagueness, but they have little to say about certainty and clarity. Realizing that a rule cannot determine its own application does not apply to algorithms. Thus, a subject-less "reign of the rule" arises.[28] As such, it is seen as a decisive breakthrough in the history of the development of the computer when the process of rule application becomes mechanized[29] and decoupled from any kind of judgement technique. This exclusion of any kind of personal contribution to the process of application is the endpoint of formalization as understood in the sense developed here (pp. 167–68). This leads to the question of what is lost out of sight by this kind of formalization, or whether the contingencies contained in the application of rules fulfill any useful function.

Now, algorithms as such are not norms. However, they can be deployed as normative or normatively relevant practices. This should allow for routinely applied legal norms being taken over by algorithms, such as in the case of processing damage cases. The upside is obvious: such cases should be decided quickly, equally, and without the risk of chance. At the same time it is obvious that such practices are not merely of interest as an entrance into a more comprehensive structural evolution of normativity, but that they also challenge traditional notions of normativity. Admittedly, the attempt to narrow down discretion in decision-making procedures as much as possible enjoys a long history. So in what exactly does the novelty consist? Well, as long as people apply a norm, a decision is being made that could have had a different outcome. This is just as much the case for decision-makers who find themselves at the very bottom of an organizational hierarchy.[30] If it is true that even such decisions with comparably little reach cannot be purely formally determined, but rather inevitably incorporate informal factors, then we see the dramatic degree of change that is set into motion by applying algorithmic procedures.

Seen in this light, the application of algorithms already absolutizes the formal side of norm application even in rather trivial contexts, and it radically sidelines

[28] Bettina Heintz, *Die Herrschaft der Regel. Zur Grundlagengeschichte des Computers*, Frankfurt/M. 1993.

[29] Ibid., pp. 99–101.

[30] This is the convincing claim of the remarkable administrative-anthropological study by Bernardo Zacka, *When the State Meets the Street*, Cambridge, Mass. 2017.

informality. As long as one views informality simply as an impurity of the form that only serves to question a norm's obligatory effect as well as the positive qualities connected to the normative form, such as equal treatment, then this poses no problem. But very little would seem to indicate that this is the case. All too rarely do we tackle the question of how the two aspects of normative practices, the fact of being formally bound by a rule and the addressing of subjects by means of a rule, are related to each other. If a normative order emphasizes that its norms are applied by subjects, then we must ask which end this serves—beyond all too frequent invocations of the relationship between freedom and responsibility—or vice versa, what is lost when the application is automatized. One important function of making the application subjective—which should not be confused for personalization or randomness—seems to lie in making visible in the act of application the concrete form, shape, and import of the applied norm such as to subject the norm to an additional round of scrutiny and control. The subject observes the result of the application and adjusts her rule interpretation and exercise of judgement in case the two do not "fit" with each other.[31] At times, this is criticized as an impermissible observation of consequences.[32] But not only can there be no application of concepts to cases without a follow-up assessment;[33] what is more the very purpose of having rational subjects apply norms arguably lies in their ability to assess separately this act of application after the fact. The whole point of this procedure, then, is to place the application of the formalized norm into a separate decision context that is not equally formalized. The context is what remains of the formalization when the form is subtracted. In other words, making decisions means using the inevitable openness of the rule in order to carry along normative criteria other than the formalized ones into a specific context. This is inevitable as long as one cannot apply norms other than in the form of a decision because in this context we can only be concerned with figuring out how to deal with the informal side of the decision, and not with whether we can do without it. This changes when algorithms introduce an alternative to the scenario.

Such a complete formalization of the application will obfuscate numerous factors of the decision-making process that otherwise would have been part of the decision. We can see this in the fact that algorithms do not simply turn an input into an output, rather they already become effective in the selection of the input.[34] They confer relevance. Whatever is permitted as an input gains meaning. Whatever can be embedded into formalized decision structure gains normative

[31] Concerning the concept of a fit, Sabine Müller-Mall, "Entfaltungen des Rechts im Gefühl" in: Sigrid G. Köhler et al. (eds), *Recht fühlen*, Paderborn 2015, pp. 159–76, here pp. 171–3.

[32] Specifically, by Luhmann, *Das Recht der Gesellschaft*, pp. 377–9.

[33] Convincingly critiquing Luhmann in this regard: Gertrude Lübbe-Wolff, *Rechtsfolgen und Realfolgen*, Freiburg im Breisgau, 1981.

[34] Tarleston Gillespie, "The Relevance of Algorithms" in: Id., Pablo J. Boczkowski, and Kirsten A. Foot (eds), *Media Technologies*, Cambridge, Mass. 2014, Chapter 9.

relevance. Other aspects are lost. But in order to be able to observe such losses of decisive quality, we would need a more precise investigation of norm application practices, and one that is not idealized from the outset. For the time being, we are empty-handed in this regard, as we lack any cognitively substantive models of judgement.[35] Assuming that good decision-making does not merely consist in the diligent application of normative standards but also requires an appropriate engagement with actual circumstances, we currently face a deficit in this regard.

So how do we proceed with algorithms threatening to not only metaphorically turn the "king-judge" into a mere automaton of judgement?[36] Two paths seem conceivable. One would consist in formalizing the informal; that is, incorporating observations of the consequences and contexts of a decision into the program. This is discussed under headings such as "machine ethics."[37] However, it is questionable whether the achievements brought about by what we call judgement can be reduced to the ethical. Another path would consist in diversifying programs; that is, to ponder how the application could be made plural in that various different algorithms are deployed together. Neither option would be a return to the ideal of subjective-human decision formation—which would probably be lost slowly but surely once human communities were to open themselves up to such techniques.

3.2 Governance by Rules and Responsibility

The deployment of machines does not simply lead to the impoverishment of social decision-making practices, but it frequently depicts an impoverished human decision-making practice which in turn invites automatization.[38] Elsewhere, this impoverishment shows itself in the increasing recourse to rules in authoritarian systems, which only leave ample room for political decision in the center but otherwise strongly insist on ever-more detailed prescription. Such regimes have little in common with arbitrary rule, neither should we speak of a structure governed by the rule of law (*Rechtsstaatlichkeit*), because the decisions in place leave no space for independent checks and control. However, other functions of the rule of law such as providing for rule-bound decision-making and for the reliability of expectations can indeed be accounted for in such systems.

We see a similar tendency in the increasing relevance of compliance rules for organizations. These rules may not be formally binding, but factually, they take on a fiercely determining role. Extensive efforts in self-regulation are made with

[35] Compare, however, with Müller-Mall, "Entfaltungen des Rechts."

[36] According to Regina Ogoroek, *Richterkönig oder Subsumtionsautomat? Zur Justiztheorie im 19. Jahrhundert*, Frankfurt/M., 1986.

[37] Cathrin Misselhorn, "Maschinenethik und ›Artificial Morality‹: Können und sollen Maschinen moralisch handeln?" in: *Aus Politik und Zeitgeschichte* 68 (2018), pp. 29–33.

[38] See also the concluding comment in Heintz, *Herrschaft der Regel*, p. 298.

the aim of conveying the impression that everything imaginable has been done in order to comply with legal requirements. Here, formally non-binding yet precisely formulated internal standards of behavior merge with broadly formulated but binding legal norms that stipulate the payment of damages or criminal sanctions. What lurks behind such technical-sounding arrangements is the tendency to minimize the contribution from smaller actors within the organization. These kinds of models are concerned with using rules as a means to substitute subjective responsibility.[39]

Such ideals of perfect governance—and this is the crucial point here—are not simply the consequence of a certain technology, even if they can make particularly good use of certain technologies. Furthermore, this does not imply that other ideals have to be displaced by the development of automatization, such as the ideal of a normative order which grants plenty of room for both a plurality of application possibilities and for debate about the meaning of one and the same norm. They would have to be designed in a more complex way. Maybe Alan Turing's insight applies here, which states that variance of behavior could be a function of storage capacity.[40]

3.3 The End of Social Normativity as the End of Deviance

Overly normativized communities draw all existing practices into question, under-normativized communities leave all existing practices unchallenged (pp. 287–89). A substantial part of the discussion surrounding normative problems of digitalization concerns the ethical content of automatized actions, such as the question of which alternative paths should be predetermined for an autonomous car in the case of a pending accident. My book has nothing to say with regards to these interesting questions. However, the book's line of inquiry concerns the conditions of possibility for normativity as such, an issue whose social relevance continues to be underappreciated. It addresses the possibility of the end of deviant behavior, and as such—so runs the argument—also the end of social normativity which hinges on deviance.

The possibility of deviance vanishish[41] is at least partially promoted by conceptions of normative individualism that tend to identify freedom and rationality. For if rationally justified individual actions serve as the general standard for normativity, then it becomes difficult to develop reasons why deviant behavior should

[39] Critical overview in Ralf Kölbel, "Wirtschaftkriminalität und unternehmensinterne Strafrechtsdurchsetzung" in: *Monatsschrift für Krimonologie und Strafrechtsreform* 101 (2018), pp. 22–35.

[40] Alan Turing, "Computing Machinery and Intelligence" in: *Mind* 49 (1950), pp. 433–60, here p. 449.

[41] Literature on this topic is quite scarce, but see Michael L. Rich, "Should We Make Crime Impossible? " in: *Harvard Journal of Law & Public Policy* 36 (2013), pp. 795–848.

have its own merit. Surprisingly, a systematic perspective from this view, one which—just like the sociology of classical modernity—is capable of expressing deviance's normative advantage for individuals, proves to be more gentle in dealing with the realm of possibility of normative orders.

There are various ways to argue for the justification of deviant behavior vis-à-vis a norm that itself is justified. In the sociology of classical modernity, deviance serves the stabilization of community formation, the criminal is a "regular effective factor in social life."[42] For an instrumentalist conception of norms, deviance becomes attractive because ensuring perfect compliance with all norms is too costly for the community. Furthermore, instances of deviance help to reaffirm the existing inventory of norms (p. 102). Deviation can clarify why we recognize certain norms, or why we want to change or get rid of them. Most of all, deviance highlights the fact that our practices respond to norms, that is, to social formations that could be different, just as the practices could be different which they regulate. A community's sense of possibility is shaped by norms for as long as deviation remains an option.

However, due to recent technological advances the costs of implementation could be drastically reduced, and the remaining tolerance of deviant behavior might thus fade. Maybe it will become factually more difficult to act in a deviant manner because methods of indirect control, such as "nudging"[43] and other limitations make it more cumbersome to act other than expected, even if that which is "expected" is not actually prescribed in a norm. In debates on indirect control of decision-making, it became obvious how much individual decisions are shaped by a malleable social context that is not freely chosen. This insight could be put to use in clarifying decisions, yet it is more frequently used to control decisions in the name of general criteria of well-being, and in eliminating decision alternatives.

These developments as well are promoted by technology—the ubiquity of surveillance is but one such example—but they cannot be reduced to it. Once more, the emphasis has to be on enabling deviance in normative orders. If one presumes that technological innovation per se cannot be stopped, then the positive achievements of normative orders must be integrated into them. Some possibilities to do so might include diversifying commands and putting them into competition with each other, as well as enriching them with mechanisms of chance. The strategy of protecting normative orders by limiting the possibilities of their implementation is nothing new, but rather a core feature—albeit at times unnoticed—of the rule of law (*Rechtsstaatlichkeit*).[44] Of course, by using automatic barriers we would be

[42] According to Émile Durkheim, *The Rules of Sociological Method*, New York 1982, p. 102.

[43] For critical perspectives, see the contributions in: Alexander Kemmerer et al. (eds), *Choice Architecture in Democracies*, Baden-Baden 2016.

[44] Christoph Möllers, *Zweckverfolgung und Zweckreflexion: Zur Legitimität modernen Rechts*, Discussion Paper, XXIV. Congress of the German Society for Philosophy, Subsection of Legal Philosophy, Berlin 2017, manuscript available from author.

able to arrange car traffic in such a way that the question of whether someone ran a red light becomes obsolete. But one can also view red lights as a space in which a responsible engagement of norms is instituted even by those who ignore them.

4. *Empirical Research Perspectives*

4.1 Problems of Normative-Individualist Models of Empirical Norm Research

In recent years, new impulses for empirical research into normative practices have arisen from numerous disciplines. Evolutionary biology investigates the genesis of normative structures out of the practical need for cooperation in primates and human beings;[45] in sociological research on complexity, behavioral models are developed that seek to explain the rise and fall of social norms as formalized social theory;[46] an experimental branch of norm research conducts investigations into the effects of norms on action patterns of individuals in order to develop models that go beyond and fine-tune existing models of rational cost–benefit calculus.[47] Some of these efforts are tied to normative concerns such as improving regulatory models, others are limited to descriptive aspirations. What they have in common is that they are only loosely oriented along disciplinary lines, instead bringing together statistical, economic, biological, psychological, and other models.

What is of interest for our purposes is that while such research regularly approaches things in a methodical-individualist manner, that is, by departing from models of action and from observable individual actions, it often arrives at empirical observations and theoretical models that prove the individualist perspective to be insufficient to adequately grasp normative practices. To the contrary, it seems necessary from a theory-immanent perspective to incorporate into the description factors that have become autonomous from the individual level of action, that is, to presume an independent, objective level of social normativity. It is in this sense that, in his modeling of the evolution of moral norms, Michael Tomasello speaks of a necessary "cultural common ground" in order for objective norms to evolve.[48] By this he means a shared world view, a common cognitive framework of the

[45] Michael Tomasello, *A Natural History of Human Morality*, Cambridge, Mass. 2016.

[46] Herbert Gintis, *Individuality and Entanglement*, Princeton 2017; Id. and Dirk Helbing, "Homo Socialis: An Analytical Core for Sociological Theory" in: *Review of Behavioral Economics* 2 (2015), pp. 1–59.

[47] Exemplary and with results that confirm the conflict-inducing effects of norms (129 f.): Fabian Winter, Heiko Rauhut, and Dirk Helbing, "How Norms Can Generate Conflict: An Experiment on the Failure of Cooperative Micro-Motives on the Macro-Level" in: *Social Forces* 90 (2012), pp. 919–48.

[48] Tomasello, *Natural History*, pp. 92–7. In the book, I critically discuss this kind of argumentation in the context of Robert Brandom's theory because of the unclarified transition from the cognitive to the normative (pp. 26–28).

individuals involved. In Herbert Gintis' sociological model, the figure of a "choreograph" is introduced.[49] By this he means a signaler who informs the participants about the status of social norms which the signaler, however, has neither posited nor can he enforce them. In both models, mentioned here simply as representative, the transition from subjective coordination and cooperation to objective norms clearly raises problems and seems to necessitate the inclusion of further assumptions. Furthermore, methodical-individualist models frequently have to introduce a notion of internalization, that is they have to re-subjectivize the hard-won objective character of norms in order to bring their models in line with the postulates of methodical individualism.[50]

This points toward it being advisable for empirical norm research to operate with other approaches too. Admittedly, the question of the origin of norms—which the two approaches mentioned above tackle at times empirically, at times by developing theoretical models—deserves independent inquiry. At the same time, it is not self-evident that there is a clear path from a given starting point to a privileged access to and understanding of any existing, fully developed state of normative practices. Maybe the methodical path from a model of origins to a description of the status quo is simply too far. If individuals are socialized into an inventory of social norms which displays a high level of contingency, then we will not be able to explain this from any starting point. At the same time, the model of "internalization" of norms is quickly overburdened under such conditions, not only because there are too many norms that cannot all be internalized but also because their validity and meaning will most likely remain often contentious and vague. For this reason, practices external to subjects, ones that require no internalization, play such a large role in modern normative orders. People need to be reminded of norms, and norms need to be implemented. The very ubiquity of such mechanisms speaks against the idea that they might be secondary to normative practices. For this reason, it is too easy to claim that social norms are only abided by if they are viewed as legitimate.[51] This assumption is more in accord with the theoretical model than with the experience of social normative orders. The fact that a norm is contentious, that there is cognitive uncertainty regarding its content, and that it requires enforcement, are not secondary phenomena of social practices. They all serve to maintain a perpetually precarious stock that was not established upon a stabilizing foundation of moral rightness or efficiency. For this reason, the investigation of institutional practices, one that does not take its departure point from individual actions, remains indispensable. This critique does not entail any objection to quantitative research. It only

[49] Gintis (n 46), *Individuality and Entanglement*, p. 113, tying into Aumann's concept of a "correlated equilibrium." But for Aumann, this mechanism depends on a presumption of probability which the participants themselves can carry out. By contrast, Gintis' notion of the choreograph has become autonomous, in other words: The self-coordination of actors becomes a coordination from outside by others.

[50] Ibid., pp. 124–6.

[51] Gintis (n 46), *Individuality and Entanglement*, p. 113.

appears at times that quantitative social science prefers more easily quantifiable and formalizable models, and thus leans more toward methodical-individualist social theories than toward institutional ones without any substantial methodological justification for that choice. That all being said, quantitative research focusing on other units than action, such as texts and their forms[52]—if proceeding in a historically informed way—could certainly be applied to normative practices in a useful manner.

4.2 Historicization

A further dominant strategy for investigating into normative practices can be found in the realm of historicization. While the historicization of norms is nothing new, what is novel is the attempt to historicize norms that have traditionally been assumed to operate universally in terms of time and space, particularly human rights. Discussion surrounding the history of human rights gives tremendous insight into the conditions of a theory of social norms. To begin with, this debate confronts us with the notion that human rights refer to a past that reaches as far back as antiquity, not only considering the dramatic evolution of the human rights discourse after the Atlantic revolutions or the Second World War, but even in the 1970s and after 1989.[53] This effort at historicization goes well with the perspective taken in my book, in so far as it also questions the explanatory value of exceedingly universalist theorizing.[54] Of course, working on the historical phenomenon does not replace the work on the concept. After all, it seems uncertain whether the various responses to the question of where relevant turning points in history should be made out take their starting point from one and the same concept, or whether they simply juxtapose very different practices under the heading of a single word. If that were the case, one would still have to justify how such forms of historicization challenge models that claim human rights to be the product of "classical antiquity" or the "Christian West," as troublesome as even these epoch labels may be. This stems from the observation that, in historical research, normativity is frequently equated with the proximate description of practices, that is, one claims to have captured the history of a norm by describing a ritually determined practice without having considered how it accords with the normative aspirations which also arise in the practice but elsewhere in it (pp. 280–81).[55] The approach that seeks to downsize

[52] Franco Moretti, *Distant Reading*, London 2013; Matthew Jockers, *Macroanalysis*, Urbana 2013.

[53] See Lynn Hunt, *Inventing Human Rights*, New York 2007; Samuel Moyn, *The Last Utopia*, Cambridge, Mass. 2010; Jan Eckel, *Die Ambivalenz des Guten*, Göttingen 2014, as well as the contributions in: Stefan-Ludwig Hoffmann (ed.), *Human Rights in the Twentieth Century*, Cambridge 2011.

[54] This is criticized by Alexy, "Besprechung p. 789, with the demand to work out universal structures. But what is the reason for this demand? Human rights themselves?

[55] Concerning this problem, but with an eye toward the history of national socialist law: Christoph Möllers, "Ernst Rudolf Huber's letzte Fußnote. Die normative Ordnung des Nationalsozialismus und die Grenzen der Kulturgeschichte" in: *Zeitschrift für Ideengeschichte* 2016, pp. 47–65, here pp. 51–60.

norms that claim universality, such as human rights or democracy, reaches limits if the object of this historicization is not adequately described. When Pierre Rosanvallon, assessing the historiography of democracy, observes: "In order to appropriately think democracy, one must thus abandon the idea of a model in favor of that of experience,"[56] this is the historicist version of Oliver Wendell Holmes' observation that the essence of law is experience, not logic.[57] Both statements pit experience against concept. But can we even dispute that there is no experience without concepts—and no concepts without experience? For the historicization of norms, it is less crucial to do without concepts than it is to shape concepts in such a manner that they can bring about descriptively rich distinctions.

Debates about the historicization of norms draw their energy from that which they point beyond, that is, from the implicit pretense that normative conclusions could be drawn from historical experience. It is no coincidence if historical outlines which draw on antiquity or early modernity to describe human rights tell stories of success, whereas the shorter-term historicization frequently highlights contingency and failure of human rights discourse. But the question remains as to the degree to which historical experience, in dealing with a normative concept, is capable of criticizing it, or even disproving it. There will be no clear answer to this question. Whether instigating a war in the name of "humanitarian intervention" compromises said mission, and whether the same goes for "real existing socialism," could not be answered with mere recourse to historical experience. This holds true even if this experience could be completely and impartially reconstructed, which seems methodically impossible as it is. There is certainly no general rule for answering the question of how bad experiences with certain norms or kinds of norms justify renouncing them. This basic insight arguably severely limits the normative objectives of many historical projects. More pointedly, as insightful as histories about colonial engagement of human rights may be, nothing normative immediately follows from such accounts.

The historicization of normative practices is inevitable. To name just two, the temporal structure of norms (pp. 190–93), as well as the frequently fluid transition between descriptions of a certain state of affairs and normative commands with regards to it—the greatest indicator of this being the word »constitution«—account for the fact that there can be no normativity without an affirmative or critical reference to past events. If the practical interwovenness and conceptual distinction (not necessarily the practical distinguishability in each case) of normative and other practices necessarily exist side-by-side (pp. 126–127), then we should more decidedly relativize the normative aspirations and imports of efforts at the

[56] Pierre Rosanvallon, "Democratic Universalism as a Historical Problem" in: *Constellations Journal* 16 (2009), pp. 539–49, here p. 547.

[57] "The life of the law has not been logic; it has been experience," Oliver W. Holmes, *The Common Law* (1881), London 1968, p. 5.

historicization of norms. A historical argument alone is insufficient for justifying a norm. Even a normative order building on tradition has to select from the past, privilege some things over others, and in doing so apply criteria that extend beyond the historicization.[58] By contrast, the problem of an openly normatively selective engagement of past events lies in its limiting the realm of experience that could arise from observing history, and in failing to recognize the foreignness of past norms (p. 190 ff.).

4.3 My Own Perspectives: Order, Comparison, Dispositif

The argument offered in the book has three conceptual vanishing points which would lend themselves to being further pursued in the future. On the whole, the argument moves from a philosophy-critical conceptualization to a sociological line of inquiry. This necessitates thinking about the concept of order more precisely, which is tied to many normative practices, even if not to all of them. Just like rules, orders are not necessarily normative phenomena; an order can develop against a norm. But similarly to norms arising negatively from an experience of disappointment, when an expected course of events does not materialize, normative orders seem to develop from the world being experienced as cognitively ordered. This, in turn, might be due to our need to find an order. "In our search for rules, we create them."[59]

Secondly, as mentioned at the outset, I take the book to be a pre-study for a comparative study of normative practices (pp. 285–86). The technique of comparison is fundamentally crucial, as it is my impression that all normative practices implicitly operate in comparative fashion. Even a normative standard with an aspiration to absoluteness rests on a horizon of its applicability, a horizon which compares, even if only by taking note of cases in which it has not yet been applied. In more recent sociological literature, there is a preference for investigating into the practices of comparison in the context of quantification and standardization of social practices that frequently feature a normative aspiration.[60] But qualitative forms of making normative evaluations as well seem often to proceed in a comparative fashion. If one pauses to reflect for a moment, it actually is quite difficult to make out any normative practices that get by without an at least implicit comparative element. In the realm of theoretical inquiry, however, the concept of comparison hardly plays any role at all, arguably because, similar to the concept of analogy, it faces a dominant

[58] Waldenfels (n 5), *Ordnung im Zwielicht*, p. 158.

[59] Thus runs the fortunate expression in Ryan Muldoon, Chiara Lisciandra, and Stephan Hartmann, "Why Are There Descriptive Norms? Because We Looked for Them" in: *Synthese* 191 (2014), pp. 4409–29.

[60] A good overview in Michèle Lamont, "Towards a Comparative Sociology of Valuation and Evaluation« in: *Annual Review of Sociology* 38 (2012), pp. 201–21.

understanding of rationality for which it is either (qualitatively) too soft or (quantitatively) too mechanical.

Thirdly, the book's emphasis on a realization perspective allows for a more precise investigation into the relationship between social norms and the material substance of social practices. In the segment on the normative pretense of art, a sociological reviewer saw the core of the formation of a sociological model.[61] The problem here is that many theories which emphasize the social effectiveness of objects describe these in the conceptuality of agency (pp. 151–53 ff.) and thereby miss their distinctiveness. It is no surprise that the concept of an "object" simply cannot separate from that of "subject." The same holds for proximate alternative concepts, such as "things." For this reason, it appears more promising to operate with procedural concepts, such as "script" or "dispositif." The latter in particular has yielded a substantial amount of research on normative practices in recent years. It is crucial that such research emphasizes that dispositifs—in contrast to Foucault, who helped the term gain credence—should not be understood as normative per se, but to distinguish between them and their evaluation.[62] This is an important step away from unifying theories of social practices.

4.4 Outlook: Escapism or Agnosticism?

One of the most interesting experiences entailed in the book's reception has been the disagreement over how to categorize it politically: the readings range from the accusation of conservative status quo positivism, to the claim it provides a superstructure for the democratic constitutional State, all the way to the diagnosis of a gleeful freedom from values.[63] Epistemologically speaking, one could ask whether it is possible or desirable to develop a non-normative concept of normativity.

But even if I must concede that every descriptive expression represents an intervention that has its own normative effects, such effects should still be distinguished from their descriptive pretense. Theories that claim that this "simply does not work" are currently plentiful, such as critical theory and theories of performativity. I engaged with some of them in the book (pp. 131–38, 196–201). I suspect that it would be much more difficult consistently to do without any

[61] Wolfgang Knöbl, "Die Möglichkeit der Normen. Soziologische Anmerkungen zu Christoph Möllers" in: *Soziopolis* from 23 November 2015 (= Möllers-Buchforum [1]), https://soziopolis.de/beobachten/recht/artikel/moellers-buchforum-1-die-moeglickeit-der-normen/ (last accessed: August 21, 2019).

[62] Nicolas Dodier and Janine Barbot, "The Force of Dispositifs" in: *Annales HHS* (English edition) 71 (2016), pp. 291–317, here p. 306.

[63] Rainer Schmalz-Bruns, "Paradoxie als Erkenntnisform? " in: *Soziopolis* from 7 December 2015 (= Möllers-Buchforum [3]), https://soziopolis.de/beobachten/recht/artikel/moellers-buchforum-3-paradoxie-als-erkenntnisform/ (last accessed: 12 February 2018); Auer, "Hundert Klassiker" and Michael Pawlik, "Demokratie lebt nicht vom großen Zusammenhang" in: *Frankfurter Allgemeine Zeitung* 16 December 2015.

non-normative concept of normativity. The fact that a concept does not have to share in the feature which it describes does not appear odd, and in this specific case, any talk of an unjustified norm precisely presumes such a concept. I am unable to see how the attempt to take a step back and observe normative orders beyond their justification, in and of itself, could have any justifying effect. I do not even see why every engagement with normative orders should also turn toward their dark sides. Quite to the contrary, the question arises of how one should even be able to defend something that one—albeit being able to justify it—cannot describe, how one could praise something that one cannot not define. However, this does not mean that this approach is free of normative consequences.

A first such consequence has already been mentioned: If one does not reduce norms to their restraining effect, then a normativity of second order arises. Norms have to maintain a measure of distance to the practices to which they refer, without either becoming too detached from them or too narrowly embedded in them. This is what is meant by successful normativity, even if the norm itself has no justification. A practice of successful normativity in this sense does not have to be a good practice in any imaginable sense.

A second implication concerns the unintended effects of justificatory discourses. It arises systematically from the element of realization in my concept of a norm, that is by there being no such thing as "justification" *tout court*, but always and only justificatory regimes and practices. At the moment, in political theory, liberal theories are being criticized both for their idealizing model assumptions and for their truncated concept of politics.[64] In a different way, and with a different intention, the book leads into a similar direction. It is not about bestowing more reality on justificatory theories of action or power structures. As long as they limit themselves in their pretense, this is not necessary. It is, instead, about observing what happens when certain models of justification are to be institutionally realized, that is, for example, asking what an order looks like that tries to pit normative correctness against the majority rule (pp. 16–19). On this view, what is of interest are the unintended consequences of normative models. For jurists, observing these is a daily task, but not for philosophers, and this difference could in turn affect theory formation.

A third implication systematically follows from my notion of norms not resting on the processes of functional differentiation: Normativity is a mode of social self-differentiation which lies across and bears no direct relation with these processes. This is why it must be observed in an integrated fashion. On the one hand, this is what it means not to reduce normative practices to their respective provenance but also to look for the hidden origins outside of this provenance-centered categorization: for crypto-juridical ideas in the arguments of ethics-committees,[65] or for the

[64] On the distinction between the two, see Matt Sleat, "Liberalism and Non-Ideal Theory Or, Are there two Ways to do Realistic Political Theory?" in: *Political Studies* 64 (2016), pp. 27–41.

[65] Gordian Ezazi, *Ethikräte in der Politik*, Wiesbaden 2016.

religious motives of sociological models of secularization.[66] On the other hand, normativity must be discovered wherever it is consistently denied, most obviously today in art institutions that draw "on the yearning for the norm,"[67] thereby justifying that they both posit and deny norms in order to satisfy a need for normativization and standardization, which art theory and the market simultaneously declare as illegitimate and also inflame. If these implications were taken to be of "political" relevance, I would not object; if not, this too would not have any further effect on my intentions.

[66] Manuel Borutta, "Genealogie der Säkularisierungstheorie. Zur Historisierung einer großen Erzählung der Moderne" in: *Geschichte und Gesellschaft* 36 (2010), pp. 347–76.

[67] Stefan Germer, "Wie finde ich mich aus diesem Labyrinth? Über Möglichkeit und Unmöglichkeit von Kriterien zur Beurteilung zeitgenössischer Kunst" in: *Jahresring* 46 (1999), pp. 233–44, here p. 238 (= *Germeriana. Unveröffentlichte oder übersetzte Schriften von Stefan Germer zur zeitgenössischen und modernen Kunst*, ed. by Julia Bernard).

Index

Note: *For the benefit of digital users, indexed terms that span two pages (e.g., 52–53) may, on occasion, appear on only one of those pages.*